Why We Evaluate
Functions of Attitudes

Why We Evaluate
Functions of Attitudes

Edited by

Gregory R. Maio
Cardiff University

James M. Olson
University of Western Ontario

 LAWRENCE ERLBAUM ASSOCIATES, PUBLISHERS
2000   Mahwah, New Jersey   London

#4137694

Lawrence Erlbaum Associates, Inc., Publishers
10 Industrial Avenue
Mahwah, NJ 07430

Cover design by Kathryn Houghtaling Lacey

Library of Congress Cataloging-in-Publication Data

Why we evaluate: functions of attitudes / edited by Gregory R.
Maio, James M. Olson.

p. cm.

Includes bibliographical references and index.
ISBN 0-8058-2770-6(cloth : alk. paper)
1. Attitude (Psychology) 2. Social influence. I. Maio, Gregory R. II.
Olson, James M., 1953-
HM1181.W48 ~~1999~~ *2000*
152.4—dc21

99-28185
CIP

Books published by Lawrence Erlbaum Associates are printed on
acid-free paper, and their bindings are chosen for strength and durability.

Printed in the United States of America
10 9 8 7 6 5 4 3 2 1

Contents

Preface

In the classic film, *Citizen Kane*, the opening scene shows the death of a wealthy publishing tycoon, Charles Foster Kane, whose last word before dying is the name "Rosebud." In the rest of the film, the audience is led through a journalist's attempt to uncover the identity of Rosebud. At the end, the audience discovers that Rosebud is not the name of a cherished partner or family member, but rather the name of a sled that Kane played with as a child.

When they discover that Rosebud is Kane's sled, movie watchers inevitably wonder why he was so enamored by it. This question addresses the topic of the present book, attitude functions. An initial guess might be that Kane adored his sled because of its features, such as its color, blades, and speed, but this explanation is incomplete and fatuous because it is unclear why these features would be so important to Kane. The movie provides clues that Kane possessed unique needs and goals that are relevant to his attitude. Specifically, Kane was an ambitious man who tirelessly built a publishing empire, and his ambition led him to forego pleasure and family leisure. Consequently, his sled may have been the one object that he associated most strongly with enjoyment and pleasure. This example illustrates how psychological needs and motives are relevant to attitudes.

Classic social psychological theory and research have supported the importance of needs and motives. For example, Lewin (1938) suggested that individuals' behavior toward objects is influenced by distinct motivational "force fields" to approach and avoid the objects. Also, in the influential monograph *Communication and Persuasion*, Hovland, Janis, and Kelley (1953) proposed that a persuasive message elicits attitude change when the message provides a motivating incentive to adopt a new attitude.

In the latter half of the 20th century, however, social psychological research has been dominated by a structural zeitgeist. For example, models of attitude–behavior relations have focused on determining how the beliefs and feelings associated with an attitude predict attitude-relevant behaviors (Fishbein & Ajzen, 1975) and moderate attitude–behavior relations (Millar & Tesser, 1989). In addition, contemporary models of persuasion tend to focus on the cognitive responses that are elicited by persuasive messages (e.g., Chaiken, Liberman, & Eagly, 1989; Petty & Cacioppo, 1986).

This focus on structural variables has occurred despite the existence of two seminal theories of attitude function that were proposed by Smith, Bruner, and White (1956) and Katz (1960). These theories did not inspire abundant research when they first appeared, because they proposed many functions that were difficult to measure. Fortunately, recent developments in techniques for manipulating and measuring attitude function have helped to facilitate research on attitude function. As a result, the past two decades have seen an increase in research inspired by these seminal theories of attitude function, and the structural and motivational approaches are quickly approaching a rapprochement.

The seminal theories of attitude function share some tenets, despite being developed independently. First, both theories claim that a basic function of attitudes is to simplify knowledge about objects in the environment, consistent with Allport's (1935) classic description of the attitude construct. That is, attitudes help people to approach things that are good for them and avoid things that are bad for them, without the need to constantly reassess pros and cons. Smith et al. (1956) labeled this motivation the *object appraisal function*. In contrast, Katz (1960) divided this motivation into two functions: a *knowledge function*, which represents the ability of attitudes to summarize information about objects in the environment, and a *utilitarian function*, which exists in attitudes that maximize rewards and minimize punishments obtained from the environment.

In addition, both theories propose that attitudes can subsume a motivation to defend the self against internal conflict. For example, a new mother might feel badly about herself after experiencing a sudden urge to strike her child, and, to defend against this threat to self-esteem, the mother might develop a positive attitude toward spoiling the child (see Freud, 1966). Smith et al., (1956) labeled this motivation the *externalization function*, whereas Katz (1960) labeled this motivation the *ego-defensive function*.

Some of the proposed functions were not shared by the two theories. For instance, Smith et al. (1956) proposed a *social-adjustment function*, which is served by attitudes that help individuals identify with people whom they admire and dissociate from people whom they dislike. Presumably, this function underlies people's attitudes toward fashionable consumer items. In addition, Katz (1960) proposed a *value-expressive function*, which exists in attitudes that express the self-concept and central social values (e.g., equality, freedom; Rokeach, 1973; Schwartz, 1992). For example, some people favor affirmative action programs because they believe that the programs promote equality.

Together, these theories provided a good foundation for research on attitude function. As illustrated by the chapters in this volume, however, recent research has moved beyond the original models to develop new hypotheses and theories. Moreover, new theories have been applied in many areas of practical importance, such as attitudes toward people with AIDS and attitudes toward volunteering. Although the extant literature may not yet enable us to understand perfectly Kane's attitude toward Rosebud, a new generation of studies of attitude function is emerging, which focuses on a wider variety of motivations and on the psychological mechanisms that mediate the effects of attitude function.

The present volume is intended to help facilitate this new generation of research. As such, the volume includes contributions from many of the leading researchers in the field. They have all written interesting and stimulating chapters that integrate and describe their latest research relevant to the study of attitude function. The chapters are roughly organized in the following manner: specific attitude functions (chapters 1 and 2), persuasion (chapters 3–6), individual–differences approaches (chapters 7 and 8), the unique role of motivation (chapters 9 and 10), practical implications (chapters 11–14), and theoretical elaborations of attitude functions (chapter 15). Of course, there is some overlap in focus. In particular, all of the chapters are relevant to both theory and application. For example, the chapters on practical implications raise interesting issues for theories of attitude function, consistent with the adage that practice informs theory (and vice versa).

The book begins with Fazio's chapter describing how accessible attitudes fulfill an object appraisal function. This chapter provides a useful beginning because it is widely believed that the object-appraisal function is the primary function of attitudes. Fazio's evidence supports this claim and raises the intriguing possibility that there are psychological costs associated with this function. In chapter 2, Shavitt and Nelson provide evidence that the social identity function of attitudes is important as well, because people use others' attitudes and possessions to form impressions of them. This communicative aspect of attitudes is often underappreciated.

Chapter 3 provides a provocative introduction to the chapters that focus on persuasion. In this chapter, Thompson, Kruglanski, and Spiegel present their new unimodel of persuasion, which draws on Kruglanski's theory of lay epistemology and emphasizes the importance of object appraisal in the process of persuasion. In chapter 4, Lavine and Snyder reexamine the classic attitude function match hypothesis, which states that message arguments are more persuasive when they address the psychological function that is served by the message recipient's attitude. This chapter describes evidence examining the psychological mechanisms that underlie the match effect and demonstrates the effects of matching on subsequent behavior. The match effect is examined again in chapter 5. In this chapter, Petty, Wheeler, and Bizer use the Elaboration Likelihood Model of persuasion to predict when match effects should and should not occur and they note similarities between attitude function match effects and similar effects in other studies of attitude change. In chapter 6, Levin, Nichols, and Johnson describe how different attitude functions might evoke different types of involvement with issues, causing people to process issue-relevant messages in a biased manner.

Chapters 7 and 8 examine attitude function from an individual difference perspective. This perspective emphasizes the notion that there is at least some consistency in the functions that are served by an individual's attitudes and that some functions will be more dominant in an individual than other functions. In chapter 7, DeBono uses a number of engaging studies that demonstrate effects consistent with the notion that individual differences in self-monitoring might potentially reflect differences in the tendency to adapt social-expressive versus value-expressive (and utilitarian) attitudes. In chapter 8, Prentice and Carlsmith present interesting evidence that there are consistencies in the motivations served by people's attitudes, possessions, and psychological attachment to others.

Chapters 9 and 10 tackle an important issue in the study of attitude function: To what extent can we disentangle effects of motivation from effects of cognition? In chapter 9, we scrutinize the value-expressive function, showing that this function might actually encompass many different distinct motivations. In chapter 10, Marsh and Julka attempt to manipulate several attitude functions in a manner that unconfounds relevant cognitions. Using their manipulations, they discover interesting potential caveats to the attitude function match hypothesis.

Chapters 11 begins a series of four chapters that examine important practical applications of attitude function research. In this chapter, Reeder and Pryor describe their research on the functions of attitudes toward persons with AIDS and present a model that incorporates the role of preconscious affect. The functions of attitudes toward people with AIDS are also examined in chapter 12. In this chapter, Herek presents a methodology for testing whether the functions fulfilled by a particular attitude (e.g., toward persons with AIDS) are similar or varied within a target population. In chapter 13, Snyder, Clary, and Stukas examine the functions of volunteering. Their research identifies several specific motivations that are not included in other theories of attitude function, illustrating the potential variety of attitude functions in real-world settings. In chapter 14, Ennis and Zanna examine the functions of attitudes toward the automobile, showing that different types of automobile serve different attitude functions.

Finally, in chapter 15, we summarize some general themes and issues that have emerged in the recent research. In an attempt to integrate these themes and issues, we present a new model of attitudes that explicitly incorporates both attitude function and attitude structure.

In summary, we believe that these chapters illustrate the vitality and growth in research on the functions fulfilled by attitudes, and we hope that this book stimulates future research and theorizing on this topic. We are indebted to Robert Kidd (formerly of Lawrence Erlbaum Associates), Kate Graetzer, and the people at Lawrence Erlbaum Associates for their patience and support.

—*Gregory R. Maio*
James M. Olson

REFERENCES

Allport, G. W. (1935). Attitudes. In C. Murchison (Ed.), *Handbook of social psychology* (pp. 798–844). Worcester, MA: Clark University Press.

Chaiken, S., Liberman, A., & Eagly, A. H. (1989). Heuristic and systematic processing within and beyond the persuasion context. In J. S. Uleman & J. A. Bargh (Eds.), *Unintended thought* (pp. 212–252). New York: Gilford.

Fishbein, M., & Ajzen, I. (1975). *Belief, attitude, intention, and behavior: An introduction to theory and research.* Reading, MA: Addison–Wesley.

Freud, A. (1966). *The ego and the mechanisms of defense.* New York: International Universities Press.

Hovland, C. I., Janis, I. L., & Kelley, H. H. (1953). *Communication and persuasion: Psychological studies of opinion change.* New Haven, CT: Yale University Press.

Katz, D. (1960). The functional approach to the study of attitudes. *Public Opinion Quarterly, 24,* 163–204.

Lewin, K. (1938). *The conceptual representation and the measurement of psychological forces.* Durham, NC: Duke University Press.

Millar, M. G., & Tesser, A. (1989). Effects of affective and cognitive focus on the attitude–behavior relation. *Journal of Personality and Social Psychology, 51,* 259–269.

Petty, R. E., & Cacioppo, J. T. (1986). The elaboration likelihood model of persuasion. In L. Berkowitz (Ed.), *Advances in experimental social psychology* (Vol. 19, pp. 123–205). San Diego, CA: Academic Press.

Rokeach, M. (1973). *The nature of human values.* New York: Free Press.

Schwartz, S. H. (1992). Universals in the content and structure of values: Theoretical advances and empirical tests in 20 countries. In M. P. Zanna (Ed.), *Advances in experimental social psychology* (Vol. 25, pp. 1–65). San Diego, CA: Academic Press.

Smith, M. B., Bruner, J. S., & White, R. W. (1956). *Opinions and personality.* New York: Wiley.

1

Accessible Attitudes as Tools for Object Appraisal: Their Costs and Benefits

Russell H. Fazio
Indiana University

During the course of their daily lives, individuals encounter a multitude of objects. In fact, they are bombarded by a diverse array of stimuli and forced to make innumerable decisions about which to approach and which to avoid. These stimuli include not only such physical objects as foods, clothing, and toys but also other people, events, and activities. Moreover, societal matters, as well as conversations with others, often require that individuals adopt a position regarding various social and political issues. Thus, merely proceeding through a day involves individuals making a continuous series of choices based on their appraisals of objects.

When considered in this way, daily existence appears to be astoundingly burdensome. One can readily imagine an individual who is paralyzed by the need to assess and then weigh the pros and cons of the choice alternatives for each successive decision. Yet, few people—at least not those who can be considered mentally healthy—experience day-to-day life as so phenomenologically troublesome. How do we manage?

1

We are extremely adaptive creatures who have the capacity to learn from experience. We have memory for these experiences. We develop and remember vast storehouses of knowledge regarding the attributes that characterize the objects, people, issues, and events that we either encounter directly or learn about indirectly from others. As helpful as this knowledge base might be, however, it represents only an initial step toward individuals' successful coping with the multitude of stimuli that impinge on them. Having knowledge regarding a given object available in memory provides a basis for choice, but still requires that individuals engage in extensive and effortful deliberation. They must retrieve the relevant stored information, consider its implications for approach or avoidance, and integrate those implications into a final judgment.

Although individuals unquestionably engage in such deliberation at times (see Fazio, 1990a; Sanbonmatsu & Fazio, 1990), even these processes do not seem to capture the ease with which individuals typically function in their daily lives. People do not simply acquire knowledge about the objects in their social world. Instead, individuals employ this knowledge—be it information about the positively and negatively valued attributes of the object, about their past behavioral experiences with the object, and/or about emotions that the object has evoked in the past—as the basis for forming for an *attitude* toward, or summary evaluation of, the object. In other words, individuals categorize objects along an evaluative dimension (see Fazio, Chen, McDonel, & Sherman, 1982; Zanna & Rempel, 1988, for further discussion of this definition of attitude). It is such categorizations into likes and dislikes—objects that we wish to approach and those that we wish to avoid—that enable individuals to progress easily through daily life. By imposing an evaluative structure on their social world, individuals can more easily cope with the demands of the social environment. Their attitudes provide an indication of which objects to approach and which to avoid, all in the interest of maximizing positive outcomes and minimizing negative outcomes.

THE OBJECT APPRAISAL FUNCTION

This argument regarding the functional utility of attitudes as readily available indicators of whether approach or avoidance is to be preferred has long been recognized in social psychology. In his classic discussion of attitudes, Allport (1935) stated:

> Without guiding attitudes the individual is confused and baffled.... Attitudes determine for each individual what he will see and hear, what he will think and what he will do. To borrow a phrase from William James, they "engender meaning upon the world"; they draw lines about and segregate an otherwise chaotic environment; they are our methods for finding our way about in an ambiguous universe. (p. 806)

Similarly, both Katz (1960) and Smith, Bruner, and White (1956) commented on this knowledge or object appraisal function when they delineated an entire set of functions that can be served by attitudes. For example, Smith et al. (1956) argued as follows:

> The holding of an attitude provides a ready aid in 'sizing up' objects and events in the environment from the point of view of one's major interests and going concerns.... [It] permits the individual to check more quickly and efficiently the action-relevancy of the event in the environment around him. Presented with an object or event, [the individual] may categorize it in some class of objects and events for which a predisposition to action and experience exists. Once thus categorized, it becomes the focus of an already-established repertory of reactions and feelings, and the person is saved the energy-consuming and sometimes painful process of figuring out *de novo* how he shall relate himself to it.... In sum, then, attitudes aid us in classifying for action the objects of the environment, and they make appropriate response tendencies available for coping with these objects. (p. 41)

The object appraisal function was only one of many noted by these attitude theorists. They also discussed, for example, how attitudes can provide a means of communicating one's social identity, expressing one's core values, and maintaining or enhancing one's self-esteem. Attitudes toward a given object may assume a particular valence because that valence allows one to communicate valued group memberships, is congruent with one's values, and/or bolsters one's self-esteem. Unquestionably, attitude formation and expression can be affected by such factors. However, I believe that the inclusion of the object appraisal function as one entry in a list of such benefits potentially provided by attitudes both obscures a critical distinction and undervalues its importance. The other functions that theorists have discussed concern the basis for an attitude (i.e., the reasons that the attitude assumed a particular direction or valence). In contrast, the object appraisal function is unique in that it concerns the general utility of simply holding an attitude, regardless of its valence. That is, regardless of why the individual's attitude took on a particular valence, the mere possession of any attitude is useful to the individual in terms of orienting him or her to the object in question. In this sense, the object appraisal function can be considered the primary value of possessing an attitude. *Every* attitude, regardless of any other functional benefits that it also might provide, serves this object appraisal function.

THE ATTITUDE–NONATTITUDE CONTINUUM

However, I also argue that not all attitudes are equally successful in serving an object appraisal function, for attitudes vary in the extent to which they are capable of providing the "ready aid" that Smith et al. (1956) mentioned. The theoretical model that underlies the research my colleagues and I have conducted on the functionality of attitudes views attitudes as associations in memory between the attitude object and a given summary evaluation of the object (see Fazio, 1995; Fazio et al., 1982, for a general review). The strength of such object-evaluation associations is presumed to vary across people and attitude objects. This associative strength is viewed as the major determinant of the attitude's accessibility from memory (i.e., the likelihood that the evaluation will be activated from memory automatically on the individual's encountering the attitude object). My colleagues and I argued that attitudes involving stronger object-evaluation associations more adequately fulfill the object appraisal function (e.g., Fazio, Blascovich, & Driscoll, 1992).

Although some researchers have argued that individuals automatically evaluate *all* attitude objects when they encounter them (Bargh, Chaiken, Raymond, & Hymes, 1996; Pratto, 1994), I believe that any such tendencies involve, at most, a very rudimentary surveillance of signals regarding safety versus threat. The extent to which individuals form what can be considered attitudes varies across situations. Attitude formation is not inevitable, but instead depends upon the presence of situational cues implying that it may be beneficial to have a summary evaluation of the attitude object stored in memory.

Evidence supporting this hypothesis is provided by research conducted by Fazio, Lenn, and Effrein (1984). This research took advantage of the often-observed finding that individuals who "compute" a judgment for the first time require substantially more time to do so than is required to express the judgment a second time. A number of experiments have found that individuals who have been forced to develop and express a judgment are capable of responding more quickly to a similar inquiry than are individuals who did not form judgments earlier (e.g., Carlston & Skowronski, 1986; Fazio et al., 1982; see Fazio, 1990b, for a general discussion of this issue). In each of two experiments, Fazio et al. (1984) exposed participants to a set of novel intellectual puzzles. Some participants, the consolidation condition, were forced to develop attitudes toward the puzzles; they were required to complete a questionnaire on which they rated the puzzles. No such questionnaire was administered in the no consolidation condition. When the participants were later asked to respond to a series of inquiries regarding their attitudes toward the puzzles, the expected effect was observed. Participants in the consolidation condition had faster response latencies.

However, what is of primary interest in this research are the response latencies in a third condition—among participants who, although not forced to consolidate by the need to complete a questionnaire, received a cue implying that it may be functional to develop attitudes toward the puzzles. In one experiment, the cue led participants to expect future questioning regarding the puzzles; the researcher, who was employing the puzzles as items for an aptitude test, was to interview the participants in the second half of the experiment. In a second experiment, the cue involved an expectation of future interaction; these participants were led to believe that they would have the opportunity to work more with any of the puzzle types that they wished in the second part of the experiment. In both experiments, the participants who received a cue responded just as quickly to the attitudinal inquiries as did the consolidation participants (who had been forced to develop and express attitudes) and more rapidly than the no consolidation participants (who received neither a cue nor a questionnaire forcing them to develop attitudes). Thus, the findings suggest that situational cues implying the functional value of possessing an attitude can prompt individuals to engage in relevant cognitive work, comparable to that pursued by individuals directly asked to provide an attitudinal judgment. Apparently, individuals do not spontaneously engage in the level of attitude development that is required to express an attitude unless they are motivated to do so by a cue suggesting that it may prove functionally beneficial to consider one's attitude toward the novel objects.

Just as situations can vary in the extent to which they entail cues that will prompt attitude formation, individuals appear to vary in their chronic tendencies to engage in evaluative responding. Recent research by Jarvis and Petty (1996) has identified such an individual difference. Individuals with a higher "need to evaluate" were more likely to report having attitudes (i.e., less likely to select a "no opinion" option) toward a variety of social and political issues. They also were more likely to provide evaluative thoughts in a free-response listing about unfamiliar paintings or about a typical day in their lives.

Regardless of any pervasive predispositions that influence the likelihood that individuals will form attitudes, people's general interests and knowledge also are bound to affect the extent to which they form attitudes toward novel objects. For example, some people are very unaware of national politics, whereas others follow the political scene closely. The latter are much more likely to develop an evaluative association regarding a newly emerging figure on the national political scene. Likewise, some people are avid basketball fans with highly rehearsed attitudes toward teams, players, and coaches; such individuals also quickly and easily form judgments about new players and coaches. Others, who have no evaluation of such basketball-related attitude objects available in memory, will have little reason to make evaluative judgments of such entities, and will find doing so difficult if and when the need arises. As a result of such varying interests and knowledge, people can vary in the extent to which they are, in effect, "attitudinally expert" in any given domain.

Thus, situations may vary in the extent to which they prompt attitude formation. Individuals vary in the extent to which they are generally predisposed to evaluate attitude objects, and individuals themselves exhibit varying degrees of attachment to various domains of attitude objects. For these reasons, considerable variability is to be expected across both people and attitude objects with respect to the strength of their attitudes. My colleagues and I have referred to such variation in the strength of object-evaluation associations as the *attitude–nonattitude continuum* (see Converse, 1970). Objects toward which an individual has no associated evaluation available in memory are characterized as falling at the nonattitude end of the continuum. When faced with an attitudinal inquiry or a decision, the individual is forced to construct an evaluative judgment "on the spot" using whatever relevant attributes of the object might be available in memory or in the current situational context. As we move along the continuum, an evaluation is now available in memory and the strength of the association between the object and the evaluation increases, as does the attitude's capability for automatic activation. Thus, toward the upper end of the continuum is the case of a well-learned association—sufficiently so that the evaluation is capable of being activated automatically on observation of the attitude object.

Research testing this view of attitudes has involved either measuring or manipulating the strength of the object-evaluation association. Measurement has been accomplished via response latency techniques; the more quickly an individual can respond to a query about his or her attitude, the stronger the association. In other work, the strength of the association has been manipulated by having some participants express their attitudes repeatedly in an early phase of the experiment. Each attitudinal expression induces individuals to note and rehearse the association and, hence, enhances the strength of the association. Such research has provided converging evidence for the proposition that the likelihood of automatic attitude activation increases as the strength of the object-evaluation association increases (e.g., Bargh, Chaiken, Govender, & Pratto, 1992; Fazio, 1993; Fazio, Sanbonmatsu, Powell, & Kardes, 1986). Moreover, both correlational investigations (in which associative strength has been measured) and laboratory research (in which it has been manipulated experimentally) have found that position along the attitude–nonattitude continuum moderates the influence of attitudes on judgments and behavior (e.g., Bassili, 1995, 1996; Fazio, Powell, & Williams, 1989; Fazio & Williams, 1986; Houston & Fazio, 1989; see Fazio, 1995, for a general review).

As mentioned earlier, the implications of this view of attitudes for the matter of attitude functionality are very straightforward. The degree to which an attitude provides the individual with a functional "ready aid" depends on the extent to which the attitude is capable of being activated automatically from memory when the individual observes the attitude object. The likelihood of such automatic activation depends on the strength of the object–evaluation association. Thus, it is attitudes that involve a strong association that are truly functional. By virtue of their accessibility from memory, such attitudes free the individual from the processing required for reflective thought about his or her evaluation of the object.

Over the past decade, my colleagues and I have conducted a variety of empirical investigations related to the functional value of attitudes, especially ones that are accessible from memory. In what follows, I review this research and, in so doing, illustrate the many senses in which accessible attitudes serve an object appraisal function. Individuals attain a variety of functional benefits as a consequence of possessing accessible attitudes.[1] However, I also review some recent research that suggests that these benefits are achieved at some cost to the individual.

THE BENEFITS OF ACCESSIBLE ATTITUDES

The research that we have conducted on what can be viewed as functional benefits of attitudes is quite varied. All the research concerns attitudes as convenient summaries that guide appraisal processes in a functional manner and, consequently, ease decision making. However, in considering the potential influence of attitudes on appraisal processes, we have focused on a variety of phenomena, ranging from fundamental cognitive processes such as attention and categorization to higher order judgmental and decision processes.

Accessible Attitudes Orient Visual Attention. Individuals cannot attend to all the stimuli that enter their visual fields. Research by Roskos-Ewoldsen and Fazio (1992) indicates that accessible attitudes play a very useful role in directing attention to certain objects in the visual field. In a series of experiments, these researchers obtained evidence that objects toward which individuals held highly accessible attitudes (termed *attitude-evoking* objects) automatically attracted attention. Across the experiments, attitude accessibility was either manipulated by inducing participants to note and rehearse their attitudes or measured by assessing the latency with which individuals could respond to an attitudinal inquiry. In the visual attention portion of the experiments, the participants were shown displays consisting of six line drawings of objects. The more attitude-evoking objects were more likely to be noticed on very brief exposures of the displays than were the objects toward which participants possessed less accessible attitudes. In another experiment, attitude-evoking objects were more likely to have been noticed incidentally when they were presented in the context of a task that did not require attending to the objects.

The final experiment in the series yielded evidence that attitude-evoking objects interfered with performance on a visual search task when the

---

[1]Some of the research presented in this chapter has been reviewed in related chapters written earlier (see Fazio, 1995; Fazio, Roskos-Ewoldsen, & Powell, 1994). Research reviewed in these earlier chapters is summarized briefly. Greater attention is devoted to newer work conducted since the preparation of those earlier reviews.

objects were presented as distractors. On each trial, participants were required to search the display for the present or absence of a target item. Through instructions and training, the participants were led to understand that a target would never appear in certain positions of the visual display. Thus, these locations could be ignored when searching for the target. However, when these to-be-ignored positions depicted objects toward which the participants had rehearsed attitudes, their presence interfered with search performance. Participants were slower to indicate that the display did or did not include the target item when the distractors were attitude-evoking objects. Apparently, these attitude-evoking objects automatically attracted attention as they entered the visual field.

These findings led Roskos-Ewoldsen and Fazio (1992) to suggest that attitudes, if they are sufficiently accessible from memory, can be activated from memory at a very early stage in the processing of visual information and that, once activated, such evaluative information directs further attention to the visual stimulus. As a result, attitude-evoking objects are at an advantage in terms of their being consciously noticed and reported. What we "see" appears to be influenced by our possession of accessible attitudes.

This effect of accessible attitudes certainly has functional value. The attitudes alert us to the presence of objects that have the potential for hedonic consequences. We are likely to notice those objects that can provide reward or satisfaction, those that we have personally defined as likable and from which we can benefit by approaching. Likewise, we are likely to notice those objects toward which we have developed strongly associated negative evaluations, ones that we wish to avoid if at all possible. By orienting our attention to objects that have such hedonic significance, accessible attitudes ready appropriate approach or avoidance tendencies and, hence, promote individuals' maximization of positive outcomes and minimization of negative outcomes.

Accessible Attitudes Promote Hedonically Meaningful Categorizations. Attitude objects, whether they be physical objects, people, or issues, often can be thought of in multiple ways. They are categorizable in multiple ways. For example, a chainsaw can be viewed as an environment-damaging artifact by a forest conservationist, but as a valued symbol of one's livelihood by a logger. Likewise, kung pao chicken is likely to be categorized as a Szechuan dish, but to a person with an allergy to peanuts it may be viewed as a dish that contains peanuts. An African-

American, female cashier can be considered in terms of her race, gender, or occupation. Affirmative action can be viewed as a race issue, as a gender issue, as a setting of hiring quotas, or as a means of providing for equal opportunity. Which potential categorization will predominate?

Smith, Fazio, and Cejka (1996) noted the parallel between this question and the question posed by Roskos-Ewoldsen and Fazio (1992) regarding which of the multitude of objects present in the visual field at any moment in time attract attention. Smith et al. (1996) suggested that each of the various potential categorizations of a given object may receive some activation when the object is encountered. However, they noted that each of these possibilities may itself be associated with an evaluation. On the basis of findings of Roskos-Ewoldsen and Fazio (1992), Smith et al. argued that the strength of any such evaluative associations is critical. The more attitude-evoking a potential categorization is, the more likely it is that attention will be drawn to that particular attribute of the stimulus. Models of categorization (e.g., Medin & Schaffer, 1978; Nosofsky, 1986; Smith & Zarate, 1992) posit a pivotal role for such attentional mechanisms. These models suggest that categorization follows from the allocation of attention to particular dimensions of the stimulus. Greater attention to a given attribute increases the likelihood that the stimulus will be categorized accordingly. Therefore, it would appear that possessing highly accessible attitudes toward a given attribute of a stimulus object could lead to greater attention being drawn to this specific attitude-evoking characteristic of the object. In turn, this greater attention increases the likelihood that the target will be categorized in terms of this attitude-evoking category.

The experiments conducted by Smith et al. (1996) focused on multiple categorizable objects and people. For example, yogurt can be viewed as a health food or as a dairy product, sunbathing as an activity that can lead to cancer or as something one does at the beach, Pete Rose as a baseball player or as a gambler. Using triads consisting of a target and two alternative categorizations of the target, Smith et al. had research participants rehearse their attitudes toward one of the two alternative categories. For the other category, the participants indicated whether it was animate or inanimate. In this way, the accessibility of attitudes toward one of the two potential categorizations was enhanced. That is, one of the categories was experimentally made more attitude evoking.

Smith et al. (1996) employed a cued-recall measure as the dependent variable assessing categorization. Later in the experiment, the participants were presented, for the first time, with the target words from each triad. They were instructed to use these words as cues to aid their recall of the stimuli that had been presented in the two earlier tasks (i.e., the attitude rehearsal task and the animate/inanimate task). Smith et al. reasoned that the potential categorizations of the target should receive varying degrees of activation on presentation of the object name. However, those categories that evoke attitudes should be at an advantage. They should attract attention and, other factors being equal, more strongly influence how the target object is categorized at that moment in time. Thus, the targets were expected to more effectively cue the categories for which attitude accessibility had been enhanced.

This reasoning was confirmed in each of the two cued-recall experiments that Smith et al. (1996) conducted. The targets more effectively cued the categories that had been assigned to the attitude rehearsal task. For example, when the accessibility of attitudes toward health food had been experimentally enhanced, yogurt was more likely to cue health food; when attitudes toward dairy products had been rehearsed, yogurt was more likely to cue dairy product. Moreover, in the second of the two Smith et al. experiments, this effect of attitude rehearsal on cued recall was observed despite the imposition of a 1-week delay between the manipulation tasks and the recall measure.

A final experiment by Smith et al. (1996) served to test the hypothesis with a completely different dependent variable that did not involve memory for the terms presented during the two manipulation tasks. The time required to verify that a given target was a member of a given category was examined. Following the manipulation of attitude accessibility, participants engaged in a task in which they were shown a category label followed by a target and answered "yes or no" as quickly as possible to indicate whether or not the target was a member of the specified category. Participants verified category membership more quickly when the accessibility of attitudes toward the category had been enhanced. Thus, this experiment provided converging evidence for the proposition that the potential category toward which the individual had the more accessible attitude was more likely to dominate the categorization process.

A recent investigation by Fazio and Dunton (1997) also tested this same general hypothesis regarding the influence of attitude accessibility on categorization. However, this research tested the hypothesis in a very different manner—with photos of people, instead of words, as the stimuli of interest. The photos that were presented to participants varied in race, gender, and occupation. Each photo included context information, such as uniforms, tools, equipment, or background settings, that provided cues regarding the occupation of the individual. Included were such targets as a White, female police officer; a White, male bricklayer; a Black, female cashier; and a Black, male Air Force officer. Thus, each photo was potentially categorizable in multiple ways.

In order to assess categorization, Fazio and Dunton employed a similarity judgment task. The participants were presented with pairs of photos and asked to rate the similarity of the individuals in each pair. The resulting similarity matrices were subjected to a multidimensional scaling procedure, which revealed the similarity judgments to be largely a function of four dimensions. Two dimensions concerned the occupations depicted in the photos. The other two were clearly identifiable as concerning the targets' race and gender.

Fazio and Dunton were interested primarily in the race dimension. The multidimensional scaling procedure INDSCAL yielded not only the four-dimensional space previously summarized, but also a set of weights for each individual respondent showing the extent to which the individual weighted each dimension in making his or her similarity ratings. When squared, these weights are readily interpretable; they indicate the proportion of variance in the given respondent's similarity ratings that is accounted for by each dimension. The squared weights for the race dimension revealed considerable variability among the respondents in the extent to which they used race as a basis for judging similarity. Some participants used race little, whereas others used it heavily.

The question that concerned Fazio and Dunton was whether the extent to which individuals categorized by race was itself a function of the accessibility of their racial attitudes. Both the findings regarding visual attention (Roskos-Ewoldsen & Fazio, 1992) and the findings regarding the categorization of verbal stimuli (Smith et al., 1996) point to the importance of the extent to which a possible categorization is attitude evoking or evaluatively laden. In the present case, Fazio and Dunton reasoned that the more race was attitude evoking for a given perceiver, the more likely it was that the target's race would automatically attract attention and, hence, the more likely that the perceiver would categorize by race and use race heavily as a basis for judging similarity.

In order to assess the extent to which race might be attitude evoking for a given individual, Fazio and Dunton (1997) used a priming procedure that provides a direct assessment of any evaluations that are automatically activated on exposure to a Black target person. This *bona fide pipeline* procedure was developed in recent research by Fazio, Jackson, Dunton, and Williams (1995) as an unobtrusive measure of racial attitudes. The participant's task on each trial is to indicate the connotation of an evaluative adjective as quickly as possible. Does the adjective mean "good" or "bad"? The latency with which this judgment is made and how it is affected by the prior presentation of a prime is the focus. Essentially, the pattern of facilitation that is exhibited on positive versus negative adjectives can provide an indication of the individual's attitude toward the primed object, which in this case are high-resolution color images of Black and White undergraduates. Relatively more facilitation on positive adjectives would be indicative of a more positive attitude, and relatively more facilitation on negative adjectives would be indicative of a more negative attitude. Obviously, what is of major interest is the amount of facilitation on positive versus negative adjectives when those adjectives are preceded by Black faces versus White faces. In fact, for each individual participant, the effect size of this interaction between race of photo and valence of adjective serves as an estimate of the individual's racial attitude. Previous research using such estimates of racial attitudes has established their predictive validity (Dunton & Fazio, 1997; Fazio et al., 1995).

The individuals in the study of Fazio and Dunton (1997) participated in the bona fide pipeline procedure 1 week prior to having completed the similarity judgment task, in what was ostensibly a separate study. Because the unobtrusive measure is based on evaluations that are automatically activated from memory, the resulting attitude estimates have the advantage of providing an indication of the extent to which race is attitude evoking for any given individual. For some individuals, positivity is automatically evoked in response to the Black faces; for others, negativity is automatically evoked. For other people, neither occurs. Fazio and Dunton (1997) predicted a curvilinear, U-shaped relation between the attitude estimates derived from the priming procedure and categorization by race. Those individuals for whom race is attitude evoking should have their attention automatically drawn to the target's skin color and, hence, should be more likely to use race as a basis for judging similarity.

A multiple regression predicting the INDSCAL subject weights for the race dimension from the estimates of automatically activated attitudes and from the squared values of these attitude estimates revealed the predicted curvilinear relation to be significant. Those participants for whom negativity was automatically activated in response to Blacks had weights indicating that they used the race dimension heavily in making their similarity ratings. The same was true of those participants for whom positive attitudes were automatically activated. Individuals for whom little or no attitude activation automatically occurred tended not to use the race dimension much.

Together, the investigations of Smith et al. (1996) and Fazio and Dunton (1997) provide converging evidence regarding the importance of attitude accessibility as a determinant of categorization. The various investigations differed markedly in their empirical approaches. Smith et al. experimentally manipulated the accessibility of attitudes toward a potentially relevant category, whereas Fazio and Dunton directly measured the extent to which race was attitude evoking for a given individual. Smith et al. employed verbal stimuli consisting of the names of objects or people that could be categorized in multiple ways, whereas Fazio and Dunton examined photos that varied in race, gender, and occupation. Across the studies, cued recall, the latency with which category membership could be verified, and the extent to which race was employed as a basis for judging similarity served as the dependent measures. Despite these differences, all the studies provided evidence consistent with the proposition that categorization depends, at least in part, on the extent to which the relevant categories are evaluatively laden. Because categories that are attitude evoking attract attention, they are relatively likely to dominate the categorization process.

Once again, such an effect of possessing accessible attitudes appears to have functional value. Of the many possible ways to construe a given object, the categorization that the individual most strongly associates with an evaluation is at an advantage. Thus, the individual is likely to view the object in a way that is most hedonically meaningful for him or her. By guiding how an object is construed in this way, accessible attitudes alert the individual to the presence of objects that have, for that individual, the potential for hedonic consequences. Recognizing its hedonic significance, the individual is now prepared to either approach or avoid the object, whichever is more appropriate given the valence of the activated attitude.

Ultimately, then, the outcome of such categorization processes should influence both perceptions of the object in the immediate situation and behavior toward the object. Having categorized a stimulus in a given way, the individual is now positioned to use any information about the category that may be available in memory as a basis for drawing further inferences about the object. In the case of a physical object, such inferences would involve beliefs about the category of objects; in the case of a stimulus person, the inferences would involve beliefs about the category of persons (i.e., stereotypes). Any such inferential processes should contribute all the more to construal of the object in a manner that is consistent with the valence of the attitude whose accessibility influenced the categorization process. For example, consider how categorization of a Black, male Air Force officer might vary as a consequence of the differential accessibility of a negative attitude toward Blacks versus a positive attitude toward military officers. If the latter is more accessible, the person is likely to be categorized as an officer, construed positively, and, ultimately, approached and treated positively. Moreover, any inferences regarding the traits that the person is apt to exhibit will be based on the stereotype of military officers. In contrast, the findings suggest that if the negative racial attitude is more accessible, then the person is likely to be categorized by his race and, hence, construed negatively. Trait inferences will be based on the perceiver's stereotype of Blacks and may provide a further basis for avoidance of, or generally negative responses to, the individual.

Accessible Attitudes Ease Decision Making. Attitude theorists' discussion of the object appraisal function explicitly postulates that one of the benefits of possessing an attitude is that the individual does not need to engage in an extensive process of deliberative reflection regarding the value of the object every time it is encountered. Instead, the preexisting attitude provides a "ready aid" for appraising the object. As argued earlier, such benefits should be especially true of more accessible attitudes.

Research motivated by this reasoning (Blascovich et al., 1993; Fazio et al., 1992) has provided direct evidence concerning the value of possessing accessible attitudes—such attitudes actually ease decision making. These experiments employed measures of autonomic reactivity to assess effort expenditure during decision making. The experiments involved a paradigm in which the critical task required participants to express a preference between pairs of abstract paintings. Moreover, the task was intentionally made quite difficult by having the trials proceed at a fairly rapid rate; a new pair of paintings was presented every 2.5 seconds.

An attitude-rehearsal manipulation occurred prior to this pairwise preference task. Participants judged their liking for each painting repeatedly, or performed a "color-naming" task in which they announced the predominant color, the percentage of the painting that consisted of that color, and any other colors appearing in the painting. Thus, the manipulation permitted a comparison of individuals whose attitudes were relatively accessible as a result of their having rehearsed their evaluations to individuals who had been exposed to the paintings equally often but not provided with the opportunity to develop and rehearse attitudes. In other words, the two conditions involved individuals whose attitudes were at different positions along the attitude–nonattitude continuum. As expected, those in the attitude-rehearsal condition displayed less reactivity when they later performed the pairwise preference task than did participants in the color-naming condition.

Importantly, similar effects were obtained in an experiment in which the attitude-rehearsal manipulation was conducted within-subjects instead of between-subjects (Blascovich et al., 1993, Experiment 2). The within-subjects design ensured that all participants were equivalently familiar with the task of evaluating paintings and that they had received equivalent practice at the procedure of doing so. Despite task novelty and procedural efficiency having been equated in this way, participants displayed greater reactivity when the pairwise preference task involved paintings that had been in the color-naming set than when it involved paintings that had been in the attitude-rehearsal set. Analogous findings were obtained in a within-subjects experiment in which the latency with which respondents made their pairwise preference decisions served as the dependent measure (Fazio et al., 1992, Experiment 4). Decisions were made more quickly when individuals were deciding between two alternatives from the attitude-rehearsal set than when they were deciding between two alternatives from the color-naming set.

These findings indicate that accessible attitudes can ease decision making. The attitude-rehearsal task led participants to develop associations in memory between each painting and their evaluation of the painting. Activation of these evaluations during the pairwise preference task made that task less demanding. Having an attitude freed the individual from the processing required to construct an evaluation of the object. Hence, fewer resources were required to cope with the demands of the task.

Accessible Attitudes Enhance the Quality of Decision Making.   The experiments involving this pairwise preference paradigm also yielded evidence that suggests that accessible attitudes improve the quality of decision making. At the end of each experiment, participants were asked to rank order the paintings in terms of their liking for them. Unlike the situation for the pairwise preference trials, which had proceeded at a demanding and rapid rate, participants were provided unlimited time to accomplish this ranking. Each participant's rank ordering was compared to the preferences that he or she expressed during the pairwise preference task by counting the number of times that the pairwise preference concurred with the rank ordering. For example, if a participant ranked Painting 4 as more likable than Painting 12, then the participant was given credit for a concurrence if he or she had chosen Painting 4 over Painting 12 when the two had been presented together during the pairwise preference task. In each experiment, the scores were well above chance in both conditions, which indicates that the participants did take the tasks seriously. However, concurrences were significantly more numerous when the participants had rehearsed their attitudes toward the paintings at the beginning of the experiment, which suggests that the rushed decisions participants were required to make during the pairwise preference task were of better quality when individuals could rely on previously developed attitudes.

This finding points to an advantage of making decisions on the basis of accessible attitudes relative to doing so on the basis of quick, on-the-spot appraisals of the object. When an individual possesses an accessible attitude, the attitude is likely to be activated automatically upon his or her encountering the attitude object. Hence, the individual is likely to arrive at a perception of the object in the immediate situation that concurs with his or her attitude. In contrast, the individual's only recourse when lacking an accessible attitude is to construct an appraisal of the object on-the-spot. The problem with this is that these on the spot appraisals may be unduly influenced by momentarily salient characteristics of the object. As a result, the individual may, in effect, make a mistake (i.e, arrive at a decision that is not reflective of his or her true attitude).

Recent research by Wilson and his colleagues illustrates this difficulty with on-the-spot appraisals (Wilson et al., 1993; Wilson & Schooler, 1991). In various experiments concerned with attitudes toward different jams, college courses, or posters, individuals were induced to analyze the reasons underlying their attitudes. Doing so is known to focus attention on at least some attributes and criteria that typically do not receive consideration during decision making. When thinking about reasons for their attitudes, people appear to focus unduly on attributes of the objects that are easy to verbalize, even though those attributes may not be important causes of their evaluations. The increased salience of these attributes can influence individuals' immediate appraisals of the objects and, ultimately, their choice behavior. The end result is a decision that corresponds less with expert opinion (Wilson & Schooler, 1991), or that the individual comes to regret over time (Wilson et al., 1993), relative to what is observed among participants who have not analyzed such reasons. Especially relevant to the present concerns is the fact that attitude accessibility has been shown to moderate the influence of analyzing reasons on the evaluations that are expressed immediately after having generated the reasons (Hodges & Wilson, 1993). Individuals with more accessible attitudes are less likely to base their attitude expressions on the somewhat unrepresentative thoughts temporarily made salient by the reasons analysis, presumably because they have no need to "compute" an attitude on the spot. These findings, then, provide further support for the argument that a lack of accessible attitudes can leave people open to the possibility of making decisions on the basis of momentarily salient characteristics of the object that do not necessarily concur with their true attitudes toward the object.

Accessible Attitudes Free Resources for Coping with Stressors. The research summarized earlier concerning ease of decision making indicates that benefits result from having accessible attitudes toward objects when one has to make decisions about those objects. Fewer resources are required when one already possesses accessible attitudes toward the decision alternatives. This may have considerable adaptive value in that the resources freed by having accessible attitudes may assist the individual in coping with other, potentially more pressing, matters.

This adaptive value is illustrated by a recent longitudinal study concerned with individuals' adjustment to a new life setting. In an investigation assessing the mental and physical health of students during their first semester in college, Fazio and Powell (1997) found the accessibility of academically related attitudes (e.g., attitudes toward specific courses and possible majors) to play an important role. The study was prospective in nature. Students participated in two sessions separated by a 2-month interval. The initial session occurred within the first 2 weeks of the semester. It began with an assessment of the accessibility of students' attitudes toward a variety of academic concerns. These included specific courses (e.g, taking introductory biology), possible majors (e.g., majoring in business), and types of classes (e.g., early morning classes, small seminar classes, large lecture classes), as well as a variety of academic activities (e.g., studying in the library, pulling an all-nighter, giving an oral presentation, doing extra credit assignments, talking to a professor after class). A large number of filler trials also were included for the purpose of obtaining an estimate of the respondent's baseline speed of responding. These filler items involved a wide variety of issues, including various recreational activities, national and social policy issues, political figures, and celebrities. On each trial, a word or phrase was displayed on the monitor in the individual's cubicle and the participants indicated whether they liked or disliked the object by pressing one of two buttons on a response pad as quickly as possible. Attitude accessibility toward the academic issues was indexed as the participant's average z score for the target latencies, with z computed relative to the individual's own mean and standard deviation for the filler trial latencies. In effect, a high score means that the participant knows his or her likes and dislikes with respect to academic concerns relatively well compared to those with respect to the filler issues.

Following the attitude latency task, the participants completed a number of measures related to stress and mental and physical health. They first completed the College Student Life Events Scale (see Levine & Perkins, 1980; Linville, 1987). This questionnaire asked whether each of a number of events had occurred within the last month and, if it did, whether the event had a negative impact. Following Linville (1987), the number of negative events served as the measure of stress. Participants then completed two standard mental health measures: the Hopkins Symptom Checklist (or SCL-90), which asks about the extent to which one has experienced each of a number of symptoms of distress in the past week (Derogatis, Lipman, & Covi, 1973), and the Beck Depression Inventory (BDI; Beck, Ward, Mendelson, Mock, & Erbaugh, 1961). They also completed some measures regarding their physical health, including the Cohen–Hoberman Inventory of Physical Symptoms (Cohen & Hoberman, 1983), which asks about the extent to which one has experienced a number of specific physical symptoms in the previous month, such as headache, nausea, diarrhea, back pain, cold, or cough. When the participants returned 2 months later, they completed the same battery of self-report instruments regarding health.

The data were analyzed via hierarchical multiple regression. Participants' scores on a given health measure at Time 1, their stress scores at Time 1, and their attitude accessibility scores were used to predict scores on the same health measure at Time 2. Cross products representing the two-way interactions among these variables were then entered into the equation, followed by the three-way interaction term. Such analyses were conducted for each health measure—the SCL-90, the BDI, and self-reported physical health. In each case, a significant three-way interaction between attitude accessibility, stress at Time 1, and the given health measure at Time 1 emerged.

The three-way interaction indicated that the relation between stress and Time 2 health depended on both initial health and attitude accessibility. It is best understood by considering the nature of the relation when health scores at Time 1 are relatively good versus relatively poor. Among those who entered college in relatively good health, greater stress at Time 1 was related to poorer health at Time 2. However, the relation became less pronounced as attitude accessibility increased. The possession of accessible attitudes appeared to insulate individuals from the negative consequences of stress in that this relation was attenuated among those individuals whose academically related attitudes were relatively accessible. In other words, attitude accessibility served as a buffering variable. If negative life events were imposing additional stress on the students, then their having accessible attitudes in the academic domain seems to have freed resources for coping with such stressors. Apparently, knowing their likes and dislikes and, thus, not having to deliberate extensively in order to make academically relevant decisions permitted individuals to focus their cognitive and emotional resources on coping more effectively with the stressors that they were experiencing.

Consideration of the relation between Time 1 stress and Time 2 health among those students who entered college in a state of relative dysphoria or poor physical health indicated that attitude accessibility also was related to recovery from that poor initial state. Generally speaking, the degree of recovery from this initial dysphoria was a function of the stress factor. Those experiencing lesser stress displayed greater recovery (i.e., better health at Time 2). However, this relation grew stronger with increasing attitude accessibility. The more accessible their attitudes toward the academically related issues, the more these initially dysphoric, yet relatively unstressed, students showed improvement from their initially negative state. Those who lacked accessible attitudes and, hence, were forced to reflect and deliberate more extensively about academic decisions were less able to recover than were those whose accessible attitudes permitted them the luxury of foregoing extensive deliberation.

Thus, it appears that freshmen who enter college knowing their likes and dislikes regarding academically relevant issues have an easier time coping with any life stressors that they may experience and recovering from any earlier episodes of dysphoria or physical illness that they may have experienced. The findings suggest that there are indeed benefits to knowing one's likes and dislikes. Obviously, the correlational nature of this investigation does not permit us to draw causal inferences about the role of attitude accessibility. The study was intended only to complement the picture that has emerged from the laboratory experiments regarding attitude functionality. It is important that it be viewed in conjunction with those much more controlled laboratory experiments. Those experiments provide a clear indication of the causal role of accessible attitudes in easing decision making. The findings from this longitudinal study are consistent with our theoretical model and with the inferences that we have drawn from the laboratory experiments, but ultimately they must be replicated by research in which attitude accessibility is manipulated experimentally. Nevertheless, the findings suggest that accessible attitudes may play an important role in a real-world context involving very significant outcome measures of mental and physical health.

Summary. There now exists a variety of evidence regarding the functional value of accessible attitudes. Such attitudes orient visual attention and categorization processes in a useful manner (Fazio & Dunton, 1997; Roskos-Ewoldsen & Fazio, 1992; Smith et al., 1996), both ease decision making and enhance the quality of the ultimate decisions (Blascovich et al., 1993; Fazio et al., 1992), and leave more resources available for coping with other stressors that one is experiencing (Fazio & Powell, 1997). Each of these research findings is consistent with the object-appraisal function that attitudes have been postulated to serve. An attitude, at least to the extent that it is readily accessible from memory, "provides a ready aid in 'sizing up' objects and events in the environment" (Smith et al., 1956, p. 41), which yields a number of benefits for the individual.

Shortly, I argue that these benefits are not without accompanying costs. However, before doing so, it will prove useful to digress briefly to review research concerned with the effect of attitudes, especially accessible ones, on perceptions and judgments.

ATTITUDES, PERCEPTION, AND JUDGMENT

Social psychology has long recognized the constructive nature of perception and judgmental processes. Indeed, this perspective formed the essence of the New Look movement (e.g., Bruner, 1957), which viewed perception not as the mere outcome of sensory processes but as an inferential act of categorization. The constructs that a perceiver brings to bear when witnessing an event can be very influential in determining what is perceived. As a result, two perceivers can arrive at very divergent perceptions of the very same event.

Included among the many relevant constructs that can influence perception is the perceiver's attitude toward the object. It is well established that attitudes can bias the processing and judgment of information relevant to the attitude object. For example, documenting a phenomenon well known to any sports fan, Hastorf and Cantril (1954) observed divergent perceptions of possible infractions committed during the course of a football game as a function of team allegiance. Relatively more infractions were thought to have been committed by the opposing team. Regan, Straus, and Fazio (1974) found that attitudes toward a confederate influenced attributions regarding the confederate's behavior, such that attitudinally inconsistent behavior was attributed to external forces and attitudinally consistent behavior was attributed to internal causes. Carretta and Moreland (1982) found that Nixon supporters (as identified by earlier voting behavior) were more likely than McGovern supporters to evaluate Nixon's involvement with Watergate as within legal limits and to maintain their positive attitudes toward Nixon through the course of the Watergate hearings. Research by Lord, Ross, and Lepper (1979) revealed that judgments of the quality of two purported scientific studies concerning the deterrent efficacy of capital punishment varied as a function of the participants' own attitudes toward the death penalty. Subsequent research employing this same paradigm has found that this biasing effect of attitudes is all the more pronounced as the accessibility of individuals' attitudes toward capital punishment increases (Houston & Fazio, 1989; Schuette & Fazio, 1995). Similarly, Fazio and Williams' (1986) investigation of the 1984 U.S. presidential election revealed a relation between attitudes toward the candidates and judgments of the quality of the candidates' performance during the nationally televised debates—a relation that, once again, increased as attitude accessibility increased.

These are just a few examples of the many investigations available in the literature that illustrate the influence that attitudes can have on perceptions and judgments. It is interesting to note that this accumulated evidence typically involves judgments made in the context of a complex, enriched environment. That is, social psychologists generally have studied biased processing in environments that readily allow for multiple interpretations of the target event. If one were to imagine a continuum ranging from sparse to rich environments, it seems quite plausible that the role of the perceiver would be more marked for the richer end of the continuum. The richer the environment and, hence, the more features that are available, the greater the latitude the individual enjoys in terms of the specific features that he or she might notice and consider. The features that receive consideration are likely to vary from perceiver to perceiver. It is not surprising that different samples of information lead to different interpretations.

However, an experiment by Powell and Fazio (summarized in Fazio, Roskos-Ewoldsen, & Powell, 1994) demonstrates just how extensive and fundamental the influence of attitudes on perception can be. This experiment differed from typical research on attitudinally biased processing, like the studies previously mentioned, in two important ways. First, it involved what could be considered an informationally sparse event. The experiment concerned the possibility that attitudes may bias what people report seeing even when the situation is stripped of elements that allow for differential feature sampling. Essentially, the participants saw a flash of light on a computer screen and were required to note its location on the screen. Obviously, this is a very simple perceptual event, much less complex than, for example, the presidential debates. In addition, the judgment that the participants were asked to make also was quite simple. They indicated whether the flash was within or beyond a boundary line. This is unlike previous research in which judgments involved making causal attributions or arriving at an overall interpretation of a series of events. The judgment does not require the integration of many pieces of information.

The participants' responses were collected in the context of what was described as a computerized "tennis" game that was under development. The flash of light represented the "ball" and the participant decided whether each volley of the ball was in or out-of-bounds. Biased perception was examined as a function of the participant's liking or disliking of the target individual who ostensibly was playing against the computer. The liking manipulation occurred earlier in the experiment. It involved an entire series of events, including the confederate's wearing a sweatshirt with the insignia of the participants' own university or a rival university, behaving politely or rudely to both the experimenter and the participant, and offering the participant a cookie or eating cookies in front of the participant without ever offering any.

Through a rigged drawing, the participant learned that she was to play a role similar to that of a linesman for the tennis match between the confederate and a computerized opponent. Her task was to press a button on a response box to indicate after each and every volley (flash of light) whether the ball landed in- or out-of-bounds. However, the participant was told explicitly that she had no control over the game. Her calls would simply provide information for the experimenter on the adequacy of the resolution of the video display. The computer itself would determine whether a given ball was out-of-bounds and, if so, would terminate the point. Thus, the participant knew that her responses were to be compared to the true position of the ball as determined by the computer.

On target trials, the computer randomly selected and executed shots that appeared within 5 pixels of either side of the end line. The participants' responses (key presses of "in" or "out") to the target trials, as well as the latencies of those responses, were recorded by the computer.

The conceptual reasoning underlying this experiment was based upon Bruner's (1957) arguments regarding two major effects of category accessibility. According to Bruner, category accessibility both readies one to perceive an event that fits the category and widens the range of input characteristics that will be accepted as fitting the category. The investigators reasoned that attitudes toward the confederate, and the expectations and hopes that they generated, would have corresponding effects on the participants' responses. That is, the participant's attitude would lead her to hope that a given event (the disliked confederate's loss of the point or the liked confederate's winning of the point) would occur. This enhanced readiness for a particular scenario would increase the likelihood that she in fact would see it that way. Bruner's widening notion implies a greater likelihood of errors that match one's attitudinally driven hopes. Similarly, his readiness notion implies a faster latency to correctly detect a ball's location when the true location matches one's hopes than when it does not.

Despite the experimental instructions emphasizing accuracy, the participants responses were affected by their liking or disliking of the confederate. Both the error rates and the response latencies revealed effects consistent with Bruner's arguments. Errors that showed bias in favor of the confederate (calling a ball hit by the confederate as "in" when it truly was "out" or calling a ball hit by the computerized opponent as "out" when it truly was "in") were more numerous than errors that did not favor the confederate (calling a ball hit by the confederate as "out" when it truly was "in" or calling a ball hit by the opponent as "in" when it actually was "out") when the confederate was liked. In contrast, participants who had been induced to dislike the confederate showed a pattern of errors that favored the confederate's computerized opponent.

The latency data also revealed attitude-consistent bias. Participants who liked the confederate were faster to make correct calls that favored the confederate, whereas those who disliked the confederate were faster to make correct calls that favored the computerized player, the confederate's opponent. Thus, participants displayed a greater readiness to perceive events that matched their attitudinally based hopes.

The experimental findings attest to the powerful influence of attitudes on perception. Indeed, the results demonstrate the presence of biased processing, due to attitudinally driven hopes, at a basic perceptual level. Even when such a simple stimulus event was presented in so sparse an environment, participants instructed to strive for accuracy showed very disparate (and attitudinally congruent) responses. The results imply that attitudes can create expectancies (or wishes) that make one very receptive to attitude-consistent perceptual events. Given that attitudinally congruent events enjoy this distinct advantage even in informationally sparse environments, it is no wonder that attitudes have been found to exert such a strong biasing influence on the interpretation and judgment of the informationally richer and more complex events that typically have been investigated.

THE "FLIP SIDE":
COSTS OF ACCESSIBLE ATTITUDES

Attitudes, then, exert a pervasive influence on perception and judgments. However, in the present context where our concern is with the functionality of having an attitude, it certainly is reasonable to pose the question, is such attitudinally biased processing functional for the individual? There are senses in which it does appear functional. Attitudinally biased processing helps maintain the individual's attitudes and thus maintains a consistent view of objects in social world. In that sense, it simplifies existence.

Furthermore, a number of studies have indicated that attitudes provide a useful basis for making a decision when the situation does not permit sufficient opportunity to consider the details of the stimulus information carefully (e.g., Jamieson & Zanna, 1989; Kruglanski & Freund, 1983; Sanbonmatsu & Fazio, 1990). When the time pressure to reach a decision is such that it does not permit careful deliberation, attitudes, and the impact they have on perceptions of the object in the immediate situation, provide a convenient and easy basis for deciding. Thus, attitudes can serve a very useful role when situational circumstances make extensive analysis and reasoning impossible. In such situations, it appears that an individual who has a relevant preexisting attitude is better off than one who does not.

However, there is another sense in which the biasing effects of attitudes, especially relatively accessible ones, leave the individual fairly closed minded and inflexible (see Cooper & Aronson, 1992; Zanna, 1993). Instead of being open to the implications of new information regarding the attitude object, individuals with such attitudes display information-processing and judgmental tendencies that are biased by their preexisting attitudes. As a result, such attitudes can inhibit the individual from according sufficient merit to the qualities of the object that might be viewed as incongruent with the attitude. Opportunities for experiencing a "change of heart" are likely to be diminished. In a case in which both the object and one's likely outcomes on interacting with the object have not changed since the accessible attitude was developed, this poses no difficulty. It is this presumed constancy that makes accessible attitudes generally functional; the individual approaches (or avoids) objects that are likely to yield positive (or negative) outcomes, as personally defined.

However, what if the attitude object actually has changed over time? Accessible attitudes may prevent individuals from judging the object in terms of the new qualities that it exhibits. In this sense, the individual is less open to a new experience with the object and may continue to approach an object that may now produce a negative outcome or fail to approach an object that may now provide a positive, rewarding outcome. This, then, appears to be a cost associated with possessing an accessible attitude. The attitude may actually do one a disservice in the case of an object that has changed over time.[2]

In considering this possibility that individuals with accessible attitudes may accord insufficient weight to new qualities exhibited by the attitude object, Fazio and Ledbetter (1998) suggested that the reasoning could

---

[2]One potential cost of accessible attitudes does not depend on the object having changed over time. Recall the summary of the research by Roskos-Ewoldsen and Fazio (1992) concerning the effects of attitude accessibility on visual attention. Objects toward which individuals possessed accessible attitudes automatically attracted attention when they entered the visual field. In fact, when such objects were presented as distractors during a visual search task, they interfered with search performance. Thus, although such attention attraction has the functional benefit of alerting the individual to the presence of hedonically significant stimuli, it also can be dysfunctional when the individual's attention *should* be directed elsewhere for the purpose of optimizing task performance.

actually be extended a step further. Individuals with accessible attitudes might also be relatively unlikely even to *detect* that the object has changed. To introduce the reasoning that prompted the initial research, consider a task in which one is required to indicate whether a stimulus is the same as or different from what it was previously. A judgment of this sort obviously is made by assessing one's degree of familiarity with the current stimulus (i.e., by at least implicitly comparing the features of the current stimulus with the features represented in memory). However, let us also assume that the object, although it has changed somewhat, remains sufficiently similar to its original state that the changed object still automatically activates the evaluation associated with the original object for anyone who possesses an accessible attitude. In this case, the judgment of familiarity might involve not only a featural comparison process, but also an affective or attitudinal comparison. The evaluation that is activated may be compared to one's memory for the evaluation of the original stimulus ("Yes, I remember liking her before, too"). This similarity contributes positively to a global sense of familiarity with the changed object. Thus, the automatically activated attitude provides a cue that the object has not changed—a cue that is absent among individuals for whom no attitude was activated automatically. Unless the cue is countered by the featural comparisons, it will lead to an error. If it is countered by the featural comparisons, then an error might be avoided, but at the cost of some additional time and effort as one attempts to reconcile the conflicting cues. Hence, in the case of new stimuli that remain somewhat similar to the original, more confusability is expected when attitudes are relatively more accessible.

Fazio and Ledbetter (1998) tested this reasoning by taking advantage of commercially available morphing software. The stimuli in this experiment consisted of pairs of color photos of male and female undergrads. Each photo displayed the individual's head and shoulders, much like the typical yearbook photo. After digitizing each photo, we used morphing software to construct composites of each pair of photos. Because the software allows one to weigh the extent to which the composite resembles one photo or the other, we were able to create morphs that varied systematically with respect to their similarity to the original. In the detection phase of the experiment, participants were asked to indicate as quickly as possible whether an image was exactly the same as one to which they had been exposed in an earlier part of the experiment or different in any way.

Prior to this detection task, the participants were exposed to one of the two original photos in each pair under one of two conditions. Just as in the earlier research concerning the functional value of accessible attitudes (Blascovich et al., 1993; Fazio et al., 1992; Roskos-Ewoldsen & Fazio, 1992; Smith et al., 1996), some participants engaged in an attitude-rehearsal task while being exposed to the original images, whereas others saw the images equally often but were engaged in a control task that was intended to occupy them sufficiently to prevent them from rehearsing and developing accessible attitudes. Each photo was presented once for 4 seconds in each of four blocks. Participants in the attitude-rehearsal condition were instructed to examine each photo for the full time that it was on the screen and then announce aloud into a tape recorder whether they personally found the photo attractive, very attractive, unattractive, or very unattractive. Participants in the control condition were asked to estimate the person's height.

The next part of the experiment concerned the detection of change. Participants were told that we had taken several photos at different times of the people they had seen in Part 1. Their task was to indicate whether a photo was the exact same one they had seen in Part 1 or different in any way. They were explicitly told that the photos could be different either because they were different photos of the same people from Part 1 or because they were photos of people that they had not seen in Part 1. The instructions emphasized accuracy, but the participant was told to respond as quickly as possible without making errors. During the course of the task, participants were exposed to originals and to morphs of varying weights. The morphing levels included were based on the decision to have the experiment focus on the latency data. We employed morphing weights for which a correct response was relatively likely, according to pilot data. The percentages of each photograph contained in the morphs were 63/37, 50/50, 37/63, 25/75, and 13/87, where the first percentage refers to the weight given to the original and the second to that given to its morphing partner. In effect, these morphing weights provided a metric for the amount of change exhibited by a given stimulus.

The data regarding the original photos, i.e, trials on which the participant should be answering "same," revealed no differences between the attitude-rehearsal and the height estimate conditions. The two groups were equivalently accurate and their average latency to correctly respond "same" also was equivalent. This equivalence is important, for it suggests that the original photos were encoded equally well in the two experimental conditions. Any differences observed on the morphed stimuli cannot be due to differences in encoding.

Analyses of error rates for the changed stimuli revealed only a large main effect of morphing weight. Participants were more accurate at identifying a morph as "different" when the morph differed more markedly from the original. Accuracy rates ranged from 58% for the morphs that most closely resembled the originals to 94% for the morphs that most differed from the originals. No effects of attitude rehearsal were obtained on these accuracy data. However, the latency data indicated that participants in the attitude-rehearsal condition required more time to achieve this equivalent level of performance. These data revealed not only the main effect of morphing level, but also a significant attitude rehearsal × morphing level interaction. For morphs that were relatively close to the original (63% weight assigned to the original), attitude-rehearsal subjects took more time to correctly detect that a photo was different. This difference grew smaller the less the morphed photo resembled the original.

These results suggest that the 63% composites were sufficiently similar to the original to evoke the previously formed and accessible attitude. Once evoked, this attitude interfered with the participant's ability to identify the morph as "different." The morph's evocation of the original evaluative response contributed positively to a global sense of familiarity with the morphed stimulus. On the other hand, differences between the actual features of the original and the morphed images detracted from the sense of familiarity. Resolution of conflicting cues was time consuming. However, if the photo did not resemble the original and hence did not activate the evaluation associated with the original, the attitude-rehearsal subjects did not experience this interference.

Fazio and Ledbetter (1998) conducted a second experiment with two aims in mind. The primary aim was to examine the extent to which participants *spontaneously* detected change. In Experiment 1, participants' very mission was to detect change. They were explicitly told that some of the images they would see were different from those that they had seen earlier and were instructed to detect those that were different, no matter how small the differences might be. In everyday situations, individuals are not usually given advance notice that something or someone may be changing, nor are they told when it is in their best interest to look for any changes that may be occurring at a given time. Instead, they must notice the change spontaneously.

Fazio and Ledbetter (1998) were interested in determining whether accessible attitudes might interfere with the spontaneous detection of unannounced change, just as they did with the goal-directed detection of announced change in Experiment 1. Like Experiment 1, Experiment 2 began with the attitude-rehearsal manipulation. However, Part 2 was very different in the two experiments. Instead of making same–different responses to individual images, the participants in Experiment 2 underwent a procedure whose purpose was deliberately left vague. They watched a presentation of an entire series of images on their computer monitors, knowing only that they would be asked questions about the presentation later. At the end of the presentation, they were asked for their reconstruction of what they had seen, for example, how many were photographs of new people, ones that had not been shown in Part 1 of the experiment?

During the presentation, 12 morphs were displayed. This time all the morphs were very confusable. Eight of them weighted the original 75%, 2 weighted the original 63%, and 2 weighted the original 50%. The presentation included these 12 morphs, as well as 10 originals and 3 new photos, for a total of 25 photos. These numbers were deliberately selected, with the thought that new photos, by virtue of their being relatively infrequent and, hence, distinctive, might be noticed as new. It is this information that should provide participants with a basis for their subsequent reconstructions of the presentation. The participants were to indicate how many of the 25 photos were same, different, and new. That is, how many of the photographs that they saw in Part 2 were the *exact same photographs* they had seen in Part 1? How may were just *different photographs of the same people* they had seen in Part 1? And how many were *photographs of new people* they had not seen in Part 1?

The two conditions did not differ in terms of the number of photos participants estimated to have been the same as the originals. However, the conditions did differ with respect to the other two estimates. Attitude-rehearsal participants recalled seeing more different photos of original persons and fewer photos of new persons. So, even in terms of the spontaneous detection of change, accessible attitudes seem to have interfered with individuals' sensitivity to change.

The second aim of Experiment 2 was to examine directed detection in a manner slightly different from what manner than had been done in Experiment 1. Because Experiment 1 had focused on latency to detect change, the response options were necessarily dichotomous. Change had or had not occurred. We were not able to collect information regarding how extensive participants viewed any change they detected because we did not want to compromise the sensitivity of the latency data. In Experiment 2, immediately following the spontaneous detection measure, participants were shown the very same images that had appeared in the presentation, but this time they were required to respond to each one individually. Unlike in Experiment 1, participants were given three response options: (a) it is exactly the same as an original photo, (b) it is a different photo of a person that was seen earlier, or (c) it is a photo of a new person. This measure provided an indication of the extent to which a test photo was judged to differ from the original.

The participants were quite accurate in judging the same and new photos. Accuracy rates exceeded 90% and did not differ as a function of condition. Once again, this equivalence provides evidence that the original photos were encoded equally well in the two conditions. However, the two conditions did differ with respect to their judgments of the morphs. Attitude-rehearsal participants were significantly more likely to view the morph as a different photo of an original person and significantly less likely to view it as a photo of a new person. Thus, they did not perceive as much change in the stimuli.

These findings suggest that, as functionally beneficial as accessible attitudes might be in terms of their providing a "ready aid" for responding to the attitude object, they do leave one relatively insensitive to any changes the object might exhibit. Regardless of whether individuals are purposefully attempting to detect change or must notice any such change spontaneously, those with more accessible attitudes appear to have more difficulty doing so. Further research is needed to identify more definitively the mediating mechanisms responsible for these effects. Fazio and Ledbetter (1998) suggested that the mediating processes may differ somewhat for directed versus spontaneous detection of change. The spontaneous detection data suggest that a perceptual process may play a role. At the time of their exposure to the presentation, the participants in Experiment 2 were not aware of the interest in change relative to what had been seen in Part 1, nor of the claim that multiple photos of the people seen in Part 1 were available. They had no reason to consider and weight the extent to which a given photograph might differ from the original. Thus, their reconstructions of the presentations are likely to have reflected elements that happened to capture their attention during the presentation. Given the relative infrequency of truly new photos (3 vs. 10

originals) during the presentation, these new photos, as well as any morphs for which change was spontaneously perceived, are likely to have appeared distinctive. As they watched the presentation, attitude-rehearsal partici- pants appear to have had their attention drawn to fewer instances of "newness." Because the morphs closely resembled the originals, the origi- nal attitudes are likely to have been automatically activated by the morphs. The activated attitudes may have led the participants to perceive the altered features in an attitudinally congruent manner and, hence, may have lessened the actual perception of change. Such a mechanism of assimilation toward the original attitude may underlie the attitude-rehearsal participants' reports of having seen relatively fewer photos of entirely new people.

This assimilation process may be supplemented by an additional mechanism when the individual's very goal is to detect the presence or absence of change. It is in such a situation that an activated attitude can provide the sort of cue that was mentioned earlier. The fact that the attitude activated by a morph closely resembling the original concurs with one's memory for the earlier evaluation of the original may provide a cue that there has not been any change, or that any such change is minimal. Given sufficient motivation and opportunity, the implications of this cue can be overcome and the presence of change can be detected, as shown by the equivalent accuracy rates of the attitude-rehearsal and control participants in Experiment 1. However, this vigilance is achieved at the cost of some time and effort, as demonstrated by the longer latencies exhibited by the attitude-rehearsal participants in Experiment 1. Once change is detected, however, individuals with accessible attitudes are still at a relative disadvantage, for their automatically activated attitudes imply that any such change must be minimal. In the directed detection task of Experiment 2, attitude rehearsal participants were less likely to view a morph as sufficiently different from the original for it to be considered a photo of a new person, instead of simply a different photo of the original person. Thus, individuals with accessible attitudes appear to discount the magnitude of any change that they do perceive, weighting it less than individuals with less accessible attitudes.

CONCLUSIONS:
BALANCING THE COSTS AND BENEFITS

Where, then, do these findings leave us with respect to the question of the functional value of accessible attitudes? As hinted at earlier, the answer appears to depend on whether the attitude object remains stable over time. If so, an earlier formed and accessible attitude serves the individual very well.

Given the complexity of the social world, individuals must somehow structure the numerous objects, issues, and people they encounter daily. The development of attitudes is one of the means by which individuals manage to function effectively in their environment. Attitudes structure objects, issues, and people along an evaluative dimension. To the extent that these attitudes are accessible from memory, they are activated automatically from memory when the object is encountered; they guide attention, categorization, information processing, and, ultimately, behavior. Moreover, they do so without requiring the individual to engage in deliberate reflection, which has the consequence of easing decision making regarding such objects and, hence, frees the individual from some of the impinging demands and stresses of the social environment. Accessible attitudes foster approaching objects that have been personally defined as hedonically positive and avoiding those that have been defined as producing negative outcomes. In effect, they plot a safe route through the social environment.

However, when the attitude object changes over time, i.e., sometime after an accessible attitude has been developed, the attitude actually may prove dysfunctional for the individual. An accessible attitude can leave the individual relatively insensitive to any change the object exhibits, thus interfering with the individual's ability to detect change and to weight such change sufficiently when it is detected. As a result, the individual may needlessly avoid an object that he or she now might find enjoyable, and may approach an object that no longer provides the satisfaction it once did or, even worse, that now proves harmful. That is the price one must pay for the functional benefits that accessible attitudes provide. The safety that they provide comes at the cost of a lack of receptivity to new experiences.

ACKNOWLEDGMENTS

Preparation of this chapter, as well as much of the research that is summarized within the chapter, was supported by Senior Scientist Award MH01646 and Grant MH38832 from the National Institute of Mental Health. The author thanks Michael Olson for his helpful comments on an earlier draft of the chapter.

REFERENCES

Allport, G.W. (1935). Attitudes. In C. Murchison (Ed.), *Handbook of social psychology* (pp. 798–844). Worcester, MA: Clark University Press.

Bargh, J. A., Chaiken, S., Govender, R., & Pratto, F. (1992). The generality of the automatic attitude activation effect. *Journal of Personality and Social Psychology, 62*, 893–912.

Bargh, J. A., Chaiken, S., Raymond, P., & Hymes, C. (1996). The automatic evaluation effect: Unconditional automatic attitude activation with a pronunciation task. *Journal of Experimental Social Psychology, 32*, 104–128.

Bassili, J. N. (1995). Response latency and the accessibility of voting intentions: What contributes to accessibility and how it affects vote choice. *Personality and Social Psychology Bulletin, 21*, 686–695.

Bassili, J. N. (1996). Meta-judgmental versus operative indexes of psychological attributes: The case of measure of attitude strength. *Journal of Personality and Social Psychology, 71*, 637–653.

Beck, A., Ward, C., Mendelson, M., Mock, J., & Erbaugh, J. (1961). An inventory for measuring depression. *Archives of General Psychiatry, 4*, 53–63.

Blascovich, J., Ernst, J. M., Tomaka, J., Kelsey, R. M., Salomon, K. L., & Fazio, R. H. (1993). Attitude accessibility as a moderator of autonomic reactivity during decision making. *Journal of Personality and Social Psychology, 64*, 165–176.

Bruner, J. S. (1957). On perceptual readiness. *Psychological Review, 64*, 123–152.

Carlston, D. E., & Skowronski, J. J. (1986). Trait memory and behavior memory: The effects of alternative pathways on impression judgment response times. *Journal of Personality and Social Psychology, 50*, 5–13.

Carretta, T. R., & Moreland, R. L. (1982). Nixon and Watergate: A field demonstration of belief perseverance. *Personality and Social Psychology Bulletin, 8*, 446–453.

Cohen, S., & Hoberman, H. M., (1983). Positive events and social support as buffers of life change stress. *Journal of Applied Social Psychology, 13*, 99–125.

Converse, P. E. (1970). Attitudes and non-attitudes: Continuation of a dialogue. In E. R. Tufte (Ed.), *The quantitative analysis of social problems* (pp. 168–189). Reading, MA: Addison-Wesley.

Cooper, J., & Aronson, J. M. (1992). Attitudes and consistency theories: Implications for mental health. In D. N. Ruble, P. R. Costanzo, & M. E. Oliveri (Eds.), *The social psychology of mental health: Basic mechanisms and applications* (pp. 279–300). New York: Guilford.

Derogatis, L., Lipman, R., & Covi, L. (1973). SCL-90: An outpatient psychiatrist rating scale—Preliminary report. *Psychopharmacology Bulletin, 9*, 13–28.

Dunton, B. C., & Fazio, R. H. (1997). An individual difference measure of motivation to control prejudiced reactions. *Personality and Social Psychology Bulletin, 23*, 316–326.

Fazio, R. H. (1990a). Multiple processes by which attitudes guide behavior: The MODE model as an integrative framework. In M. P. Zanna (Ed.), *Advances in experimental social psychology* (Vol. 23, pp. 75–109). New York: Academic Press.

Fazio, R. H. (1990b). A practical guide to the use of response latency in social psychological research. In C. Hendrick & M. S. Clark (Eds.), *Review of personality and social psychology* (Vol. 11, pp. 74–97). Newbury Park, CA: Sage Publications.

Fazio, R. H. (1993). Variability in the likelihood of automatic attitude activation: Data re-analysis and commentary on Bargh, Chaiken, Govender, and Pratto (1992). *Journal of Personality and Social Psychology, 64*, 753–758, 764–765.

Fazio, R. H. (1995). Attitudes as object-evaluation associations: Determinants, consequences, and correlates of attitude accessibility. In R. E. Petty & J. A. Krosnick (Eds.), *Attitude strength: Antecedents and consequences* (pp. 247–282). Hillsdale, NJ: Lawrence Erlbaum Associates.

Fazio, R. H., Blascovich, J., & Driscoll, D. M. (1992). On the functional value of attitudes: The influence of accessible attitudes upon the ease and quality of decision making. *Personality and Social Psychology Bulletin, 18*, 388–401.

Fazio, R. H., Chen, J., McDonel, E. C., & Sherman, S. J. (1982). Attitude accessibility, attitude–behavior consistency, and the strength of the object-evaluation association. *Journal of Experimental Social Psychology, 18*, 339–357.

Fazio, R. H., & Dunton, B. C. (1997). Categorization by race: The impact of automatic and controlled components of racial prejudice. *Journal of Experimental Social Psychology, 33*, 451–470.

Fazio, R. H., Jackson, J. R., Dunton, B. C., & Williams, C. J. (1995). Variability in automatic activation as an unobtrusive measure of racial attitudes: A bona fide pipeline? *Journal of Personality and Social Psychology, 69*, 1013–1027.

Fazio, R. H., & Ledbetter, J. E. (1998). *On the costs of accessible attitudes: Detecting that the attitude object has changed.* Unpublished manuscript, Indiana University, Bloomington, IN.

Fazio, R. H., Lenn, T. M., & Effrein, E. A. (1984). Spontaneous attitude formation. *Social Cognition, 2*, 217–234.

Fazio, R. H., & Powell, M. C. (1997). On the value of knowing one's likes and dislikes: Attitude accessibility, stress, and health in college. *Psychological Science, 8*, 430–436.

Fazio, R. H., Powell, M. C., & Williams, C. J. (1989). The role of attitude accessibility in the attitude-to-behavior process. *Journal of Consumer Research, 16*, 280–288.

Fazio, R. H., Roskos-Ewoldsen, D. R., & Powell, M. C. (1994). Attitudes, perception, and attention. In P. M. Niedenthal & S. Kitayama (Eds.), *The heart's eye: Emotional influences in perception and attention* (pp. 197–216). New York: Academic Press.

Fazio, R. H., Sanbonmatsu, D. M., Powell, M. C., & Kardes, F. R. (1986). On the automatic activation of attitudes. *Journal of Personality and Social Psychology, 50*, 229–238.

Fazio, R. H., & Williams, C. J. (1986). Attitude accessibility as a moderator of the attitude– perception and attitude–behavior relations: An investigation of the 1984 presidential election. *Journal of Personality and Social Psychology, 51*, 505–514.

Hastorf, A. H., & Cantril, H. (1954). They saw a game: A case study. *Journal of Abnormal and Social Psychology, 49*, 129– 134.

Hodges, S. D., & Wilson, T. D. (1993). Effects of analyzing reasons on attitude change: The moderating role of attitude accessibility. *Social Cognition, 11*, 353–366.

Houston, D. A., & Fazio, R. H. (1989). Biased processing as a function of attitude accessibility: Making objective judgments subjectively. *Social Cognition, 7*, 51–66.

Jamieson, D. W., & Zanna, M. P. (1989). Need for structure in attitude formation and expression. In A. R. Pratkanis, S. J. Breckler, & A. G. Greenwald (Eds.), *Attitude structure and function* (pp. 383–406). Hillsdale, NJ: Lawrence Erlbaum Associates.

Jarvis, W. B. G., & Petty, R. E. (1996). The need to evaluate. *Journal of Personality and Social Psychology, 70*, 172–194.

Katz, D. (1960). The functional approach to the study of attitudes. *Public Opinion Quarterly, 24*, 163–204.

Kruglanski, A. W., & Freund, T. (1983). The freezing and unfreezing of lay-inferences: Effects of impressional primacy, ethnic stereotyping, and numerical anchoring. *Journal of Experimental Social Psychology, 19*, 448–468.

Levine, M., & Perkins, D. V. (1980, August). *Tailor making life events scale.* Paper presented at the meeting of the American Psychological Association, Montreal.

Linville, P. W. (1987). Self-complexity as a buffer against stress-related illness and depression. *Journal of Personality and Social Psychology, 52*, 663–676.

Lord, C. G., Ross, L., & Lepper, M. R. (1979). Biased assimilation and attitude polarization: The effects of prior theories on subsequently considered evidence. *Journal of Personality and Social Psychology, 37*, 2098–2109.

Medin, D. L., & Schaffer, M. M. (1978). Context theory of classification learning. *Psychological Review, 85*, 207–238.

Nosofsky, R. M. (1986). Attention, similarity, and the identification–categorization relationship. *Journal of Experimental Psychology: General, 115*, 39–57.

Pratto, F. (1994). Consciousness and automatic evaluation. In P. M. Niedenthal & S. Kitayama (Eds.), *The heart's eye: Emotional influences in perception and attention* (pp. 115–143). New York: Academic Press.

Regan, D. T., Straus, E., & Fazio, R. H. (1974). Liking and the attribution process. *Journal of Experimental Social Psychology, 10,* 385–397.

Roskos-Ewoldsen, D. R., & Fazio, R. H. (1992). On the orienting value of attitudes: Attitude accessibility as a determinant of an object's attraction of visual attention. *Journal of Personality and Social Psychology, 63,* 198–211.

Sanbonmatsu, D. M., & Fazio, R. H. (1990). The role of attitudes in memory-based decision making. *Journal of Personality and Social Psychology, 59,* 614–622.

Schuette, R. A., & Fazio, R. H. (1995). Attitude accessibility and motivation as determinants of biased processing: A test of the MODE model. *Personality and Social Psychology Bulletin, 21,* 704–710.

Smith, E. R., Fazio, R. H., & Cejka, M. A. (1996). Accessible attitudes influence categorization of multiply categorizable objects. *Journal of Personality and Social Psychology, 71,* 888–898.

Smith, E. R., & Zarate, M. A. (1992). Exemplar-based model of social judgment. *Psychological Review, 99,* 3–21.

Smith, M. B., Bruner, J. S., & White, R. W. (1956). *Opinions and personality.* New York: Wiley.

Wilson, T. D., Lisle, D. J., Schooler, J. W., Hodges, S. D., Klaaren, K. J., & LaFleur, S. J. (1993). Introspecting about reasons can reduce post-choice satisfaction. *Personality and Social Psychology Bulletin, 19,* 331–339.

Wilson, T. D., & Schooler, J. W. (1991). Thinking too much: Introspection can reduce the quality of preferences and decisions. *Journal of Personality and Social Psychology, 60,* 181–192.

Zanna, M. P. (1993). Message receptivity: A new look at the old problem of open- versus closed-mindedness (pp. 141–162). In A. A. Mitchell (Ed.), *Advertising exposure, memory, and choice.* Hillsdale, NJ: Lawrence Erlbaum Associates.

Zanna, M. P., & Rempel, J. K. (1988). In D. Bar-Tal & A. W. Kruglanski (Eds.), *The social psychology of knowledge* (pp. 315–354). New York: Cambridge University Press.

2

The Social-Identity Function in Person Perception: Communicated Meanings of Product Preferences

Sharon Shavitt
University of Illinois at Urbana–Champaign

Michelle R. Nelson
Emerson College

A recent survey of 500 people across England for the supermarket chain Somerfield reveals that the vast majority of people (71 percent) believe that the contents of shopping carts send out powerful messages about the persons pushing them.... What's more, 11 percent of singles under 25 said they regularly, deliberately communicate with prospective partners via the contents of their shopping baskets.
—D. Lewis (cited in Mistiaen, 1997).

One of the fundamental assumptions of functional theory is that people often hold or express their attitudes and preferences in order to communicate something about themselves to other people (Katz, 1960;

---

*Michelle R. Nelson is currently Manager of Marketing Communications at Math Engine, Inc., Oxford, UK.

Smith, Bruner, & White, 1956). That is, attitudes toward specific issues, products, or ideas serve to convey broader information about us to interested parties.

To date, this *social-identity function* of attitudes (Shavitt, 1989) has primarily been investigated from the perspective of the attitude holder—in terms of the persuasiveness of appeals targeted at that function. For instance, studies have consistently shown that, for attitudes that serve this type of functional goal, social image appeals, status appeals, and other "soft-sell" strategies that describe the impression conveyed by an attitudinal position or a consumer choice are particularly persuasive (e.g., Shavitt 1990; Snyder & DeBono, 1985, 1987).

However, an equally important implication of the social identity function that has yet to be explored is the role of attitudes in creating an impression in the eye of the beholder. To the extent that an attitude serves a social-identity function, one would expect it to affect the judgments that observers make about the attitude holder based on their knowledge of that person's attitude. That is, the notion of a social-identity function implicates person perception processes. In this sense, then, the "social-identity function of attitudes" refers to the informativeness of attitudes for person impressions, or how much attitudes appear to convey about the persons who hold them.

In what follows, we explore these person perception implications of the social-identity function. Our program of research shifts the focus from the attitude holder to the observer, and the conclusions drawn by that observer on the basis of attitudinal information. Specifically, we examine the communicated meanings of product attitudes in a person perception context, that is, the types of judgments that observers make about targets based on the products that the targets select.

PREVIOUS RESEARCH

Although social signaling via the display of one's attitudes and preferences is presumably a ubiquitous social communication process, only limited research in psychology has investigated its characteristics. Prior psychological research, using conceptual frameworks other than functional theory, has demonstrated that observers do make judgments about targets based on knowledge of their attitudes. Indeed, exchanging information about one's attitudinal stands is a common part of the acquaintanceship process (Kent, Davis, & Shapiro, 1981). The effects of attitude similarity on person judgments have been studied extensively (e.g., Byrne, 1971; Schachter, 1951), and it is well established that the expression of similar and/or dissimilar attitudes influences interpersonal attraction (e.g., Byrne & Clore, 1970; Byrne et al., 1971; Rosenbaum, 1986).

Psychologists have rarely addressed the person inferences elicited specifically by product usage or consumption preferences. One exception is judgments based on a person's attire: Manipulations of attire have been used to assess the effects of status, authority, and other person characteristics on behavior, and numerous studies have demonstrated that clothing serves as an important cue to such person characteristics (e.g., Darley & Cooper, 1972; Hamid, 1968, 1972; Lambert, 1972; Satrapa et al., 1992; Suedfeld, Bochner, & Matas, 1971; Thibaut & Riecken, 1955).[1]

In contrast, there has been extensive research in marketing, communication, and sociology demonstrating that observers readily make person judgments based on knowledge of targets' purchase decisions (e.g., Baran, Mok, Land, & Kang, 1989; Belk, 1981; Belk, Bahn, & Mayer, 1982; Calder & Burnkrant, 1977; Fram & Cibotti, 1991; Haire, 1950; see Belk et al., 1982, for an excellent review). One of the earliest empirical demonstrations of this phenomenon was a classic and widely cited study published in 1950 by Mason Haire, which focused on women's perceptions of the types of people who purchase instant coffee (a newly introduced product) versus traditional drip-grind coffee. This study used a unique technique in which homemakers were shown a shopping list ostensibly written by another homemaker and were asked to describe the writer's personality and character. Haire found that, compared to those who saw a list containing "Maxwell House coffee (drip ground)," those who saw a list containing "Nescafé instant coffee" were more likely to describe the woman who wrote the list as being lazy, a poor planner, and a bad wife!

Happily, more recent research suggests that judgments of instant coffee users have improved substantially (see Fram & Cibotti, 1991), in part reflecting the evolution of women's social positions since 1950. However, coffee and many other products continue to be used as a basis for making personality judgments about their users. For instance, Baran et al. (1989) found that people made judgments of a person's responsibility and character based on the target's gender and purchase of various "practical"

---

[1]We do not include here studies that have assessed responses to uniforms or other prescribed professional attire (e.g., Bushman, 1988; Frank & Gilovich, 1988) because such attire may not be perceived to reflect the wearers' personal selections or preferences.

versus "upscale" brands of supermarket goods. They concluded that "variously positioned products do indeed provide a social stock of knowledge that people use in typifying those they meet" (p. 52).

Our approach to functional theory makes specific predictions about *when* person impressions are likely to be informed by targets' product attitudes. Such person judgments reflect the social-identity function of product attitudes. Thus, we would expect person impressions to be based on product attitudes to the extent that those attitudes are perceived to serve a social-identity function. However, as described in what follows, for many products, attitudes do not tend to serve a social-identity function.

THE ROLE OF ATTITUDE OBJECTS
IN ATTITUDE FUNCTIONS

In previous research, we have demonstrated that products (and other attitude objects) differ in the degree to which they engage social identity and utilitarian attitude functions (Nelson, Shavitt, Schennum, & Barkmeier, 1997; Shavitt, 1990; Shavitt, Lowrey, & Han, 1992). Products tend to engage a utilitarian function to the extent that they are intrinsically associated with rewards or punishments, and that consumption and maintenance behaviors toward them are generally aimed at maximizing product rewards. Products tend to engage a social-identity function to the extent that they are seen as expressing identity and values, consumption behaviors are likely to be performed in public, the product is generally displayed or is visible to others, or the product is widely seen as symbolizing membership in a particular group (Shavitt, 1989). Note, therefore, that the functions of attitudes toward a product are determined not only by characteristics of the product itself (e.g., its active ingredients, its cost per use), but also by shared societal definitions of the product (e.g., its "status"). Thus, the functions served by attitudes toward a product are in part a reflection of social consensus about the meanings or goals associated with the product.

A variety of factors may influence the types of meanings or goals that become associated with a product. For instance, the more universal the use of a product (e.g., over-the-counter painkillers), the less it will be perceived to convey discriminating information about its users and, thus, the less it may be likely to engage a social-identity function. On the other hand, products that are much less commonly used will not necessarily be relevant to social-identity goals. Consider, for example, the use of an antibiotic to treat a specific infection. Also, some products that are very commonly used (e.g., a university sweatshirt among college students) can nevertheless be strongly associated with social-identity goals (Shavitt, 1990). Thus, the degree to which a product's use is widespread will not be sufficient to predict the functions it is likely to engage. It is crucial to consider the types of goals associated with the product and the degree to which those goals are intrinsically associated with the product (e.g., pain relief), as opposed to socially mediated (e.g., popularity).

Importantly, some objects or products (e.g., air conditioners, aspirin) are predominantly relevant to utilitarian goals, and thus typically tend to engage attitudes that serve a utilitarian function and not those that serve a social-identity function. In contrast, some objects or products (e.g., team banners, perfumes) are primarily relevant to social-identity goals, and thus typically tend to engage attitudes that serve a social-identity function and not those that serve a utilitarian function. These differences make product or object variation a viable strategy for manipulating attitude functions (Shavitt, 1989).

Our prior research has shown that these differences between objects are consequential in that they predict a number of things. For instance, they predict the content of the cognitive representation underlying an attitude (Shavitt, 1990, Study 1). Attitudes toward products and objects that are expected primarily to engage a utilitarian function tend to be based on beliefs about object attributes and the rewards and punishments intrinsically associated with them. In contrast, attitudes toward products and objects that are expected primarily to engage a social-identity function tend to be based on beliefs about what the objects symbolize and what they express to others.

These differences between product categories also have implications for the persuasiveness of appeals (Shavitt, 1990, Studies 2 and 3). For products that predominantly engage a utilitarian function, claims regarding product attributes and benefits are particularly persuasive (e.g., "the special construction that makes Coolcraft air conditioners so efficient also makes them quiet"). However, for products that typically engage a social-identity function, claims regarding what the product symbolizes or conveys to others are particularly persuasive (e.g., "Astoria is the sophisticated scent that tells people you're *not* one of the crowd"). Indeed, for products that primarily engage a single (utilitarian or social-identity) function, these differences between product categories appear to be more important in predicting the persuasiveness of appeals than are individual differences in self-monitoring (Shavitt et al., 1992).

Furthermore, these product differences also appear to predict the relation between cognitive responses to an advertising appeal and long-term persuasion. Nelson et al. (1997) assessed cognitive responses to ads that contained both utilitarian and social-identity claims for different types of products. At a 1-week delay, attitudes toward the advertised brands as well as recall of the listed cognitive responses were also assessed. The types of recalled thoughts that tended to be more predictive of delayed attitudes were those that reflected the functions engaged by the products (i.e., for utilitarian products, the favorability of thoughts that were recalled about attributes and benefits of the brand; for social-identity products, the favorability of thoughts that were recalled about what the brand symbolizes or conveys to others).

Implications for Person Judgments. In the present context, such differences in the functions engaged by products imply that attitudes toward different types of products may also vary in the degree to which they are seen as informative in forming person impressions[2]. Specifically, we argue that to the extent that a product engages attitudes that serve a social-identity function, attitudes toward the product should be more likely to elicit individuating person judgments. Our research addresses this hypothesis.

It should be noted that, as a description of the stimuli will reveal, we use the term "attitude" loosely here. Participants were not exposed to any attitudinal statements purportedly made by the targets (as in studies of attitude similarity; Byrne & Clore, 1970; Byrne et al., 1971). Rather, they were given information about targets' purchase decisions. It is assumed that, if a perceiver knows that a target bought a given item, they will infer that the target has a favorable disposition toward that item (although there are conditions under which such attributions are less likely to be made; see, e.g., Calder & Burnkrant, 1977).

---

[2]Indeed, in 1981, Russell Belk obtained some evidence for this notion. Belk's predictions were based on specific characteristics of products rather than a unifying theoretical framework. Nevertheless, his findings provided partial support for the hypothesized role of those characteristics: Participant's ratings of a variety of products and services indicated that products that were rated as informative about users' personalities were also seen as having greater visibility, higher cost, greater time and thought invested in the purchase decision, and greater selection/variety (but not greater uniqueness, stylistic change, or complexity). Experimental data for a specific product (attaché case) indicated that manipulations of cost and time/thought invested in the decision (but not selection variety) affected specific personality ratings of the typical customer.

It should also be noted that by "individuating" person judgments we mean any of a variety of dispositional judgments (e.g., personality judgments and impressions about other preferences, tastes, or interests of the target) rather than inferences that place the target into a demographic category. Inferences about, say, gender or age can be made without reference to the individual consumer simply by considering the uses associated with the product (e.g., cosmetics, denture adhesives). However, individuating judgments are more likely to reflect impression-formation processes. Thus, although we examined all types of person inferences, we were primarily interested in judgments about target persons' personality or preferences.

Finally, it should be noted that our focus in this research is on the person perception implications of the functions engaged by products and not by specific brands of those products. Of course, brands can themselves engage a variety of attitude functions, and thus both a person's product selections and a person's brand selections can be informative. However, the functions engaged by the various brands of a product may or may not be the same as those engaged by the product category itself. For instance, the purchase and display of a U.S. flag or a team banner may be driven primarily by social-identity goals. However, the selection of a specific *brand* of flag or banner may be made to maximize utilitarian goals (e.g., durability, fade resistance, cost savings). In this research, therefore, we did not include brand names in the information about targets' purchase decisions.

Next, we describe a series of studies that attempted to demonstrate the person perception implications of product attitudes, dimensionalize the person judgments made in response to those attitudes, and examine the role of product categories in moderating the degree to which individuating judgments are elicited.

STUDY 1

One straightforward way to assess the person perception implications of product attitudes is simply to ask respondents to describe the typical consumer of a given product. This offers the advantage of obtaining rich person descriptions without constraining respondents to any particular dimensions of judgment.

In the present study, we asked 123 participants to consider the typical consumer of one of a variety of products in three function categories. The utilitarian products selected were aspirin and air conditioner. The social-identity products selected were team banner and class ring. There was also a multiple-function product category for products that were expected to readily engage both utilitarian and social-identity functions, and this comprised mineral water and coffee (presented as instant, automatic drip, or gourmet coffee).

These products were selected based on previous research on the functional goals people associated with their own attitudes toward these and similar products (Nelson et al., 1997; Shavitt et al. 1992). We used these products to examine the personal qualities inferred from others' attitudes toward them. We expected that to the extent that products engage attitudes that serve a social-identity function they will elicit individuating descriptors of their users, with social-identity products eliciting the greatest number of such descriptors and utilitarian products the least.

Respondents were instructed as follows: "Sometimes you can characterize people by the types of products they buy. Please describe your view of the type of person who buys/uses _____. List as many words as you can think of that describe the person. Make a list and then number them." Respondents were randomly assigned to one of the products listed above and were given as much time as they needed to complete this task.

The words or descriptors listed by respondents were subsequently coded. Those responses were readily codable into three broad categories (see Table 2.1): (a) personality traits, as well as other individuating descriptors regarding the activities, interests, and opinions of the targets

TABLE 2.1

Categorization and Percentage of Descriptors Listed

Descriptive type	Study 1	Study 2	Examples
Personality or individuating descriptors	66%	66%	Artsy Likes sports Smart Sentimental
Demographic descriptors	20%	20%	Older Wealthy Middle class Homeowner
Other descriptors	14%	14%	Sweaty Has a headache Sick Hungover

(descriptors typically referred to by market researchers as "psychographics"; Piirto, 1991); (b) demographic characteristics (descriptors referring to gender, age, socioeconomic status, and the like); and (c) other words (descriptors that were not relevant to either personality/individuating or demographic judgments; these did not describe anything enduring about the target person, but tended instead to focus on product-related needs).

Respondents had little difficulty characterizing the typical users of these products. Indeed, the great majority (86%) of descriptors that were listed represented enduring characteristics of the targets. Moreover, most of the time (66%), respondents listed individuating impressions of the traits, activities, interests, or opinions of those persons. The remainder of the descriptors were classified as "other" words.

How did the functional category of the product influence the target descriptions listed? Overall, there was no difference between product categories in the total number of descriptors listed. However, several differences emerged in the types of descriptors provided, as presented in Fig. 2.1.

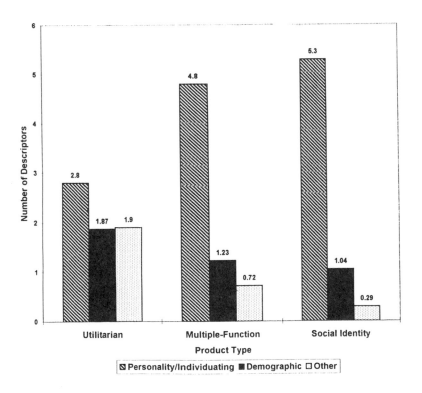

FIG. 2.1. Mean number of descriptors as a function of product type: Study 1.

As expected, participants used significantly more personality/individuating descriptors (such as "loud" or "flashy") to describe users of social-identity or multiple-function products than users of utilitarian products. Conversely, "other" words (e.g., "sick" or "hot") appeared more often for users of utilitarian products than for users of multiple-function products, and more often for users of multiple-function products than for users of social-identity products. Similarly, demographic descriptors (e.g., "office workers" or "rich") appeared more often in describing users of utilitarian products than in describing users of multiple-function and social-identity products.

Table 2.2 provides a look at the actual content themes emerging in the target descriptions. As these themes illustrate, users of social-identity products were described primarily in terms of their traits, interests, and activities. In contrast, users of utilitarian products were described primarily in terms of their product-related needs and demographic characteristics—apparently, the types of needs or benefits associated with these products were ascribed to particular demographic groups (indeed, "older" was the most common descriptor for users of aspirin).

Users of multiple-function products were described mostly in terms of their traits, interests, and activities, along with a variety of demographic descriptors. It is also worth noting that different types of coffee elicited somewhat different descriptions of their users. This is consistent with several previous studies (see Fram & Cibotti, 1991, for a review) and indicates more generally that differences *within* a product category, including differences between brands, can also have substantial implications for person perception.

Overall, the results confirmed that product attitudes are likely to elicit individuating person descriptions to the extent that those product attitudes tend to serve a social-identity function. When products engaged attitudes that typically served a utilitarian function (aspirin, air conditioner), participants made fewer individuating judgments of product users than they did when the products engaged attitudes that served a social-identity function. In other words, some product attitudes appeared to communicate substantially more dispositional information than did others.

STUDY 2

The results of the initial study provided clear evidence that different product attitudes have differential implications for person perception. In

TABLE 2.2

Most Common Themes Emerging From Personality Descriptors: Study 1

Utilitarian Products	
Aspirin	*Air Conditioner*
Older (D)	Wealthy/rich (D)
Stressed (O)	Hot (O)
Sick/has a headache (O)	Wants to be comfortable (O)
Busy (P/I)	Intolerable/irritable (P/I)
Concerned/worried (O)	Family (D)
Old-fashioned (P/I)	Smart (P/I)
Tired (O)	Lazy (P/I)
Social-Identity Products	
Class Ring	*Team Banner*
School spirit/loyal (P/I)	School spirit/loyal (P/I)
Wealthy/rich (D)	Social/fun (P/I)
Sentimental/nostalgic (P/I)	Athletic/likes sports (P/I)
Smart (P/I)	Competitive (P/I)
Athletic/likes sports (P/I)	Energetic/lively (P/I)
Showy/flashy (P/I)	Loud (P/I)
Successful/achiever (P/I)	Follower (P/I)
Multiple-Function Products	
Mineral Water	*Gourmet Coffee*
Healthy/health-conscious (P/I)	Wealthy/rich (D)
Athletic/likes sports (P/I)	Sophisticated (P/I)
Wealthy/rich (D)	Intellectual (P/I)
Yuppie (D)	Picky/choosy (P/I)
Snobby (P/I)	Snobby (P/I)
Well-dressed/trendy (P/I)	Yuppie (D)
Natural/down-to-earth (P/I)	Artsy (P/I)
Instant Coffee	*Automatic Drip*
"Working" people (D)	Middle income (D)
Cheap (P/I)	Older (D)
Hurried/fast pace (P/I)	Office workers (D)
Not picky about taste (P/I)	Do not like to cook (P/I)
Older (D)	Busy (P/I)
Economical (P/I)	Caffeine addicts (P/I)
Hyper (P/I)	Average (O)

Note. Descriptors: P/I = personality/individuating; D = demographic; O = other.

the second study, we sought to address both the replicability and the generalizability of these results by extending the findings to a broader set of products. Thus, for each functional category, we chose one product from the previous study and one new product. The utilitarian products selected were aspirin and orange juice. The social-identity products selected were team banner and men's cologne. The multiple-function products selected were gourmet coffee and sweatshirt. As in Study 1, these products were chosen based on previous research on the functions that they typically engage.

We also sought to ensure that respondents did not feel obliged to generate a person description if they felt unable to characterize the target. In this way, one would have greater confidence that any descriptions provided reflect participants' actual perceptions of the target persons. Thus, in addition to instructions similar to those for the previous study in which they were asked to describe the type of person who buys a given product, the 70 participants in this study were told, "If you do *not* feel you can characterize this person based on their use of that product, please note that below and wait for further instructions." Results indicated that more than 91% of respondents freely provided some descriptor(s) of the target person.

As before, respondents in this study appeared able and willing to characterize the typical users of these products in personality/individuating and/or demographic terms (see Table 2.1). Moreover, most of the descriptors they listed (66%) reflected individuating impressions of the targets.

The results as a function of product category replicated those of Study 1. As in that study, no difference between product categories was obtained in the total number of descriptors listed. However, as shown in Fig. 2.2, several differences emerged in the types of descriptors listed. As expected, participants used significantly more personality/individuating descriptors (e.g., "competitive" or "loyal") to describe users of social-identity or multiple-function products than users of utilitarian products. Conversely, "other" words (e.g., "has a headache" or "thirsty") appeared more often for users of utilitarian products than for users of multiple-function products, and more often for users of multiple-function products than for users of social-identity products. This time, there was no difference between product categories in the number of demographic descriptors used (e.g., "older" or "middle class").

Taken together, the results of these two studies demonstrate that respondents will readily provide target judgments of product users.

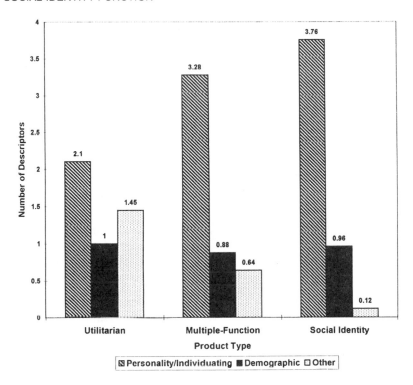

FIG. 2.2. Mean number of descriptors as a function of product type: Study 2.

Moreover, for the sets of products examined here, most of the descriptions of product users offered by respondents involved individuating judgments. These were inferences about the traits, activities, interests, or opinions of those target persons. Only 14% of descriptors were not obviously relevant to any enduring characteristics of the target persons. This is consistent with a large literature in marketing, communications, and sociology that has suggested a pervasive tendency to form person impressions based on product usage (see Belk et al., 1982, for a review).

Importantly, our findings have pointed to boundary conditions for this phenomenon. Specifically, the tendency to make individuating person judgments about product users is moderated by the functional category of the product. Products that primarily engage attitudes that serve a utilitarian function (e.g., aspirin, air conditioner, orange juice) appear much less likely to elicit individuating impressions of their users than other products do. Products that engage social-identity attitudes (primarily or partially, e.g., class rings, team banners, gourmet coffee, sweatshirts) are seen as a better basis for forming person impressions about their users. Indeed, the pattern of data in both studies suggests that the more a product engages social-identity attitudes, the more individuating information it is perceived to communicate about its users.

STUDY 3

In this final study, we considered the implications of these results for judgments of individual persons. The prior studies examined respondents' judgments about product users as a category, in effect asking respondents to apply their product-user stereotypes to the judgment task. However, those concepts may or may not be applied to the judgment of a specific individual.

A separate condition in Study 2, not described here for the sake of brevity, attempted to address this issue. In this condition, respondents were led to believe that the product purchase information they were shown about the target came from the "purchase diary" of an actual person named "Joe M." They were given the same instructions as the other participants except that they were asked specifically to characterize Joe M. As expected, respondents provided more "other" descriptors of the target in response to utilitarian products as compared to other types of products. They provided fewer demographic descriptors to utilitarian versus other types of products. Somewhat surprisingly, however, there was no difference in the tendency to offer personality/individuating descriptors as a function of product type—for all product types, the number of such descriptors was equally low (comparable to the number offered in response to utilitarian products in the other conditions of Study 2).

These findings suggested that perceivers will not necessarily use product information to judge specific persons in individuating terms, even when products are perceived to be informative along these lines. For instance, perceivers may consider their product-user stereotypes to be an invalid basis for the judgment of a specific individual and may not feel entitled to judge the target person on that basis alone (cf. Yzerbyt, Schadron, Leyens, & Rocher, 1994). Product-user stereotypes may instead be more likely to affect the evaluation of a specific target person when purchase information is provided incidentally, in the context of other information about the target, such that perceivers are not explicitly asked to consider the implications of a purchase for judgment of the target.

Thus, in this study, we examined the influence of product purchase information on judgments of an individual target person when attention is not drawn to the product information. The central questions we sought to address were as follows: When evaluating a specific target person, under what conditions would incidental product-purchase information be used to inform that judgment? Does the predominant function engaged by a product, which in the previous studies moderated person judgments of the "type of person" who uses the product, also predict these conditions?

If products that engage social-identity attitudes are seen as a better basis for forming person impressions than products that do not, then one might make the following prediction: The more important it is to form an impression of a target, the *more* one would expect target judgments to be influenced by social-identity product purchases, and the *less* one would expect target judgments to be influenced by utilitarian product purchases. This is because, when attempting to carefully form a person judgment, one would presumably want to use facts that are perceived to be informative for the judgment (such as social-identity purchases) and avoid using facts that are seen as uninformative (such as utilitarian purchases).

Testing of these hypotheses required a different design from that used in Studies 1 and 2. In this study, respondents were provided with product purchase information embedded in other information about the person, and the effect on person judgments was then assessed. However, we did not focus on the frequency with which personality/individuating inferences were made about the target because pretests had suggested that the other, filler information was eliciting a large proportion of these inferences. Rather, the favorability of the product information (i.e., whether the product is viewed positively or negatively) was manipulated within each function category so that the effects of that product information would be reflected in differences in the *favorability of person judgments*. Focusing on the favorability of person judgments as the main dependent variable, we examined the conditions under which the favorability of the target's product-purchase information had the greatest effects. We compared the influence of utilitarian and social-identity product-purchase information.

A pretest was conducted to identify product pairs that differed in their favorability but were similar in their functional meaning. For a variety of products, respondents were asked to rate (a) their overall attitude toward the product, (b) importance of the product's quality or performance in deciding whether to buy/use it (utilitarian function rating) and,

(c) importance of the product's image in deciding whether to buy/use it (social-identity function rating). Product favorability was a between-subjects factor, such that respondents rated only products that were expected to be viewed favorably (or unfavorably).

Based on these ratings, four pairs of products were selected for use in Study 3 (one product from Study 2 and one new product for each function category). The utilitarian products selected were orange juice (favorable version: fresh squeezed orange juice; unfavorable version: instant orange drink) and corn (favorable version: fresh sweet corn; unfavorable version: canned creamed corn). The social-identity products selected were team banner (favorable version: Illini banner; unfavorable version: University of Michigan banner) and flowers (favorable version: fresh flowers, unfavorable version: plastic flowers). Some of these selections are obviously quite specific to our subject population (University of Illinois undergraduates). Within favorability category, pretest participants' average attitude ratings toward these products were very similar across utilitarian and social-identity products. However, the functional meaning of these products (i.e., the relative importance of utilitarian and social-identity criteria in participants' ratings) differed as expected.

Information about purchase of these products was embedded in a printed, one-page scenario in which "you" (the reader) encounter three acquaintances, including the target person (Sara), while shopping at a grocery superstore. Participants were instructed to read the scenario and to try to project themselves into the situation as much as possible (i.e., to imagine that they were interacting with the other people in the story). In the scenario, several products and purchases were mentioned incidentally. Sara was described as purchasing both of either the utilitarian or the social identity products, and both of the products were either favorable or unfavorable. That is, product favorability and product function were between-subjects factors in the design. The portion of the scenario describing Sara read,

> ...Up ahead you see Sara—who recognizes you immediately and smiles. She asks how you've been and you chat for a short time about your new classes. Sara says she is taking 18 hours this semester. She picks out a _____ from the display but then drops it. You bend down to pick it up and put it into her cart next to _____. Nothing is damaged and Sara thanks you. You and Sara talk for a couple more minutes and then you say goodbye and move on....

To examine how the importance of the person judgment affects the role of product information in making that judgment, participants' level of involvement in evaluating Sara was also manipulated. Thus, the complete design was a 2 (involvement: high vs. low) × 2 (product function: utilitarian vs. social identity) × 2 (product favorability: favorable vs. unfavorable) factorial. In the high-involvement version, after the initial instructions, participants were further instructed to imagine that they are looking for a housemate for next semester and that Sara is a potential candidate. This provided a reason for forming a careful evaluation of Sara. In the low-involvement version, participants were instructed to imagine that they are looking for a job for next semester and that Terry (one of the non-target persons in the story) is a potential employer. Thus, low-involvement participants had no reason to form a careful evaluation of Sara. We anticipated that, as the motivation to form a careful evaluation increased, evaluations of Sara would be more in line with the favorability of social-identity product information and less in line with the favorability of utilitarian product information.

After reading the scenario, participants responded to a number of measures including providing an open-ended description of Sara. That is, similar to the previous studies, respondents were also asked to write as many words as they could think of to describe the target. These descriptors were subsequently coded for their favorability. Manipulation checks for involvement and product favorability were also included, and these validated the effectiveness of the manipulations.

Results indicated that the role of product-purchase information in influencing impressions of Sara under high-involvement conditions, as opposed to low-involvement conditions, depended on the function engaged by the products. Figure 2.3 shows an index of the favorability of descriptions of Sara (the number of favorable minus unfavorable descriptors that respondents wrote) by product function, product favorability, and involvement. For utilitarian products, the favorability of impressions of Sara was less in line with the favorability of her product selections for high-involvement conditions than for low-involvement conditions. In fact, under high-involvement conditions it appeared that overcorrection for the influence of the utilitarian product selections may have occurred, so that impressions of Sara were somewhat better when she selected unfavorable as opposed to favorable products. This is consistent with the notion that, when they were motivated to form a careful evaluation of Sara, participants avoided using information about utilitarian product selections because this was perceived to be uninformative for the judgment.

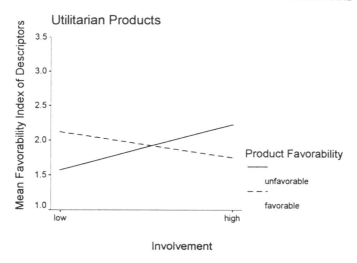

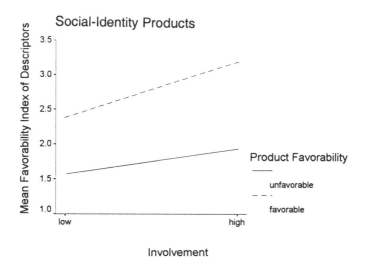

FIG. 2.3. Favorability index of descriptions of Sara: Study 3.

For social-identity products, favorable (compared to unfavorable) product selections elicited more favorable descriptions of Sara. Yet this effect appeared to be greater under high-involvement conditions. That is, although unfavorable product selections yielded slightly more favorable descriptions of Sara under high-involvement conditions than low-involvement conditions, this was offset by a larger increase in the favorability of descriptions elicited by favorable product selections. Thus, for social-identity products, as the level of involvement in evaluating Sara increased, impressions of Sara were more informed by the favorability of the product information.

Direct evaluative ratings of Sara were generally consistent with these patterns across social-identity and utilitarian products. Overall, then, these findings indicate that product-purchase information can indeed influence judgments of a specific target person when that information is acquired incidentally in the context of other information about the person. Importantly, however, the functional meaning of the product information affects the impact of that information. When the motivation to form a careful evaluation of the target was high (vs. low), evaluations were more in line with the favorability of social-identity product information and less in line with the favorability of utilitarian product information. This pattern of results suggests that, when seeking to form a careful evaluation of a target person, social-identity product selections are seen as providing information that has more implications for evaluation than the information provided by utilitarian product selections.

CONCLUSIONS

Functional theory has fundamental implications for the processes by which people use their attitudes and preferences to communicate information about the self to others. To date, little psychological research has been conducted to address this aspect of the social-identity function of attitudes. The studies described here represent a step toward elucidating a functional perspective on the social identities communicated by one's attitudes, possessions, and purchase preferences.

What we have demonstrated so far is that product attitudes sometimes have significant implications for judging their owners. This is consistent with research in other areas on the implications of product usage for person judgments. We have shown specifically that perceivers can and will infer considerable dispositional (personality/individuating) information from product attitudes.

However, the degree to which a given product attitude is seen as informative about dispositional characteristics of the target person depends on the functions engaged by the product. Social-identity product selections appear to be perceived as a better, more informative basis for making person judgments than are utilitarian product selections. To the extent that a product engages a social-identity function, information about persons' product attitudes or selections will elicit more individuating person impressions. Moreover, when one's judgment of a given individual matters, one is more likely to use the individual's attitudes toward social-identity products (compared to utilitarian products) to inform one's impressions of the person. In other words, attitudes toward social-identity products are more likely to serve a communicative social-identity function than attitudes toward utilitarian products.

This is very much in line with what has been shown in past research. Objects and products differ in the attitude functions that they tend to engage (e.g., Nelson et al., 1997; Shavitt, 1990; Shavitt et al., 1992), and these differences have a number of consequences—for the nature of attitudes, the persuasiveness of appeals, and so it seems for person perception.

REFERENCES

Baran, S. J., Mok, J. J., Land, M., & Kang, T. Y. (1989). Your are what you buy: Mass-mediated judgments of people's worth. *Journal of Communication, 39*(2), 46–54.

Belk, R. W. (1981). Determinants of consumption cue utilization in impression formation: An associational derivation and an experimental vertification. In K. B. Monroe (Ed.), *Advances in consumer research* (Vol. 8, pp. 170–175). Ann Arbor, MI: Association for Consumer Research.

Belk, R. W., Bahn, K. D., & Mayer, R. N. (1982). Developmental recognition of consumption symbolism. *Journal of Consumer Research, 9*, 4–17.

Bushman, B. J. (1988). The effects of apparel on compliance: A field experiment with a female authority figure. *Personality and Social Psychology Bulletin, 14*, 459–467.

Byrne, D. E. (1971). *The attraction paradigm.* San Diego, CA: Academic Press.

Byrne, D. E., & Clore, G. L. (1970). A reinforcement model of evaluative responses. *Personality: An International Journal, 1*, 103–128.

Byrne, D. E., Gouaux, C., Griffitt, W., Lamberth, J., Murakawa, N., Prasad, M. B., Prasad, A., & Ramirez, M. III. (1971). The ubiquitous relationship: Attitude similarity and attraction. A cross-cultural study. *Human Relations, 24*, 201–207.

Calder, B. J., & Burnkrant, R. E. (1977). Interpersonal influences on consumer behavior: An attribution theory approach. *Journal of Consumer Research, 4*, 29–38.

Darley, J. M., & Cooper, J. (1972). The "Clean for Gene" phenomenon: The effect of students' appearance on political campaigning. *Journal of Applied Social Psychology, 2*, 24–33.

Fram, E. H., & Cibotti, E. (1991, December). The shopping list studies and projective techniques: A 40-year view. *Marketing Research*, 14–22.

Frank, M. G., & Gilovich, T. (1988). The dark side of the self and social perception: Black uniforms and aggression in professional sports. *Journal of Personality and Social Psychology, 54*, 74–85.

Haire, M. (1950). Projective techniques in marketing research. *Journal of Marketing, 14*, 649–656.

Hamid, P. N. (1968). Style of dress as a perceptual cue in impression formation. *Perceptual and Motor Skills, 26,* 904–906.

Hamid, P. N. (1972). Some effects of dress cues on observational accuracy, a perceptual estimate and impression formulation. *Journal of Social Psychology, 86,* 279–289.

Katz, D. (1960). The functional approach to the study of attitudes. *Public Opinion Quarterly, 24,* 163–204.

Kent, G. G., Davis, J. D., & Shapiro, D. A. (1981). Effect of mutual acquaintance on the construction of conversation. *Journal of Experimental Social Psychology, 17,* 197–209.

Lambert, S. (1972). Reactions to a stranger as a function of style of dress. *Perceptual and Motor Skills, 35,* 711–712.

Mistiaen, V. (1997, April 6). Take a pass on the fish sticks. *Chicago Tribune,* Section 13, p. 9.

Nelson, M. R., Shavitt, S., Schennum, A., & Barkmeier, J. (1997). Prediction of long-term advertising effectiveness: New cognitive response approaches. In W. D. Wells (Ed.), *Measuring advertising effectiveness* (pp. 133–155). Mahwah, NJ: Lawrence Erlbaum Associates.

Piirto, R. (1991). *Beyond mind games: The marketing power of psychographics.* Ithaca, NY: American Demographics Books.

Rosenbaum, M. E. (1986). The repulsion hypothesis: On the nondevelopment of relationships. *Journal of Personality and Social Psychology, 51,* 1156–1166.

Satrapa, A., Melhado, M. B., Coelho, M. M. C., Otta, E., Taubemblatt, R., and Siqueira, W. D. F. (1992). Influence of style of dress on formation of first impressions. *Perceptual and Motor Skills, 74,* 159–162.

Schachter, S. (1951). Deviation, rejection, and communication. *Journal of Abnormal and Social Psychology, 46,* 190–207.

Shavitt, S. (1989). Operationalizing functional theories of attitude. In A. R. Pratkanis, S. J. Breckler, & A. G. Greenwald (Eds.), *Attitude structure and function* (pp. 311–337). Hillsdale, NJ: Lawrence Erlbaum Associates.

Shavitt, S. (1990). The role of attitude objects in attitude functions. *Journal of Experimental Social Psychology, 26,* 124–148.

Shavitt, S., Lowrey, T. M., & Han, S. (1992). Attitude functions in advertising: The interactive role of products and self-monitoring. *Journal of Consumer Psychology, 1*(4), 337–364.

Smith, M. B., Bruner, J. S., & White, R. W. (1956). *Opinions and personality.* New York: Wiley.

Snyder, M., & DeBono, K. G. (1985). Appeals to image and claims about quality: Understanding the psychology of advertising. *Journal of Personality and Social Psychology, 49,* 586–597.

Snyder, M., & DeBono, K. G. (1987). A functional approach to attitudes and persuasion. In M. P. Zanna, J. M. Olson, & C. P. Herman (Eds.), *Social influence: The Ontario Symposium* Vol. 5 (pp. 107–125.). Hillsdale, NJ: Lawrence Erlbaum Associates.

Suedfeld, P., Bochner, S., & Matas, C. (1971). Petitioners' attire and petition signing by peace demonstrators: A field experiment. *Journal of Applied Social Psychology, 1,* 278–283.

Thibaut, J. W., & Riecken, H. W. (1955). Some determinants and consequences of the perception of social causality. *Journal of Personality, 24,* 113–133.

Yzerbyt, V. Y., Schadron, G., Leyens, J., & Rocher, S. (1994). Social judgeability: The impact of meta-informational cues on the use of stereotypes. *Journal of Personality and Social Psychology, 66*(1), 48–55.

3

Attitudes as Knowledge Structures and Persuasion as a Specific Case of Subjective Knowledge Acquisition

Erik P. Thompson
Washington University

Arie W. Kruglanski
Scott Spiegel
University of Maryland, College Park

One of the most fundamental questions social psychologists have addressed within the past 50 years is that of why people have attitudes, that is, why we evaluate the people, objects, and events we encounter in terms of whether they are "good" or "bad." What purpose or purposes do attitudes serve? How might the evaluation of objects facilitate effective adaptation to, and functioning within, our physical and social worlds? In their seminal treatment of this subject, Smith and his colleagues (Smith, 1947; Smith, Bruner, & White, 1956) emphasized the *object appraisal function* of attitudes, which enables people to categorize entities as either conducive or nonconducive to their goals and objectives, as a prelude to behaving toward those entities. From this perspective, attitudes provide a basis for taking action that is personally adaptive, which leads people to approach entities that are beneficial and to avoid entities that are harmful. Subsequently, Katz (1960) distinguished between what he termed the *knowledge function* of attitudes, which emphasizes their role in cognitively structuring and organizing the barrage of information in the stimulus environment, and the *instrumental or utilitarian function* of attitudes, by which attitudes provide guidance in maximizing rewards and minimizing punishments. These early theoretical insights into attitude function have withstood the test of time, enjoying considerable support among contemporary researchers and theorists. Although other important attitude functions, such as social adjustment, value expression, and ego defense, continue to be of great interest (see Pratkanis, Breckler, & Greenwald, 1989), many writers consider object appraisal (and its constituent instrumental and knowledge functions) to be the universal or master function of all attitudes (Eagly & Chaiken, 1998; Fazio, 1989, Greenwald, 1989).

It follows that attitudes may be considered to be motivationally relevant knowledge structures that can be characterized by properties such as accessibility (Fazio, 1989), complexity (Judd & Lusk, 1984), and centrality (Kitayama & Burnstein, 1989) that have been attributed to mental representations in general. If attitudes and opinions are, in fact, a special case of subjective knowledge (Kruglanski, 1990), then the process of persuasion—through which attitudes and opinions may be formed and revised—may occur according to processes that more generally govern the formation of subjective knowledge (Kruglanski, Thompson, & Spiegel, 1999). In the pages that follow, we propose a single-mode model of persuasion, based on Kruglanski's "lay epistemic theory" (Kruglanski, 1989), that builds on the seminal empirical research and theoretical insights of the extant dual-process models of persuasion (Chaiken, Liberman, & Eagly, 1989; Petty & Cacioppo, 1986).

The principal way in which our persuasion unimodel (Kruglanski & Thompson, 1999; Kruglanski et al., 1999; Thompson, Kruglanski, & Spiegel, 1999) is different from the traditional dual-process models (reviewed later) derives from the former's emphasis on the knowledge function of attitudes. In particular, our model treats the contents of both persuasive messages and message-extraneous information in the persuasion context (i.e., "cues" or "heuristics") as functionally equivalent forms of evidence, potentially experienced by the persuasion target as relevant to evaluative conclusions about an attitude object, the processing of which is governed by the same quasi-syllogistic reasoning structure. Our model posits that persuasion occurs to the extent that prior beliefs establishing the perceived relevance of the evidence are available and accessible to the perceiver.

However, it also holds that persuasion depends on the perceiver's motivation to sort through available evidence and to construct new beliefs that determine the relevance of available evidence. As such, the unimodel acknowledges the role that various qualitatively different motivations, related to different attitude functions (such as object appraisal, social adjustment, and ego defense), may play in the persuasion process.

Because our persuasion unimodel has just begun to be articulated in the literature, we first review its evolution as a synthesis of the insights of the dual-process approaches and earlier, single-mode process theories of persuasion. We contrast our formulation with the current dual-process models, clarify the former's unique features, and review some initial evidence supporting our approach. Along the way, we draw connections between our formulation and research and theory on attitude functions. Finally, we return to a consideration of the implications of our single-mode approach for current and future research on the role of attitude functions and related motivations in the processes governing attitude formation and change.

THE STUDY OF PERSUASION

Given the ubiquity and importance of persuasion in today's world, it is hardly surprising that the study of persuasion has had high priority on the research agenda of many social psychologists. Over the past 30 years or so, persuasion and attitude change have been among the most thoroughly investigated topics in social psychology, yielding many intriguing conceptual developments and a plethora of fascinating empirical results (for a comprehensive review see Eagly & Chaiken, 1993).

This hasn't always been the case. "Persuasion" as a term did not even figure in the indices of major early volumes introducing social psychology as a systematic field of study (e.g., Allport, 1924; McDougal, 1908; Ross, 1908), and influential mid-century texts (Asch, 1952; Newcomb, 1950) barely mentioned it in passing while discussing "propaganda". It was not until Carl Hovland and his coworkers at Yale University (Hovland, 1957;

Hovland & Janis, 1959; Hovland, Janis & Kelley, 1953) launched their seminal communication and persuasion program that these issues began to receive an appropriate degree of attention as major topics of social psychological inquiry.

The Yale research was based on a classification system of persuasion variables growing out of Laswell's (1948, p. 37) comprehensive question, "Who says what in what channel to whom with what effect?" Initially, this led to a rather descriptive approach to persuasion research, for example, listing the variables within the *communicator* (i.e., the "who"), the *message* (i.e., the "what"), and the *audience* (the "to whom") categories. Over time, persuasion research has moved from the mere itemization and interrelation of variables in Laswell's scheme to an exploration of the basic cognitive and motivational processes that underlie attitude formation and change.

Significant milestones along this road have been McGuire's (1968; 1969; 1972) reception-yielding model and the cognitive response model of persuasion (Greenwald, 1968; Petty, Ostrom & Brock, 1981; for discussion see Eagly & Chaiken, 1993). Yet, the lion's share of current persuasion work has been inspired by two major theoretical frameworks: Petty and Cacioppo's elaboration likelihood model (ELM) (e.g., Petty & Cacioppo, 1986) and Chaiken and Eagly's heuristic–systematic model (HSM). Although they may significantly differ in some respects (for recent comparisons see Eagly & Chaiken, 1993; Petty, 1994), the ELM and HSM share a fundamental commonality in that they both posit that persuasion may be accomplished via two qualitatively dissimilar "routes" or "modes". In the ELM, these are the central and the peripheral routes; in the HSM these are the systematic and heuristic modes. Both models also stress that conditions that promote the extensive elaboration of message arguments will produce opinion change via one of the modes (the central one in ELM and the systematic one in HSM), whereas conditions that restrict the effortful elaboration of message arguments will bring opinion change via the remaining mode (the peripheral one in ELM and the heuristic one in HSM).

Both the theoretical developments made in the dual-process models and the empirical research conducted under their auspices have greatly advanced understanding of the cognitive and motivational determinants of persuasion. Nonetheless, our conceptualization substantially differs from the dual-process paradigm. We suggest a way to integrate two component processes into one, and in this sense feature a unimodel of persuasion. The unimodel (a) adopts a more abstract level of analysis in which the two persuasive modes (of either ELM or HSM) are viewed as special cases of the same underlying process and (b) deconstructs the "Laswellian" partition between persuasively relevant categories.

It is not that the Laswellian categories are not real. What is important, however, is that they may not be meaningful distinctions that matter to persuasion. Take the distinction between the categories "who" and "what," that is, the distinction between source and message. Even though these two may appear to be quite different, in one sense their differences are irrelevant to persuasion. That is, they constitute surface differences that share the same deep structure.

Moreover, even though contemporary dual-process models have gone far beyond the variable-listing approach inspired by Laswell's classification, they remain at least somewhat constrained by his scheme. This is because they retain, as a basic premise, the Laswellian partition between persuasion based on source factors, which function for the most part as peripheral cues in the ELM and as heuristic cues within the HSM, and persuasion based on the message as such—referred to as the central route in the ELM and as systematic processing in the HSM. The unimodel, in contrast, unequivocally parts ways with the Laswellian scheme.

TWO DUAL-PROCESS MODELS

The two dual-process models, the ELM and the HSM, are discussed at length elsewhere (Chaiken et al., 1989; Chen & Chaiken, 1999; Petty, 1994; Petty & Cacioppo, 1986; Petty & Wegener, 1999). In addition, a more detailed review of those aspects of the dual-process models pertinent to our new single-mode approach may be found in Kruglanski and Thompson (1999), and in Kruglanski et al., (1999). Therefore, we briefly summarize only those aspects of the dual-process models most relevant to our current discussion of the unimodel.

ELM

The ELM highlights the notion that there are two routes to persuasion that operate in different circumstances and that have different consequences for persuasion (Petty, 1994). The ELM proposes a continuum of elaboration likelihood bounded at one end by the total absence of thought about issue-relevant information available in a persuasion situation, and at the other end by complete elaboration of all the relevant information (Petty, 1994). Extensive elaboration of the message information refers to persuasion via the central route, and reliance on message-irrelevant cues refers to persuasion via the peripheral route. The ELM holds that "any variable that increases the likelihood of thinking increases the likelihood of engaging the central route" (Petty, 1994, p. 2). Prominent such variables are (a) personal relevance of the message, (b) expertise of the source, (c) attractiveness of the source, (d) number of communicators, and (e) message recipient's need for cognition (Cacioppo & Petty, 1982).

Although the notion of peripheral processing usually calls to mind brief and simple cues, this need not necessarily be the case. As Petty and Cacioppo (1986) note, in addition to relatively simple acceptance/rejection rules, attitude change by the peripheral route can occur via more complex, and potentially demanding, reasoning processes, such as those based on balance theory or certain attributional principles. Nevertheless, according to the ELM, reliance on such complex inferences is defined as peripheral, rather than central, processing, if it eliminates the need for careful scrutiny of the issue-relevant arguments in a persuasive communication.

Although the ELM allows for some co-occurrence of central and peripheral processing, it also suggests a tradeoff between these processes. Specifically, factors that increase the likelihood of message elaboration (e.g., issue involvement) not only increase the persuasive impact of message contents, but also reduce the impact of nonmessage "cues," such as information about the expertise of the communicator.

Finally, an important aspect of the ELM is its attention to motivational factors. This model assumes that the default motive in persuasion settings is to develop veridical, well-informed views. Strengthening this motive should increase a relatively objective scrutiny of the points made in a persuasive message. However, the ELM also proposes that other motives—such as psychological reactance, and ego-defensive and self-presentational concerns—can come into play and shape the impact of a communication on one's attitude through relatively biased processing of its arguments (Fleming & Petty, 1999; Petty, 1994; Petty & Cacioppo, 1986).

HSM

Chaiken et al. (1989) define systematic processing as a "comprehensive, analytic orientation in which perceivers access all informational input for its relevance and importance to their judgment task, and integrate all useful information in forming their judgments..." (p. 212). In comparison, heuristic processing is portrayed as a more limited mode, whereby people use only information that enables them to apply simple inferential rules, heuristics, or cognitive schemata that might be relevant to a particular judgment or decision. As such, heuristic (vs. systematic) processing is thought to require substantially less cognitive effort and capacity. According to the HSM, the difference between systematic and heuristic processing is not only quantitative (i.e., a matter of the extent of processing), but also qualitative, because the former is thought to be more exclusively theory driven, and the latter more exclusively data driven. Additionally, the HSM suggests that factors that increase the desire to form valid attitudes, such as the personal relevance of an issue, can increase both systematic processing, through increased scrutiny of a message, and also heuristic processing, by increasing the search for relevant heuristic cues.

Much like the ELM, the HSM assumes that the dominant motivational concern of persons in persuasion settings is the desire to form or hold valid or accurate attitudes. And, like the ELM, the HSM assumes that defensive and impression-management concerns also can play an important role in persuasion. However, in the HSM, these alternate motivations, like the motivation for accuracy, also can stimulate both systematic and heuristic processing.

A major emphasis in the HSM concerns the relation of persuasion phenomena to broader social cognition principles. This emphasis is particularly apparent in the treatment of persuasion heuristics, because their impact is assumed to be moderated by their availability, accessibility, and perceived reliability (Chaiken et al., 1989). It is of interest, however, that according to the HSM, accessibility considerations may also enter into the systematic processing of persuasive messages, because they can "influence perceivers' interpretation and evaluation of information)..." (p. 213).

Commonalities Between the ELM and the HSM

Certainly, the ELM and the HSM differ in some respects (see Eagly & Chaiken, 1993, Chapter 7; Petty, 1994, p. 4). More relevant to our purpose are features that the two frameworks share in common. First, both posit the existence of two qualitatively different modes of persuasion, of which one is more thorough and extensive than the other. Second, both assume that engagement of the more extensive mode (i.e., the central or the systematic mode) depends on sufficient motivation and ability to process information. Third, both assert that the two persuasive modes can co-occur, although the exact manner of their co-ocurrence is depicted somewhat differently in the ELM and the HSM. Though it permits co-occurrence, the ELM adheres, nonetheless, to the notion of a continuum whereby a tradeoff (hence, a negative correlation) governs the use of the two modes. The HSM, on the other hand, allows orthogonality in use of the modes so that they can augment each other, or clash in their influence. Finally, although both the ELM and the HSM imply that the desire to hold accurate attitudes and opinions is often the "default" motivation in persuasion contexts, both models assume that beyond accuracy strivings, extensive processing (i.e., central or systematic) can be affected by alternate motivations.

Even though they may differ in specific emphasis, the ELM and the HSM share considerable features in common, the most important of which is the presumption of two qualitatively different persuasion modes. But are these two modes truly different? Next, we address the question of how such a qualitative difference (or its absence) might be ascertained.

PERSUASION BY A SINGLE ROUTE

Rules for Establishing Process Uniformity

Our basic argument is simple. The crucial distinction between cues/heuristics on the one hand and message arguments on the other refers to informational contents relevant to a conclusion, rather than to a principled difference in the persuasion process as such. Cues and message arguments, then, should be subsumed as special cases of the more abstract category of persuasive evidence. We contend that the informational contents corresponding to the cue versus message argument partition do not, intrinsically, have a general effect on persuasion, nor are they impacted differently by variables relevant to persuasion. Instead, the same overall process may occur regardless of whether the informational grist for the persuasive mill is of the cue or message type.

For instance, a specific cue may appear less (or more) relevant to a conclusion than a specific message argument, and this degree of relevance may in fact constitute a significant characteristic of persuasion. A specific cue may be less (or more) complex, salient, or accessible than a specific message argument, and complexity, salience or accessibility may be important elements of persuasion. Finally, a specific cue may appear either before or after a specific message argument, and the order of appearance or presentation may comprise an important dimension of persuasion (Hovland, 1957). The foregoing does not imply that cues, as a category, must systematically differ from message arguments as a category in those particular ways. For example, a given message argument might be more relevant than, more complex than, or presented before another message argument. Any particular cue might be less relevant than, less complex than, or presented after some other particular cue.

Although the existence of within-category variability does not rule out the possibility of between-category variability, we contend, and now proceed to demonstrate, that there is little reason to believe that arguments must systematically differ from cues/heuristics on parameters relevant to persuasion. Once one controls for differences on features relevant to persuasion (e.g., length and complexity), cue-based and message argument-based persuasion should be impacted similarly by various processing variables (e.g., motivation and cognitive capacity). Such an outcome, if obtained, suggests that the two modes of persuasion lack discriminant validity, or functional independence, a known criterion for arguing the dissociation of psychological systems (Sloman, 1996; Tulving, 1983). In order to apply the functional independence criterion to the present case, however, it is necessary first to outline what variables are, in fact, relevant to persuasion, as well as what the underlying process of persuasion may be. These issues are addressed in our unimodel of persuasion, described next.

The Unimodel

Our persuasion unimodel is based on the lay epistemic theory (LET) of the processes governing the formation of subjective knowledge (Kruglanski, 1989). Such knowledge may consist of judgments, opinions, or attitudes individuals may acquire or alter in various circumstances. Thus, in agreement with Chaiken et al. (1989), we view persuasion as integrally related to the general epistemic process of judgment formation. We believe it to be a motivated process of hypothesis testing and inference dependent on individuals' cognitive capacity, and affected by the availability and accessibility (Higgins, 1996) of pertinent information. More generally speaking, it is a process by which beliefs are formed on the basis of appropriate evidence.

The Concept of Evidence.   According to LET, "evidence" refers to information relevant to a conclusion. Relevance, in turn, implies a prior linkage between general categories (e.g., "political experience" and "presidential potential") such that affirmation of one in a specific case (e.g., "Steve Forbes has no political experience") affects one's belief in the other (e.g., "Steve Forbes has little presidential potential"). Such a linkage is assumed to be mentally represented in the knower's mind, and it constitutes a premise to which he or she subscribes (e.g., "presidential potential requires prior political experience"). In this example, granting our knower's beliefs, the candidate's lack of political experience becomes relevant evidence for his expected presidential performance. More formally speaking, the conditional belief linking the evidence to the conclusion is the *major premise* of a syllogism. Affirmation of the evidence in a particular instance (e.g., compelling information that Forbes lacked any political experience) constitutes the *minor premise*. Jointly, the two premises yield the (logical or probabilistic) conclusion regarding his future presidential attainments.

The LET notion of evidence is compatible with major analyses of this concept within the philosophy of inference (e.g., Achinstein, 1983; Carnap, 1962, sec. 86; Glymour, 1980; Hempel, 1965) and, more to the point, with treatment of this topic in major social psychological models of persuasion. Most explicit recognition of this approach can be found in the probabilogical models of belief inference introduced by McGuire (1960) and by Wyer (1970, 1974), and in the Bayesian analysis of persuasion offered by Fishbein and Ajzen (1975; Ajzen, 1988).

In terms of the present discussion, the valence of an object's attributes, as well as of the outcomes the object may mediate (e.g., the health promoting consequences of a given drug), constitutes relevant evidence for its overall "goodness" or "badness" and thus determines one's attitude toward the object. Perceived relevance is determined by a major premise, whereby the overall positivity of an object is conditional on the positivity of its attributes or mediated outcomes (e.g., "anything that promotes health is good"). In other words, if the object appears to have certain attributes or mediated outcomes (minor premise), and those attributes or outcomes are believed to be positive (major premise), then the object merits a positive evaluation. In contrast, if the object appears to have attributes or outcomes believed to be negative (e.g., "a side effect of the drug is acute nausea"), then the result is a more unfavorable attitude.

The Dual Modes of Persuasion as Specific Contents of Evidence.
The present notion of evidence is the integrative glue that binds together
the dual modes of persuasion. Specifically, the distinction between heuristic (or peripheral) cues and message arguments is now assumed to
represent a difference in contents of evidence relevant to a conclusion,
rather than a qualitative difference in the persuasive process as such.
Consider a statement ascribed to Dr. Smith, a fictitious environmental
specialist, that "the use of freon in household appliances destroys the
ozone layer, and therefore ought to be prohibited." This argument may
be evaluatively relevant evidence for a recipient whose background
knowledge included the (major) premise that "if something contributes
to the thinning of the ozone layer (then) it should be prohibited." Dr.
Smith's specific argument supplies the minor premise that "the use of
freon in everyday appliances does destroy the ozone layer." In other
words, Dr. Smith's pronouncement constitutes the evidence that, granting the major premise, warrants the conclusion that "the use of freon
ought to be prohibited." Such orderly and logical processing of a message
argument from evidence to conclusion has been typically considered the
hallmark of persuasion by the "systematic" or "central" route.

But consider now a recipient who does not subscribe to the notion that
"anything that causes the thinning of the ozone layer ought to be
prohibited." Alternatively, this same recipient might be strongly committed to the assumption that "if an opinion is offered by an expert, (then)
it is valid." This assumption may serve as a major premise of a syllogism,
and the realization that "Dr. Smith is an expert" may serve as a minor
premise and hence furnish evidence that (granting the major premise)
points to the conclusion that "Dr. Smith's opinion (that the use of freon
ought to be prohibited) is valid." Such reliance on source attributes (such
as expertise) has been typically regarded as characteristic of persuasion via
the "peripheral" or the "heuristic" route. Yet from our unimodel's
perspective, the two persuasion types share a fundamental similarity in
that both are mediated by "if–then," or syllogistic, reasoning leading from
evidence to a conclusion.

Motivation and Cognitive Capacity. The foregoing, highly schematic depiction of the evidence concept belies the substantial amount of
cognitive work often involved in identifying more relevant evidence from
less relevant background material, in summoning less accessible "major
premises" from memory, and in imagining and evaluating the possible

attributes and consequences of an attitude object that may not have been overtly presented in a persuasion situation. Collectively, these processes comprise cognitive responses to persuasion (Petty et al., 1981). Because of the effort required to sustain such processes, they may often require considerable motivation and cognitive capacity. This dependence on processing resources should be most pronounced when information under consideration is relatively lengthy, complex, or unclear, but should not depend on whether that information consists of message arguments or of "cues" external to the semantic content of the message.

Motivation

Deriving as it does from Kruglanski's (1989) LET, the unimodel assumes that persuasion, like the process of knowledge formation and change more generally, is importantly affected by motivation. Within the LET framework, the initiation and termination of this process are governed by the relative strength of the perceiver's desire for accuracy and confidence in a particular judgment or decision. When the desire for confidence outweighs that for accuracy, the perceiver's motivation for nonspecific cognitive closure is heightened (Kruglanski & Webster, 1996), and, on achieving an acceptable degree of judgmental confidence, the perceiver becomes relatively closed to new information. However, when the desire for accuracy outweighs that for confidence, the individual seeks to avoid premature closure and remains fairly open to new information.

Some have noted a conceptual correspondence between the need for nonspecific closure and the object appraisal function of attitudes (see Maio & Olson, 1998, chap. 15). Indeed, the emphasis on attaining certain knowledge as a prelude to taking action or making a decision suggests that attitudes formed under the press of such a need may function primarily to provide some clear orientation toward the attitude object, regardless of what that orientation may be. For example, Kruglanski, Webster, and Klem (1993) found that experimental participants given insufficient (vs. sufficient) information with which to form an initial attitude were more (less) persuaded by an appeal delivered under conditions that promoted a need for nonspecific closure, regardless of whether the appeal argued for or against the issue in question. However, recent evidence suggests that in the former case, such a motivation does not induce mindless acceptance of the appeal. Thompson and Kruglanski (1998) found that heightened need for nonspecific closure led participants to be more persuaded by appeals with strong (vs. weak) arguments when participants had little basis for an initial opinion. Thus, this form of motivation may spur considerable cognitive effort if necessary in order to achieve an attitude in which one can have sufficient confidence to serve as an enduring basis for action.

The knowledge formation process also may be affected by needs for specific closure (Kruglanski, 1989; 1990). For example, an individual may wish to establish or maintain favorable self-perceptions, or may wish for significant others to view him or her favorably. When such motives are aroused, the perceiver selectively processes information, accepting the implications of that which maintains preferred conclusions, and avoiding or rejecting the implications of that which defies them. Thus, the LET assumes that motivation affects not only the extent of information processing, but also the direction of cognitive activity accompanying persuasion or judgment. For example, motivation may affect selective attention to relevant stimuli. The attention-grabbing properties of goal-relevant objects has been demonstrated in several studies (Berscheid, Graziano, Monson, & Dermer, 1976; Erber & Fiske, 1984; Ruscher & Fiske, 1990; Taylor, 1975).

Our earlier analysis of relevant to attitudes evidence appears to emphasize the object appraisal function of attitudes—the extent to which they summarize positive and negative implications of attitude objects and provide a stable, ready basis for relating to them. However, as we have just suggested, our framework is not unresponsive to other potential functions of attitudes. Relevant directional motivations such as instrumentality, social adjustment, ego defense, and value expression may play a role in determining precisely what constitutes the positive and negative implications of an attitude object when any particular motivation is dominant, and thus what constitutes subjectively relevant evidence for one's attitude.

For example, when utilitarian concerns are paramount, hedonic and material consequences may be salient; when social-adjustive motives are aroused, implications for one's social acceptance and desirability may become most accessible; when an ego-defensive stance is evoked, consequences for one's sense of self-esteem may come to mind most easily; and when value-expressive concerns are activated, implications for one's self-integrity may constitute the most subjectively relevant evidence (see also Maio & Olson, 1998, chap. 15). From our perspective, particular motivations may increase the cognitive accessibility of those "major premises" that establish the evaluative relevance of evidence congruent with those concerns. For example, if one's opinion serves an ego-defensive function, then evidence supportive of one's view will appear more germane than evidence contradictory to it. This may occur partly because the beliefs linking the proattitudinal evidence to evaluative conclusions are (or become) more accessible than those establishing the evaluative relevance of the counterattitudinal evidence. Thus, different types of motivations may determine what evidence is experienced as subjectively relevant, and the magnitude of these motivations may determine the extent to which evidence is processed.

Recently a number of researchers have demonstrated that message arguments have a greater persuasive impact, or receive greater attention, when they target attitude functions that reflect chronic or temporary motivations of the persuasion recipient (DeBono & Harnish, 1988; Lavine & Snyder, 1996; Petty & Wegener, 1998; Shavitt, 1990). From our perspective, the operation of different motivations may involve the marshaling of different beliefs that determine the perceived relevance, and hence persuasive impact, of available evidence. Whereas these researchers have focused on matching the motives that underlie various attitude functions to the content of messages or appeals, our unimodel suggests that the match of other forms of evidence (such as information about the communicator) might moderate its persuasive impact as well. For example, the arousal of ego-defensive concerns might enhance the perceived relevance of information impugning the veracity of counterattitudinal arguments and stimulate biased, effortful processing of a persuasive message. However, it might also enhance the perceived relevance of information impugning the credibility of the message source, and hence increase attention to and processing of such information.

In sum, the LET assumes that all instances of knowledge formation, including persuasion, are potentially impacted by a broad variety of motivations which affect the course of the judgmental process, i.e., its extent (or depth) and direction. Later we argue that these motivational effects are the same irrespective of whether the evidence for the judgments is contained in heuristics or cues, versus message arguments.

Cognitive Capability and Capacity

Both the ELM and the HSM stress that persuasion depends on the recipient's cognitive ability. It seems important to further distinguish between a "software" aspect of ability, referred to as *capability*, and a "hardware" aspect, referred to as *capacity*. Capability refers to the knower's possession of those beliefs that render particular evidence relevant to a conclusion. These beliefs need to be mentally represented (or *available*), and also sufficiently *accessible* to be used in a specific instance (Higgins, 1996). Thus, for particular evidence to affect one's opinion, these "bridging" cognitions must be both available and accessible. If such knowledge is available, but not accessible, one may need to actively search one's memory for it. If such knowledge is neither accessible nor available, one may need to construct such beliefs "on-line," on the basis of other knowledge, which requires an extra effort. Thus, capability may affect the extensiveness of information processing.

Recent empirical evidence has confirmed the importance of belief accessibility in the processing of both message and cue information in persuasion situations. With respect to message processing, Fabrigar, Priester, Petty, and Wegener (1998) found that experimentally increasing the cognitive accessibility of participants' attitudes toward an issue increased processing of subsequent persuasive communications, as demonstrated by an enhanced persuasive impact of strong (vs. weak) message arguments. According to one explanation proposed by the authors, this was due to spreading activation from the primed attitude to related knowledge and beliefs, which subsequently were utilized in participants' elaboration of the message arguments. With respect to the impact of heuristic/peripheral cues, Maio and Olson (1998) found that misrepresenting one's attitudes toward a likable communicator increased subsequent agreement with the communicator's position toward an issue, presumably because dissimulation heightened the accessibility of participants' genuine attitude toward the source and thus enhanced the operation of a "likability heuristic." Thus, recent research, as well as theoretical statements within the dual-process models, confirm our unimodel's position that availability and accessibility of relevant knowledge structures can enhance the judgmental impact of both heuristics/cues and persuasive arguments.

Cognitive capacity refers to attentional limitations on the amount of processing the knower is capable of carrying out at any given moment (Kahneman, 1973). Thus, under conditions that tax the knower's cognitive capacity, the knower should be less able to process extensive bodies of information than under conditions in which his or her capacity is relatively unencumbered. Again, we assume that cognitive capability or capacity considerations are unrelated to whether persuasion is accomplished via cues/heuristics or message arguments. Although cognitive capability and capacity are similar in that they both affect information processing, they may differ in ways that are important. For example, the accessibility component of capability may be responsive to current goals or motivations, whereas one's attentional resources (capacity) are generally thought to be fixed and unresponsive to varying levels of motivation.

The Unimodel and the Dual-Mode Frameworks

The unimodel agrees with the dual-process models in that the elaboration of persuasively relevant information can vary in extent because of variations in motivation and cognitive ability. However, it is different in two very important ways. First, it makes a specific distinction between cognitive capability and capacity. Second, and more important, it is more explicit about the evidence concept, which it shares in common with prior, classic models of persuasion (McGuire, 1960; Wyer, 1970, 1974). It is this concept that warrants our essential claim for the unimodel, namely that heuristics or cues, as well as message arguments, constitute forms (or content categories) of persuasive evidence. We propose that message arguments and cues (i.e., information extraneous to message content) are *functionally equivalent* in that, controlling for differences in important parameters such as length/complexity, order of presentation, and relevance, they are processed in a similar fashion during persuasion (for more details, see Kruglanski & Thompson, 1999).

As noted earlier, there is no inherent reason that information extraneous to a message is necessarily shorter or simpler than the message content itself. Both may be either brief and succinct, or long and unwieldy. For both cues and arguments, the message content should require a higher level of perceiver motivation and ability in order to affect the perceiver's attitude. Also, cues/heuristics need not necessarily be encountered prior to the contents of a message, because order of presentation is controlled by the presenter, and is not intrinsic to the essential distinction between cues and arguments. For example, in many magazine editorials, information regarding the author or contributor is presented after the essay itself. It follows that any information (be it cue or argument) presented later in an informational sequence may yield a greater persuasive effect when the recipient has sufficient motivation and ability to continue processing through to the end of the sequence.

Finally, cues and arguments need not necessarily differ in perceived relevance. For example, Chaiken et al. (1989) have noted that heuristics can vary in their perceived reliability. In addition, the notion of argument strength, central to the ELM, specifically allows that some ("weak") arguments are seen as less relevant than other ("strong") arguments. Thus, it not difficult to imagine that in a situation involving highly reliable heuristics and weak arguments, the persuasive impact of the latter actually might be stronger, even under conditions of high issue involvement.

Our review thus far has cues and arguments share a similar evidential structure, and thus may affect persuasion through the same quasi-syllogistic process that governs the formation of knowledge in general. The impact of processing motivation and ability depends on critical informational features such as length/complexity, order of presentation, and perceived relevance (i.e., the cognitive availability and accessibility of beliefs linking evidence to conclusions). However, the impact of motivation and ability should not depend on the cue versus argument distinction per se because both types of information theoretically can vary considerably on each of the critical features. Consistent with the unimodel, the processing outcomes based on cues/heuristics versus arguments do not necessarily appear to be functionally independent. Despite this congenial analysis, it is important for us to account for the considerable mass of published empirical data that suggest precisely the opposite.

Empirical Evidence for the Dual Modes

A major empirical point for the functional independence of psychological processes can be made through demonstrations that they are impacted differently by, and hence that they "interact with," other variables (Tulving, 1983). In the case of the dual-process models, the large body of empirical findings (for reviews see Eagly & Chaiken, 1993; Petty & Cacioppo, 1986) is commonly taken to suggest the presence of interactions between evidential content type (i.e., cue vs. argument) and determinants of "depth of processing" (e.g., motivation and cognitive capacity) for such significant persuasion outcomes as attitude change, its persistence over time, its resistance to counterpersuasion, and its relation to relevant, overt behaviors. Two categories of such interaction effects may be discerned. One we call *inferred* interactions because these are cases in which a variable's effect (e.g., that of distraction) is empirically observed in research that incorporates one evidence type only (e.g., message arguments). The implicit, albeit untested, assumption in such a case is that the effect in question would fail to be manifest with the alternative evidence type (e.g., with cues or heuristics). The other category we call *manifest* interactions. These are cases in which one evidence-type (e.g., heuristic cues) is actually observed to interact with a determinant of processing extent (e.g., issue relevance or need for cognition) in a way patently different from that of the other evidence-type (e.g., message arguments). Since manifest interactions provide the strongest support for the dual-process models, we focus here on the evidence for these.

Manifest Interactions

Prototypical of research on manifest interactions is the classic study by Petty, Cacioppo, and Goldman (1981), in which the following variables were manipulated orthogonally: (a) the personal relevance of the issue to message recipients, (b) the quality of the arguments in the communication, and (c) the apparent expertise of the source. The data from this study clearly indicated that personal relevance differentially moderated the persuasive impact of the source expertise and argument quality manipulations. Whereas argument quality was the more important determinant of persuasion for high (vs. low) relevance participants, source expertise was the more important determinant for low (vs. high) relevance participants. Taken at face value, these interactive results, and many similar ones reported in the literature (for reviews see Eagly & Chaiken, 1993; Petty & Cacioppo, 1986), appear to constitute powerful support for the dual-process models. They imply that the content type of evidence does, in fact, matter and that cues/heuristics (vs. message arguments) are impacted in diametrically opposite ways by the very same moderator variables. Confirmation of the dual-process approach appears virtually inescapable unless an alternative account of these results is possible.

Reinterpreting Manifest Interactions

Interestingly, in Petty et al. (1981), cue information (regarding source expertise) (a) was presented to participants prior to the message arguments and (b) was considerably briefer than the message arguments. As a consequence, it seems plausible that the cue/heuristic information in this case was much easier to process than the message argument information It is entirely possible, in other words, that message arguments have had a greater impact under high (vs. low) issue involvement because they both were more extensive and appeared later in the informational sequence, either of which would have made them less likely to be thoroughly processed. As such, message arguments were particularly likely to benefit from the enhanced processing motivation engendered in the high (vs. low) involvement condition. Similarly, because the more extensive, and secondarily presented, message arguments failed to be processed carefully in the low involvement condition; the brief, easily processed, and initially presented cue/heuristic information may have enjoyed a persuasive advantage in this situation.

The covariation in the research of Petty et al. (1981) between information length and ordinal position on the one hand, and the evidential type of the information on the other, is hardly unique. Quite the contrary, it is representative of much of the work conducted within the ELM and HSM research programs. Thus, Petty's (1994) "State of the Art" review describes six major (most frequently cited) ELM studies, and chapter 7 in Eagly and Chaiken (1993) discusses seven influential HSM studies. In all of this research, listed in Table 3.1, the message argument information was considerably more extensive, elaborate, and/or easy to process than the cue or heuristic information. Furthermore, in 9 of the 13 studies the cue/heuristic information appeared before the message arguments, and in the remaining 4 it appeared concomitantly with the message arguments. For instance, in the Wells & Petty (1980) research the cue consisted of the communicator's head movements that occurred as he was delivering the message arguments. If our analysis is correct, controlling for informational extent and ordinal position should eliminate the apparent differences in the way cues/heuristics versus message arguments have interacted with various factors known to affect persuasion (e.g., involvement) in past research. These notions were examined empirically by Thompson, Kruglanski, and Spiegel (1999). We summarize their results in what follows.

TESTING THE UNIMODEL

We conducted four experiments in which we began to reveal the informational properties of length/complexity and type of evidence (cues/heuristics vs. message arguments). Because the particulars of these

TABLE 3.1

Characteristics of Message Arguments and Peripheral/Heuristic Cues from Studies Featured in Petty (1994) and Eagly and Chaiken (1993)

	Types of Cue or Heuristic	Order of Presentation	Length of Arguments (A) and Cues, Heuristics (C)	Cues Seem Easier to Process?
< ELM Studies >				
Heesacker, Petty, & Cacioppo (1983)	Source expertise	Cue first	A: *Several arguments* C: 30-word statement	Yes
Petty & Cacioppo (1984)	Number of arguments	Simultaneous	A: 3 to 9 arguments C: —	Yes
Petty, Cacioppo, & Goldman (1981)	Source expertise	Cue first	A: *8 elaborated arguments* C: Short statement	Yes
Petty, Cacioppo, & Schumann (1983)	Celebrity status	Cue first	A: 5 one-sentence arguments C: —	Yes
Petty, Harkins, & Williams (1980)	Group size	Cue first	A: *5-minute videotape* C: Short statement	Yes
Wells & Petty (1980)	Head movements	Simultaneous	A: Short spoken editorial C: —	Yes
< HSM Studies >				
Axsom, Yates, & Chaiken (1987)	Audience response	Simultaneous	A: 5-minute audiotape C: —	Yes
Chaiken (1979)	Source attractiveness	Cue first	A: 2 brief oral arguments C: —	Yes

Table 3.1 continued

Table 3.1 continued

	Types of Cue or Heuristic	Order of Presentation	Length of Arguments (A) and Cues, Heuristics (C)	Cues Seem Easier to Process?
Chaiken (1980)	Source likeability	Cue first	A: 2 or 6 short arguments C: Paragraph	Yes
Chaiken & Eagly (1983)	Source likeability	Cue first	A: 5-minute message C: Paragraph	Yes
Chaiken & Maheswaran (1994)	Source credibility	Cue first	A: 450-word description C: Short statement	Yes
Maheswaran & Chaiken (1991)	Consensus	Cue first	A: 450-word description C: Short statement	Yes
Ratneshwar & Chaiken (1991)	Source expertise	Cue first	A: 9-sentence paragraph C: 2 short paragraphs	Yes

Note. In column 3, the longer set of information is italicized; in some cases, cues had no length per se. Also, in Chaiken, 1980, and Ratneshwar and Chaiken, 1991, cue and argument information were roughly equal in length.

experiments are reported elsewhere (Kruglanski & Thompson, 1999; Thompson et al., 1999), they are reviewed here in a more general fashion.

Motivation and Cue Usage

A major finding in the dual-mode literature has been that only message arguments drive attitude change when the issue personally involves the recipient (e.g., Petty et al., 1981). In contrast, when personal involvement is low, attitude change is influenced primarily by cues or heuristics. This may be because cue information is brief in the typical dual-mode study, whereas message argument information is relatively lengthy. When the issue involves the recipient, the recipient's motivation may be sufficiently high to prompt the relatively laborious processing that lengthy informational passages may require in order to yield a persuasive impact. According to the unimodel, however, the critical feature here is not whether the information is of the heuristic/cue versus message argument variety, but rather how long and complex is.

In our first study, participants read a one-page proposal that advocated the implementation of comprehensive exams either at nearby colleges and universities, including their home institution (high involvement condition), or at a set of geographically remote schools (low involvement condition). The proposal was designed to be moderate in the quality of its arguments, containing four known through earlier pretesting to be "moderately weak" and two known to be "strong." Prior to this, participants read a biographical résumé of equal length allegedly pertaining to the background of the proposal's author. This information, if examined carefully, established that the author's credentials were either relevant to the topic of the proposal (expert condition) or irrelevant to the topic (inexpert condition). After reading all the information, participants completed an unexpected, four-item, self-report measure of their attitude toward the proposal and a timed listing of their cognitive responses while reading the materials. Finally, they completed a set of checks on the manipulations of source expertise and issue involvement, later analysis of which confirmed that these manipulations were indeed successful.

We predicted that the "heuristic" information in this case would have greater persuasive impact in the high (vs. low) personal relevance condition. Specifically, the tendency of recipients to be more persuaded by the expert source than by the inexpert source should have been greater when personal involvement was high than when it was low. Indeed, the means for the aggregate measure of attitude (displayed in Fig. 3.1) show a reliable persuasive advantage for the expert (vs. inexpert) in the high involvement condition. In the low involvement condition, the manipulation of expertise had no significant impact on participants' support for the proposal. Thus, in the present case, when the source information was made more difficult to process, increased motivation to determine the merits of the proposal caused the persuasive implications of that information to become manifest.

Cognitive Capacity and Cue Usage

Adequate processing of relatively lengthy and complex information requires not only the proper degree of motivation, but also sufficient

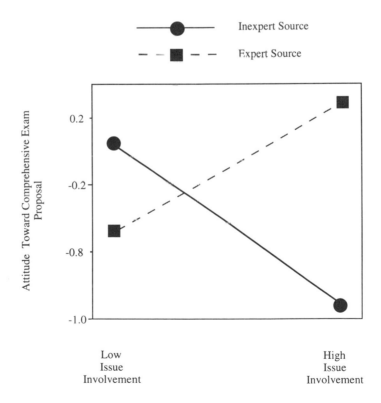

FIG. 3.1. Impact of Issue Involvement (low, high) and Lengthy Source Background Information (inexpert, expert) on Attitude Toward Exam Policy in First Study.

cognitive capacity. Capacity-depleting events such as distraction or cognitive load should, therefore, attenuate the persuasive impact of such information. Indeed, prior research (e.g., the classic experiment by Petty, Wells, & Brock, 1976) has demonstrated that distraction does interfere with the processing of message information, thus increasing the persuasive impact of low quality arguments and reducing the persuasive impact of high quality arguments. In our second study, we endeavored to demonstrate that cognitive distraction also could attenuate the persuasive impact of lengthy and complex information about source expertise under conditions of high processing likelihood. The procedure and materials were identical except that all participants read information establishing high issue involvement, and, to manipulate cognitive load, half were instructed to rehearse a nine-digit number string while reading the information.

The results for the attitude measure are displayed in Fig. 3.2. Consistent with predictions, the persuasive impact of lengthy source expertise infor-

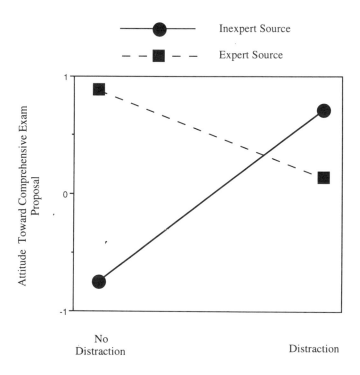

FIG. 3.2. Impact on Distraction (absent, present) and Lengthy Source Background Information (inexpert, expert) on Attitude Toward Exam Policy in Second Study.

mation in the no distraction condition (paralleling our finding in the high involvement condition of our first study) was attenuated in the distraction condition. Whereas participants agreed more with the expert (vs. inexpert) in the no distraction condition, in the distraction condition the manipulation of source expertise had no reliable effect on attitude.

Cognitive Capacity and Cue Usage: Cue Complexity

In our first two studies, by using relatively lengthy and complex source background information, we demonstrated that differences in apparent source expertise could have a greater, rather than lesser, impact under conditions of either high motivational involvement or high processing capacity compared to conditions under which those variables were constrained to be low. However, in those studies we did not attempt to replicate past findings using the more traditional, briefer presentation of source information. In a third study, we employed the design and procedure of the second, but extended it by adding a short source background condition to create a 2: source background (inexpert, expert) x 2: distraction (no, yes) x 2: source background length (short, long) experimental design. We expected to replicate the source expertise x distraction effect from the second study when the source information was relatively long, as before. However, when the source information was shorter, and therefore less difficult to process when one is distracted, we expected to find only a main effect of expertise.

The materials and procedure were the same as in the second study, with the exception of the short source background condition, in which the implications of the longer, one-page résumés each were summarized in two brief, straightforward sentences. The means for the measure of attitude appear in Fig. 3.3. As expected, in the brief source background condition, there was only a simple main effect of expertise, such that the expert source elicited more agreement than the inexpert, regardless of the level of distraction. However, when the source information was longer, we replicated the source expertise x distraction interaction found earlier in the second study. Thus, it appears that distraction does not interfere with the processing of short cue/heuristic information of the type traditionally used in prior research, but it does significantly interfere with the processing of cue/heuristic information when it is sufficiently lengthy and complex.

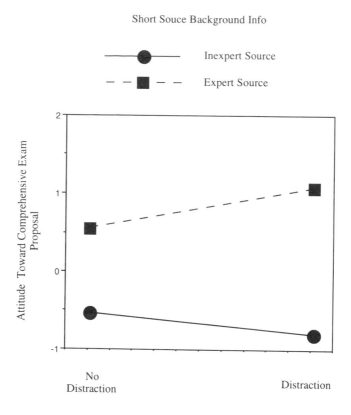

FIG. 3.3a. Impact of Distraction (absent, present) and Source Expertise (inexpert, expert) on Attitude Toward Exam Policy in Brief Source Background Condition of Third Study.

Motivation and Content Effects

As we have seen, in a typical persuasion experiment brief heuristic information (e.g., about source expertise) is followed by much lengthier and more complex message argument information. According to the present analysis, the length/complexity of the information and/or its position in the sequence, rather than its content (i.e., being composed of message arguments or cues/heuristics), determine its persuasive impact. If so, the same pattern of interactions (e.g., with issue involvement) previously found to distinguish cue/heuristics from message arguments should be obtained with any two informational sets, the first of which is relatively brief and simple, the subsequent one being relatively lengthy

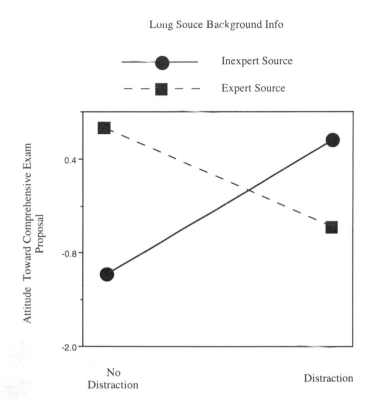

FIG. 3.3b. Impact of Distraction (absent, present) and Source Expertise (inexpert, expert) on Attitude Toward Exam Policy in Lengthy Source Background Condition of Third Study.

and complex. Consider, for example, two separate sets of arguments that exhibit these characteristics. If the unimodel analysis is valid, then early appearing, brief arguments ought to exert greater persuasive impact under low involvement than under with high involvement, whereas later appearing, lengthier arguments ought to exert greater persuasive impact under high involvement than under low involvement.

In a fourth study, we put these ideas to an empirical test. To this end, we independently manipulated the persuasive strength of two brief, initial arguments that supported the comprehensive exam issue, as well as the strength of six subsequent, extensive arguments that comprised a traditional persuasive communication. These were crossed with a manipulation of the recipients' personal involvement in the issue. In line with our

Initial, Brief Arguments

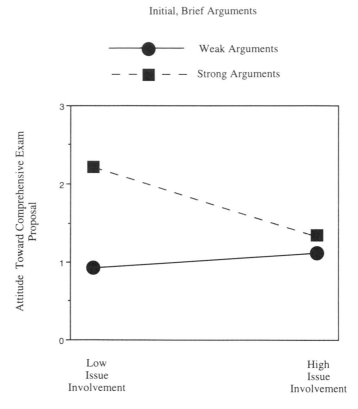

FIG. 3.4a. Impact of Initial, Brief Arguments' Quality (weak, strong) and Issue Involvement (low, high) on Attitude Toward Exam Policy in Fourth Study.

single-process approach, we predicted that exposure to strong (vs. weak) initial, brief arguments would result in greater agreement with the communicator's position when issue involvement was low. Conversely, we expected that exposure to strong (vs. weak) subsequent, lengthy arguments would result in a more favorable attitude toward the communicator's position when issue involvement was high.

Indeed, as seen in Fig. 3.4, an interaction between issue involvement and initial, brief argument quality indicated that strong (vs. weak) arguments elicited more agreement with the exam proposal in the low involvement condition, but not in the high involvement condition. In addition, an interaction between issue involvement and subsequent, lengthy argument quality indicated a persuasive advantage for strong arguments only when involvement was high.

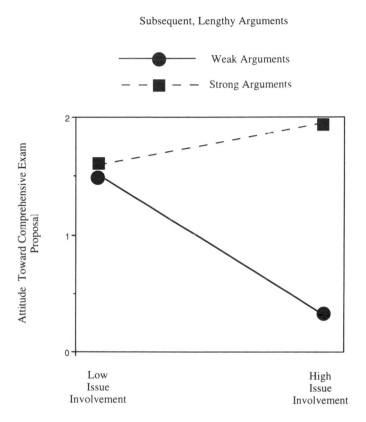

FIG. 3.4b. Impact of Subsequent, Lengthy Arguments' Quality (weak, strong) and Issue Involvement (low, high) on Attitude Toward Exam Policy in Fourth Study.

These results lend greater generality to the evidence in support of our persuasion unimodel. In particular, they speak to its proposition that the important characteristics of persuasive evidence (such as length/complexity, order, perceived relevance) are independent of whether such evidence constitutes cues or arguments. Previously, we demonstrated that nonargument cue information (e.g., pertaining to the expertise of the source) can have a greater, rather than lesser, impact on participants' attitudes when that information is made similar in length/complexity to message argument information. In the present study we showed further that variations in participants' processing motivation had precisely the same moderating effect on the impact of brief, initially encountered persuasive evidence when that information was of the "argument" type as it has had in past research when that information was of the "cue/heuristic" type.

Processing motivation in our current studies was manipulated via the arousal of utilitarian or instrumental concerns (e.g., "Will the exams benefit me or not?") or what Johnson and Eagly (1989) referred to as "outcome-relevant involvement." That is, information in these studies emphasized either the objective, material benefits of the attitude object (in the case of the strong arguments) or the extent to which the communicator's position was likely to be based on a veridical knowledge of those benefits.

However, we suspect that motivation based on other functional concerns could enhance the persuasive impact of substantial nonmessage (e.g., source) information in a similar fashion. For example, Chen, Shechter, and Chaiken (1996) found that inducing "impression-relevant involvement" (based on social-adjustive concerns) heightened the impact of expected partner attitude on participants' subsequently reported opinions by increasing the extent to which participants elaborated a set of issue arguments in the direction of the partner's expected position. However, virtually no effort was necessary to deduce the relevant "heuristic cue" involved (i.e., the partner's expected attitude); it was directly given to participants in the form of a scale rating. Consider an alternative situation, in which the partner's attitude was not readily obvious, but instead could be derived only from extensive scrutiny of available information (e.g., examination of discursive essays written by the partner). We suspect that, in such a case, high levels of impression motivation could determine participants' attitude via heightened processing of such heuristic information, as participants strive to ascertain their partner's opinion before expressing their own. Importantly, in such a case, a manipulation of partner opinion might affect participants' attitude only when impression motivation was strong enough to prompt extensive processing of the partner information and could occur even without exposure to a set of issue-related arguments to process selectively.

Implications of the Unimodel

The unimodel represents a fundamental critique of the dual-process frameworks in one sense only. It disputes the central assumption of these frameworks that a qualitative difference in the persuasion process hinges on whether persuasion is accomplished by the processing of message arguments versus the processing of information exogenous to the message, that is, by "cues" or heuristics. Our conclusion regarding the uniformity of process in these two instances is supported not only by our own analysis and empirical results, but also, strikingly, by statements of the dual-mode theorists themselves. As noted throughout, many of the present arguments (e.g., for the similar way in which various factors affect heuristic/or cue-based and message-based persuasion), were either explicitly articulated or at least strongly implied in the dual-mode literature. In this sense, the present conceptualization merely spells out the logical consequences of considerations recognized at some level, but not fully followed through, within the dual-mode frameworks. Also, we essentially agree with the dual-mode theorists regarding the role that motivational and cognitive factors play in determining the extent to which available evidence is processed. In addition, as ample evidence attests (see Eagly & Chaiken, 1993, for a review), the dual-mode frameworks work very well in situations where brief cue, or heuristic, information is followed by more extensive message arguments. Where such situations are encountered the dual-mode frameworks may work well, indeed. How often they occur outside the lab, however, is more difficult to ascertain. The unimodel offers the advantage of flexibility in accounting for persuasion occurring in situations where, for example, potentially relevant nonmessage information is relatively complex and occurs after briefer, more straightforward message arguments. In such (possibly common) situations, the current dual-mode analyses may not apply. In short, because of the infinite heterogeneity of real world situations, the frequentist argument—that in the real world the cue/heuristic versus message argument distinction is confounded actuarially with the length/complexity of information, its relevance, or its ordinal position—is difficult to verify.

More importantly, the unimodel offers a number of serious advantages for persuasion researchers. Not the least of these is its considerable generative potential as a source of novel, testable predictions. In this regard, our present studies merely scratch the surface. Although they call attention to the need to control for different types of persuasive information (i.e., heuristics/cues vs. message arguments) for length, complexity, and ordinal position, additional research is needed to demonstrate the need to control also for its perceived relevance to the conclusion, and for the availability and accessibility of its premises (see Spiegel, Kruglanski, & Thompson, 1998).

In general, the present unimodel forms a bridge between prior persuasion work that stressed the syllogistic (or probabilogical) processes, whereby people's attitudes and opinions are formed or altered (McGuire,

1960; Wyer, 1970; 1974), and contemporary work that highlights both the extent or depth of information processing involved in persuasion, and the motivational and capacity factors that affect it. Whereas previous work affirmed that people's conclusions are largely consistent with their premises (cf. McGuire, 1960; Wyer, 1976) we assume that when persuasively relevant information is extensive and/or complex, this degree of consistency will be maximized when sufficient processing motivation and attentional resources allow recipients to fully apply their premises to the information at hand. These issues could be fruitfully investigated in future research.

Of special significance, the unimodel offers the fundamental conceptual advantages of parsimony and integration. Such integration consists not only in synthesizing the ubiquitous dual modes into one, but also in forging linkages to previous models of persuasion and attitude change, such as McGuire's (1960, 1968) and Wyer's (1970, 1974) probabilogical notions, the theories of reasoned action or planned behavior (Ajzen, 1988; Fishbein & Ajzen, 1975), or the various cognitive consistency models of attitude change like those of Festinger (1957) or Heider (1958). In all these approaches, as in the unimodel, the concept of persuasive evidence that supports (i.e., is consistent with) or undermines (i.e., is inconsistent with) a conclusion plays a major role (see Kruglanski, 1989, Chapter 6; Kruglanski & Klar, 1987). These explicit ties to past theorizing and research both highlight the cumulative nature of our progress in understanding persuasion and also take advantage of important prior insights and discoveries.

Further Implications for Research on Attitude Functions

The data we have gathered thus far in support of the unimodel suggest that cues and arguments may share a similar evidentiary structure and may be processed according to a similar reasoning structure. Although we have employed exclusively manipulations of instrumental or utilitarian motives, future research could explore the same basic issues with fundamentally different processing motivations. Indeed, there is some evidence already that enhanced persuasion through matching particular attitude functions with the content of persuasive evidence may occur both for message arguments and for source information. For example, Lavine and Snyder (1996) presented low and high self-monitors (for whom value-expressive and social-adjustive motives respectively, are dominant) with persuasive appeals that emphasize either positive value-expressive or positive social-adjustive implications of supporting the advocated position (voter participation). Participants were more persuaded when the appeals matched their chronic motivational concerns, and this effect was mediated (in two studies) by perceptions of the quality of the arguments in the appeals. From our perspective, perceived argument quality reflected the perceived evaluative relevance of the evidence contained in the appeals.

In another study of function matching and persuasion, Shavitt, Swan, Lowrey, and Wanke (1994) primed utilitarian (sensory) and social-adjustive (image) concerns in participants before asking them to read about and evaluate a series of restaurant ads. Furthermore, some participants were specially motivated to attend to one of the ads through the offer of a gift certificate for that restaurant (allegedly in exchange for their participation in the experiment), and others were offered a gift unrelated to the restaurant. In one version of the target ad, the faces and identities of the endorsers were designed to be particularly socially attractive, and in another version they were designed to be less attractive. Shavitt et al. found that endorser attractiveness had a greater impact both on attitude toward the restaurant and on participants' valenced cognitive responses under high (vs. low) involvement, but only when a social-adjustive goal was primed. Furthermore, the valence of participants' thoughts about the endorsers reliably predicted both attitude and behavioral intention in the high involvement condition, but again, only when the social-adjustive goal was primed.

These results suggest, consistent with our unimodel perspective, that both the nature and magnitude of motivation are important in determining not only what evidence is deemed relevant, but whether that evidence is processed sufficiently to exert a detectable persuasive impact. Taken together with the studies of Lavine and Snyder (1996) they argue that our emphasis on the functional equivalence of cues and message arguments extends to processing motivations other than those directly examined in our own studies. In the future, as we continue to explore the fundamental implications of our emphasis on evidential properties such as length, complexity, relevance, and ordinal position (rather than on the cue/message argument distinction per se), an increased consideration of the processing motivations that reflect various attitude functions will play an important role in the development of our single-mode model of persuasion.

REFERENCES

Achinstein, P. (1983). Concepts of evidence. In P. Achinstein (Ed.), *The concept of evidence*. New York: Oxford University Press.

Ajzen, I. (1988). *Attitudes, personality, and behavior*. Chicago: Dorsey.

Allport, F. H. (1924). *Social psychology*. Cambridge, MA: Riverside.

Asch, S. E. (1952). *Social psychology*. Englewood Cliffs, NJ: Prentice Hall.

Axsom, D., Yates, S., & Chaiken, S. (1987). Audience resoponse as a heuristic cue in persuasion. *Journal of Personality and Social Psychology, 53*, 30–40.

Berscheid, E., Graziano, W., Monson, T., & Dermer, M. (1976). Outcome dependency: Attention, attribution, and attraction. *Journal of Personality and Social Psychology, 34*, 978– 989.

Cacioppo, J. T., & Petty, R. E. (1982). The need for cognition. *Journal of Personality and Social Psychology, 42*, 116–131.

Carnap, R. (1962). *Logical foundations of probability*. Chicago: Chicago University Press.

Chaiken, S. (1979). Communicator physical attractiveness and persuasion. *Journal of Personality and Social Psychology, 37*, 1387–1397.

Chaiken, S. (1980). Heuristic versus systematic information processing and the use of source versus message cues in persuasion. *Journal of Personality and Social Psychology, 39*, 752– 766.

Chaiken, S., & Eagly, A. H. (1983). Communication modality as a determinant of persuasion: The role of communicator salience. *Journal of Personality and Social Psychology, 45*, 241– 256.

Chaiken, S., Liberman, A., & Eagly, A. H. (1989). Heuristic and systematic processing within and beyond the persuasion context. In J. S. Uleman, & J. A. Bargh (Eds.), *Unintended thought* (pp. 212–252). New York: Guilford Press.

Chaiken, S., & Maheswaran, D. (1994). Heuristic processing can bias systematic processing: Effects of source credibility, argument ambiguity, and task importance on attitude judgment. *Journal of Personality and Social Psychology, 66*, 460–473.

Chen, S., & Chaiken, S. (1999). The heuristic–systematic model in its broader context. In S. Chaiken & Y. Trope (Eds.), *Dual-process theories in social psychology* (pp. 73–96). New York: Guilford Press.

Chen, S., Shechter, D., & Chaiken, S. (1996). Getting at the truth or getting along: Accuracy- versus impression-motivated heuristic and systematic processing. *Journal of Personality and Social Psychology, 71*, 262–275.

DeBono, K.G., & Harnish, R.J. (1988). Source expertise, source attractiveness, and the processing of persuasive information: A functional approach. *Journal of Personality and Social Psychology, 55*, 541–546.

Eagly, A. H., & Chaiken, S. (1993). *The psychology of attitudes*. Fort Worth, TX: Harcourt Brace Jovanovich.

Eagly, A. H., & Chaiken, S. (1998). Attitude structure and function. In D. Gilbert, S. Fiske, & G. Lindzey (Eds.), *Handbook of social psychology* (4th ed., pp. 269–322). New York: McGraw Hill.

Erber, R., & Fiske, S. T. (1984). Outcome dependency and attention to inconsistent information. *Journal of Personality and Social Psychology, 47*, 709–726.

Fabrigar, L. R., Priester, J. R., Petty, R. E., & Wegener, D. T. (1998). The impact of attitude accessibility on elaboration of persuasive messages. *Personality and Social Psychology Bulletin, 24*, 339–352.

Fazio, R. H. (1989). On the power and functionality of attitudes: The role of attitude accessibility. In A. R. Pratkanis, S. J. Breckler, & A. G. Greenwald (Eds.), *Attitude structure and function* (pp. 153–179). Hillsdale, NJ: Lawrence Erlbaum Associates.

Festinger, L. (1957). *A theory of cognitive dissonance*. Stanford, CA: Stanford University Press.

Fishbein, M., & Ajzen, I. (1975). *Belief, attitude, intention, and behavior: An introduction to theory and research*. Reading, MA: Addison-Wesley.

Fleming, M. A., & Petty, R. E. (1999). Identity and persuasion: An elaboration likelihood approach. In M. A. Hogg, & D. J. Terry (Eds.), *Attitudes, behavior, and social context: The role of norms and group membership* (pp. 171–199). Mahwah, NJ: Lawrence Erlbaum Associates.

Glymour, C. N. (1980). *Theory and evidence*. Princeton, NJ: Princeton University Press.

Greenwald, A. G. (1968). Cognitive learning, cognitive response to persuasion, and attitude change. In A. G. Greenwald, T. C. Brock, & T. M. Ostrom (Eds.), *Psychological foundations of attitudes* (pp. 147–170). San Diego, CA: Academic Press.

Greenwald, A. G. (1989). Why attitudes are important: Defining attitude and attitude theory 20 years later. In A. R. Pratkanis, S. J. Breckler, & A. G. Greenwald (Eds.), *Attitude structure and function* (pp. 429–440). Hillsdale, NJ: Lawrence Erlbaum Associates.

Heesaker, M., Petty, R. E., & Cacioppo, J. T. (1983). Field dependence and attitude change: Source credibility can alter persuasion by affecting message-relevant thinking. *Journal of Personality, 51,* 653–666.

Heider, F. (1958). *The psychology of interpersonal relations.* New York: Wiley.

Hempel, C. G. (1965). *Aspects of scientific explanation.* San Francisco: Free Press.

Higgins, E. T. (1996). Knowledge activation, application, and salience. In E. T. Higgins & A. W. Kruglanski (Eds.), *Social psychology: Handbook of basic principles.* New York: Guilford Press.

Hovland, C. I. (Ed.). (1957). *The order of presentation in persuasion.* New Haven, CT: Yale University Press.

Hovland, C. I., & Janis, I. L. (Eds.). (1959). *Personality and persuasibility.* New Haven, CT: Yale University Press.

Hovland, C. I., Janis, I. L., & Kelley, H. H. (1953). *Communication and persuasion: Psychological studies of opinion change.* New Haven, CT: Yale University Press.

Johnson, B. T., & Eagly, A. H. (1989). The effects of involvement on persuasion. *Psychological Bulletin, 106,* 290–314.

Judd, C. M., & Lusk, C. M. (1984). Knowledge structures and evaluative judgments: Effects of structural variables on judgmental extremity. *Journal of Personality and Social Psychology, 46,* 1193–1207.

Kahneman, D. (1973). *Attention and effort.* Englewood, NJ: Prentice Hall.

Katz, D. (1960). The functional approach to the study of attitudes. *Public Opinion Quarterly, 24,* 163–204.

Kitayama, S., & Burnstein, E. (1989). The relation between opinion and memory: Distinguishing between associative density and structural centrality. In J. N. Bassili (Ed.), *On-line cognition in person perception* (pp. 91–122). Hillsdale, NJ: Lawrence Erlbaum Associates.

Kruglanski, A. W. (1989). *Lay epistemics and human knowledge: Cognitive and motivational bases.* New York: Plenum Press.

Kruglanski, A. W. (1990). Motivations for judging and knowing: Implications for causal attribution. In E. T. Higgins & R. M. Sorrentino (Eds.), *The handbook of motivation and cognition: Foundations of social behavior* (Vol. 2, pp. 333–368). New York: Guilford Press.

Kruglanski, A. W., & Klar, Y. (1987). A view from a bridge: Synthesizing the consistency and attribution paradigms from a lay epistemic perspective. *European Journal of Social Psychology, 17,* 211–241.

Kruglanski, A. W., & Thompson, E. P. (1999). Persuasion by a single route: A view from the unimodel. *Psychological Inquiry.*

Kruglanski, A. W., Thompson, E. P., & Spiegel, S. (1999). Separate or equal? Bimodal notions of persuasion and a single-process "Unimodel." In S. Chaiken and Y. Trope (Eds.), *Dual process models in social cognition: A source book* (pp. 293–322). New York: Guilford.

Kruglanski, A. W., & Webster, D. M. (1996). Motivated closing of the mind: "Seizing" and "freezing." *Psychological Review, 103,* 263–283.

Kruglanski, A. W., Webster, D. M., & Klem, A. (1993). Motivated resistance and openness to persuasion in the presence or absence of prior information. *Journal of Personality and Social Psychology, 65,* 861–876.

Laswell, H. D. (1948). The structure and function of communication in society. In L. Bryson (Ed.), *The communication of ideas: Religion and civilization series* (pp. 37–51). New York: Harper & Row.

Lavine, H., & Snyder, M. (1996). Cognitive processing and the functional matching effect in persuasion: The mediating role of subjective perceptions of message quality. *Journal of Experimental Social Psychology, 32,* 580–604.

Maheswaran, D., & Chaiken, S. (1991). Promoting systematic processing in low motivation settings: The effect of incongruent information on processing and judgment. *Journal of Personality and Social Psychology, 61,* 13–25.

Maio, G. R., & Olson, J. M. (1998). Attitude dissimulation and persuasion. *Journal of Experimental Social Psychology, 34,* 182–201.

McDougall, W. (1908). *Social psychology.* New York: Luce & Co.

McGuire, W. J. (1960). A syllogistic analysis of cognitive relationships. In C. I. Hovland & M. J. Rosenberg (Eds.), *Attitude organization and change: An analysis of consistency among attitude components* (pp. 65–111). New Haven, CT: Yale University Press.

McGuire, W. J. (1968). Personality and attitude change: An information-processing theory. In A. G. Greenwald, T. C. Brock, & T. M. Ostrom (Eds.), *Psychological foundations of attitudes* (pp. 171–196). San Diego, CA: Academic Press.

McGuire, W. J. (1969). The nature of attitudes and attitude change. In G. Lindzey & E. Aronson (Eds.), *Handbook of social psychology* (2nd ed., Vol. 3, pp. 136–314). Reading, MA: Addison-Wesley.

McGuire, W. J. (1972). Attitude change: The information processing paradigm. In C. G. McClintock (Ed.), *Experimental social psychology* (pp. 108–141). New York: Holt, Rinehart, & Winston.

Newcomb, T. M. (1950). *Social psychology.* New York: Dryden.

Petty, R. E. (1994). Two routes to persuasion: State of the art. In G. d'Ydewalle, P. Eelen, & P. Berteleson (Eds.), *International perspectives on psychological science* (Vol. 2, pp. 229–247). Hillsdale, NJ: Lawrence Erlbaum Associates.

Petty, R. E., & Cacioppo, J. T. (1984). The effets of involvement on responses to argument quantity and quality: Central and peripheral routes to persuasion. *Journal of Personality and Social Psychology, 46,* 69–81.

Petty, R. E., & Cacioppo, J. T. (1986). The elaboration likelihood model of persuasion. In L. Berkowitz (Ed.), *Advances in experimental social psychology* (Vol. 19, pp. 123–205). San Diego, CA: Academic Press.

Petty, R. E., Cacioppo, J. T., & Goldman, R. (1981). Personal involvement as a predictor of argument-based persuasion. *Journal of Personality and Social Psychology, 41,* 847–855.

Petty, R. E., Cacioppo, J. T., & Schumann, D. (1983). Central and peripheral routes to advertising effectiveness: The moderating role of involvement. *Journal of Consumer Research, 10,* 135–146.

Petty, R. E., Harkins, D. G., & Williams, K. D. (1980). The effects of group diffusion of cognitive effort on attitudes: An information processing view. *Journal of Personality and Social Psychology, 38,* 81–92.

Petty, R. E., Ostrom, T. M., & Brock, T. C. (Eds.), (1981). *Cognitive responses in persuasion.* Hillsdale, NJ: Lawrence Erlbaum Associates.

Petty, R. E., & Wegener, D. T. (1998). Matching versus mismatching attitude functions: Implications for scrutiny of persuasive messages. *Personality and Social Psychology Bulletin, 24,* 227–240.

Petty, R. E., & Wegener, D. T. (1999). The elaboration likelihood model: Current status and controversies. In S. Chaiken & Y. Trope (Eds.), *Dual-process theories in social psychology* (pp. 41–72). New York: Guilford.

Petty, R. E., Wells, G. L., & Brock, T. C. (1976). Distraction can enhance or reduce yielding to propaganda: Thought disruption versus effort justification. *Journal of Personality and Social Psychology, 34,* 874–884.

Pratkanis, A. R., Breckler, S. J., & Greenwald, A. G. (Eds.), (1989). *Attitude structure and function.* Hillsdale, NJ: Lawrence Erlbaum Associates.

Ratneshwar, S., & Chaiken, S. (1991). Comprehension's role in persuasion: The case of its moderating effect on the persuasive impact of source expertise. *Journal of Consumer Research, 18,* 52–62.

Ross, E. A. (1908). *Social control: A survey of the foundations of order.* New York: MacMillan.

Ruscher, J. B., & Fiske, S. T. (1990). Interpersonal competition can cause individuating processes. *Journal of Personality and Social Psychology, 58,* 832–843.

Shavitt, S. (1990). The role of attitude objects in attitude functions. *Journal of Experimental Social Psychology, 26,* 124–148.

Shavitt, S., Swan, S., Lowrey, T. M., & Wanke, M. (1994). The interaction of endorser attractiveness and involvement in persuasion depends on the goal that guides message processing. *Journal of Consumer Psychology, 3,* 137–162.

Sloman, S. A. (1996). The empirical case for two systems of reasoning. *Psychological Bulletin, 119,* 3–22.

Smith, M. B. (1947). The personal setting of public opinions: A study of attitudes toward Russia. *Public Opinion Quarterly, 11,* 507–523.

Smith, M. B., Bruner, J. S., & White, R. W. (1956). *Opinions and personality.* New York: Wiley.

Spiegel, S., Kruglanski, A. W., & Thompson, E. P. (1998, May). *Accessibility effects in a unimodel theory of persuasion.* Paper presented at the 10th meeting of the American Psychological Society, Washington, DC.

Taylor, S. E. (1975). On inferring one's attitudes from one's behavior: Some delimiting conditions. *Journal of Personality and Social Psychology, 31,* 126–131.

Thompson, E. P., & Kruglanski, A. W. (1998). *"Freezing" on high (but not low) source expertise prevents "seizing" on the content of a communication: The role of time pressure in message-based persuasion.* Manuscript in preparation.

Thompson, E. P., Kruglanski, A. W., & Spiegel, S. (1999). *Evidence for a single-mode "unimodel" of motivated reasoning in persuasion: The role of "cue" length and complexity.* Unpublished manuscript.

Tulving, E. (1983). *Elements of episodic memory:* Oxford, England: Oxford University Press.

Wells, G. L., & Petty, R. E. (1980). The effects of overt head movements on persuasion: Compatibility and incompatibility of responses. *Basic and Applied Social Psychology, 1,* 219–230.

Wyer, R. S., Jr. (1970). Quantitative prediction of belief and opinion change: A further test of a subjective probability model. *Personality and Social Psychology, 16,* 559–570.

Wyer, R. S., Jr. (1974). *Cognitive organization and change: An information processing approach.* Hillsdale, NJ: Lawrence Erlbaum Associates.

Wyer, R. S., Jr. (1976). Effects of previously formed beliefs on syllogistic inference processes. *Journal of Personality and Social Psychology, 33,* 307–316.

4

Cognitive Processes and the Functional Matching Effect in Persuasion: Studies of Personality and Political Behavior

Howard Lavine
State University of New York at Stony Brook

Mark Snyder
University of Minnesota

Following the development of formal attitude scaling techniques in the 1920s and 1930s, social scientists have been intensely interested in measuring the public's opinions on a wide range of topics (see McGuire, 1986). The birth of the science of public opinion afforded investigators the ability to forecast presidential elections, helped companies to peddle their goods, and aided the government in raising money to defeat the Nazis in World War II (Hovland, Lumsdaine, & Sheffield, 1949). Not until the 1950s and 1960s, however, did the attitude researchers turn their attention to matters of attitude *theory* such as how attitudes are formed, structured, and changed.

97

Most theories of the attitude formation/change process focus on questions of *what* information people may use in forming their attitudes or *when* persuasion attempts will be successful in bringing about attitude change (e.g., Chaiken, Liberman, & Eagly, 1989; Petty & Cacioppo, 1986). In contrast to these approaches, functional theories of attitude formation and change focus on the question of *why* people hold their attitudes. That is, functional approaches attempt to identify the various psychological benefits that people can and do derive from forming, expressing, and changing their attitudes. Functional approaches are thus directed to "the reasons and the purposes, the needs and the goals, the plans and the motives that underlie and generate psychological phenomena" (Snyder & Cantor, 1999, p. 642).

Both classic functional theories (e.g., Katz, 1960; Katz & Stotland, 1959; Sarnoff & Katz, 1954; Smith, Bruner, & White, 1956) and more contemporary taxonomies of social behavior (Chaiken et al., 1989; Herek, 1986; Snyder, 1992; Thomsen, Borgida, & Lavine, 1995) suggest that the holding and expressing of attitudes enable people to experience specific types of psychological benefit, such as gaining accurate knowledge of the social world (the knowledge function) defending the self from intrapsychic conflict or shoring up one's self-esteem (the ego-defensive function), expressing one's values and other important aspects of one's identity (the value-expressive function), and obtaining rewards from and fitting into one's social environment (the social-adjustive function), among others (see Pratkanis, Breckler, & Greenwald, 1989). The theoretical implications of a functional analysis of attitudes have been examined most frequently within the domain of persuasion. Recent studies have consistently shown that persuasion attempts will produce more recommended attitude change when they directly address the psychological function on which the attitude is based than when they address an irrelevant or less relevant function (DeBono, 1987; DeBono & Harnish, 1988; Lavine et al., 1999; Lavine & Snyder, 1996; Prentice, 1987; Shavitt, 1990; Snyder & DeBono, 1985; although see Petty & Wegener, 1998). This phenomenon has been termed the *functional matching effect* in persuasion (Lavine & Snyder, 1996).

In our recent work (Lavine et al., 1999; Lavine & Snyder, 1996), we have pursued three unexplored aspects of the functional matching effect. First, although the logic of the functional approach explains *why* functionally matched messages typically produce more attitude change than functionally mismatched ones (i.e., because the former allow the message recipient to obtain the desired type of psychological benefit), the cognitive processes that mediate the functional matching effect have—until recently—received little empirical attention. Thus, the question of *how* functionally matched messages produce their effects is not well understood. By directly examining these cognitive processes, we stand to gain a more complete understanding of the functional dynamics that underlie persuasion. Our first objective is therefore to identify what these processes might be.

Second, our research is aimed at gathering more direct evidence of the influence of functionally relevant persuasive communications on *overt behavior*. Previous research that tests the functional matching hypothesis has predominantly focused on attitudinal reactions to consumer products (e.g., DeBono & Telesca, 1990; Petty & Wegener, 1998; Shavitt, 1990; Snyder & DeBono, 1985) and has rarely sought behavioral evidence (although Shavitt, 1990, assessed hypothetical purchasing intentions, and Snyder & DeBono, 1985, assessed participants' hypothetical willingness to use a new product). Both the theoretical power and the practical utility of the functional approach to persuasion rest in part on its ability to influence overt behaviors toward socially meaningful issues and events.

Third, our interest in the influence of functional matching on behavior change has centered on a specific and socially consequential type of behavior, namely, the act of voting in presidential elections. As can be seen in Fig. 4.1, scarcely half of the eligible American electorate turn out to vote on election day; voter turnout is especially low among young voters.[1] In our studies, we investigate the motivational underpinnings of voting behavior within a functional framework. By studying the voting process from a functional perspective, we hope to evaluate strategies with which to bring people's behavior into line with their democratic values, attitudes, and beliefs. At the same time, we seek to shed light on the various types of psychological benefit that may accrue from voting and to gain insight into the processes through which voting-related persuasive messages mediate voting behavior.

In this chapter, we outline two cognitive processes through which the functional matching effect in persuasion might occur. We then discuss voter turnout in presidential elections within a functional framework. Finally, we present several studies that test our proposed mediational

---

[1]Voting turnout rates obtained by self-report are consistently higher than those obtained through more formal channels such as county records (Silver, Abramson, & Anderson, 1986). It is thus likely that these self-reports somewhat overestimate actual turnout rates.

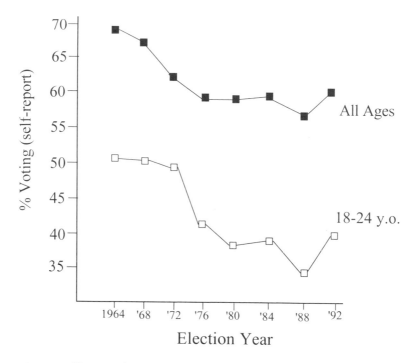

FIG. 4.1. Self-reported voting rates in presidential elections from 1964 to 1992 for all ages and for the youngest eligible voting group.

framework within the context of attitudes about and voting in presidential elections.

THE FUNCTIONAL MATCHING EFFECT
IN PERSUASION

The contemporary literature on the functional approach to persuasion has consistently shown that messages that make direct contact with the function served by an attitude produce more attitude change than do messages that address a function irrelevant or less relevant to that attitude (DeBono, 1987; DeBono & Harnish, 1988; Lavine et al., 1999; Lavine & Snyder, 1996; Prentice, 1987; Snyder & DeBono, 1985). Consistent with the view of early functional attitude theorists (e.g., Katz, 1960; Smith et al., 1956) that the psychological needs served by attitudes vary widely across individuals, these contemporary studies have tested the functional matching hypothesis using a dispositional strategy to identify attitude functions. The logic of this strategy is that psychological processes can be meaningfully understood by studying people who characteristically exhibit those processes (see Snyder & Ickes, 1985). For example, if we wish to examine whether attitudes are formed and expressed to facilitate value attainment (the value-expression function), we should attempt to identify and study those individuals who consistently seek to express their values. Similarly, if we wish to know whether attitudes can serve a social-adjustive function, we should attempt to identify and study people who consistently seek to monitor and regulate their behavior according to their social circumstances (Lavine & Snyder, 1996).

In a program of research exemplifying this investigative strategy, Snyder, DeBono and Lavine and their colleagues (e.g., DeBono, 1987; DeBono & Harnish, 1988; DeBono & Telesca, 1990; Lavine et al., 1999; Lavine & Snyder, 1996; Snyder & DeBono, 1985) have argued that individuals who differ in their self-monitoring propensities systematically differ in the functions that underlie their attitudes. Specifically, these authors reasoned that if the interpersonal behavior of high self-monitors is guided by the desire to appropriately fit into their social circumstances (Snyder, 1974, 1979, 1987), the attitudes and behaviors of high self-monitors may be especially likely to serve the social-adjustive function. In contrast, if the interpersonal behavior of low self-monitors is guided by the desire to express their dispositions, the attitudes and behavior of low self-monitors may be especially likely to serve the value-expressive function. In a series of studies, Snyder and DeBono (1985) found that functionally relevant consumer product ads (i.e., social-adjustive or "image-oriented" ads for high self-monitors and value-expressive or "product-quality" ads for low self-monitors) produced more favorable reactions and higher levels of behavioral intention to purchase the product than did functionally irrelevant ads. Providing somewhat more direct evidence that functionally relevant persuasive messages produce greater shifts in attitude than functionally irrelevant ones, DeBono (1987) found that low self-monitors adopted a more favorable attitude toward the issue of deinstitutionalization of the mentally ill after learning that this position was associated with their values (a value-expressive argument) than after learning that the position was favored by 70% of their peers (a social-adjustive argument). By contrast, high self-monitors adopted a more prode-institutionalization attitude after learning that a majority of their peers favored the position than after learning that the position was associated with their values (for another dispositional approach to testing the functional matching hypothesis, see Prentice, 1987).

Beyond dispositional strategies for assessing the functional matching hypothesis, both object-centered (e.g., Shavitt, 1990) and situational (e.g., Robertson, Lavine, & Borgida, 1993) approaches to identifying attitude functions have been employed. Shavitt (1990), for example, argued that attitude objects intrinsically vary in their functional affordances. That is, Shavitt reasoned that attitude objects such as air conditioners and coffee serve a utilitarian function because they are "*intrinsically* associated with rewards and punishments" (p. 129, our italics), whereas attitude objects such as wedding rings and the American flag serve a social identity function because they are "commonly considered as symbols of identity and values, or ...represent social classifications or reference groups" (p. 129). In two experiments, Shavitt (1990) found strong support for the functional matching hypothesis: functionally matched product appeals produced greater liking for the ads, more favorable attitudes toward the target products, and greater purchasing preferences than did functionally mismatched ads (i.e., a utilitarian attitude object paired with a social identity-based persuasive appeal).

In sum, across a variety of approaches for identifying attitude functions, it appears that persuasive messages that make direct contact with the motivational underpinnings of the attitude produce more persuasion than do messages that address an irrelevant or less relevant function. The question we wish to pursue now is that of *how* the functional matching effect occurs. That is, what cognitive processes are responsible for the differential persuasiveness of functionally relevant versus irrelevant message arguments?

WHAT PROCESSES MEDIATE THE FUNCTIONAL MATCHING EFFECT?

In our recent work (Lavine et al., 1999; Lavine & McBride, 1996; Lavine & Snyder, 1996; see also Petty & Wegener, 1998), we have explored the idea that the functional relevance of a persuasive message can influence both the *manner* in which the message arguments are evaluated and the *extent* to which those arguments are scrutinized. With respect to the former, we have examined the idea that functionally relevant messages are processed in a positively biased manner such that their arguments are perceived as more valid and convincing than those of functionally irrelevant messages. This might occur through the influence of an attitude's underlying function on the attitude's supporting cognitive structure (see Ennis & Zanna, this volume; Pratkanis & Greenwald, 1989). Specifically, the function(s) that an attitude serves should influence the contents of the attitude's resulting structure; for example, attitudes based on the value-expressive function should contain strong value-attitude linkages (see Thomsen, Lavine, & Kounios, 1996). In turn, the contents of attitude structures may bias the message recipient's judgment of the strength of the message, thereby mediating persuasion.

Moreover, consistent with the idea that self-relevant information is processed more deeply (e.g., Chaiken et al., 1989; Fiske & Taylor, 1991; Petty & Cacioppo, 1986; Rogers, Kuiper, & Kirker, 1977), we and others (e.g., DeBono & Harnish, 1988; Petty & Wegener, 1998) have proposed that messages that directly address the function served by an attitude engender greater processing motivation than messages that address an irrelevant function and thus produce more persuasion *so long as argument quality is high.*

In what follows, we sketch out the logic of how both biased processing and differences in processing motivation may mediate the functional matching effect in persuasion. We then turn to a consideration of the behavior of interest—voting in presidential elections. Specifically, we discuss how the act of voting may serve a variety of motivational functions. Finally, we present several experiments that test our mediational framework within the voting context.

Direction of Thinking: Perceived Message Quality.

It seems reasonable to assume that people devote more attention and thought to function-relevant information than to function-irrelevant information (DeBono & Packer, 1991; Lavine & McBride, 1996; Petty & Wegener, 1998). For example, a person with a value-expressive attitude should be especially interested in ascertaining an attitude object's value-related qualities, whereas a person with a social-adjustive attitude should be more interested in sizing up the object's normative qualities. Over time, this selective attention to and elaboration of function-relevant information should lead to the formation of organized cognitive structures based largely on the attitude's instrumentality in bringing about the desired type(s) of psychological benefit. As Ennis and Zanna (chap. 14 this volume) suggest, "...belief structures are formed largely on the bases of experience with stimulus objects, and, in particular, the ability of those objects to meet specific needs". Thus, the cognitive structures of value-expressive attitudes should contain well-organized, accessible information about an attitude object's instrumentality in facilitating or blocking cherished values, whereas the cognitive structures of social-adjustive attitudes should contain well-organized, accessible information about the relationship between the attitude and interpersonal rewards and punishments (Eagly & Chaiken, 1993, p. 151; Pratkanis & Greenwald, 1989). Attitude structures, then, may provide the necessary cognitive apparatus to appraise and respond to attitude-relevant information in a way that facilitates need attainment.

According to social cognition theory and research (e.g., Neisser, 1976; for reviews, see Fiske & Taylor, 1991; Lavine, Borgida, & Rudman, 1994; Markus & Zajonc, 1985), cognitive structures can exert an important influence on both *what* and *how* information is processed. Specifically, cognitive structures can bias the perception and evaluation of new information in a structure-consistent manner. As Markus and Zajonc noted in their review of the influence of cognitive structure on information processing, "An understanding of *how* perceivers process information in the social environment, how they categorize, evaluate, and assign causality, or what they remember or infer from a situation depends on an understanding of the cognitive structures that are responsible for selectivity in information processing" (Markus & Zajonc, 1985, p. 144, italics added).

Previous work on the cognitive underpinnings of attitudes suggests that such structures influence how new attitude-relevant information is evaluated. One line of research that examines the influence of attitude structures on attitude-based information processing stems from Lord, Ross, and Lepper's (1979) study on selective judgment, which presented participants who held extreme attitudes for or against capital punishment with two ostensible empirical reports on the efficacy of the policy as a deterrent to murder. One article provided evidence in support of the policy whereas the other article suggested that capital punishment increases murder. Lord et al. found an attitude-congruence effect on participants' judgments of the perceived quality of the empirical studies: Those with positive attitudes toward capital punishment found the study that supported the efficacy of the policy to be more convincing and better conducted than the study that opposed the efficacy of capital punishment, and the reverse was true for participants with negative attitudes toward capital punishment. More recent work has shown that this biased processing effect is stronger among individuals with well-developed attitude structures. For example, Houston and Fazio (1989) showed that this effect occurs only among those with highly accessible attitudes (i.e., those for whom the structural link between the object and the evaluation is strong), and Pomerantz, Margolies, and Chaiken (1993) found that the effect occurs to a greater extent among those whose attitudes are consistent with the evaluative implications of underlying beliefs (i.e., those whose attitudes are high in evaluative-cognitive consistency; for a review, see Chaiken, Pomerantz, & Giner-Sorolla, 1995).

Within the persuasion domain, message recipients' attitude structures, as well as other types of knowledge structures, have been found to exert biasing effects on their perceptions and evaluations of persuasive messages. Social-judgment theorists, for example, conceptualize attitudes as a tripartite structure of latitudes along the evaluative continuum (M. Sherif & Hovland, 1961; C. Sherif & M. Sherif, 1967). The latitude of acceptance (rejection) is the area of the evaluative continuum that represents acceptable (unacceptable) positions; the latitude of noncommitment represents positions that are neither acceptable nor unacceptable. According to the theory, latitude width (i.e., attitude structure) determines the manner in which persuasive messages are perceived. Messages falling within or near the latitude of acceptance are assimilated (i.e., perceived as closer to one's attitude than they really are); however, messages falling within or near the latitude of rejection are contrasted (i.e., perceived as further from one's attitude than they really are). In turn, these perceptual biases lead to biases in message evaluation; assimilated messages are judged as being valid and fair (thereby facilitating persuasion), whereas contrasted messages are judged as being invalid and propagandistic (thus inhibiting persuasion).

Similarly, self-schemas have been shown to influence the perceived quality of the message arguments. Cacioppo, Petty, and Sidera (1982), for example, found that message recipients with a religious (legalistic) self-schema judged religious (legalistic) message arguments to be more persuasive than schema-irrelevant message arguments. Cacioppo et al. proposed that recipients' self-schemas "...serve as a subjective theory that biases the assimilation of the message arguments; ...that messages consistent with self-schemas ...may guide a filling-in, or strengthening, of the arguments presented, therefore leading to the perception of the message being more persuasive" (p. 328).

These diverse lines of theory and research strongly suggest that the cognitive process of evaluating the contents of a persuasive message is an inherently subjective enterprise that may be biased by a variety of cognitive structures (e.g., the width of attitude latitudes, self-schemas, structural properties of attitude strength). We previously argued that the motivational (i.e., functional) origins of an attitude should influence the contents of its supporting cognitive structure (see also Pratkanis & Greenwald, 1989). If this is the case, it follows that these function-influenced cognitive structures are likely to bias message recipients' judgments of the quality of a persuasive message. Specifically, persuasive messages that contain functionally relevant information—and therefore make direct contact with the contents of the attitude's supporting cognitive structure—should be perceived as more valid and more persuasive than messages that contain functionally irrelevant information. For example, value-expressive attitudes should be associated with well-developed value-attitude structures; message arguments framed in terms of value attainment should thus be perceived as more persuasive and valid than message arguments that link the recommended attitude to the mediation of one's social relationships. In contrast, social-adjustive attitudes should contain well-developed structures that relate the attitude to normative behavior; therefore, message arguments that link the recommended attitude to the facilitation of one's social relationships should be perceived as more persuasive and valid than message arguments that link the recommended attitude to the facilitation of value-related goals. In essence, then, we propose that the functional match of a persuasive message should directly influence the recipient's perceptions of message validity and quality. In turn, these biased perceptions of message quality should determine the extent to which message recipients accept the recommendations of the message.

Amount of Thinking: Degree of Argument Scrutiny

In addition to producing biased processing, functionally matched messages may also be expected to heighten processing motivation. This should be the case because, by definition, matched messages impinge more strongly on the recipient's relevant needs and goals than do mismatched messages, and thus are more self-relevant than mismatched messages (DeBono, 1987; Study 1; DeBono & Packer, 1991; Petty & Wegener, 1998; Robertson, Lavine, & Borgida, 1993). For example, an attitude held because of its instrumentality in bringing about important values is likely to serve the value-expressive function as well as induce self-relevance (a factor known to heighten processing motivation, see, e.g., Petty & Cacioppo, 1986) based on the attitude's linkage to important values (see Eagly & Chaiken, 1993, for a discussion of the relation between attitude function and type of attitudinal involvement). Similarly, an attitude held because of its utility in mediating an individual's social relationships is likely to serve the social-adjustive function as well as lead to self-relevance based on the attitude's linkage to impression management goals. If functionally matched messages heighten argument scrutiny and if the arguments are strong, such messages should facilitate persuasion because the arguments will be processed more deeply than those contained in functionally mismatched messages. Thus, instead of or in addition to biasing message recipients' message-relevant processing, functionally matched messages may lead to greater interest in and thus scrutiny of the message arguments, and thus mediate persuasion through the central or systematic processing route (Chaiken et al., 1989; Petty & Cacioppo, 1986; Petty & Wegener, 1998).

In sum, the functional matching effect in persuasion is likely to be mediated by biased processing and/or enhanced processing motivation. Before we present evidence bearing directly on these mediational ideas, we present an analysis of voting behavior within a functional framework.

A FUNCTIONAL ANALYSIS OF VOTING BEHAVIOR

As we noted at the beginning of the chapter, voting rates in the United States are comparatively low (see Current Population Reports of the U. S. Census Bureau, 1993). Turnout rates hover around half of the eligible electorate and are considerably lower among young voters (see Fig. 4.1). In the face of seeming widespread support for democracy in principle, why is it that relatively few potential voters translate this core belief into action?

Explanations of the causes of nonvoting range from legal–institutional battles over voter registration requirements (e.g., the recently enacted "Motor Voter Law"; see also Campbell, Converse, Miller, & Stokes, 1960; Powell, 1986) to demographic factors such as low education or social status (Berelson, Lazarsfeld, & McPhee, 1954; Verba & Nie, 1972) to rationalistic decision-making explanations in which the perceived benefits of voting are outweighed by the perceived costs (e.g., Downs, 1957). Although social psychological explanations for the problem of nonvoting have been offered (e.g., Lazarsfeld, Berelson, & Gaudet, 1948), social psychologists have more often directed their efforts toward the prediction of vote choice (Fazio & Williams, 1986; Sears & Funk, 1991) and more recently to the cognitive processes associated with the appraisal of political candidates (Lavine, Sullivan, Borgida, & Thomsen, 1996; Lodge, McGraw, & Stroh, 1989; Ottati & Wyer, 1990; Rahn, Aldrich, Borgida, & Sullivan, 1990).

Although voting can undoubtedly be understood from legal, demographic, and cognitive perspectives, such explanations often provide little insight into the individual psychological dynamics of *why* people actually *choose* to vote rather than to stay home. We argue that voting behavior can be meaningfully understood within the larger motivational context of an individual's ongoing purposeful and goal-directed social behavior, that is, in terms of the psychological benefits that people can and do derive from such behavior.

So, what are the motivations that lead people to vote? One frequently cited response to this question is that people who vote do so to maximize their economic self-interests (Downs, 1957; for a review, see Sears & Funk, 1991). Although it is scarcely debatable that people sometimes vote for the candidate whose policies will benefit them the most, the self-interest motive alone is unlikely to be entirely satisfactory in accounting for voting because any one vote has virtually no impact on the outcome of an election. In fact, it could be argued that the truly selfish thing to do on voting day is to stay home. If voting conveys little utilitarian benefit, of what use is it? We suggest that among the motivations that underlie people's voting-related behaviors is the desire to express important attributes of one's identity and the desire to fit into one's social circumstances. Attitudes and behavior related to voting are well positioned to serve the value-expressive function because voting may provide an opportunity to express one's core values (e.g., voting may serve to symbolize one's devotion to the principle of living in a democracy). Value-expressive attitudes toward voting may also result from voters' perceptions that voting enables them to express their attitudes toward the candidates and toward salient campaign issues. Alternatively, attitudes toward voting may be based on social-adjustive considerations. Attitudes that serve a social-adjustive function fulfill a person's need to fit into and reap rewards from his or her social situation. Because in democratic societies voting is generally perceived to be highly desirable, such behavior may also serve to provide opportunities for the individual to manage his or her public image in an effort to win social approbation. Attitudes and behavior related to voting would thus serve a social-adjustive function if they were motivated by self-presentational goals.

In the following sections, we directly examine this functional framework for heightening voting behavior. We also examine the cognitive processes (i.e., biased message processing and increased processing motivation) through which functionally matched messages may increase provoting attitudes and heighten voting-related behavior.

TESTING THE BIASED PROCESSING EXPLANATION OF THE FUNCTIONAL MATCHING EFFECT

Experiment 1

In our first study (Lavine & Snyder, 1996, Experiment 1), high and low self-monitoring participants were exposed to either a value-expressive or a social-adjustive message in favor of voting in upcoming local elections in Minneapolis. A final group of participants was exposed to a mixed message that contained both value-expressive and social-adjustive arguments in favor of voting.[2] To evaluate our hypothesis that functionally matched messages (e.g., the value-expressive message for low self-monitors) are seen as containing stronger and more persuasive arguments than mismatched messages, we assessed two indicators of perceived message quality. First, immediately following message exposure, participants completed a thought-listing task (e.g., Mackie & Worth, 1989; Petty & Cacioppo, 1979) in which they listed any ideas, feelings, thoughts, or images that occurred to them as they read the persuasive messages. An index of the favorability of these thoughts was constructed by subtracting topic- and message-relevant negative elaborations from topic- and message-relevant positive elaborations. Second, participants completed a 12-item index of structured perceptions of message quality (e.g., "I found the material to be convincing," "the material did not contain persuasive arguments," and "the arguments in the material make good sense to me"). In addition to these measures and a 16-item measure of attitudes toward

---

[2]In this chapter, we do not provide an in-depth analysis of the relative utility of functionally mixed messages. For a treatment of this issue, see Lavine and Snyder (1996).

voting, participants were invited to complete an address card to receive a voter information guide in the mail pertaining to upcoming elections in the St. Paul/Minneapolis area.

We tested three primary hypotheses. First, we assessed the idea that functionally matched messages would be perceived as containing stronger and more persuasive arguments than functionally mismatched messages, and that participants would therefore also exhibit more favorable cognitive responses to matched than mismatched messages. Second, we determined whether functionally matched messages would produce more favorable attitudes toward voting and whether such messages would result in a greater number of requests for the voter information guide (i.e., whether functional matching produces more proattitudinal overt behavior). Third, to evaluate the role of perceived message quality, we assessed whether any influence of functional matching on voting-related attitudes and behavior was mediated by differences in perceived message quality.

As can be seen in Table 4.1, our first two hypotheses were supported. Rows 1 and 2 of Table 4.1 show that functionally matched messages led to significantly higher levels of perceived message quality (Message type $\times$ Self-monitoring $F[2, 176] = 7.86, p = <.001$) and more favorable cognitive responses (Message type $\times$ Self-monitoring $F[2, 174] = 7.22$,

TABLE 4.1

Effects of Message Type and Self-Monitoring on Cognitive Responses and Structured Perceptions of Message Quality, Attitudes toward Voting, and Voting-Related Behavior

Dependent Variable	Low Self-Monitoring			High Self-Monitoring		
	VE	SA	Mixed	VE	SA	Mixed
Valenced index of Cognitive responses	1.32[a]	−0.48[b]	1.00[a]	−0.32[x]	1.00[y]	0.38[x,y]
Perceptions of message quality	1.12[a]	0.14[b]	0.86[a]	0.66[x]	1.15[y]	0.70[x,y]
Attitudes toward voting	5.57[a]	5.59[a]	5.70[a]	5.53[x]	5.91[y]	5.36[x]
Voting behavior	0.68[a]	0.35[b]	0.52[a,b]	0.26[x]	0.50[y]	0.54[y]

Note. VE = value-expressive message; SA = social-adjustive message. Voting behavior entries represent the proportion of participants who requested the voter's guide within each condition. Entries with different superscripts within in each row within each self-monitoring condition are significantly different at $p < .05$ according to Duncan's multiple range test (for comparisons involving the mixed message) or planned contrasts (for comparisons not involving the mixed message).

$p = <.001$) than functionally mismatched messages. Specifically, low self-monitors perceived the value-expressive message to contain more cogent and convincing arguments than the social-adjustive message, and high self-monitors perceived the social-adjustive message to contain more cogent and convincing arguments than the value-expressive message ($p < .05$). These results suggest that when a persuasive message makes direct contact with the attitude's underlying function, it is perceived as containing stronger and more persuasive arguments than when the message is addressed to a less relevant or irrelevant function.

The effects of functional matching on attitudes and behavior were similar. As can be seen in row 3 of Table 4.1, functionally matched messages produced more favorable attitudes toward voting among high ($p < .05$) but not low self-monitors (Message type × Self-monitoring $F[2, 176] = 2.59, p < .08$). Finally, as seen in row 4 of Table 4.1, functionally matched messages led to higher levels of voting-related behavior (i.e., requests for the voter guide) than mismatched messages among both low and high self-monitors (Message type × Self-monitoring $F[2, 176] = 5.18$, $p < 01$). That is, low self-monitors exhibited more behavioral interest in the voter guide when informed that voting can help in translating one's values and attitudes into action than when informed that voting is the popular thing to do and creates a positive social image; in contrast, high self-monitors exhibited more behavioral interest in the voter guide when informed that voting is image enhancing than when informed that voting provides a context for expressing one's cherished values and other dispositions.

Finally, to evaluate whether the influence of functional matching on voting-related attitudes and behavior was mediated by perceived message quality, we used LISREL 8 (Jöreskog & Sörbom, 1993) to estimate the maximum likelihood parameters of the observed variable path model shown in Fig. 4.2 (participants in the mixed message condition were excluded from this analysis). As can be seen in the figure, all of the paths are significant: The functional match of the message exerted a direct effect on perceived message quality, which in turn influenced postmessage attitudes toward voting. Finally, recipients' postmessage attitudes exerted a direct effect on their behavioral decisions of whether to request the voter information guide. To examine more formally our hypothesis that perceived message quality mediates the influence of functional matching on postmessage attitudes and behavior, we examined the indirect paths from functional match through perceived message quality to attitudes and voting-related behavior (see J. Cohen & P. Cohen, 1983). These coeffi-

Functional Relevance of the Message — .40*** → Perceptions of Message Quality — .31*** → Attitudes toward Voting — .21* → Voting-Related Behavior

Note: *p<.05; **p<.01; ***p<.001.

FIG. 4.2. The influence of functional matching on perceptions of message quality and voting-related attitudes and behavior.

cients determine whether functional matching had its influence on post-message attitudes and behavior by initially influencing perceived message quality. Each of these indirect (mediated) paths proved significant (β = .12 and .03, $p < .05$, from functional match through perceived message quality to attitudes and to behavior, respectively), which confirms that recipients' perceptions of the validity and cogency of the arguments contained in the message mediated the influence of the functional match of the message on voting-related attitudes and behavior.

Experiment 2

In our next study (Lavine & Snyder, 1996, Experiment 2), we attempted to replicate Experiment 1 and to extend it in several ways. First, we wanted to enquire into whether our functional framework could be extended to real voting behavior—behavior that occurs not in the lab, but in the field. In addition, we wanted to determine whether the mediation of functional matching by perceived message quality would be generalizable to a setting in which the time period between message exposure and message-related behavior was more substantial (5 days instead of 45 minutes).

To accomplish these goals, we examined whether functionally matched voting appeals (value-expressive messages for low self-monitors and social-adjustive messages for high self-monitors) enhanced message recipients' perceptions of the quality of the message arguments, and whether, in turn, differences in perceived message quality predicted postmessage attitudes toward voting in the 1992 presidential election. As in Experiment 1, we assessed structured perceptions of message quality (but not cognitive responses). We also assessed attitudes toward voting in the presidential election and obtained voting information from the Hennepin County Board of Elections regarding whether each participant voted in the election.[3] Because we exposed participants to the message 5 days before the election, we also considered the role of behavioral intention. Consistent with Fishbein and Ajzen's (1975) theory of reasoned action, we hypothesized that attitudes toward voting in the election

---

[3]For postmessage attitudes (assessed 5 days before the election) to influence subsequent voting behavior, participants should not be restricted from voting due to not being registered to vote. In the state of Minnesota, where we conducted these experiments, citizens need not be registered before election day to vote in the election.

would indirectly influence whether participants actually voted by directly shaping their voting intentions. Within the theory of reasoned action, behavioral intentions represent people's conscious and deliberate plans for engaging in volitional behavior, and are hypothesized to be influenced (in part) by attitudes toward the behavior in question.

As Table 4.2 shows, the results of Experiment 2 replicated those of Experiment 1: Participants who received functionally matched messages found the arguments to be more convincing and persuasive than did participants who received mismatched messages (Message type × Self-monitoring $F[1,62] = 9.85$, $p < .01$). Moreover, functionally matched messages produced more favorable postmessage attitudes toward voting in the upcoming election (Message type × Self-monitoring $F[1, 62] = 4.40$, $p < .05$). Because voting behavior and voting intentions were predicted to be directly regulated by voting intention and postmessage attitudes, respectively, we neither predicted nor found that the functional match of the message exerted a *direct* effect on either voting intention or voting behavior (Message type × self-monitoring $F < 1$).

To determine whether perceived message quality mediated the influence of functional match on postmessage attitudes toward voting in the election and whether voting intentions mediated the relationship between postmessage attitudes and voting behavior, we estimated the observed variable path model in Fig. 4.3. As the figure shows, all of the paths in the model are significant, and the model accounted for 28% of the variance in voting behavior. More important, the indirect path from functional match through perceived message quality to postmessage attitudes was significant ($\beta = .08$, $p < .06$), as was the indirect path from postmessage attitudes through voting intentions to voting behavior ($\beta = .18$, $p < .05$).

TABLE 4.2

Effects of Message Type and Self-Monitoring on Perceptions of Message Quality and Attitudes toward Voting in the 1992 Presidential Election

	Low Self-Monitoring		High Self-Monitoring	
Dependent Variable	*VE*	*SA*	*VE*	*SA*
Perceptions of Message Quality	0.71[a]	0.16[b]	0.96[x]	0.33[y]
Attitudes toward voting in the Election	6.02[a]	5.71[b]	5.62[x]	6.01[y]

Note. VE = value-expressive message; SA = social-adjustive message. Entries with different superscripts within in each row within each self-monitoring condition are significantly different at p .05, except the comparison among low self-monitors for attitudes, in which p .10.

Functional ── .35** ──▶ Perceptions of ── .22* ──▶ Attitudes toward Voting ── .34** ──▶ Voting ── .53*** ──▶ Voting
Match Message Quality in the 1992 Election Intentions Behavior

Note: *p<.05; **p<.01;***p<.001.

FIG. 4.3. The influence of functional matching on perceptions of message quality and attitudes toward and behavior related to voting in the 1992 presidential election.

Taken together, these studies suggest that the functional matching effect in persuasion is mediated (at least partly) by the perception that functionally matched messages contain more valid and convincing argumentation than do functionally mismatched messages. However, this conclusion is based on contemporary personality-based work that has focused exclusively on a single personality construct (i.e., self-monitoring) and on only two attitude functions (i.e., value expressive and social adjustive; e.g., DeBono, 1987; DeBono & Harnish, 1988; Lavine & Snyder, 1996; Petty & Wegener, 1998; Snyder & DeBono, 1985; 1989). Given the theoretical generality of the functional attitude theory, one expects that functionally matched messages could be crafted to address a wide variety of personality dispositions.

Our next experiment was designed to broaden the scope of the functional matching effect within the voting context by using a different personality construct (i.e., authoritarianism) and engaging different types of attitude functions (i.e., ego defensive). In Experiment 3, we sought to examine not only whether a dispositional approach to the functional matching effect could be generalized beyond self-monitoring, but also whether our mediational framework explained the influence of functional matching on postmessage voting-related attitudes and behavior in the context of attitude functions other than value expression and social adjustment.

Experiment 3

Increasingly, our social and political environment is permeated with threatening message of all types—threats to our personal safety, to our loved ones, to our pocketbooks, to our psychological well-being, to our health, to our social relationships, to our political values, and so on. With respect to voting, the Rock the Vote organization relied heavily on nonpartisan, threat-laden ads to motivate young people to vote in the 1992 and 1996 presidential elections. Some of these ads emphasized the idea that unnamed others such as uncaring cynical politicians or vaguely described people with values diametrically opposed to those held by the viewer would seize power and use it against the interests of young people (see Lavine et al., 1999, p. 4). These messages appeared to be quite effective in gaining and holding viewers' attention.

Social scientists have examined the impact of threat perceptions and fear reactions on a range of political attitudes and behavior, including extreme forms of political aggression and intolerance toward racial (e.g.,

Feldman & Stenner, 1997; Kinder & Sanders, 1996; Mendelberg, 1997) and political outgroups (e.g., Marcus, Sullivan, Theiss-Morse, & Wood, 1995; Stouffer, 1955). These perceptions of and reactions to threat can be conceptually understood as manifestations of authoritarianism (Adorno, Frenkel-Brunswik, Levinson, & Sanford, 1950; Altemeyer, 1988, 1996). Individuals who are chronically fearful and who perceive a great deal of threat in their immediate and broader social environments have a greater propensity to develop authoritarian attitudes and behaviors. Moreover, individuals who exhibit a high degree of authoritarianism are likely to hold their attitudes for ego-defensive (i.e., threat reduction) reasons and are thus likely to be responsive to threatening stimuli (as well as to stimuli that suggest ways in which threats may be averted).

Given the robust link between threat and authoritarianism, and especially the notion that authoritarians are highly receptive to threatening stimuli, in Experiment 3 we examined whether individuals who exhibited a high degree of authoritarianism were especially receptive to a voting-related persuasive message framed in terms of threat. Specifically, 5 days before the 1996 presidential election, we (Lavine et al., in 1999) presented high and low authoritarian recipients (based on a median split on a 10-item version of Altemeyer's, 1998, Right-Wing Authoritarianism Scale) with a persuasive message that advocated that they vote in the upcoming election. Some participants received a message framed in terms of the rewards that may accrue for engaging in such behavior. Other participants received a message framed in terms of the threatening personal and political consequences that may occur for failing to engage in such behavior. The remainder of Experiment 3 was similar to Experiment 2 (i.e., we assessed perceptions of message quality and attitudes toward voting in the 1996 presidential election, and subsequently confirmed with the Hennepin County Board of Elections whether participants actually voted in the election).

Our key prediction was that message type (reward vs. threat) would interact with recipients' authoritarianism propensities such that high authoritarian recipients would perceive the threat message as more valid and persuasive than the reward message (see also Janis, 1967). Because high authoritarians perceive the world as a dangerous and threatening place, they should resonate to a message that highlights the potential negative consequences of not voting. Specifically, high authoritarians should be more likely than their low authoritarian counterparts to find threat-related persuasive arguments to be credible and valid.

Results of Experiment 3 are presented in Table 4.3. As seen in the table, perceptions of the quality of the message depended on recipients' authoritarianism propensities (Message type × Authoritarianism $F[1, 81] = 8.63$ $p < .01$). As predicted, high authoritarians perceived the message that emphasized threat as containing stronger and more convincing arguments than the message that emphasized reward ($p < .01$). Interestingly, a marginally significant opposite pattern occurred for low authoritarians: They perceived the reward message to contain stronger and more convincing arguments than the threat message ($p < .10$, two-tailed). As can be seen in row 2 of Table 4.3, high authoritarians held more positive attitudes toward voting in the 1996 presidential election when exposed to the matched threat- based message than when exposed to the mismatched reward-based message. However, this effect did not reach significance.

To examine whether matched messages influenced attitudes *indirectly* (i.e., through perceptions of message quality), we used LISREL 8 (Joreskog & Sorbom, 1993) to estimate the maximum likelihood parameters of a structural equation model. As seen in Fig. 4.4, all of the paths in the model are significant. Moreover, the model provided a very good fit to the data, chi-square ($df = 34$) $= 35.62$, $p = .39$. Message match directly influenced perceived message quality, which in turn influenced postmessage attitudes toward voting in the election. Also, postmessage attitudes exerted a direct effect on voting intentions, which in turn exerted a direct influence on whether participants voted in the 1996 presidential election. More important, the indirect paths from message match through perceptions of message quality to post-message attitudes ($\beta = .08$, $p < .05$) and from post-message attitudes through voting intentions to voting behavior ($\beta = .18$, $p < .05$) were significant. This indicates that recipients' perceptions of message quality significantly mediated the influence of

TABLE 4.3

Effects of Message Type and Authoritarianism Perceptions of Message Quality and Attitudes toward Voting in the 1996 Presidential Election

	Low Authoritarianism		High Authoritarianism	
Dependent Variable	Threat	Reward	Threat	Reward
Perceptions of message quality	0.10^a	0.63^b	0.69^x	$-.04^y$
Attitudes toward voting in the election	5.57^a	5.60^a	5.60^x	5.38^x

Note. Entries with different subscripts within in each row within each authoritarianism condition are significantly different at p .05.

Functional Match $\xrightarrow{.29^*}$ Perceptions of Message Quality $\xrightarrow{.29^*}$ Attitudes toward Voting in the 1996 Election $\xrightarrow{.69^{**}}$ Voting Intentions $\xrightarrow{.26^*}$ Voting Behavior

Note: *$p<.05$; **$p<.01$.

FIG. 4.4. The influence of functional matching on perceptions of message quality and attitudes toward and behavior related to voting in the 1996 presidential election.

119

message match on post-message attitudes and that voting intentions mediated the influence of postmessage attitudes toward voting on actual voting behavior.

As a group, Experiments 1–3 (Lavine et al., 1999; Lavine & Snyder, 1996) indicate that persuasive messages that are specifically tailored to the personality disposition of the recipient (and are therefore presumably of some functional relevance) are perceived to contain stronger and more convincing argumentation than functionally irrelevant messages. In other words, when the message provides the recipient with an explicit strategy for obtaining the psychological end states for which the attitude stands, the recipient tends to view those message arguments in a favorable light. Moreover, on the basis of the path models, perceptions of message quality seem to constitute one cognitive mechanism through which functionally matched messages influence persuasion. These studies thus provide one explanation to the question of *why* the functional matching effect occurs.

TESTING THE PROCESSING MOTIVATION EXPLANATION OF THE FUNCTIONAL MATCHING EFFECT

As we suggested at the beginning of the chapter, in addition to heightening perceptions of message quality, functionally matched messages might also produce more persuasion than functionally mismatched messages because the former induce recipients to scrutinize and process the arguments more deeply. Because functionally matched messages directly impinge on the individual's attitude-related goals, such messages should be perceived as self-relevant. Indeed, DeBono and Packer (1991) found that functionally matched messages were judged to be more relevant to the self than were mismatched messages (see also Thomsen, Borgida, & Lavine, 1995). Consistent with dual-process theories of persuasion (Chaiken et al., 1989; Petty & Cacioppo, 1986), self-relevant persuasive messages should heighten the recipient's motivation to give careful thought to the arguments in the message. So long as these arguments are strong (and thus persuasive), functionally matched messages should produce more persuasion. In what follows, we present evidence from our lab that functionally matched messages induce greater interest and are processed more deeply.

Experiment 4

To test the hypothesis that functionally matched messages are viewed with greater interest than mismatched messages, we (Lavine & McBride, 1996) conducted a selective exposure study. Specifically, to determine whether message recipients prefer to expose themselves to and gain information about function relevant rather than function irrelevant information, we provided low and high self-monitoring undergraduates with the opportunity to learn more about the issue of senior comprehensive exams. We expected that participants would be more interested in reading function-relevant than function-irrelevant information about the issue, especially if the issue were framed in a highly involving or self-relevant manner. To manipulate involvement, undergraduates were informed that either their university (*high involvement condition*) or a distant university (*low involvement condition*) was considering implementing senior comprehensive exams in the following year (Petty & Cacioppo, 1979). Participants were then given the opportunity to read one of four articles concerning the policy. The titles did not advocate one side of the issue or the other. However, two of the articles implied a social-adjustive function (e.g., development of an attitude on the issue would enhance the participant's social image), whereas the other two titles implied a value-expressive function (e.g., development of an attitude on the issue would allow the participant to express his or her educational values). The design was thus a 2 (Involvement) × 2 (Self-monitoring) × 2 (Information type: value expressive vs. social adjustive) with repeated measures on the last factor. Participants selected the article that they most wanted to read and then ranked their preferences for the four articles.

The prediction that participants prefer function-relevant to function-irrelevant information to a greater extent when involvement is high than when it is low implies a three-way interaction between involvement, self-monitoring, and information type. This prediction was confirmed. The three-way interaction (Involvement × Self-monitoring × Information type) on participants' ranked preferences was marginally significant, $F(1, 135) = 2.91, p = < .09$. When involvement was high, low self-monitors (*M* rank = 4.46[4]) preferred to read the value-expressive titles more than did high self-monitors (*M* rank = 5.10), and high self-monitors (*M* rank = 4.94) preferred to read the social-adjustive titles more than did low self-monitors (*M* rank = 5.53; $p < .05$). These effects did not occur when involvement was low (*M* ranks ranged 4.91 to 5.10). Moreover, χ^2 tests of association revealed that when involvement was high, low self-monitors were more likely to select the value-expressive title than the

---

[4]Means represent summed ranks for the two value-expressive and two social-adjustive articles. Means could thus range from 3 to 7, with lower numbers indicating greater exposure preference.

social-adjustive title, whereas high self-monitors were more likely to select the social-adjustive title than the value-expressive title chi-square (1) = 5.43, p < .05. However, this effect did not approach significance when involvement was low, chi-square (1) = .001, *ns*. These results provide evidence that people are particularly interested in attending to and gaining information about function-relevant information, especially when that information is perceived to be highly relevant to the self.

Experiment 1 Revisited

Recall that participants in Experiment 1 performed a thought-listing task in which they listed any ideas they had while reading the message. We previously reported that the valence of recipients' message- and topic-relevant elaborations varied according to functional match, in support of the notion that functional matching biased their processing of the message. In addition, it is possible to construct an index of the amount of thought in which recipients engaged by summing the total number of message- and topic-relevant elaborations they generated. To more directly test the hypothesis that functionally matched messages heighten processing motivation, we examined the sum rather than the valence of recipients' cognitive responses to the message in Experiment 1. A 3 (Message type) × 2 (Self-monitoring) ANOVA performed on the sum (positive + negative + neutral) of message recipients' topic- and message-relevant cognitive responses produced the expected interaction $F(2, 176) = 7.00$, $p = .001$. High self-monitors listed more relevant thoughts when exposed to the functionally matched social-adjustive message ($M = 2.50$) than when exposed to the mismatched value-expressive message ($M = .76$), $t(56) = 4.46, p$ < .001. Although there was a trend such that low self-monitors listed more thoughts when exposed to the matched value-expressive message ($M = 1.52$) than the mismatched social-adjustive message ($M = 1.19$), this effect did not approach significance ($t < 1$). Nonetheless, low self-monitors did list significantly more thoughts when exposed to the value-expressive message than did high self-monitors (p < .05), and high self-monitors listed significantly more thoughts when exposed to the social-adjustive message than did low self-monitors (p < .01).

We can also assess whether message recipients *selectively* elaborated on functionally relevant (versus nonrelevant) arguments by examining the cognitive responses of those participants in the mixed message condition (i.e., those who were exposed to a message that contains both value-expressive and social-adjustive message arguments). To examine this issue, we separately computed the number of thoughts generated to the social-adjustive and value-expressive message arguments and subjected them to a 2 (Self-monitoring) × 2 (Cognitive response type: value expressive vs. social adjustive) mixed message ANOVA with repeated measures on the second factor. This analysis produced a significant interaction, $F(1, 66) = 5.73, p < .01$. Consistent with the selective elaboration hypothesis, high self-monitors in the mixed message condition listed more functionally relevant (social-adjustive; $M = 0.97$) than functionally irrelevant (value-expressive, $M = 0.15$) thoughts ($p < .001$). In contrast, low self-monitors did not show a comparable selective elaboration tendency ($M = 0.66$ and 0.55 for thoughts in response to social-adjustive and value-expressive arguments, respectively ($|t| < 1$). However, consistent with the selective elaboration hypothesis, low self-monitors listed more thoughts in response to value-expressive arguments than did high self-monitors (p .05, one-tailed), and high self-monitors listed marginally more thoughts in response to social-adjustive arguments than did low self-monitors ($p < .08$, one-tailed).

These effects were paralleled by those for memory of the message arguments (assessed approximately 45 minutes after reading of the message) such that high but not low self-monitors recalled functionally relevant message arguments better than functionally irrelevant ones. Taken together, these analyses provide some support for the contention that people are willing to carefully think about message arguments when the latter are directly addressed to the presumed function that underlies the attitude.

Finally, strong evidence for the view that functionally matched messages enhance processing motivation comes from a recent set of studies by Petty and Wegener (1998). They argued that if functionally matched messages increase argument scrutiny, the influence on persuasion of functional matching versus mismatching arguments should depend on argument quality. Consistent with the Elaboration Likelihood Model of persuasion (Petty & Cacioppo, 1986), Petty and Wegener reasoned that functionally matched messages should facilitate persuasion when argument quality is strong, but should reduce persuasion (compared to functionally irrelevant messages) when argument quality is weak. This should be the case because recipients for whom the message is functionally relevant are more likely to recognize whether the arguments are cogent or specious and change their attitudes accordingly.

Petty and Wegener (1998, Experiment 2) confirmed this hypothesis among message recipients whose baseline level of processing was not already high (i.e., those low in need for cognition, see Cacioppo & Petty, 1982). Specifically, among message recipients low but not high in need for cognition, low (high) self-monitors formed more positive attitudes toward consumer products (e.g., shampoo, toothpaste) when exposed to *strong* value-expressive (social-adjustive) message arguments than when exposed to strong social-adjustive (value-expressive) message arguments. However, when the message arguments were designed to be specious, the reverse occurred: In this case, functionally mismatched message arguments led to more persuasion than did functionally matched arguments.

This latter result is a novel one in the functional matching literature and strongly suggests that when baseline motivation to process is low, enhanced argument scrutiny—produced by exposure to a functionally matched message—is an important mediator of the functional matching effect. This may not be the case, however, when baseline levels of motivation to process are high. In this case, functional matching may not exert an additional effect in enhancing argument scrutiny. Instead, when baseline motivation to process is high, biased processing of the message arguments may be the prime mediator of the functional matching effect.

CONCLUSIONS

Understanding the Functional Matching Effect

The contemporary literature on the functional approach to persuasion indicates that persuasive messages that are matched or targeted to a relevant disposition of the recipient (and are presumably therefore of some functional relevance) produce more recommended attitude change than do messages that are addressed to an irrelevant or less relevant function. Until recently, however, the cognitive processes that underlie the functional matching effect have not been well understood. In our recent work (Lavine et al., 1999; Lavine & McBride, 1996; Lavine & Snyder, 1996), we have attempted to craft a psychological account of the functional matching phenomenon.

As we noted earlier, the functional match of a persuasive message should influence both the manner in which and the degree to which the message is processed. Specifically, we believe that functionally matched messages are processed in a positively biased manner (compared to mismatched messages) and that such messages enhance motivation to scrutinize the message arguments (see also DeBono & Harnish, 1988; DeBono & Packer, 1991; Petty & Wegener, 1998). These variables are likely to mediate the functional matching effect in different circumstances. Consistent with Petty and his colleagues' (Fleming & Petty, in press; Petty & Wegener, 1998) recent analysis, the operative mediating process is likely to depend on the recipient's baseline level of processing motivation. If message or recipient characteristics (e.g., self-relevance, need for cognition) render processing motivation high, it is *how* and not *how much* the arguments are processed that causes the functional matching effect. When baseline motivation to process is high, the arguments should be perceived as convincing and strong to the extent that the message promises to provide the recipient with a strategy (i.e., attitude change) for attaining a recipient-relevant goal (e.g., social rewards for high self-monitors; threat reduction for high authoritarians). Across three experiments that used two different personality traits and two different types of messages, our results were consistent with this biased processing explanation. Moreover, these effects seem to occur above and beyond any matching-based effects on processing motivation (see Lavine & Snyder, 1996, p. 600).

However, as Petty and his colleagues (Fleming & Petty, in press; Petty & Wegener, 1998) noted, when the persuasion situation does not constrain processing to be particularly high or low, the functional matching effect on persuasion may occur through heightening the degree of argument scrutiny (without necessarily biasing processing), which can increase or decrease persuasion depending on the quality of the message arguments (Petty & Wegener, 1998). On the basis of the current studies (see also Petty & Wegener, 1998), it appears that functional matching can influence persuasion through multiple routes, either by biasing the manner in which the information is perceived or by increasing the extent to which the information is processed.

Functional Matching and Political Participation

A second goal of our research has been to apply the functional matching approach to the political domain with the aim of increasing basic forms of political participation. To date, we have focused on heightening voting behavior in local and national elections. The reasons for our selection of voting behavior as an exemplar of political participation are twofold. First, as Fig. 4.1 indicates, turnout rates are low in presidential elections, and even lower in congressional elections. Second, the right to participate in free and open elections of government leaders is perhaps the single most important cornerstone of a democratic society. With each presidential election, civic organizations spend increasing amounts of money to try to induce people to vote (and candidates spend more and more on advertising), while fewer and fewer people turn out to vote. This state of affairs suggests a surprising lack of understanding of why people do and do not vote in such elections. In their book *Why Americans Don't Vote*, political theorists Piven and Cloward (1988) argue that the scholarly consensus of why so many people do not vote is that they lack attitudes on the issues or toward the candidates or are insufficiently educated on the virtues of voting.

On the basis of our research, we argue that the problem of nonvoting is at least partly due to motivational causes. Therefore, interventions that seek to increase voting behavior may benefit from a consideration of the psychological benefit that individuals are likely to derive from such behavior. In our experiments, we first identified individuals who are chronically responsive to outlets for their value-expressive, social-adjustive, and ego-defensive needs. Consistent with the functional matching hypothesis, we found that these individuals were favorably disposed toward voting appeals that informed or reminded them of the ways in which voting behavior can be instrumental to these chronic needs. In Experiment 1, this led to higher rates of behavior related to obtaining a voter information guide. In Experiments 2 and 3, voting in presidential elections was indirectly increased by exposure to functionally matched voting appeals.

Finally, how might an understanding of the motivational underpinnings of voting be used to increase other forms of civic participation? Although it is not yet possible to offer a definitive answer to this question, we can think of two such strategies. The first strategy involves constructing persuasive messages that emphasize the value-expressive, social-adjustive, or ego-defensive benefits of voting, as we did in our study. These messages could then be simultaneously placed in the media marketplace in the hope that each message would be consumed by its own intended audience. To the extent that people selectively expose themselves to motivationally congenial information (as we observed in Experiments 1 and 4), we expect high self-monitors to selectively attend to, process, and encode messages pertaining to the social-adjustive benefits associated with the message topic, and low self- monitors to selectively attend to, process, and encode messages pertaining to the value-expressive benefits of the message topic. To the extent, however, that such selective effects are weak, this approach might have the unintended consequence of actually reducing the likelihood of voting for some individuals. Such an outcome might occur, for example, if low self-monitors find social-adjustive voting appeals to be noxious and not merely motivationally irrelevant.

There may be, however, an alternative strategy for delivering motivationally relevant messages to their intended audiences. Specifically, this projective strategy would entail the construction of persuasive messages that could be interpreted as containing either value-expressive or social-adjustive information. Thus, for example, low self-monitors would find such messages to contain information about the ways in which voting can serve to express important values and attitudes, whereas high self-monitors would construe the same message as providing information about the ways in which voting conveys a positive image. Such messages would thus function as projective tests onto which people could project their own (self-expressive or social-adjustive) needs. Although it remains for future research to determine whether high and low self-monitors would assimilate identical voting-related messages to their own motivational orientations, there is some evidence that high and low self-monitors do interpret the same information in motivationally congenial ways (e.g., DeBono & Snyder, 1989).

Functional Explanations
for Negative Attitudes toward Voting

In our work to date, we have examined the functions underlying *positive* attitudes toward voting. However, because approximately half of the eligible electorate fails to vote in presidential elections, it seems important as well to understand why so many Americans hold relatively *negative* attitudes toward voting. We believe that functional approaches may hold answers to this question. Perhaps most obviously, negative attitudes toward voting may stem from utilitarian concerns related to the belief that "my vote won't do anything, so why bother?" Thus, low levels of political efficacy may underlie negative attitudes toward voting. More interestingly, negative attitudes toward voting may stem from value-expressive considerations related to rejection of the government, the candidates, or the political system. For example, those who decry the increasingly central role that money plays in the election process may choose not to participate in a system that they view as fundamentally undemocratic. Negative attitudes toward voting may also be based on social-adjustive concerns within subcultures where participation in the political process is regarded as undesirable (e.g., militias). By identifying the motivational origins that underlie negative attitudes toward voting, researchers may be in a better position to design strategies intended to increase political participation.

In conclusion, our research suggests that to better understand people's decisions to vote or not to vote, and to intervene to increase voting behavior, we need to move beyond an analysis of legal, demographic, and cognitive variables. Rather, or in addition, we argue for the importance of examining and appealing to the larger motivational contexts within which people live their lives. By connecting socially desirable behavior (such as voting) with relevant psychological goals and motivational functions at the individual level, we can both gain a better understanding of the underlying causes of such behavior and develop techniques (such as the functionally matched persuasion appeals employed in our work) to actually increase such behavior.

REFERENCES

Adorno, T. W., Frenkel-Brunswik, E., Levinson, D. J., & Sanford, R. N. (1950). *The authoritarian personality*. New York: Harper.

Altemeyer, B. (1988). *Enemies of freedom*. San Francisco: Jossey–Bass.

Altemeyer, B. (1996). *The authoritarian specter*. Cambridge; MA: Harvard University Press.

Berelson, B., Lazarsfeld, P. F., & McPhee, W. (1954). *Voting*. Chicago: University of Chicago Press.

Campbell, A., Converse, P. E., Miller, W., & Stokes, D. (1960). *The American voter*. New York: Wiley.

Caccoppo, J. T. & Petty, R. E. (1982). The need for cognition. Journal of Personality and Social Psychology, *42*, 116–131.

Cacioppo, J. T., Petty, R. E., & Sidera, J. (1982). The effects of a salient self-schema on the evaluation of proattitudinal editorials: Top-down versus bottom-up message processing. *Journal of Experimental Social Psychology, 18*, 324–338.

Chaiken, S., Liberman, A., & Eagly, A. H. (1989). Heuristic and systematic processing within and beyond the persuasion context. In J. S. Uleman & J. A. Bargh (Eds.), *Unintended thought* (pp. 212–252). New York: Guilford Press.

Chaiken, S., Pomerantz, E. M., & Giner-Sorolla, R. (1995). Structural consistency and attitude strength. In R. E. Petty & J. A. Krosnick (Eds.), *Attitude strength: Antecedents and consequences*. Mahwah, NJ: Lawrence Erlbaum Associates.

Cohen, J., & Cohen, P. (1983). *Applied multiple regression/correlation analysis for the behavioral sciences*. Hillsdale NJ: Lawrence Erlbaum Associates.

Current Population Reports (1993). *Voting and registration in the election of November 1992.* Washington, DC: U. S. Department of Commerce, Bureau of the Census.

DeBono, K. G. (1987). Investigating the social-adjustive and value-expressive functions of attitudes: Implications for persuasion processes. *Journal of Personality and Social Psychology, 52,* 279–287.

DeBono, K. G., & Harnish, R. J. (1988). Source expertise, source attractiveness, and the processing of persuasive information: A functional approach. *Journal of Personality and Social Psychology, 55,* 541–546.

DeBono, K. G., & Packer, M. (1991). The effects of advertising appeal on perceptions of product quality. *Personality and Social Psychology Bulletin, 17,* 194–200.

DeBono, K. G., & Snyder, M. (1989). Understanding consumer decision-making processes: The role of form and function in product evaluation. *Journal of Applied Social Psychology, 19,* 416–424.

DeBono, K. G., & Telesca, C. (1990). The influence of source physical attractiveness on advertising effectiveness: A functional perspective. *Journal of Applied Social Psychology, 20,* 1383–1395.

Downs, A. (1957). *An economic theory of democracy.* New York: Harper & Brothers.

Eagly, A. H., & Chaiken, S. (1993). *The psychology of attitudes.* New York: Harcourt Brace Jovanovich.

Fazio. R. H., & Williams, C. J. (1986). Attitude accessibility as a moderator of the attitude-perception and attitude-behavior relations: An investigation of the 1984 presidential election. *Journal of Personality and Social Psychology, 51,* 505–514.

Feldman, S., & Stenner, K. (1997). Perceived threat and authoritarianism. *Political Psychology, 18,* 741–770.

Fishbein, M., & Ajzen, I. (1975). *Belief, attitude, intention, and behavior: An introduction to theory and research.* Reading, MA: Addison–Wesley.

Fiske, S. T., & Taylor, S. E. (1991). *Social cognition.* New York: McGraw-Hill.

Fleming, M. A., & Petty, R. E. (in press). Identity and persuasion: An elaboration likelihood approach. In D. J. Terry & M. A. Hogg (Eds.), *Attitudes, behavior and social context: The roles of norms and group membership.* Mahwah, NJ: Lawrence Erlbaum Associates.

Herek, G. M. (1986). The instrumentality of attitudes: Toward a neofunctional theory. *Journal of Social Issues, 42,* 99–114.

Houston, D. A., & Fazio, R. H. (1989). Biased processing as a function of attitude accessibility: Making objective judgments subjectively. *Social Cognition, 7,* 51–66.

Hovland, C. I., Lumsdaine, A. A., & Sheffield, F. D. (1949). *Experiments on mass communication.* Princeton, NJ: Princeton University Press. Janis, I. L. (1967). Effects of fear arousal on attitude change: Recent developments in theory and experimental research. In L. Berkowitz (Ed.), *Advances in experimental social psychology* (Vol. 3, pp. 166–224). San Diego, CA: Academic Press.

Jöreskog, K. G., & Sörbom, D. (1993). *LISREL 8: Structural equation modeling with the SIMPLIS command language.* Hillsdale, NJ: Lawrence Erlbaum Associates.

Katz, D. (1960). The functional approach to the study of attitudes. *Public Opinion Quarterly, 24,* 163–204.

Katz, D., & Stotland, E. (1959). A preliminary statement to a theory of attitude structure and change. In S. Kroch (Ed.), *Psychology: A study of a science* (Vol. 3, pp. 423–475). New York: McGraw-Hill.

Kinder, D., & Sanders, L. (1996). *Divided by color: Racial politics and democratic ideal.* Chicago: The University of Chicago Press.

Lavine, H., Borgida, E., & Rudman, L. A. (1994). Social Cognition. In V. S. Ramachandran (Ed.), *Encyclopedia of Human Behavior.* San Diego, CA: Academic Press.

Lavine, H., Burgess, D, Snyder, M., Transue, J., Sullivan, J. L., Haney, B., & Wagner, S. H. (1999). Threat, authoritarianism, and voting: An investigation of personality and persuasion. *Personality and Social Psychology Bulletin, 25,* 337–347.

Lavine, H., & McBride, T. (1996, May). *The influence of attitudinal involvement on selective exposure to functionally relevant information.* Paper presented at the annual meeting of the Midwestern Psychological Association, Chicago, IL. Lavine, H., & Snyder, M. (1996). Cognitive processing and the functional matching effect in persuasion: The mediating role of subjective perceptions of message quality. *Journal of Experimental Social Psychology, 32,* 580–604.

Lavine, H., and Snyder, M. (1996). Cognitive processing and the functional matching effect in persuasion: The mediating role of subjective perceptions and message quality. *Journal of Experimental Social Psychology, 32,* 580–604.

Lavine, H., Sullivan, J. L., Borgida, E., & Thomsen, C. J. (1996). The relationship of national and personal issue salience to attitude accessibility on foreign and domestic policy issues. *Political Psychology, 17,* 293–316.

Lazarsfeld, P. F., Berelson, B., & Gaudet, H. (1948). *The people's choice.* New York: Columbia University Press.

Lodge, M., McGraw, K., & Stroh, P. (1989). An impression-driven model of candidate evaluation. *American Political Science Review, 83,* 399–419.

Lord, C., G., Ross, L., & Lepper, M. R. (1979). Biased assimilation and attitude polarization: The effect of prior theories on subsequently considered evidence. *Journal of Personality and Social Psychology, 37,* 2098–2109.

Mackie, D. M., & Worth, L. T. (1989). Cognitive deficits and the mediation of positive affect in persuasion. *Journal of Personality and Social Psychology, 57,* 27–40.

Marcus, G., Sullivan, J. L., Theiss-Morse, E. & Wood, S. L. (1995). *With malice toward some: How people make civil liberties judgments.* New York: Cambridge University Press.

Markus, H., & Zajonc, R. B. (1985). The cognitive perspective in social psychology. In G. Lindzey & E. Aronson (Eds.), *Handbook of social psychology* (3rd ed., pp. 137–230). New York: Random House.

McGuire, W. J. (1986). The vicissitudes of attitudes and similar representational constructs in twentieth century psychology. *European Journal of Social Psychology, 16,* 89–130.

Mendelberg, T. (1997). Executing Hortons: Racial crime in the 1988 presidential campaign. *Public Opinion Quarterly, 61,* 134–157.

Neisser, U. (1976). *Cognition and reality: Principles and implications of cognitive psychology.* San Francisco: Freeman.

Ottati, V. C., & Wyer, R. S. (1990). The cognitive mediators of political choice: Toward a comprehensive model of political information processing. In J. A. Ferejohn & J. H. Kuklinski (Eds.), *Information and democratic process.* Urbana, IL: University of Illinois Press.

Petty, R. E., & Cacioppo, J. T. (1979). Issue involvement can increase or decrease persuasion by enhancing message-relevant cognitive responses. *Journal of Personality and Social Psychology, 37,* 1915–1926.

Petty, R. E., & Cacioppo, J. T. (1986). The elaboration likelihood model of persuasion. In L. Berkowitz (Ed.), *Advances in experimental social psychology* (Vol. 19, pp. 123–205). San Diego, CA: Academic Press.

Petty, R. E., & Wegener, D. T. (1998). Matching versus mismatching attitude functions: Implications for scrutiny of persuasive messages. *Personality and Social Psychology Bulletin, 24,* 227–240.

Piven, F. F., & Cloward, R. A. (1988). *Why Americans don't vote.* New York: Pantheon.

Pomerantz, E. M., Margolies, D., & Chaiken, S. (1993). *Selective judgment and structural consistency.* Poster presented at the American Psychology Association Meetings, Toronto, Ontario, Canada.

Powell, G. B. (1986). Voter turnout in comparative perspective. *American Political Science Review, 80,* 17–43.

Pratkanis, A. R., Breckler, S. J., & Greenwald, A. G. (Eds.) (1989). *Attitude structure and function.* Mahwah, NJ: Lawrence Erlbaum Associates.

Pratkanis, A. R., & Greenwald, A. G. (1989). A sociocognitive model of attitude structure and function. In L. Berkowitz (Ed.), *Advances in experimental social psychology* (Vol. 22, pp. 245– 85). San Diego, CA: Academic Press.

Prentice, D. A. (1987). Psychological correspondence of possessions, attitudes, and values. *Journal of Personality and Social Psychology, 53,* 993–1003.

Rahn, W. M., Aldrich, J. H., Borgida, E., & Sullivan, J. L. (1990). A social-cognitive model of candidate appraisal. In J. A. Ferejohn & J. H. Kuklinski (Eds.), *Information and democratic process.* Urbana, IL: University of Illinois Press.

Robertson, B., Lavine, H., & Borgida, E. (1993, May). *Self-interest-and value-based involvement: Implications for persuasion processes.* Paper presented at the annual meeting of the Midwestern Psychological Association, Chicago, IL.

Rogers, T. B., Kuiper, N. A., & Kirker, W. S. (1977). Self-reference and the encoding of personal information. *Journal of Personality and Social Psychology, 35,* 677–688.

Sarnoff, I., & Katz, D. (1954). The motivational basis of attitude change. *Journal of Abnormal and Social Psychology, 49,* 115–124.

Sears, D. O., & Funk, C. L. (1991). The role of self-interest in social and political attitudes. In M. P. Zanna (Ed.), *Advances in experimental social psychology* (Vol. 24). New York: Academic Press.

Shavitt, S. (1990). The role of attitude objects in attitude functions. *Journal of Experiment Social Psychology, 26,* 124–138.

Sherif, M., & Hovland, C. I. (1961). *Social judgment: Assimilation and contrast effects in communication and attitude change.* New Haven, CT: Yale University Press.

Sherif, M., & Sherif, C. W. (1967). Attitude as the individual's own categories: The social judgment-involvement approach to attitude and attitude change. In C. W. Sherif & M. Sherif (Eds.), *Attitude, ego-involvement and change* (pp. 105–139). New York: Wiley.

Silver, B. D., Abramson, P. R., & Anderson, B. A. (1986). The presence of others and overreporting of voting in American national elections. *Public Opinion Quarterly, 50,* 228– 239.

Smith, M. B., Bruner, J. S., & White, R. W. (1956). *Opinions and personality.* New York: Wiley.

Snyder, M. (1974). The self-monitoring of expressive behavior. *Journal of Personality and Social Psychology, 30,* 526–537.

Snyder, M. (1979). Self-monitoring processes. In L. Berkowitz (Ed.), *Advances in experimental social psychology* (Vol. 12). New York: Academic Press.

Snyder, M. (1987). *Public appearances/private realities: The psychology of self-monitoring.* New York: Freeman.

Snyder, M. (1992). Motivational foundations of behavioral confirmation. In M. P. Zanna (Ed.), *Advances in experimental social psychology* (Vol. 25). New York: Academic Press.

Snyder, M., & Cantor, N. (1999). Understanding personality and social behavior: A functionalist strategy. In D. T. Gilbert, S. T. Fiske & G. Lindsey (Eds.), *Handbook of social psychology* (4th ed., pp. 635–679). Boston: McGraw-Hill.

Snyder, M., & DeBono, K. G. (1985). Appeals to images and claims about quality: Understanding the psychology of advertising. *Journal of Personality and Social Psychology, 49,* 586–597.

Snyder, M., & DeBono, K. G. (1989). Understanding the functions of attitudes: Lessons from personality and social behavior. In A. R. Pratkanis, S. J. Breckler, & A. G. Greenwald (Eds.), *Attitude structure and function* (pp. 339–359) Hillsdale, NJ: Lawrence Erlbaum Associates.

Snyder, M., & Ickes, W. (1985). Personality and social behavior. In G. Lindzey & E. Aronson (Eds.), *The handbook of social psychology* (3rd ed., pp. 883–947). New York: Random House.

Stouffer, S. (1955). *Communism, conformity and civil liberties: A cross-section of the nation speaks its mind.* New York: Doubleday.

Thomsen, C. T., Borgida, E., & Lavine, H. (1995). The causes and consequences of personal involvement. In R. E. Petty & J. A. Krosnick (Eds.), *Attitude strength: Antecedents and consequences* (pp. 191–214). Hillsdale, NJ: Lawrence Erlbaum Associates.

Thomsen, C. J., Lavine, H., & Kounios, J. (1996) Social value and attitude concepts in semantic memory: Relational structure, concept strength, and the fan effect. *Social Cognition, 14,* 191–225.

Verba, S., & Nie, N. H. (1972). *Participation in America.* New York: Harper & Row.

5

Attitude Functions and Persuasion: An Elaboration Likelihood Approach to Matched Versus Mismatched Messages

Richard E. Petty
S. Christian Wheeler
and George Y. Bizer
The Ohio State University

The functional theorists believed that people hold attitudes because these attitudes serve particular needs that people have—such as to understand the world, fit in with others, express important values, have high self-esteem, and so forth (see Katz, 1960; Smith, Bruner, & White, 1956). For example, a person might develop a prejudice toward a minority group because this negative evaluation of the out-group makes the person feel better about the in-group and him- or herself. Research on attitude functions requires some method for assessing the functions served by attitudes, and contemporary theorists have identified a number of ways in which attitude functions can be identified. One method relies on individual differences and suggests that most attitudes serve different functions for different people. For example, for some people, most attitudes might serve a value-expressive function but for others, most attitudes might serve a social-adjustive function (e.g., Clary, Snyder, Ridge, Miene, & Haugen, 1994; Snyder & DeBono, 1985, 1989). An alternative to the individual difference approach suggests that attitudes toward particular issues or objects might serve a common function for most people. For example, attitudes toward aspirin might be based primarily on utilitarian concerns (e.g., Abelson & Prentice, 1989; Prentice, 1987; Shavitt, 1990). It also seems possible that different situations could make different functions of an attitude salient for most objects and for most people. For example, when at a party, the social-adjustive functions of one's attitudes might dominate, but when in church, value-expressive motivations might be prepotent. Finally, it is possible that in some cases there is little consistency in functions, and thus one must assess functions separately for each attitude object for each person in each situation (see Herek, 1987). Various combinations could also be possible. That is, for some people, a subset of their attitudes might be chronically based on social-adjustment concerns, whereas another set is based on value-expressive concerns and a third set is subject to situational variability.

FUNCTIONAL MATCHING EFFECTS IN PERSUASION

A key notion of the functional approach is that it is important to understand the functional basis of people's attitudes in order to understand how to change those attitudes. Functional theory offers the general proposition that persuasive appeals that address or "match" the function served by an attitude will be more persuasive than appeals that are irrelevant to or "mismatch" the function served by that attitude. That is, one should offer value-relevant arguments to the person whose attitude serves a value-expressive function, for objects that have a value expressive basis, and for situations in which concerns about values dominate, but one should offer social-adjustment arguments when this function serves as the basis of the attitude to be changed (e.g., Clary et al., 1994; DeBono & Packer, 1991; DeBono & Rubin, 1995; Katz, 1960; Kiesler, Collins, & Miller, 1969; Lavine & Snyder, 1996; Shavitt, 1990; Snyder & DeBono, 1989).

Various studies have provided support for the fundamental functional hypothesis that persuasive appeals are more effective when they present information that matches the function underlying an attitude than when they present information that does not match. For example, Snyder and DeBono (1985) used the individual difference method of identifying people for whom attitudes likely served different functions. These authors reasoned that, because high self-monitors (Snyder, 1974, 1979) tailor their behavior to fit the socially appropriate considerations of different situations, their attitudes might typically serve the social-adjustive function. In contrast, Snyder and DeBono (1985) reasoned that, because low self-monitors are guided by internal sources such as values and feelings, their attitudes are more likely to serve the value-expressive function.

To examine the idea that attitudes can be changed more easily by presenting message arguments that matched different functions, Snyder and DeBono (1985) presented research participants with advertisements for a variety of products. These advertisements contained content that appealed either to the social-adjustment function (i.e., describing the social images that consumers could gain from use of the product) or to the value-expressive function (i.e., presenting content regarding the intrinsic quality or merit of the product). For example, an ad for Canadian Club whiskey that contained product image content showed a bottle of the whiskey resting on a set of blueprints for a house and stated that "You're not just moving in, you're moving up." The product quality ad for the whiskey had the same picture, but used the statement, "When it comes to taste, everyone draws the same conclusion."

Across a number of studies and using a variety of measures, Snyder and DeBono (1985) found that high self-monitors rated ads with image content as better (more effective) than ads with quality content. In contrast, low self-monitors rated quality ads as better (more effective) than image ads. Individuals high versus low in self-monitoring have also been shown to rate product quality as better when the product is advertised in a manner consistent with the functional base assumed to underlie the attitude (DeBono & Packer, 1991; see Clary et al., 1994; and Lavine & Snyder, 1996 for additional evidence consistent with matching functional message content to individuals' bases of attitudes being more persuasive than mismatching content).

Using an object-oriented approach to classifying functions, Shavitt (1990) also found support for the hypothesis that advertisements that contain function-relevant arguments are more persuasive than function-irrelevant ads. That is, people preferred advertisements when the ad content matched the function served by the product, held more favorable attitudes toward brands advertised with the matching strategy, and preferred to purchase brands advertised with an ad when the content matched rather than mismatched the function of the object. Thus, the existing literature is consistent with the functional hypothesis that, all else being equal, messages containing arguments that match functional bases are more persuasive than those that mismatch functional bases (see Shavitt, 1989; Snyder & DeBono, 1989, for reviews).

The Mediation of Functional Matching Effects

Although the effect of matching message content to the functional basis of a person's attitude has been clear and consistent in past research, the reason *why* such functional matching effects have been obtained has been less clear. As Lavine and Snyder (1996) recently noted, "the logic of the functional approach's matching hypothesis does not fully address the question of *how* such motivational appeals influence attitudes... in fact, the cognitive processes that mediate the functional matching effect are not yet well understood" (p. 581). Based on past work suggesting that existing cognitive structures can bias the evaluation of message arguments (e.g., Cacioppo, Petty, & Sidera, 1982), Lavine and Snyder (1996) hypothesized that "functional match of a persuasive message should directly influence the recipient's perception of message validity... which in turn should influence postmessage attitudes" (p. 583). That is, these investigators suggested that functional matching of arguments should "bias recipients' evaluations of the persuasiveness of the arguments" and result in the message being "perceived as more persuasive than messages that contain functionally-irrelevant information" (p. 583). In two studies in which high and low self-monitors were presented with messages that either matched or mismatched the presumed functional basis of the attitude, matched messages elicited more favorable thoughts and were rated as more persuasive. That is, low self-monitors seemed motivated to generate favorable thoughts to a message that made an appeal to values, whereas high self-monitors seemed motivated to generate favorable thoughts to a message that made an appeal to image. Of greater interest, valenced thoughts and perceptions of message quality mediated the impact of functional argument matching on postmessage attitudes. Thus, this study provided the first mediational evidence consistent with the view that arguments that match the functional basis of one's attitude produce greater attitude change because of biased processing of those arguments.

In this chapter, we provide a reexamination of the mechanisms by which functional matching effects occur and address the extent to which these mechanisms might account for other types of matching effects in persuasion. Instead of suggesting that matching always leads to enhanced persuasion, we argue that a more complex process might be responsible for the effects found to date. Before turning to this, however, we provide a very brief overview of our conceptual framework—the Elaboration Likelihood Model (ELM) of Persuasion.

The Elaboration Likelihood Model of Persuasion

In brief, the ELM (Petty & Cacioppo, 1981; 1986; Petty & Wegener, 1999) was formulated as a theory about how various source, message, recipient, and contextual variables have an impact on attitudes toward various objects, issues, and people. The theory outlines a finite number of ways in which variables can have their impact on judgments, and it specifies when variables take on these roles as well as the consequences that result from these different roles. That is, the ELM is a theory about the processes that underlie changes in judgments of objects, the variables that induce these processes, and the strength of the judgments that result from these processes. The ELM is a dual-route but multiprocess theory. The dual routes—central and peripheral—refer to attitude changes that are based on different degrees of information processing activity. Central route attitude changes refer to those that are based on relatively extensive and effortful information processing activity aimed at scrutinizing and uncovering the central merits of the issue or advocacy. Peripheral route attitude changes are based on a variety of lower effort attitude change processes.

Perhaps the most critical construct in the ELM is the elaboration continuum. Points along the elaboration continuum are determined by how motivated and able people are to assess the central merits of a person, issue, or a position (i.e., the attitude object). The more motivated and able people are to assess the central merits of the attitude object (i.e., determine how good it really is), the more likely they are to effortfully scrutinize all available object-relevant information. This is because effortful scrutiny is usually perceived to be the best way to achieve this goal. Thus, at the high end of the elaboration continuum, people assess object-relevant information in relation to knowledge that they already possess, and arrive at a reasoned (though not necessarily unbiased) attitude that is well articulated and bolstered by supporting information (the central route to judgment). At the low end of the elaboration continuum, information scrutiny is reduced. Nevertheless, attitude change can still result from a low-effort scrutiny of the information available (e.g., examining less information than when elaboration is high or examining the same information less carefully) or from a number of less resource demanding processes such as classical conditioning (Staats & Staats, 1958), self-perception (Bem, 1972), or the use of heuristics (Chaiken, 1987). Attitudes that are changed with minimal object-relevant thought are postulated to be weaker (i.e., less persistent, resistant, and predictive of behavior) than attitudes that are changed to the same extent as a result of maximal object-relevant thought (see Petty, Haugtvedt, & Smith, 1995).

At different points along the elaboration continuum, variables are postulated to take on different roles. In general, when the likelihood of elaboration is low, variables influence attitudes (if at all) through some process requiring relatively little effort such as by invoking a decision heuristic ("if I feel good, I must like it"). Under high elaboration, however, the same variable can influence attitudes through some central mechanism such as by biasing the ongoing cognitive activity (e.g., positive moods could bring positive thoughts to mind; see Petty, Schumann, Richman, & Strathman, 1993). If the elaboration likelihood is not constrained to be high or low by other factors, then a variable itself can determine the extent of issue-relevant thinking (e.g., positive mood could enhance or reduce processing of the message relative to a negative mood; see Wegener, Petty, & Smith, 1995).

The ELM and Functional Matching Effects

According to the ELM, just like other variables, matching of message arguments to the functional bases of peoples' attitudes should have an impact on attitude change by different processes along the elaboration continuum. For example, when the overall likelihood of message elaboration is high, such as when distractions are low (Petty, Wells, & Brock, 1976), and the message is high in personal relevance (Petty & Cacioppo, 1979), functional matching should work by biasing message processing (see Chaiken & Maheswaran, 1994; Petty et al., 1993). In fact, Levine and Snyder (1996) noted that in their research, in which functional matching appeared to invoke a positive bias in message processing, it was likely that "processing motivation was relatively high" (p. 600).

On the other hand, according to the ELM, if the overall likelihood of thinking is quite low, functional matching might produce attitude change by the lower effort peripheral route. For example, if the arguments simply seemed to suggest that values were relevant to the advocacy, a low self-monitor might be more inclined to agree than a high self-monitor by reasoning that "if it speaks to my values, it must be good." An analogous heuristic might be used by a high-self monitor to accept a message with arguments using terms such as "image" since the person might reason that "if the product is image related, I should buy it" (cf. Chaiken, 1987). These simple inferences could lead to message acceptance in the absence of thinking about the actual justifications for the value or image assertions contained in the message. DeBono (1987), in fact, argued that such a peripheral process was responsible for the functional matching effect he observed in one study. In this research, DeBono informed recipients which side of an issue (pro or con) was associated with the function served by their attitude, but no message was actually presented. Following exposure to this information, people expressed more agreement with the side that was said to be a functional match. Although it is possible that people generated arguments that were supportive of the position said to be consistent with the functional basis of their attitudes (i.e., biased central route processing), it seems quite reasonable that in the absence of any arguments, attitude change was the result of a low effort peripheral process.

Both the cue and biased processing explanations for functional matching effects predict statistical main effects of functional matching. The mechanisms behind the cue and biased processing explanations are quite different, of course, but the attitudinal outcome is similar. That is, messages that match the underlying basis of the attitude should be more effective than messages that mismatch—either because matching serves as a peripheral cue or because people engage in biased evaluation of functionally matched arguments (or a biased generation of arguments). It is also possible, however, that the past main effects of functional matching could be accounted for by another process highlighted by the ELM—differential processing of matched versus mismatched messages. As previously noted, if the background elaboration likelihood is not constrained to be either very high or low, a persuasion variable such as functional argument match might prompt people to effortfully scrutinize the message. In particular, people might give more careful thought to a message when the content of that message matches the functional basis of their attitudes than when the content mismatches. If past messages in the literature used relatively cogent information to support the attitude object, and content matching enhanced message processing, then people for whom the message matched the functional basis would be more persuaded than people for whom the message mismatched because they would better recognize the cogency of the arguments presented. According to this analysis, however, if the supporting evidence were specious, then matching would be *less* effective than mismatching because people for whom the message matched would better recognize the weakness of the arguments (Petty & Cacioppo, 1979). Thus, the enhanced scrutiny hypothesis suggests that functional matches of arguments could be either superior to or inferior to mismatches in producing persuasion, depending on the quality of the information presented in support of the advocated position.

A few studies are relevant to the hypothesis that functionally matched arguments are sometimes scrutinized more carefully than mismatched arguments. First, some indirect evidence for this hypothesis comes from studies that examined functional matching without varying the actual content of the arguments that comprised the message, instead varying whether the source of the message was one that appealed to individuals whose attitudes served different functional bases. DeBono and colleagues (DeBono & Harnish, 1988; DeBono & Telesca, 1990) have provided strong support for the notion that functionally relevant sources can increase message scrutiny over functionally irrelevant sources even though the messages are not varied to differ in the actual functions they address. The notion is that expert sources provide a better functional match for individuals' whose attitudes are based on values and the central merits of things (i.e., low self-monitors), but that socially attractive sources provide a better functional match for individuals whose attitudes are based on social-adjustment concerns (i.e., high self-monitors). This may be because of differential identification with these sources or because these sources might be expected to present different kinds of information (i.e., an expert might be more likely to present value-relevant arguments than an attractive source, and an attractive source might be more likely to present image arguments than an expert source). Consistent with the notion that functional source matching increases message scrutiny, De-Bono and Harnish (1988) found that attitudes were more dependent on argument quality when the source matched the presumed functional basis of the attitude than when it mismatched. The enhanced impact of argument quality on attitudes is indicative of enhanced information processing activity (Petty & Cacioppo, 1986; Wegener, Downing, Krosnick, & Petty, 1995).

Of course, in the studies that varied some feature of the communication other than the message arguments, the messages themselves never directly matched or mismatched the functional bases of peoples' attitudes. Because of this, these studies provide no information as to whether message *content* that matches functional bases (which is the focus of most of the work on functional matches) receives greater thought.

Functional Argument Matching
Can Increase Message Scrutiny

To summarize, the previous literature on functional argument matching indicates that matched arguments are more persuasive than nonmatched arguments, but it is not entirely clear why this effect is obtained. The one mediational study that has been conducted suggests that the mechanism behind the argument matching effect is biased information processing (Lavine & Snyder, 1996). However, the ELM suggests that functional argument matching effects could result from other mechanisms such as the operation of peripheral cues or enhanced scrutiny of matched messages.

In two experiments, Petty and Wegener (1998) attempted to test the hypothesis that message arguments that match the functional basis of an attitude receive greater scrutiny than those that mismatch the functional basis. This possibility is especially intriguing because if true, it implies that functional argument matching sometimes leads to less persuasion than does functional mis-matching. This should occur if the arguments are weak because if functional matching increases message scrutiny, people should better realize how specious the arguments are and thus should be more likely to reject them. If this result were obtained, it would provide a strong counterpoint to the notion that functional matching of arguments invariably increases persuasion due to favorably biased information processing.

To examine the enhanced scrutiny idea, Petty and Wegener (1998) manipulated the strength of the matching versus mismatching information in brief messages about new consumer products. If information that matches functional bases receives greater scrutiny than information that mismatches functional bases, one would expect to obtain an interaction between function match and the strength of the arguments in the message. Participants who read matching information should form more favorable opinions of the products when the latter are supported by strong, cogent information rather than by weak, specious information to a greater extent than participants who read mismatching information. If the biased processing or cue alternatives are operating in this context, however, one would expect a main effect of functional match (with matching information leading to more favorable opinions than mismatching information) instead of or in addition to the interaction between argument strength and functional match (see Petty & Cacioppo, 1986).

To summarize, rather than suggesting that arguments that match the function served by one's attitude invariably are more persuasive than arguments that mismatch, the processing view suggests that, in some circumstances at least, matching arguments are scrutinized more carefully. If information in matched messages is processed more thoroughly than information in mismatched messages, then matches should be more persuasive than mismatches if strong arguments are used (and baseline opinions are not already so favorable that little room is left for enhancement of opinions), but matches should also be less persuasive than mismatches if weak arguments are used.[1]

Students who were high or low in self-monitoring (Snyder, 1974) received messages that provided descriptions of four products (i.e., a shampoo, a shoe, a coat, and a toothpaste). Each product was introduced and described with either strong or weak claims about product quality, or with strong or weak appeals to image associated with use of the product. On the same page as the information about each product, participants provided their opinions of the product. Messages that matched the hypothesized functional bases of attitudes (i.e., image arguments to high self-monitors and quality arguments to low self-monitors) were classified as matches, and messages that mismatched the hypothe-

---

[1]As noted already, the ELM suggests that each of the explanations (i.e., cue effect, biased elaboration, enhanced elaboration) could account for functional matching effects under different baseline levels of thinking (see Petty & Cacioppo, 1986). We focus here on the enhanced elaboration hypothesis because it is the one that can accommodate the previously unobtained result that the matching of arguments to functions can actually reduce persuasion. In addition, since prior work on functional matching of arguments has never manipulated the elaboration likelihood to render it especially high or low, the elaboration conditions that characterize most past research might best be described as moderate. In any case, the current research examines the impact of functional matches when the elaboration likelihood is not constrained to be very high or low.

sized functional bases of attitudes (i.e., quality arguments to high self-monitors and image arguments to low self-monitors) were classified as mismatches. Thus, the test of the processing hypothesis could be represented as the two-way interaction between argument strength and functional match.[2] The four variations of type and strength of appeal for the shampoo ads were as follows:

Strong Image: A brand new shampoo is being introduced whose primary qualities are related to how good it makes your hair look. That is, of people who have used the shampoo in tests of the product, over half of them thought the shampoo made their hair look better than the shampoo they used at home. Also, the shampoo seemed able to make people's hair manageable and attractive for a longer period of time than other shampoos.

Weak Image: A brand new shampoo is being introduced whose primary qualities are related to how good it makes your hair look. That is, of people who have used the shampoo in tests of the product, almost half of them thought the shampoo made their hair look better than the shampoo they used at home. Also, the shampoo seemed able to make people's hair manageable and attractive for some time as long as people did not go outdoors or otherwise mess up their hair following initial styling.

Strong Quality: A brand new shampoo is being introduced whose primary qualities are related to how well it cleans your hair. That is, of people who have used the shampoo in tests of the product, over half of them thought the shampoo cleaned their hair better than the shampoo they used at home. Also, the shampoo seemed able to keep hair clean for a longer period of time than other shampoos.

Weak Quality: A brand new shampoo is being introduced whose primary qualities are related to how well it cleans your hair. That is, of people who have used the shampoo in tests of the product, almost half of them thought the shampoo cleaned their hair better than the shampoo they used at home. Also, the shampoo seemed able to keep hair clean for some time as long as people did not go outdoors or otherwise soil their hair.

Following exposure to the appropriate message, participants were given a variety of semantic differential scales on which to rate their evaluations of the products. Products were always presented in the same order (i.e., shampoo, coat, shoe, and toothpaste), and all four combinations of argument strength and type of appeal were represented across the four products. Participants received one of four orders of the message conditions that corresponded to a revised Latin square for the four combinations of argument strength and type of appeal.

---

[2]Alternatively, we could have looked for the (identical) three-way interaction of Self-monitoring (low, high) X Argument quality (weak, strong) X Message type (image, quality).

Corresponding to the experimental design previously described, the attitude measure was submitted to a 2 (Self-monitoring: low, high) X 2 (Argument quality: weak, strong) X 2 (Message type: matched, mismatched) mixed-design ANOVA. As in much prior research, strong arguments led to more favorable opinions toward the products than did weak arguments. Consistent with the hypothesis that information matching the functional base of an attitude is naturally processed more extensively than information mismatching the functional base, the argument strength main effect was qualified by the two-way interaction between argument strength and functional match (see Fig. 5.1). That is, the effect of argument strength was greater when the message content matched the functional base of product attitudes (i.e., when image messages were presented to high self-monitors or quality messages were presented to low self-monitors) than when the message content mismatched the functional base of product attitudes (i.e., when quality messages were presented to high self-monitors or image messages were presented to low self-monitors). The Functional match X Argument strength interaction did not differ across levels of self-monitoring. Because

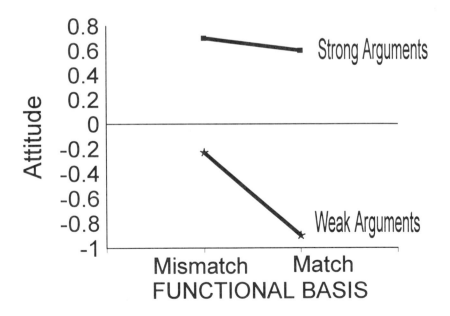

FIG. 5.1. Effects of functional matching and argument quality on attitudes (data from Petty & Wegener, 1998).

the weak arguments were especially ineffective in persuading people when the message matched the function underlying the attitude, there was also a main effect of functional match such that matches were significantly less effective than mismatches.

Why Does Functional Matching Work?

In the domain of attitude functions, the accumulated research suggests that matching of a message to the function served by one's attitude can influence attitudes in multiple ways at different points along the elaboration continuum. Specifically, when the elaboration likelihood was not constrained to be high or low, functional matching served to enhance information processing activity (Petty & Wegener, 1998). When the elaboration likelihood was low, functional matching appeared to serve as a favorable peripheral cue (DeBono, 1987), and when the elaboration likelihood was high, functional matching appeared to impart a favorable bias to the ongoing information processing activity (Lavine & Snyder, 1996).

Why does functional matching have these effects? In one study, De-Bono and Packer (1991) found that people rated matching messages to be more self-relevant than mismatching messages. If matched messages are perceived to be more self-relevant, perhaps because they are perceived to speak more directly to the kind of person the recipient is, a number of consequences follow. First, considerable prior research suggests that any feature of a message that invokes self-relevance (whether based on connections to one's personal goals, values, possessions, etc.) increases information-processing activity when other variables have not already constrained the elaboration likelihood to be high or low (Petty & Cacioppo, 1979; see Petty, Cacioppo & Haugtvedt, 1992; Thomsen, Borgida, & Lavine, 1995, for reviews).

When the likelihood of thinking is low, however, tying of the message to the self should have other consequences. First, consider that people tend to like things that are associated with themselves more than things that are associated with others. Thus, research on dissonance theory showed that an object tends to be seen as more valuable as soon as an individual chooses it (e.g., Brehm, 1956). In fact, objects are also seen as more valuable even if people are simply given the items and no choice is involved (Kahneman, Knetsch, & Thaler, 1991). People overvalue members of their in-group (Tajfel, 1981), prefer the arguments they have generated over the arguments generated by others (Greenwald & Albert,

1968), and have even shown preferences for the letters in their own names over other letters (Nuttin, 1985). This strong preference for things associated with the self suggests that people would value a message framed as linking to the self such as a message that is seen to speak to "the kind of person I am." When the likelihood of thinking is low, this "own-ness" (Perloff & Brock, 1980) or self-bias presumably operates to increase agreement with a message. When the likelihood of thinking is high, this bias presumably motivates people to see the merits of the position associated with the self. Such self-serving biases in cognitive processing are well documented in the literature (see Baumeister, 1998).

OTHER MATCHING EFFECTS IN PERSUASION

Given that functional matching effects can operate in multiple ways by making a connection to the self salient, it seems plausible that making other links between a message and the self salient might operate similarly. In the remainder of this chapter, we examine the potential similarities in operation between functional matching effects and matching effects that involve self-schemas, personal identities, and matching messages to bases of attitudes other than functional ones.

Self-Schema Matching

The Self-Schema and Persuasion. Markus (1977) defined self-schemas as "cognitive generalizations about the self...that organize and guide the processing of self-related information contained in the individual's social experiences" (p. 64). In other words, a self-schema is represented as a construct that contains information about who we are that can influence the processing of information. To find evidence of the construct, Markus identified people who were schematic on the trait of "independence," "dependence," or neither based on their answers to a questionnaire. Markus found that compared to those who were not schematic on a trait, schematics were quicker to report if a schema-relevant trait adjective was self-descriptive, were able to recall more schema-consistent prior behavior, and felt that future schema-consistent behavior was more likely.

As noted previously, functional matching effects might work because when a message is matched to the psychological function served by an attitude, the message seems more self-relevant or seems to contain information about "who I am" (e.g., "I care about image and the message is about image"; or "I think image is important for this object and the message is about image"). Unlike the work on functional matching, however, there is a paucity of research on self-schema matching and persuasion. One early study by Cacioppo et al. (1982) suggested that matching a message to a recipient's self-schema could enhance persuasiveness—much as the early work on functional matching suggested that such matching was invariably good for persuasion.

As noted earlier, Cacioppo et al. (1982) hypothesized that self-schema matching would bias processing of a persuasive message. Using the Markus (1977) procedure, they identified participants who were schematic on the concept of "religious," "legalistic," or neither, and then exposed them to a proattitudinal persuasive message that was framed in either religious or legalistic terms. That is, whereas some participants received legalistic arguments such as, "The right to life is one that is constitutionally safeguarded," others received religious arguments such as, "There is a sacramental quality to the nature of life that demands that we show the utmost reverence for it." Finally, participants were asked to report how persuasive they felt each of the messages was. Participants rated the messages framed in a schema-consistent manner as more persuasive than the messages framed in a schema-inconsistent manner. That is, participants who were schematic on the legalistic trait felt that the legalistically framed messages were more persuasive than were the religiously framed messages, whereas those who were schematic on the religious trait felt that the religiously framed messages were more persuasive. On the surface, at least, this result is similar to the early functional matching results. In addition, similar to the early functional matching studies, the mechanism behind the effect is not entirely clear. Cacioppo et al. (1982) suggested that people engaged in favorably biased processing of the schema-congruent message. Although this is a reasonable possibility, the data do not permit strong inferences concerning biased processing since argument quality was not varied, and no thought generation task was used to assess cognitive activity. Thus, it could be that the legalistic or religious wording of the arguments served as a peripheral cue and were accepted with relatively little scrutiny when they matched participants' self-schemata; or it is possible that matching the message to self-schemas enhanced the overall amount of scrutiny that the message received; or it could be that biased processing took place, but that the favorable bias required a proattitudinal message. With a counterattitudinal appeal, a schema-congruent message might be counterargued.

Self-Schema Matching Can Increase Message Scrutiny.   To examine the possibility that matching a message to a recipient's self-schema could enhance information processing activity, Bizer, Wheeler, and Petty (1998) manipulated the strength of the matching versus mismatching information in brief messages about new consumer products. If information that matches a person's self-schema receives greater scrutiny than information that mismatches one's self-schema, one would expect to obtain an interaction between self-schema match and argument strength. Participants should form more favorable opinions of the products when the products are supported by strong, cogent information rather than weak, specious information to a greater extent in the matching rather than the mismatching condition. If the biased processing or cue alternatives are operating in this context, however, a main effect of self-schema match should occur (with matching information leading to more favorable opinions than mismatching information).

To summarize, rather than suggesting that messages that match one's self-schema are invariably more persuasive than messages that mismatch, the processing possibility suggests that, in some circumstances at least, self-schema matching messages are scrutinized more carefully. If information in matched messages is processed more thoroughly than information in mismatched messages, then matches should be more persuasive than mismatches if strong arguments are used, but matches should also be less persuasive than mismatches if weak arguments are used.

Need for cognition (Cacioppo & Petty, 1982) was used as the self-schema variable. A large body of research is consistent with the idea that individuals who are high in need for cognition are more likely than those low in this trait to engage in and enjoy cognitive activity on a wide variety of tasks (see Cacioppo, Petty, Feinstein, & Jarvis, 1996, for a review). Interestingly, research by Feinstein (1996) has demonstrated that need for cognition operates as a self-schema if the Markus (1977) criteria are used. For example, in his research, people high in need for cognition were faster to respond to questions about whether schema-consistent adjectives (e.g., thoughtful, curious) characterized them than were individuals low in need for cognition. On schema-irrelevant traits, reaction times were comparable, which suggests that high need for cognition individuals chronically think of themselves in schema-consistent ways.[3] If need for cognition is a self-schema, and people are more likely to process schema-consistent than schema-inconsistent messages, this raises the interesting possibility that a message that appears to be aimed at people who are not thoughtful could enhance the information-processing activity of people who generally do not like to think (because it matches their self-schema), but reduce the information-processing activity of people who generally like to think (because it mismatches their self-schema).

In our examination of this idea, students who were high or low in need for cognition received a message about a new brand of toothpaste. The message was introduced with either a high or a low need for cognition frame, and presented either strong or weak arguments about the product. After exposure to the ad (which was embedded in a series of ads for other products), attitudes toward the product were obtained. Messages that matched individuals' self-schemas (i.e., thoughtful frame for high need for cognition individuals and unthoughtful frame for low need for cognition individuals) were expected to produce greater attention to argument quality than messages that mismatched the recipients' self-schemas (i.e., unthoughtful frame for high need for cognition individuals and thoughtful frame for low need for cognition individuals). If this result was obtained, a three-way interaction between need for cognition, message frame, and argument quality should occur. The self-schema frame was accomplished by having participants read one of the following introductions immediately prior to ad exposure:

Thoughtful Frame: The following advertisement is aimed at people who very much enjoy the process of thinking. These people prefer to think long and hard about problems because they enjoy finding the not-so-obvious answer. They love learning, asking questions, and uncovering answers. In short, they just enjoy thinking.

Unthoughtful Frame: The following advertisement is aimed at people who don't enjoy the process of thinking very much. These people prefer to make snap judgments rather than thinking things out because for them, finding a quick answer is best. They "use their heads" when necessary, but they don't waste their time trying to figure everything out. In short, they just don't like thinking.

After exposure to the appropriate introduction, the advertisement was presented. The first portion of the ad continued the frame established in the introduction. For example, the ad with the thoughtful introduction began with the line, "I'll bet you're the type of person who likes to think

---

[3]The evidence regarding whether low need for cognition was also a schema was less clear.

about the decisions you make." The ad with the unthoughtful introduction began with the line, "I'll bet you're the type of person who doesn't like to sit around and think about all of the details when you make choices." The ad continued with either the strong (cleans your breath all day) or the weak (cleans your breath for over an hour) claims about the product.

Corresponding to the experimental design described previously, the attitude measure was submitted to a 2 (Argument strength: weak, strong) X 2 (Message type: unthoughtful, thoughtful) X 2 Need for cognition (low, high) ANOVA. Not surprisingly, strong arguments led to more favorable opinions toward the product than did weak arguments. Consistent with the hypothesis that information matching a person's self-schema is considered more extensively than is information mismatching the self-schema, the argument strength main effect was qualified by the three-way interaction between argument strength, need for cognition, and message type (see Fig. 5.2). That is, for individuals both high and low in need for cognition, the effect of argument strength was greater when the message content matched the underlying self-schema (i.e., when thoughtful messages were presented to those high in need for cognition or unthoughtful messages were presented to those low in need for cognition) than when the message content mismatched the self-schema (i.e., when thoughtful messages were presented to those low in need for cognition or unthoughtful messages were presented to those high in need for cognition).

Given the paucity of work on self-schemas and persuasion, future work should examine the possibility that self-schema matching can serve multiple roles. That is, just as a self-schema match served to enhance the extent of information-processing activity in the study of Bizer et al. (1998), in which elaboration was not constrained to be high or low, self-schema match should serve other roles when elaboration is constrained. That is, similar to the analysis we provided for functional matching, we would expect self-schema matching to serve as a peripheral cue under low levels of elaboration likelihood, but to bias thinking at high levels of elaboration.

Social Identity Matching

As we noted above, a person's self-schema consists in part of information about how a person thinks about him or herself. Investigations of the self-schema have typically examined traits around which one can be schematic (e.g., I'm independent, thoughtful, etc.). Another possible

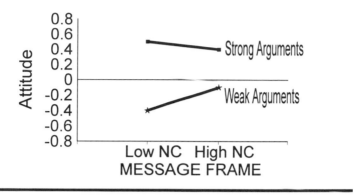

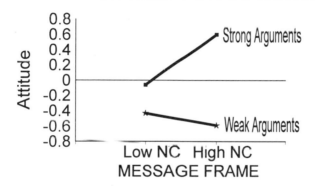

FIG. 5.2. Effects of need for Cognition, message framing, and argument quality on attitudes (data from Bizer, Wheeler, & Petty, 1998).

feature of the self-concept, however, arguably involves the groups or social categories with which people identify (e.g., I'm male, a Democrat, etc.; Tajfel, 1981). Although research on social identity and self-schemas has generally been conducted within completely separate domains, the separation of these constructs in a persuasion context may be unnecessary. That is, the impact of identity variables on attitude change may be relatively indistinguishable from that of self-schema appeals. Both personal and social identities could simply reflect a "me-ness" that is activated when a persuasive message matches some aspect of the self concept.

Indeed, Deaux (1996) has argued for the interchangeability of personal- and social-identity variables. She found that social and personal identities do not differ in their content. That is, identities do not cluster along the group versus personal dimension, but rather cluster by their conceptual meaning for the individual. Thus, it seems plausible that both personal identities (e.g., self-schemas) and social identities (e.g., group memberships) might function identically in a persuasion context insofar as their conceptual meaning matches the frame or content of the persuasive appeal.

As with some functionalist researchers (DeBono & Packer, 1991), a number of identity researchers (e.g., Festinger, 1950; Mackie, Worth, & Asuncion, 1990; Turner, 1982; Turner & Oakes, 1989) have postulated that the effects of identity appeals on persuasion stem from the importance of the message to the self. Some researchers suggest that this importance stems from the need to validate one's beliefs through agreement with similar others. Another possibility is that the importance stems from the implied or explicit relevance of the communication to the group, and therefore to the self.

A review of prior theories of social identity and persuasion is beyond the scope of this chapter (but see Fleming & Petty, 1999). Perhaps the most important point about the prior literature, however, is that past theories (e.g., Deutsch & Gerard, 1955; Festinger, 1950; Hogg & Abrams, 1993; Kelman, 1961; Sherif & Hovland ,1961; Turner & Oakes, 1989) have tended to postulate a single process by which identity variables impact on attitude change. In contrast, our analysis of functional matching and self-schema matching suggests that identity matching should be capable of operating in multiple ways (see also Fleming & Petty, 1999). Perhaps of greatest interest is the idea that identity matches or appeals from in-group members need not increase persuasion. If persuasion from in-group sources is sometimes the result of effortful message scrutiny, for example, weak messages from an in-group source should be less persuasive than weak messages from an out-group source. Next, we review some of the multiple ways in which identity matching could have an impact on persuasion.

Identity Matching as a Cue. According to the multiple-roles framework of the ELM, variables are more likely to act as a cue under conditions of low elaboration. Such conditions should be more likely, for example, when an in-group or out-group member delivers a persuasive message on a topic that is not directly relevant to the in-group. In one relevant study, Mackie et al. (1990, Experiment 2) provided a condition in which UC-Santa Barbara students read a persuasive message delivered by a member of their in-group (a student from their own school) or a member of their out-group (a student from a distant school). The message topic was not relevant to the in-group (acid rain in the Northeastern United States) and thus baseline elaboration likelihood was low. Furthermore, the position of the source was stated before the persuasive message, enabling the participants' knowledge of the source's position without processing the message. Results indicated that participants agreed more with the message when the source was a member of their in-group (i.e., matched social identity) than when the source was a member of the out-group (i.e., mismatched social identity) across both strong and weak argument conditions. In addition, cognitive responses failed to be predictive of participants' attitudes. This pattern of results is indicative of noneffortful, cue-based attitude change.

These effects might not have been driven by mere group membership, however, but by the "me-ness" aspect of identification with the group. Evidence for this perspective comes from a study by Fleming and Petty (1997a). Participants in this experiment were told the attitudes of in-group and out-group members on a series of products about which they had little or no previous knowledge. For all attitude items, the attitudes of the in-group and out-group were in the opposite direction (i.e., if one group held positive attitudes, the other held negative attitudes). Because the attitude objects were novel and unfamiliar, and because the participants were not provided with additional arguments about the products, elaboration likelihood was presumably low. Results indicated that participants held more positive attitudes when the in-group was positive than when the in-group was negative, which suggests an overall cue effect. However, this effect was moderated by level of identification with the in-group. Participants who identified highly with the in-group used the in-group position as a peripheral cue to a greater extent than people who were not identified even though the latter individuals were also nominal members of the group. This finding is consistent with the view that the "me-ness" or level of association with the self, and not in-group membership per se, is the crucial determinant of the in-group matching effect.

Identity Matching as a Determinant of Processing. According to the ELM, under conditions of moderate baseline elaboration, identity matching should serve to determine the amount of elaboration directed at a persuasive message. Evidence for this hypothesis was provided in a second set of conditions by Mackie et al. (1990). In this experiment, participants from the University of California at Santa Barbara were provided with a message from an in-group source or an out-group source. The position of the source was again announced before the persuasive message, but this time the message concerned a topic that had some potential relevance to the in-group (offshore oil drilling in the Southwestern United States). Results revealed an interaction between the strength of the arguments used in the persuasive message (strong vs. weak) and the source of the message (in-group vs. out-group member). Participants who read the message from the in-group source differentiated between strong and weak arguments, which indicates elaboration of the message. Furthermore, the cognitive responses of participants who read the message from the in-group source were predictive of their postmessage attitudes. Participants who read the message from the out-group source, however, did not differentiate between strong and weak arguments. In addition, their cognitive responses failed to be predictive of their post-message attitudes. Thus, in this experiment, identification with the in-group member appeared to instigate greater message processing from participants.

Identity Matching as a Source of Bias.   When elaboration likelihood is high, identity matching should serve to bias the thoughts an individual has in response to a persuasive message. According to our perspective, biased elaboration of arguments in response to identity appeals should be more likely to the extent that the identity appeal is seen as relevant to the self. Thus, the degree to which the appeal matches the self-identity should determine the amount of bias under high elaboration conditions.

Evidence for this hypothesis was provided in a study by Fleming and Petty (1997b). In this experiment, males and females assessed as high or low in identification with their gender were exposed to positive and negative arguments about a new snack food. All participants received both positive and negative information from both male and female sources. Thus, in one condition participants received positive information about the reactions of males and negative information about the reactions of females to the product. In another condition, participants received positive information about the reactions of females and negative information about the reactions of males to the product. Elaboration likelihood was kept high by providing participants ample time to examine the materials and by emphasizing the importance of their later judgments about the materials.

Because all participants received both positive and negative information of equal strength regardless of the frame, they should not have differed in their final attitudes as a function of the gender message frame. If participants engaged in selective scrutiny of the information based on the identity frame, however, one would expect to see differential persuasion of participants on the basis of the match between the frame and their gender, but only if they were highly gender identified. These latter predictions, in fact, were the obtained results. Males and females who were highly identified with their gender were more persuaded by, and had more positive thoughts toward, positive messages that matched their gender than positive messages that mismatched their gender. For participants who were not highly identified with their gender, no matching effects were found. Thus, the biased elaboration was not simply a function of the match between the gender frame and the gender of the individual, but rather depended on the individual's level of identification with his or her gender. When identification was low, matching did not result in bias.

Matching the Affective Versus Cognitive Bases of Attitudes

As our final example of the generality of matching effects, we discuss a type of matching that is at the same time perhaps both similar to and different from functional matching—matching the affective versus cognitive bases of attitudes. One important point of similarity is that like functional matching, this type of matching speaks to the underlying basis of the attitude itself. That is, just as a utilitarian or a social-adjustive attitude is based on a certain type of information, so too is an affective or a cognitive attitude (i.e., the former is based on feelings, whereas the latter is based on attributes; see Breckler, 1984; Rosenberg & Hovland, 1960; Zanna & Rempel, 1988). A second similarity concerns the fact that there are individual differences in the bases of the attitude. That is, just as individuals show dispositional tendencies toward holding attitudes with different functions (Snyder & DeBono, 1989), individuals presumably also differ in their propensity to hold attitudes that are primarily affectively or cognitively based. For example, a number of individual difference scales have been developed to distinguish between "thinkers" and "feelers," or those who tend to rely primarily on the facts or on their feelings in forming their attitudes (e.g., Epstein, Pacini, Denes-Raj, & Heier, 1996). Haddock and Zanna (1993), for example, demonstrated that individuals differ in their propensity to use affective or cognitive information in forming prejudicial attitudes. These propensities might therefore become a part of one's identity or self-concept, at least to the extent that an individual can indicate such thinking styles on self-report measures. Third, just as different attitude objects can differ in their association with a given attitude function for most people (e.g., air conditioners mostly serve a utilitarian function; Shavitt, 1989), attitude objects can also differ in whether they are primarily based on affect or cognition across people (Crites, Fabrigar, & Petty, 1994). For example, some research has suggested that people's attitudes toward food (Chattopadhyay & Letarte, 1996) and health detection behaviors (Millar & Millar, 1993) are primarily affectively driven.

One salient difference, however, is that functional matching effects are presumed to occur because of some underlying need or motivational state, but this has not been postulated for the affective versus cognitive bases of attitudes. Nevertheless, if the matching of a message to the basis of an attitude invokes some type of self-relevance regardless of the nature of the attitude's basis (i.e., functional or affective/cognitive), then similar mechanisms of persuasion might be revealed. That is, messages matched to the affective/cognitive bases of attitudes might serve as cues, bias processing, or determine the extent of processing.[4]

A number of different theories have attempted to account for the effects of affective and cognitive persuasive appeals. Initially, researchers sought to determine whether affective or cognitive appeals were generally more effective in eliciting attitude change. Following numerous inconclusive results, however (e.g., see Chen, 1933; Eldersveld, 1956; Knower, 1935; Matthews, 1947; Weiss, 1960), contemporary theorists have focused on whether matching affective or cognitive appeals to the underlying affective or cognitive basis of the attitude was more effective. However,

---

[4]Some might find it implausible that this type of matching (with little motivational significance) could induce a similar "me-ness" reaction as the other types of matching we described. However, a number of studies have demonstrated that relevance to the self can be noted with only minimal effort or attention. For example, Bargh (1992) demonstrated that a variety of self-relevant words, and not just one's name, can cause interference on a dichotic listening task. Thus, messages that have some link to the underlying basis of one's attitude might invoke a sense of self-relevance at an implicit if not explicit level.

in contrast to the consistent early findings that functional content matches produce greater persuasion than mismatches (e.g., Shavitt, 1990; Snyder & DeBono, 1985), the initial work on affective versus cognitive bases of attitudes has not been consistent. For example, Edwards (1990) found that matching arguments to attitude bases was better than mismatching (e.g., an affective persuasion appeal was better than a cognitive persuasion appeal when the attitude under attack had an affective basis; see also Fabrigar & Petty, 1999). On the other hand, Millar and Millar (1990) found mismatches to be more effective.

Although these various studies have arrived at seemingly opposite conclusions, their results might be rendered coherent by applying the matching framework we advocate here (see also Petty, Gleicher, & Baker, 1991). For example, consider that the Edwards (1990) studies used attitude objects that were previously unfamiliar to research participants and persuasive treatments that seem difficult to counterargue. In contrast, Millar and Millar (1990) used attitude objects familiar to participants and arguments that seem relatively easy to counterargue. Millar and Millar (1990) found that their counterattitudinal arguments were extensively counterargued, especially when the arguments attacked the basis of the attitude. Thus, if one assumes that the arguments in the Edwards (1990) studies were stronger than those in the Millar and Millar (1990) studies, then increased scrutiny of information that matched the attitudinal base could lead precisely to the results obtained by these researchers. Alternatively, it could be that the elaboration likelihood context was lower in the Edwards (1990) than in the Millar and Millar (1990) studies. If so, matching could have served as a positive cue in the Edwards (1990) research, but affected the extent of processing in the research of Millar and Millar (1990). At present, insufficient data are available to examine the notion that matching messages to the affective or cognitive bases of attitudes can serve in the multiple roles postulated for variables outlined by the ELM. Nevertheless, this seems like a reasonable possibility to examine in future research.

SUMMARY AND CONCLUSIONS

In this chapter, we argued that persuasive appeals that match the functional basis of one's attitude, one's self-schema, one's identity, or the affective–cognitive bases of attitudes might have more in common than is presently realized. That is, each of these treatments involves a self-match—a sense that the message matches the type of person the recipient is (or matches the type of attitude one has). Furthermore, we argued that this self-match could influence persuasion in one of several ways specified by the Elaboration Likelihood Model of persuasion. That is, these matches should serve as peripheral cues when the overall likelihood of thinking is low, bias the ongoing information processing when the likelihood of thinking is high, and determine the extent of information processing activity when the elaboration likelihood is not constrained to be high or low. For some of the matching variables, such as functional matching, there appears to be clear evidence for all three of these roles. For other types of matching, such as affective–cognitive matching, evidence for any of the roles is weak. For still other types of matching, such as self-schema and identity matching, there is clear evidence for some roles but not others. Future research in which the elaboration likelihood is explicitly manipulated along with different kinds of matching variables and argument quality should help to determine whether the integrative framework we offer can account for the diversity of matching variables and effects identified in the literature.

REFERENCES

Abelson, R. P., & Prentice, D. A. (1989). Beliefs as possessions: A functional perspective. In A. R. Pratkanis, S. J. Breckler, & A. G. Greenwald (Eds.), *Attitude structure and function*, (pp. 361–381). Hillsdale, NJ: Lawrence Erlbaum Associates.

Bargh, J. A. (1982). Attention and automaticity in the processing of self-relevant information. *Journal of Personality and Social Psychology, 43*, 425–436.

Baumeister, R. F. (1998). The self. In D. T. Gilbert, S. T. Fiske, & G. Lindzey (Eds.), *The Handbook of Social Psychology* (pp. 680–740). New York: McGraw-Hill.

Bem, D. J. (1972). Self-perception theory. In L. Berkowitz (Ed.), *Advances in experimental social psychology* (Vol. 6, pp. 1–62). New York: Academic Press.

Bizer, G. Y., Wheeler, S. C., & Petty, R. E. (1998, May). Appeals to self-schema as a determinant of elaboration. In R. E. Petty (Chair), *Social determinants and consequences of aspects of the self-concept*. Symposium conducted at the meeting of the American Psychological Society, Washington, DC.

Breckler, S. J. (1984). Empirical validation of affect, behavior, and cognition as distinct components of attitude. Journal of Personality and Social Psychology, 47, 1191–1205.

Brehm, J. W. (1956). Post-decision changes in the desirability of alternatives. Journal of Abnormal and Social Psychology, 52, 384–389.

Cacioppo, J. T., & Petty, R. E. (1982). The need for cognition. *Journal of Personality and Social Psychology, 42*, 116–131.

Cacioppo, J. T. , Petty, R. E., Feinstein, J., & Jarvis, W. B. G. (1996). Dispositional differences in cognitive motivation: The life and times of individuals varying in need for cognition. *Psychological Bulletin, 119*, 197–253.

Cacioppo, J. T., Petty, R. E., & Sidera, J. (1982). The effects of salient self-schema on the evaluation of proattitudinal editorials: Top-down versus bottom-up message processing. *Journal of Experimental Social Psychology, 18*, 324–338.

Chaiken, S. (1987). The heuristic model of persuasion. In M. P. Zanna, J. M. Olson, & C. P. Herman (Ed.), *Social influence: The Ontario symposium* (Vol. 5, pp. 3–39). Hillsdale, NJ: Lawrence Erlbaum Associates.

Chaiken, S., & Maheswaran, D. (1994). Heuristic processing can bias systematic processing: Effects of source credibility, argument ambiguity, and task importance on attitude judgment. *Journal of Personality and Social Psychology, 66*, 460–473.

Chattopadhyay, A., & Letarte, A. (1996). Should advertising appeals match the basis of consumers' attitudes? *Journal of Advertising Research, 36*, 82–89.

Chen, W. K. (1933). The influence of oral propaganda material upon students' attitudes. *Archives of Psychology*, No. 150.

Clary, E. G., Snyder, M., Ridge, R., Miene, P. K., & Haugen, J. A. (1994). Matching messages to motives in persuasion: A functional approach to promoting volunteerism. *Journal of Applied Social Psychology, 24*, 1129–1149.

Crites S. L., Fabrigar, L. R., & Petty, R. E. (1994). Measuring the affective and cognitive properties of attitudes: Conceptual and methodological issues. *Personality & Social Psychology Bulletin, 20*, 619–634.

Deaux, K. (1996) Social identification. In E. T. Higgins & A. W. Kruglanski (Eds.), *Social psychology: Handbook of basic principles*. New York: Guilford Press.

DeBono, K. G. (1987). Investigating the social-adjustive and value-expressive functions of attitudes: Implications for persuasion processes. *Journal of Personality and Social Psychology, 52*, 279–287.

DeBono, K. G., & Harnish, R. J. (1988). Source expertise, source attractiveness, and the processing of persuasive information: A functional approach. *Journal of Personality and Social Psychology, 55*, 541–546.

DeBono, K. G., & Packer, M. (1991). The effects of advertising appeal on perceptions of product quality. *Personality and Social Psychology Bulletin, 17*, 194–200.

DeBono, K. G., & Rubin, K. (1995). Country of origin and perceptions of product quality: An individual difference perspective. *Basic and Applied Social Psychology, 17*, 239–247.

DeBono, K. G., & Telesca, C. (1990). The influence of source physical attractiveness on advertising effectiveness: A functional perspective. *Journal of Applied Social Psychology, 20*, 1383–1395.

Deutsch, M., & Gerard, H. B. (1955). A study of normative and informational social influences upon individual judgment. *Journal of Abnormal and Social Psychology, 51*, 629–636.

Edwards, K. (1990). The interplay of affect and cognition in attitude formation and change. *Journal of Personality and Social Psychology, 59*, 202–216.

Eldersveld, S. J. (1956). Experimental propaganda techniques and voting behavior. *American Political Science Review, 50*, 154–165.

Epstein, S., Pacini, R., Denes-Raj, V., & Heier, H. (1996). Individual differences in intuitive-experiential and analytical-rational thinking styles. Journal of Personality and Social Psychology, 71, 390–405.

Fabrigar, L. R., & Petty, R. E. (1999). The role of affective and cognitive bases of attitudes in susceptibility to affectively and cognitively based persuasion. *Personality and Social Psychology Bulletin, 25*, 363–381.

Feinstein, J. A. (1996). *Need for cognition is more than "they think:" Representation and structure of cognitive activity within the self-concept*. Unpublished doctoral dissertation, Ohio State University, Columbus, OH.

Festinger, L. (1950). Informal social communication. *Psychological Review, 57*, 271-282.

Fleming, M. A., & Petty, R. E. (1997a). [Social identification with ingroup moderates the effectiveness of an ingroup source as a persuasive cue]. Unpublished raw data. Ohio State University, Columbus.

Fleming, M. A., & Petty, R. E. (1997b). [Social identification with ingroup moderates processing of social identity framed persuasive messages]. Unpublished raw data. Ohio State University, Columbus.

Fleming, M. A., & Petty, R. E. (1999). Identity and persuasion: An elaboration likelihood approach. In D. J. Terry & M. A. Hogg (Eds.), *Attitudes, behavior, and social context: The role of norms and group membership* (pp. 171–199). Mahwah, NJ: Lawrence Erlbaum Associates.

Greenwald, A. G., & Albert, R. D. (1968). Acceptance and recall of improvised arguments. *Journal of Personality and Social Psychology, 8*, 31—34.

Haddock, G., & Zanna, M. P. (1993). Predicting prejudicial attitudes: The importance of affect, cognition, and the feeling–belief dimension. *Advances in Consumer Research, 20*, 315–318.

Herek, G.M. (1987). Can functions be measured? A new perspective on the functional approach to attitudes. *Social Psychology Quarterly, 50*, 285–303.

Hogg, M., & Abrams, D. (1993). Towards a single-process uncertainty-reduction model of social motivation in groups. In M. A. Hogg & D. Abrams (Eds.), *Group motivation: Social psychological perspectives* (pp. 173–190). New York: Harvester Wheatsheaf.

Kahneman, D., Knetsch, J., & Thaler, R. (1991). The endowment effect, loss aversion, and status quo bias. *Journal of Economic Perspectives, 5*, 328–338.

Katz, D. (1960). The functional approach to the study of attitudes. *Public Opinion Quarterly, 24*, 163–204.

Kelman, H. C. (1961). Processes of opinion change. *Public Opinion Quarterly, 25*, 57–78.

Kiesler, C. A., Collins, B. E., & Miller, N. (1969). *Attitude change: A critical analysis of theoretical applications*. New York: Wiley.

Knower, F. H. (1935). Experimental studies of change in attitude. I. A study of the effect of oral arguments on changes of attitudes. *Journal of Social Psychology, 6*, 315–347.

Lavine, H., & Snyder, M. (1996). Cognitive processing and the functional matching effect in persuasion: The mediating role of subjective perceptions of message quality. *Journal of Experimental Social Psychology, 32*, 580–604.

Mackie, D. M., Worth, L. T., & Asuncion, A. G. (1990). Processing of persuasive in-group messages. *Journal of Personality and Social Psychology, 58*, 812–822.

Markus, H. (1977). Self-schemata and processing information about the self. *Journal of Personality and Social Psychology, 35*, 63–78.

Matthews, J. (1947). The effect of loaded language on audience comprehension of speeches. *Speech Monographs, 14*, 176–187.

Millar, M. G., & Millar, K. U. (1990). Attitude change as a function of attitude type and argument type. *Journal of Personality and Social Psychology, 59*, 217–228.

Millar, M. G., & Millar, K. U. (1993). Changing breast self-examination attitudes: Influences of repression–sensitization and attitude–message match. *Journal of Research in Personality, 27*, 301–314.

Nuttin, J. M., Jr. (1985). Narcissism beyond Gestalt and awareness: The name letter effect. *European Journal of Social Psychology, 15*, 353–361.

Perloff, R. M., & Brock, T. C. (1980). And thinking makes it so: Cognitive responses to persuasion. In M. Roloff, & G. Miller (Ed.), *Persuasion: New directions in theory and research* (pp. 67–100). Beverly Hills, CA: Sage.

Petty, R. E., & Cacioppo, J. T. (1979). Issue-involvement can increase or decrease persuasion by enhancing message-relevant cognitive responses. *Journal of Personality and Social Psychology, 37*, 1915–1926.

Petty, R. E., & Cacioppo, J. T. (1981). *Attitudes and persuasion: Classic and contemporary approaches*. Dubuque, IA: Wm. C. Brown.

Petty, R. E., & Cacioppo, J. T. (1986). *Communication and persuasion: Central and peripheral routes to attitude change*. New York: Springer-Verlag.

Petty, R. E., Cacioppo, J. T., & Haugtvedt, C. (1992). Involvement and persuasion: An appreciative look at the Sherif's contribution to the study of self-relevance and attitude change. In D. Granberg & G. Sarup (Eds.), *Social judgment and intergroup relations: Essays in honor of Muzafer Sherif* (pp. 147–174). New York: Springer-Verlag.

Petty, R. E., Gleicher, F., & Baker, S. (1991). Multiple roles for affect in persuasion. In J. Forgas (Ed.), *Emotion and social judgments* (pp. 181–200). Oxford: Pergamon.

Petty, R. E., Haugtvedt, C. P., & Smith, S. M. (1995). Elaboration as a determinant of attitude strength. In R. E. Petty & J. A. Krosnick (Eds.), *Attitude strength: Antecedents and consequences* (pp. 93–130). Mahwah, NJ: Lawrence Erlbaum Associates.

Petty, R. E., Schumann, D. W., Richman, S. A., & Strathman, A. J. (1993). Positive mood and persuasion: Different roles for affect under high and low elaboration conditions. *Journal of Personality and Social Psychology, 64,* 5–20.

Petty, R. E., & Wegener, D. T. (1998). Matching versus mismatching attitude functions: Implications for scrutiny of persuasive messages. *Personality and Social Psychology Bulletin, 24,* 227–240.

Petty, R. E., & Wegener, D. T. (1999). The Elaboration Likelihood Model: Current status and controversies. In S. Chaiken & Y. Trope (Eds.), *Dual process models in social psychology* (pp. 41–72). New York: Guilford Press.

Petty, R. E., Wells, G. L., & Brock, T. C. (1976). Distraction can enhance or reduce yielding to propaganda: Thought disruption versus effort justification. *Journal of Personality and Social Psychology, 34,* 874–884.

Prentice, D.A. (1987). Psychological correspondence of possessions, attitudes, and values. *Journal of Personality and Social Psychology, 53,* 993–1003.

Rosenberg, M. J., & Hovland, C. I. (1960). Cognitive, affective, and behavioral components of attitude. In M. Rosenberg, C. Hovland, W. McGuire, R. Abelson, & J. Brehm (Eds.). *Attitude organization and change.* New Haven, CT: Yale University Press.

Shavitt, S. (1989). Operationalizing functional theories of attitude. In A. R. Pratkanis, S. J. Breckler, & A. G. Greenwald (Eds.), *Attitude structure and function,* (pp. 311–338). Hillsdale, NJ: Lawrence Erlbaum Associates.

Shavitt, S. (1990). The role of attitude objects in attitude functions. *Journal of Experimental Social Psychology, 26,* 124–148.

Sherif, M., & Hovland, C. I. (1961) *Social judgment: Assimilation and contrast effects in communication and attitude change.* New Haven, CT: Yale University Press.

Smith, M. B. (1947). The personal setting of public opinions: A study of attitudes toward Russia. *Public Opinion Quarterly, 11,* 507–523.

Smith, M. B., Bruner, J. S., & White, R. W. (1956). *Opinions and personality.* New York: Wiley.

Snyder, M. (1974). The self-monitoring of expressive behavior. *Journal of Personality and Social Psychology, 30,* 526–537.

Snyder, M. (1979). Self-monitoring processes. In L. Berkowitz (Ed.), *Advances in experimental social psychology* (Vol. 12, pp. 86–128). New York: Academic Press.

Snyder, M., & DeBono, K. G. (1985). Appeals to image and claims about quality: Understanding the psychology of advertising. *Journal of Personality and Social Psychology, 49,* 586–597.

Snyder, M., & DeBono, K. G. (1989). Understanding the functions of attitudes: Lessons from personality and social behavior. In A. R. Pratkanis, S. J. Breckler, & A. G. Greenwald (Eds.), *Attitude structure and function* (pp. 361–381). Hillsdale, NJ: Lawrence Erlbaum Associates.

Staats, A. W., & Staats, C. K. (1958). Attitudes established by classical conditioning. *Journal of Abnormal and Social Psychology, 57,* 37–40.

Tajfel, H. (1981). *Human groups and social categories: Studies in social psychology.* Cambridge, England: Cambridge University Press.

Thomsen, C. J., Borgida, E., & Lavine, H. (1995). The causes and consequences of personal involvement. In R. E. Petty & J. A. Krosnick (Eds.), *Attitude strength: Antecedents and consequences* (pp. 191–214). Mahwah, NJ: Lawrence Erlbaum Associates.

Turner, J. C. (1982). Toward a cognitive redefinition of the social group. In H. Tajfel (Ed.), *Social identity and intergroup behavior* (pp. 15–40). Cambridge, England: Cambridge University Press.

Turner, J. C. (1991). *Social influence*. Bristol, England: Open University Press.

Turner, J. C., & Oakes, P. J. (1989). Self-categorization theory and social influence. In P. B. Paulus (Ed.), *The psychology of group influence* (2nd ed.). Hillsdale, NJ: Lawrence Erlbaum Associates.

Wegener, D. T., Downing, J., Krosnick, J. A., & Petty, R. E. (1995). Strength-related properties of attitudes: Measures, manipulations, and future directions. In R. E. Petty and J. A. Krosnick (Eds.), *Attitude strength: Antecedents and consequences* (pp. 455–487). Mahwah, NJ: Lawrence Erlbaum Associates.

Wegener, D. T., Petty, R. E., & Smith, S. M. (1995). Positive mood can increase or decrease message scrutiny: The hedonic contingency view of mood and message processing. *Journal of Personality and Social Psychology, 69,* 5–15.

Weiss, W. (1960). Emotional arousal and attitude change. *Psychological Reports, 6,* 267–280.

Zanna, M. P., & Rempel, J. K. (1988). Attitudes: A new look at an old concept. In D. Bar-Tal & A. W. Kruglanski (Eds.), *The social psychology of knowledge* (pp. 315–334). New York: Cambridge University Press.

6

Involvement and Persuasion: Attitude Functions for the Motivated Processor

Kenneth D. Levin
Diana R. Nichols
Syracuse University

Blair T. Johnson
University of Connecticut

> *Some of the same people who warned me against writing hastily had also cautioned me against going to Everest in the first place. There were many, many fine reasons not to go, but attempting to climb Everest is an intrinsically irrational act—a triumph of desire over sensibility. Any person who would seriously consider it is almost by definition beyond the sway of reasoned argument.*
>
> —from *Into Thin Air*, by Jon Krakauer

As is evident from the research presented in this book, attitudes can serve different functions depending on many factors. Katz (1960) wrote that a basic assumption of functional theorists is that "both attitude formation and attitude change must be understood in terms of the needs they serve and that, as these motivational processes differ, so too will the conditions and techniques for attitude change" (p. 167). According to Katz and other functional theorists (e.g., Shavitt, 1989; Smith, Bruner, & White, 1956;

163

Snyder & DeBono, 1987), attitudes can serve an instrumental function, an ego-defensive function, a value-expressive function, a knowledge function, or a social-adjustive function. Attitudes that serve an instrumental function can be characterized by the motivation to maximize rewards and minimize punishments. Attitudes that serve an ego-defensive function can be characterized by the motivation to protect against internal conflicts and external dangers. Attitudes that serve a value-expressive function can be characterized by the motivation for self-expression and maintaining self-identity. Attitudes that serve a knowledge function can be characterized by a motivation for meaningful cognitive organization. Finally, attitudes that serve a social-adjustive function can be characterized by a motivation to behave in a socially appropriate manner.

The focus of the current chapter is the role of involvement in attitude change. As is developed in this chapter, the current conceptualization of involvement nicely parallels Katz's functional analysis. Depending on how they are involved with an attitude issue, people respond differently to persuasive communications and other attempts to change their attitudes. Individuals who are involved with an attitude issue in a manner similar to the *instrumental* function are motivated to maximize rewards and minimize punishments, and therefore look for positive consequences related to the attitude issue. For example, if Cookie is shopping for a new automobile, she responds to the persuasive appeals of a salesman with the motivation to find the automobile that best suits her needs and will likely evaluate the information in a relatively objective manner. People who are involved with an attitude issue in a manner similar to the *ego-defensive* function or to the *value-expressive function* are motivated to maintain their current attitude in defense of their values and self-concept. For example, a social scientist who reads a newspaper editorial that argues that social science only confirms the obvious likely processes the editorial with a negative bias. Similarly, in the quotation about climbing Mt. Everest, Krakauer (1997) admits that although there were a number of valid reasons not to climb Mt. Everest, reason and sensibility were powerless against desire. Individuals involved with an attitude issue in a manner similar to the *social-adjustive* function are motivated to make a favorable impression. A young man who is meeting his girlfriend's parents for the first time is unlikely to disagree with any position presented by the woman's parents.

A number of different conceptions and operationalizations of involvement have been used over the years, which has led to some problems relating to clarity. Any science experiences conflict to the extent that its members disagree on the theoretical terms and their operationalizations. In the case of involvement and persuasion, however, these difficulties have even led some researchers to question the cumulativeness of the extant research (e.g., B. T. Johnson & Eagly, 1989; Poiesz & de Bont, 1995). Articulating this point, Poiesz and de Bont argued that "the cumulation of knowledge on involvement is hampered by the lack of conceptual clarity, the seemingly uncontrolled application, the overlap with presumed antecedents and consequences, and the unavoidable lack of consistent operationalisations" (p. 448). In this chapter, we present a potential solution to these difficulties. First, we discuss research that suggests that these different traditions can be represented as three different types of involvement. Next, we consider each of the three different types of involvement and discuss the different schools of thought that led to these distinctions, as well as some current research related to these topics. Finally, we discuss what happens when people experience different types of involvement simultaneously and some implications for application of this literature.

THREE TRADITIONS OF INVOLVEMENT, THREE TYPES OF INVOLVEMENT

In order to sift through the different conceptualizations and manipulations of involvement, B. T. Johnson and Eagly (1989) conducted a meta-analysis of the literature that explored the effects of involvement on persuasion. They defined involvement as "a motivational state induced by an association between an activated attitude and the self-concept" and concluded that "across these three traditions of research, the operational definitions of involvement have differed sufficiently to require that three types of involvement be distinguished at a conceptual level" (p. 290). B. T. Johnson and Eagly argued that the different types of involvement associated different aspects of the self-concept with the relevant attitude. This approach to understanding the relationship between individuals and their attitudes complements the assumption of functional theorists that "attitudes could be classified according to the psychological needs they met" (Shavitt, 1989, p. 312).

As B. T. Johnson and Eagly's (1989) definition of involvement and the functional theorists assumption make apparent, it is important to understand individuals' relationships with the attitudes in question in order to change these attitudes. To this end, B. T. Johnson and Eagly labeled three different types of involvement, which differ according to the functions that these attitudes serve and the aspect of the individual's self-concept to which the attitudes relate. They labeled the approach to involvement that stems from research on ego involvement (e.g., M. Sherif & Cantril, 1947; C. W. Sherif, M. Sherif, & Nebergall, 1965) and the relationship between values, attitudes, and the self-concept (e.g., Ostrom & Brock, 1968; Rokeach, 1973) *value-relevant involvement*. According to B. T. Johnson and Eagly, value-relevant involvement refers to "the psychological state that is created by the activation of attitudes that are linked to important values" (p. 290). When individuals are involved with an attitude issue in a value-relevant manner, those attitudes can serve value-expressive or ego-defensive functions. People employ the attitudes as a means of expressing their values or as a means of defending their self-concept. B. T. Johnson and Eagly relabeled the response-involvement tradition, which employed manipulations of the social consequences of the individual's response (e.g., H. H. Johnson & Scileppi, 1969; Zimbardo, 1960), *impression-relevant involvement*. Impression-relevant involvement characterizes the persuasion settings that "make salient to subjects the self-presentational consequences of their post-message positions" (p. 292). When people are involved with an issue in an impression-relevant manner, their attitudes will serve social-adjustive functions. They employ their attitudes as a means of advancing interpersonally oriented goals. B. T. Johnson and Eagly labeled the type of involvement manipulated via the personal relevance of the attitude issue *outcome-relevant involvement*. B. T. Johnson and Eagly suggested that the term outcome-relevant involvement be applied to those manipulations that "make salient to message recipients the relevance of an issue to their currently important goals or outcomes" (p. 292). When people are involved with an issue in an outcome-relevant manner, their attitudes serve an instrumental function. They employ their attitudes as a means of ascertaining which position will benefit them the most.

Consistent with their predictions, B. T. Johnson and Eagly (1989) found that the three types of involvement produced distinctly different patterns of persuasion across the studies in the literature. Consistent with the expectation that value-relevant involvement induces message recipients to defend their opinions, high value-relevant involvement message recipients changed their attitudes less than low involvement recipients, an effect that was reduced somewhat by very strong argumentation (see Fig. 6.1). Consistent with the prediction that outcome-relevant involvement confers a motive to be accurate, high involvement recipients agreed more following strong argumentation than did low involvement participants, an effect that usually reversed when weak arguments were used. In studies that operationalized impression-relevant involvement, high involvement message recipients changed slightly less than low involvement recipients, whether argumentation was strong or weak. The fact that argument quality interacted with outcome-relevant involvement and value-relevant involvement but did not interact with impression-relevant involvement was consistent with B. T. Johnson and Eagly's prediction that this latter form of involvement leads participants to take neutral, more socially defensible postures. Thus, as B. T. Johnson and Eagly discussed, the evidence is consistent with a conception whereby value-relevant involvement is similar to ego-defensive and value-expressive attitude functions, outcome-relevant involvement is similar to instrumental attitude functions, and impression-relevant involvement is similar to social-adjustive functions.

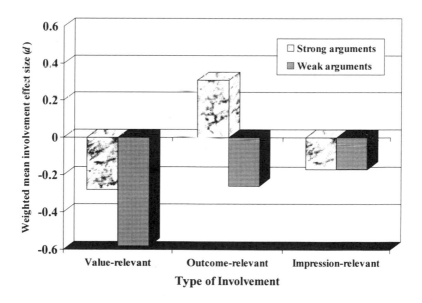

FIG. 6.1. Mean weighted effect sizes (d) by type of involvement and argument quality. Effect sizes gauge the influence of involvement on persuasion. Adapted from B. T. Johnson and Eagly (1989).

It is important to note that not all researchers agree that the three different types of involvement are different motivational states. In opposition to B. T. Johnson and Eagly's (1989) conclusion that outcome-relevant involvement and value-relevant involvement are qualitatively different motivational states, Petty and Cacioppo (1990) argued that B. T. Johnson and Eagly's finding that these two types of involvement interact with argument quality demonstrates that the same process could underlie both value-relevant and outcome-relevant involvement. Furthermore, they argued that B. T. Johnson and Eagly's demonstration of a resistance effect in the case of value-relevant involvement may be due to confounds in the ego-involvement research, rather than to a fundamentally different process. B. T. Johnson and Eagly (1990) responded that the lack of research demonstrating that the possible confounds in the ego-involvement research would lead to resistance effects and the lack of research demonstrating that the underlying processes are the same for the two types of involvement render a single-construct view unable to account for the different persuasion findings. Subsequent research to test whether value-relevant and outcome-relevant involvement are indeed different motivational states has supported B. T. Johnson and Eagly's (1989, 1990) conclusions. Zuwerink and Devine (1996) found that strong, personally important attitudes are more difficult to change than less important attitudes, and that this resistance is due to both affective and cognitive processes. Maio and Olson (1995) found that rather than a negative bias per se, value-relevant involvement is associated with reduced message processing, which can reduce persuasion. Similarly, Marsh, Hart-O'Rourke, and Julka (1997) found no differences in message processing based on personal relevance when participants were evaluating a value-relevant message.

In the rest of this chapter, we consider how various schools of persuasion relate to these types of involvement and consider recent research within each perspective.

VALUE-RELEVANT INVOLVEMENT

M. Sherif and his colleagues explored the role of involvement in persuasion through research within the social judgment–involvement approach (e.g., M. Sherif & Cantril, 1947; M. Sherif & Hovland, 1961; C. W. Sherif et al., 1965). M. Sherif and Cantril conceptualized ego involvement as the extent to which an attitude is attached to an individual's self-concept. They hypothesized that the level of ego involvement affects the strength and intensity of the attitude. Sherif and Cantril argued that "the intensity with which we hold those attitudes formed in relation to social values or those personal attitudes formed in relation to particular surroundings or experiences depends on the degree to which those attitudes are ego-involved" (p. 131). Although this conception of ego involvement was not the first consideration of this topic (see Greenwald, 1982, for a review), their seminal work on the relationship between involvement and persuasion has greatly informed this tradition of research.

According to social judgment–involvement theory, individuals evaluate persuasive messages along their own reference scales. These scales define a latitude of acceptance (the range of positions acceptable to the individual), a latitude of rejection (the range of positions unacceptable to the individual), and a latitude of noncommitment (the range of positions that fall between the latitudes of acceptance and rejection). Individuals' responses to the communication depend on the position of the message relative to their latitudes of acceptance, rejection, and noncommitment. A communication that falls in the latitude of acceptance is likely to be *assimilated*, that is, perceived as being closer to the individual's position than it actually is. A communication that falls in the latitude of rejection, however, is likely to be *contrasted*, that is, perceived as being further from the individual's position than it actually is (M. Sherif & Hovland, 1961). Hovland, Harvey, and Sherif (1957) demonstrated that "when subjects have established attitudes and are personally involved in a controversial social issue, their 'own stand' functions as the major anchorage affecting reaction to and evaluation of communication" (p. 245). Participants who were highly ego involved with an issue exhibited contrast effects in response to a communication that was in their latitude of rejection and assimilation effects in response to a communication that was in their latitude of acceptance. Furthermore, "the more involved and personally committed the individual is on the issue, the greater is the latitude of rejection in relation to the latitude of acceptance, the number of positions on which he remains non-committal approaching zero" (C. W. Sherif et al., 1965, p. 14). These effects led to the longstanding hypothesis that the more involved individuals are with an attitude issue, the less susceptible they are to attitude change.

Social judgment–involvement researchers studying ego-involvement operationalized this variable in a number of different ways. In some studies (e.g., Hovland et al., 1957; M. Sherif & Hovland, 1961), they used the *known groups technique*, in which they recruited members of groups that actively supported a particular stand as high involvement participants and individuals who were not members of these groups as low involvement participants. For example, Hovland et al. used reinstatement of prohibition as the persuasive issue, recruiting members of an active pro-prohibition group as the high involvement participants and individuals who were not active on either side of the issue as low involvement participants. A serious problem with this type of manipulation, however, is that the attitudes of the high and low involvement participants are likely to differ along with their levels of involvement. Consequently, researchers sought operational definitions of involvement that were not susceptible to this confound. Some researchers manipulated involvement by using separate persuasive issues that differed in their level of involvement. For example, Rhine and Severance (1970) used a tuition increase as the high involvement issue and the amount of park acreage that should be developed in Allentown, Pennsylvania, as the low involvement issue. However, it is difficult to find issues that differ in involvement but do not differ in other relevant dimensions (e.g., prior knowledge). As another example, C. W. Sherif, Kelly, Rodgers, Sarup, and Tittler (1973) compared high and low involvement participants by measuring, rather than manipulating, involvement. These researchers operationally defined high involvement as "a latitude of rejection greater than the sum of the frequencies accepted and those not labeled (noncommitment). If the latitude of rejection equaled or was less than the sum of the latitudes of acceptance plus noncommitment, a student was labeled as less involved" (p. 314).

Despite the large variety of operational definitions of ego involvement, researchers were able to find a good deal of empirical support for a number of hypotheses. Specifically, studies have shown that highly involved attitudes are less susceptible to change (C. W. Sherif et al., 1973; C. W. Sherif et al., 1965), that a highly involved person does not differentiate as finely between beliefs as a less involved individual (C. W. Sherif et al., 1973), and that the level of involvement influences the likelihood of action or inaction (C. W. Sherif et al., 1973).

Motivated by the social judgment–involvement approach to persuasion, some researchers began to investigate how attitudes and values relate to an individual's self-concept. In a seminal paper on the topic, Ostrom and Brock (1968) discussed the relationship between attitudes, values, and the self-concept, positing that the basic feature of an ego-involved attitude is its relation to the manner in which the individual defines himself. The individual defines himself primarily in terms of that "distinct constellation of social and personal values" he has acquired. The closer the relation between his attitude and these values and the more central these related values are, the higher the degree of attitudinal involvement. The major consequence of heightened involvement is increased resistance to persuasion. (p. 375)

Ostrom and Brock proposed three determinants of the magnitude of ego involvement: the *centrality* of the values that are related to the attitude, with more central values leading to more involved attitudes; the *relatedness* of the attitude and the values, with more relevant values leading to more involved attitudes; and the *number* of values engaged, with more values activated leading to higher involvement.

Nichols and Johnson (1997) used a technique devised by Ostrom and Brock (1968, 1969) to experimentally manipulate value-relevant involvement through the *centrality* of the values related to the attitude. They asked participants to judge the appropriateness of the relationship between a specified general value and an excerpt from a message that advocated decreased media coverage of terrorist events. At the same time, they instructed participants to draw a line connecting the related ideas in the value and message excerpt. To manipulate levels of involvement, participants judged values determined to be either central (e.g., "keeping promises made to others") or peripheral ("people sticking to their own groups") to the individual's self-concept. Nichols and Johnson expected the central values to induce higher levels of involvement because the link between a central value and an issue may cause an individual to regard the issue as central (Abelson, 1988; Katz, 1960). Following these judgments, participants read either a strong or a weak message from an expert or novice source that advocated decreased media coverage of terrorism; participants then reported their attitudes toward the reduction of media coverage of terrorism. The results revealed main effects for argument quality and message source, such that strong arguments were more persuasive than weak arguments and expert sources were more persuasive than novice sources. Although the main effect of value bonding did not achieve significance, the participants in the central values condition displayed directionally less attitude change than those in the peripheral values condition. The overall effect of involvement in this study ($d = -0.16$) is comparable with that found in Ostrom and Brock's work ($d = -0.22$), and consistent with, although smaller than, that found in B. T. Johnson and Eagly's (1989) meta-analysis of the literature ($d = -0.48$).

Studies by B. T. Johnson, Lin, Symons, Campbell, and Ekstein (1995) and Zuwerink and Devine (1996) have shed further light on the resistance to persuasion facilitated by value-relevant involvement. B. T. Johnson et al. (1995) found that a wider latitude of rejection, which has been used as an indicator of high involvement, led to greater resistance effects in response to a counterattitudinal message and increased persuasion in response to a proattitudinal message. This pattern occurred in response to both strong and weak arguments. Similarly, Zuwerink and Devine found increased resistance to a counterattitudinal message about a personally important attitude issue. Supplementing the research on the cognitive aspects of this resistance, Zuwerink and Devine found evidence that this process is affective as well as cognitive.

Rokeach (1968, 1973) hypothesized a clear relationship between attitudes and self-concept, and argued that changes in either values or attitudes resulted from discrepancies among attitudes, values, and self-concept. According to Rokeach (1973), although attitudes and values are different concepts, they are integrally related and are closely linked to the self. In his framework, an attitude referred to "an organization of several beliefs around a specific object or situation" (p. 18), whereas a value was a more enduring belief about a preferred "mode of conduct or end-state of existence" (p. 5). He argued that values are more central to an individual's personality and have a greater influence on one's cognitive system, thus determining both attitudes and behaviors. Eagly and Chaiken (1995) also discussed the consequences of these relationships in their *domino theory* of attitudinal resistance.

Rokeach's (1973) theory of attitude and value change was, in part, a modification of cognitive dissonance theory (Festinger, 1957). Although dissonance theory posited that attitude change resulted from the discrepancy between two cognitions, Rokeach suggested that attitude change resulted from the discrepancy between one's self-concept, values, and attitudes. He argued that if a value is discrepant from one's self-concept but the related attitude is not, the value changes and the attitude remains the same. In some of his experimental work, Rokeach found that when attitudes and values were consistent with each other (e.g., low value for equality and an attitude against civil rights) but inconsistent with the individual's self-concept (e.g., self as a tolerant and fair-minded person), both the attitude and the value changed to align more closely with the self-concept. However, this effect only occurred when people were made aware of the discrepancy through a *value-confrontation approach*. These changes endured for as long as 1 year after the experimental manipulation. Subsequent research has replicated these results (Kristiansen & Hotte, 1996).

If values and attitudes are indeed related and organized into a system that is coherent to the individual holding them, that system can be described as either an open or a closed system (Rokeach, 1960). An open belief system, according to Rokeach, is characterized by a wider acceptance of ideas and people, along with the evaluation of information on its own merits, with little regard to its source. A closed or dogmatic belief system, on the other hand, is associated with "an intolerance toward those with opposing beliefs, and a sufferance of those with similar beliefs" (p. 5). Furthermore, Rokeach suggested that a closed belief system often combines information about the environment with information about the source, which leads to relatively uncritical acceptance of claims made by authority figures. Rokeach's dogmatism scale (Rokeach, 1960; Rokeach & Fruchter, 1956) operationalizes these aspects of open and closed belief systems, with higher scores on the scale indicating a more dogmatic, closed system. Individual differences in the degree of openness of a belief system point to some interesting implications for the general process of value-relevant involvement.

Rokeach (1960) suggested that people who score high in dogmatism "betray more difficulty than open persons in synthesizing or integrating new beliefs into a new system" (p. 196). When new ideas are presented to people with closed systems, they are likely either to reject the new information outright or to fail to remember it because it does not fit within their system. Other work has found support for the idea that people who rank high in dogmatism are less likely to change their current beliefs. Davies (1993) suggested that those with high dogmatism ratings "tend to avoid inconsistency in their attitude and belief systems" (p. 692) by selectively forgetting, ignoring, or minimizing new information that goes against their beliefs. Davies' work, using a shortened form of Rokeach's dogmatism scale (Troldahl & Powell, 1965), found that highly dogmatic individuals were more likely to persist in holding beliefs that had been directly discredited. Consistent with the idea that dogmatism interferes with cognitive reintegration, other research has shown that highly dogmatic people (a) are less persuaded than low dogmatic people even when outcome-relevant involvement is high (B. T. Johnson & Nichols, 1997) and (b) are less objective, as reflected in responses to argument quality manipulations (DeBono & Klein, 1993; Johnson &

Nichols). In DeBono and Klein's research, people high in dogmatism used argument quality in evaluating messages only when the source was nonexpert; when the source was an expert, highly dogmatic people were equally persuaded by strong and weak arguments. This pattern indicates that highly dogmatic people are accepting of information that comes from of credible sources, regardless of the quality the information, but more objective when they receive information from a less credible source.

It is interesting to note that some research posits that people ranked high in dogmatism are actually *more* open to change than people low in dogmatism. Hunter, Levine, and Sayers (1976) highlighted the difference between dogmatism and rigidity, pointing out that when new information is consistent with the previously held beliefs of a person high in dogmatism, that person is more likely to quickly accept the new information. Slater and Rouner (1996) found that "the amount of value extremity...predicted greater message-relevant responses when the message was congruent with recipient values but not when it was discrepant with those values" (p. 227). This demonstration that highly dogmatic individuals are more open to proattitudinal information complements the work on dogmatism that has demonstrated that highly dogmatic individuals are more resistant to counterattitudinal information.

To summarize what is known about value-relevant involvement, the studies to date indicate that when an attitude issue is strongly linked to an individual's values—when the attitude is serving an ego-defensive or a value-expressive function—the individual is more resistant to a counterattitudinal message and more receptive to a proattitudinal message. Despite these fairly robust conclusions, value-relevant involvement has proven to be one of the more difficult independent variables to manipulate in the laboratory. As a result of this difficulty, much of the research exploring the effects of value-relevant involvement has operationalized value-relevant involvement by taking advantage of individual differences. Although operationalizing value-relevant involvement through these individual differences has allowed researchers to make a number of conclusions about the effects of value-relevant involvement, these individual differences have also raised concerns about confounds. Further investigation of experimental manipulations of value-relevant involvement is essential for the progress of this line of research.

Another important area for further exploration is the relationship between value-relevant involvement and attitude–behavior relations. Boninger, Krosnick, and Berent (1995) demonstrated that value relevance is an important determinant of attitude strength. Attitude strength, in turn, has been identified as an important moderator of attitude–behavior relations (see Petty & Krosnick, 1995). Similarly, attitude importance has proven to be an effective moderator of attitude–behavior relations (Krosnick, 1988). Taking a more functional perspective, Maio and Olson (1994, 1995) found support for the hypothesis that attitudes serving a value-expressive function are significantly more related to values than are attitudes serving an instrumental function. Furthermore, Maio and Olson found that values were a distinct predictor of behavioral intentions for participants whose attitudes were serving a value-expressive function but not for participants whose attitudes were serving an instrumental function. These links between value relevance and attitude–behavior relations, combined with C. W. Sherif et al.'s (1973) finding that the level of involvement affects the likelihood of action or inaction, highlight an area ripe for new research on attitude–behavior relations. These studies indicate that there is a relationship between value-relevant involvement and behavior; however, few studies have examined the direct link between this type of involvement and attitude–behavior relations.

IMPRESSION-RELEVANT INVOLVEMENT

Although much early work investigating the role of involvement in attitude change explored the relationship between attitudes, values, and self-concept, Zimbardo (1960) produced a different conceptualization of involvement. He defined involvement as "the individual's concern with the consequences of his *response* or with the instrumental meaning of his opinion" (p. 87). Zimbardo conducted an experiment to test the utility of a social-judgment interpretation of involvement effects against a cognitive dissonance interpretation of these effects. He informed high involvement participants that their responses to the issue, which was evaluation of juvenile delinquency cases, were indicative of their basic values, and he informed low involvement participants that their responses conveyed very little information about their character or values. Zimbardo theorized that if a communicator who was both attractive and credible presented a position that was far from a participant's attitude on a highly involving issue, this conflict would induce cognitive dissonance (Festinger, 1957) and motivate attitude change. He reasoned that participants would be unable to reduce dissonance by derogating the communicator because the communicator was both attractive and credible. The discrepancy between the communicator's attitude and the participant's attitude was too large for the participant to reduce dissonance by minimizing the experience of the discrepancy, and therefore, he reasoned, the participant would reduce dissonance by changing his or her attitudes. Zimbardo found the most attitude change when participants were highly involved and the position of the communicator was most discrepant from their own view.

This study was important for a number of reasons. First, until this study, researchers generally expected that involvement leads to reduced persuasion, whereas this study produced an opposite result. Second, this manipulation was qualitatively different from previous manipulations in that it was a manipulation of contextual information rather than a manipulation of the message or a measure of subject characteristics. This operationalization of involvement enabled Zimbardo (1960) to avoid many of the problems associated with manipulations of ego involvement that we mentioned in the previous section.

Researchers have used a number of different operationalizations to explore the effects of impression-relevant involvement on message processing. In another involvement manipulation that differed from the traditional manipulations of ego involvement, H. H. Johnson and Scileppi (1969) informed low involvement participants that their opinions were not relevant to the experiment and high involvement participants that the experiment was concerned with "the ability of high school students to make sound and intelligent judgments to materials used in public communications." (p. 32)[1] Crossing this involvement manipulation with manipulations of source credibility and argument plausibility, H. H. Johnson and Scileppi found less attitude change under high involvement than low involvement, and an interaction between involvement and source credibility such that the increased persuasiveness of a high credibility source was not nearly as strong under conditions of high involvement.

Using a different manipulation of response involvement, Leippe and Elkin (1987) instructed high response involvement participants that following the message, each participant would meet with another student and discuss the issue, and then be interviewed by a professor. They found that although response involvement facilitated processing, participants who were response involved but not issue involved were unaffected by

---

[1]It is important to note that although this study is discussed with research on response involvement and we label H. H. Johnson & Scileppi's (1969) manipulation "impression-relevant involvement," Johnson and Scileppi considered this a manipulation of ego involvement.

argument quality and displayed fairly neutral attitudes. Although they processed the message at a deeper level than did the participants who were neither response nor issue involved, Leippe and Elkin's response-involved participants' message processing was geared more toward ensuring a favorable impression than ascertaining the correct position on the issue. These participants' responses on a private behavioral measure were also unaffected by argument quality.

Investigating a similar issue, Chen, Shechter, and Chaiken (1996) conducted two studies in which they used two different operationalizations to explore the effects of accuracy-motivated versus impression-motivated message processing. In the first experiment, they used the well-known personality variable *self-monitoring* (Snyder, 1987) as a proxy for accuracy motivation versus impression motivation. Following from the logic that high self-monitors regulate their behavior according to what is appropriate in the social situation, whereas low self-monitors regulate their behavior according to their values and personality, Chen et al. argued that high self-monitors would be impression motivated, whereas low self-monitors would be accuracy motivated. Chen et al. found support for the prediction that high self-monitors would more readily agree with the position of a fictitious discussion partner. Impression-motivated participants also reported more thoughts about the partner than did accuracy-motivated participants. To replicate these results, Chen et al. conducted a second experiment in which they manipulated accuracy and impression-motivation using a priming task. By having participants imagine various scenarios in a seemingly unrelated task, Chen et al. made either accuracy concerns or impression concerns more salient. Their results supported the hypothesis that impression-motivated participants engaged in systematic processing that was biased by their partner's attitudes, whereas accuracy-motivated participants engaged in relatively unbiased systematic processing.

In a review relevant to impression-relevant involvement, Cialdini and Petty (1981) discussed a number of reasons that individuals often shift their opinion toward the position advocated by the communicator when they anticipate a persuasive message. Cialdini and Petty argued that

the middle is advantageous—no matter what the opponent's position—for someone wishing to be viewed as an able discussant, because defensive arguments can be selected from both sides of the issue without the appearance of inconsistency. Further, a moderate stance is usually associated with broad-mindedness—an ideal trait to project in an exchange if one is interested in conveying a favorable impression. Finally, if one wishes to assess the validity of anticipated information in an unbiased fashion, a neutral stance affords just such an opportunity. (p. 228)

When people are faced with a situation in which they may have to answer for their attitude judgments, they will often move toward a position that they can successfully defend in order to maintain a favorable impression. Similarly, if another individual yielded to their persuasion attempt on a different topic, participants are even more likely to reciprocate and yield to the other individual on a different topic (Cialdini, Green, & Rusch, 1992).

Although shifting opinion toward the communicator of the anticipated persuasive message is a robust phenomenon, researchers have argued that these shifts are elastic (Cialdini, Levy, Herman, Kozlowski, & Petty, 1976; Cialdini & Petty, 1981; B. T. Johnson, Symons, & Newman, 1991). As soon as the anticipated discussion is canceled, participants tend to revert to their original positions. This pattern suggests that the attitudes participants report are functionally social adjustive. Despite the implication that these measures do not tap into participants' true attitudes, Cialdini and Petty have argued, and the authors of this chapter agree, that this line of research is still important. Arguably, the occasions in which individuals present attitudes for a social-adjustive function occur frequently, and therefore, among other implications, it is extremely important for researchers to explore the role that impression-relevant involvement plays in attitude–behavior relations (see B. T. Johnson et al., 1991; Leippe & Elkin, 1987).

To summize what is known about impression-relevant involvement, when individuals are motivated to convey a favorable impression, they respond to persuasive messages by processing the messages systematically but displaying fairly neutral attitudes. These attitudes, which serve a social-adjustive function, enable them to convey the seemingly desirable quality of neutrality. These attitude shifts toward the center are fairly elastic and appear to last only as long as the impression motive is present. Few studies that explore the role of impression-relevant involvement as a moderator of attitude-behavior relations are available, which suggests that it is important for future research to explore this issue.

OUTCOME-RELEVANT INVOLVEMENT

Still other scholars have conceptualized involvement as a determinant of the nature and extent of message processing. Persuasion researchers (e.g.,

Greenwald, 1968; Janis & King, 1954) have long believed that receiving persuasive messages is an active rather than a passive process (see also Killeya & Johnson, 1998). In many cases, people actively process the messages and generate cognitions and arguments for or against the proposed message position. According to contemporary dual-process models of persuasion (e.g., Petty & Cacioppo, 1986; Chaiken, 1987), persuasive messages are processed in two different ways: One mode of processing involves responding to the content of a persuasive message and generating arguments and cognitions about the attitude object. Eagly and Chaiken (1993) defined *systematic processing* as "a comprehensive, analytic orientation to information processing in which perceivers access and scrutinize a great deal of information for its relevance to their judgment task" (p. 326), which is very similar to the *central route* in Petty and Cacioppo's (1986) elaboration likelihood model (ELM). The other mode of processing, referred to as the *peripheral route* in the ELM or *heuristic processing* in Chaiken's (1987) heuristic–systematic model (HSM), involves responding to cues that surround the message or the activation of learned cognitive heuristics about the cues or the message.[2]

Petty and Cacioppo (1986) argued that involvement moderates attitude change by affecting participants' motivation to process messages with high elaboration. As involvement increases, people should be more motivated to expend cognitive effort and process messages through the central route. This message processing involves the generation of cognitions in response to the arguments. These cognitions can be arguments in favor of the issue, counterarguments against the message, or other cognitive responses related to the message or the message topic. Following from this logic, attitudes formed or changed under high involvement conditions should be more predictive of behavior and more resistant to counterpersuasion than attitudes formed or changed under low involvement conditions.

Chaiken and her colleagues (Chaiken, Liberman, & Eagly, 1989; Eagly & Chaiken, 1993; Maheswaran & Chaiken, 1991) have theorized that the motivation to process a message heuristically or systematically is based on the *sufficiency principle,* which holds that receivers of persuasive messages desire a certain level of confidence in their decisions about the

---

[2]Although heuristic processing and peripheral route processing are discussed together in this chapter, there are qualitative differences between these processes. Readers interested in more information about the ELM or HSM should consult Petty and Cacioppo (1986) or Chaiken, Liberman, and Eagly (1989).

attitude object. This principle is based on the idea that people are "cognitive misers" (Taylor & Fiske, 1978); once confidence reaches this level (labeled the *sufficiency threshold*), people will not expend any more cognitive effort processing the message. If their actual level of confidence is lower than the sufficiency threshold, they will be motivated to process the information systematically in order to increase their confidence in their attitude. When their actual level of confidence is at or above the sufficiency threshold, they will not be motivated to process the message systematically and they will therefore process the message through less effortful heuristic processing. Chaiken et al. proposed the following role for involvement in determining the extent of message processing:

> Its motivating effect on systematic processing can be understood by assuming that increased personal relevance enhances recipients' desires to attain valid attitudes. Because they should therefore aspire to attain greater confidence in their assessment of message validity, their sufficiency thresholds should be higher on the judgmental confidence continuum. Because the likelihood that recipients will attain their sufficiency thresholds via heuristic processing decreases as these thresholds increase, recipients who encounter personally relevant messages should generally exhibit heightened levels of systematic processing. (p. 223)

Researchers exploring the effects of involvement on persuasion through these approaches have generally used a manipulation of involvement similar to one originally employed by Apsler and Sears (1968). In their study, high involvement participants learned that a proposal to replace professors with supervised teaching assistants would go into effect in the near future, whereas low involvement participants learned that the proposal would become valid in 10 years. In a variation of this type of manipulation, Petty and Cacioppo (1979, Experiment 2) told high involvement participants that a proposal to require students to pass a comprehensive examination in order to graduate was being considered at their own university and low involvement participants that the proposal was being considered at a distant university. This model of manipulating involvement has become quite popular not only among Petty, Cacioppo, and their colleagues (e.g., Petty & Cacioppo, 1981, 1984; Petty, Cacioppo, & Goldman, 1981; Petty, Cacioppo, & Heesacker, 1981), but also among other investigators (e.g., Axsom, Yates, & Chaiken, 1987; Burnkrant & Howard, 1984; B. T. Johnson, 1994; Killeya & Johnson, 1998; Leippe & Elkin, 1987; Schul & Knapp, 1984; Sorrentino, Bobocel, Gitta, Olson, & Hewitt, 1988). Consistent with predictions generated from the ELM (Petty & Cacioppo, 1986) and the HSM (Chaiken et al., 1989), B. T. Johnson and

Eagly (1989) found that argument quality was a significant moderator of the relationship between outcome-relevant involvement and persuasion, such that with strong arguments, higher involvement led to greater persuasion. Although the pattern was not as strong, they found that with weak arguments, high involvement tended to lead to less persuasion. Levin, Johnson, and Turco (1997) confirmed this pattern in a meta-analysis that examined the effects of argument quality on persuasion. This meta-analytic database included a broader set of studies and directly examined argument quality effect sizes, which allows a more specific test of the hypothesis that the argument quality effect is larger under conditions of high outcome-relevant involvement. The argument quality effect was significantly smaller in value-relevant involvement studies and did not occur at all in impression-relevant involvement studies, which suggests that outcome-relevant involvement can be characterized by more message elaboration. A more comprehensive examination of the variables that moderate the relationship between argument quality and persuasion would be a useful contribution to the literature.

Studying the effects of outcome-relevant involvement has helped to illuminate other issues related to attitudes. For example, outcome-relevant involvement has proven to be an effective moderator of attitude–behavior relations (Sivacek & Crano, 1982). In two experiments, Sivacek and Crano found that vested interest, which is similar to outcome-relevant involvement, is a successful moderator of attitude–behavior relations. In the first experiment, the relevant issue was a proposal to raise the drinking age. The participants who were younger than the proposed drinking age were considered high vested interest and the participants who were older than the proposed drinking age were considered low vested interest. Sivacek and Crano found that the participants in the high vested interest condition were significantly more likely to engage in behavior attempting to prevent the proposed change. In the second experiment, they replicated these results using comprehensive examinations as the persuasive issue. Those participants who felt that the exams would affect them were more willing to take action to prevent the implementation of the exams.

Complications Regarding Outcome-Relevant Involvement

Although the relationship between outcome-relevant involvement and persuasion is a robust phenomenon, a number of issues complicate the effects of outcome-relevant involvement on persuasion, including the nature of argument quality, biased systematic processing, and prior information about the proposal.

The Nature of Argument Quality.   Although most persuasion re-searchers state with confidence that argument quality is a central con-struct in involvement research, there is little agreement about the nature of the construct (cf. Areni & Lutz, 1988; Eagly & Chaiken, 1993). Typically, strong arguments have been empirically defined as arguments that elicit favorable cognitions and weak arguments have been empiri-cally defined as arguments that elicit primarily unfavorable cognitions (Petty & Cacioppo, 1986). However, there has been little investigation of the characteristics of an argument that make it strong or weak. To address this concern, B. T. Johnson, Levin, and Killeya (1997) conducted a series of experiments and found evidence that argument quality is highly related to argument valence, the extent to which the consequences engendered by an argument are good or bad. Following the logic of Fishbein and Ajzen's (1975, 1981) *expectancy-value* formulation, B. T. Johnson et al. (1997) theorized that messages are differentially persuasive depending on the valence of the arguments and the likelihood that the arguments are true. Johnson et al. (1997) conducted an initial study to examine the relationships between perceived argument strength, argu-ment valence in terms of perceived consequences for the message recipi-ent, and the perceived likelihood that the argument is actually true. In the first study, they had participants rate a series of arguments on one of these three dimensions (all arguments from Petty & Cacioppo, 1986). Confirming the findings of Areni and Lutz (1988), they found that the best predictor of argument strength was argument valence ($r_{RANK} = .81$); ratings of likelihood were unrelated to ratings of argument strength ($r_{RANK} = -.01$).

B. T. Johnson et al. (1997) then experimentally tested the expectancy-value hypothesis. Based on the argument ratings from the first study, they selected arguments that varied in valence and likelihood. For example, an argument that was both good and likely is that prestigious universities have comprehensive exams to maintain academic excellence (a likely reason to have comprehensive exams and a positive consequence—aca-demic excellence). An argument that was good but unlikely is that schools with comprehensive exams attract larger and more well-known corpora-tions to recruit students for jobs (a positive outcome—more well-known corporations recruiting students for jobs—but unlikely to be related to comprehensive exams). An argument that was bad but likely is that the difficulty of the exams would prepare one for later competitions in life (highlighting the difficulty of the exams makes a negative consequence of the exams salient, and this also seemed likely to the participants). An argument that was both bad and unlikely is that the risk of failing the exam is a challenge that most students would welcome (the risk of failing the exam is a negative consequence and it is unlikely that many students would welcome this risk). If attitudes are based on the sum of the products of beliefs and evaluations, individuals should agree the most with arguments that both are extremely likely and have positive consequences, and agree the least with unlikely, negative arguments. They should agree with likely arguments that are low in valence more than unlikely arguments that are low in valence because even the negative arguments mention an outcome that is ultimately positive, and therefore may be persuasive to some individuals, if they are likely to be true. Participants should disagree with arguments that are unlikely, whether the information has positive or negative implications. Employing a 2 (Argument valence: positive vs. negative) x 2 (Argument likelihood: likely vs. unlikely) design, they found that arguments that were positive in valence but not particularly likely were just as persuasive as arguments that were both good and likely, suggesting a "wishful thinking" effect. A third study confirmed these results and determined that they persist even in the face of high outcome-relevant involvement.

It is useful to consider these data in the context of outcome-relevant involvement. Outcome-relevant involvement includes the cases in which the individual is tied to the attitude through the outcome of the issue. Regarding comprehensive examinations, students who face the possibility of taking them have a number of outcomes to consider. First, approval of the policy could mean more work for the students. Therefore, in order to persuade the average participant that comprehensive exams are a good thing, they must be tied to good outcomes (i.e., be represented by positive valence). However, it is still unclear why the likelihood that the arguments were true did not play a more prominent role. Therefore, B. T. Johnson et al.'s (1997) results suggest that outcome-relevant involvement does not necessarily confer objectivity. Further exploration of the characteristics that determine whether arguments are strong or weak, and the conditions under which likelihood is important, is needed to gain a better understanding of this issue.

Biased Systematic Processing.   Even when people have high out-come-relevant involvement and therefore are motivated to process a message systematically in the service of an accuracy goal, people are often unable to avoid biased processing. Recent research has demon-strated that even under conditions of high outcome-relevant involve-ment, participants' message processing can be biased by directions to focus on either positive or negative thoughts regarding the message. Employing a 3 (Positive vs. negative vs. undirected cognitive response condition) X 2 (High vs. low outcome-relevant involvement) X 2 (Strong vs. weak arguments) design, Killeya and Johnson (1998) found that positively biased systematic processing increased persuasion (mir-roring the high involvement/strong argument condition) and nega-tively biased systematic processing reduced persuasion (mirroring the high involvement/weak argument condition). Killeya and Johnson concluded that "the incidental effects of directed thought were not undermined by increasing message elaboration. This finding is pro-vocative in that outcome-relevant involvement has been thought to promote relatively open-minded, accurate, message processing" (p. 31). Apparently, outcome-relevant involvement is easily disrupted by com-peting goals.

A study conducted by Liberman and Chaiken (1992) further bolsters the conclusion that competing goals can inhibit the relatively unbiased processing that should be motivated by outcome-relevant involvement. These researchers demonstrated that individuals defensively processed a personally relevant message that linked coffee drinking to a health threat. Employing a 2 (Personal relevance: high vs. low) X 2 (Message threat: high vs. low) design, Liberman and Chaiken (1992) found that although high personal relevance increased systematic processing, the processing was negatively biased when the message was threatening. In particular, participants who drank at least two cups of coffee each day defensively processed the message, whereas those participants who did not drink coffee were more likely to accept the message.

Prior Information.   There has also been evidence that demonstrates that receiving information about an attitude issue prior to receiving a persuasive message can reduce the amount of systematic processing, even under high outcome-relevant involvement (B. T. Johnson, 1994). Johnson found that prior information reduced high involvement partici-pants' motivation to process the message systematically because the prior

knowledge satisfied their need for information. Although high involvement would have motivated them to desire more information about the
issue, the information that participants received prior to the persuasive
message enabled them to make their attitude judgments without extensively processing the message. B. T. Johnson's (1994) involvement manipulation produced relatively unbiased systematic processing only when
the participants did not receive prior information.

Further complicating interpretations of outcome-relevant involvement, Liberman and Chaiken (1996) presented evidence that not only do
people respond differently to persuasive messages depending on whether
the issue is personally relevant, but also that high relevance attitudes and
low relevance attitudes evaluate different attitude objects. According to
this logic, students who read a message about comprehensive examinations at their own university are evaluating whether it is good or bad for
them to take comprehensive exams, whereas students who read about the
possibility of comprehensive exams at another university are evaluating
whether comprehensive exams are good or bad *in general*. Liberman and
Chaiken argued that this difference represents a potential violation of
Fishbein and Ajzen's (1974) *specificity principle*. Although it is unlikely
that these conclusions undermine the research on outcome-relevant involvement in a manner that negates previous conclusions, future research
looking at differences based on manipulations of this type should consider
how the difference in attitudes between high and low outcome-relevant
involvement participants may have impacted their results.

Summary of Outcome-Relevant Involvement

It is clear from the results presented here that outcome-relevant involvement is a complex variable. Although being involved with an attitude
issue in an outcome-relevant manner generally motivates a deeper level
of relatively unbiased processing in the service of accuracy, enabling the
attitude to serve an instrumental function, these goals can be thwarted by
a number of factors. Characteristics of the persuasion setting that may
bias processing (e.g., competing motives) can seriously undermine these
effects. Similarly, the amount of information that an individual may
receive before presentation of the actual message can serve to undermine
the motivating effects of outcome-relevant involvement. Further research
specifying the situations in which these factors play a role in persuasion
would be a nice addition to the literature.

WHEN WORLDS COLLIDE:
MULTIPLE MOTIVES OPERATING SIMULTANEOUSLY

Any consideration of the motivational bases of cognition cannot ignore the evidence that people often experience multiple motives simultaneously (see Kunda, 1990). There are situations in which individuals may experience an accuracy motive and a directional bias at the same time. For example, students who read about the possibility of a tuition increase at their university will likely experience these conflicting motives. Although they are presumably motivated to ascertain what will help them obtain the best educational experience (accuracy motive), most students will naturally be biased against the idea of paying more tuition (defense motive).

Practically speaking, the further one moves from the controlled confines of the laboratory, the less likely it is that only one type of involvement will be operating. Many real-world persuasion situations that involve outcome-relevant issues may also involve impression-relevant motivations. Similarly, many attitude issues that are relevant to an individual's values may also activate outcome-relevant involvement, and individuals may present value-relevant attitudes in impression-relevant settings. These possibilities highlight the need to consider how the different types of involvement interact. Leippe (1991; Leippe & Elkin, 1987) has argued that in situations in which outcome-relevant involvement and impression-relevant involvement are activated simultaneously, people engage in systematic processing, but do not respond to argument quality as strongly as people who are only experiencing outcome-relevant involvement. This argument parallels the earlier analysis concluding that the unbiased processing often motivated by outcome-relevant involvement is easily undermined by competing motives. Further research exploring the interaction of the different forms of involvement could be valuable.

Researchers who have explored the functions of different types of attitudes have also observed these potential motivational conflicts (e.g., Tetlock, 1989). Political attitudes are an excellent example of attitudes that may serve multiple functions at the same time. An individual's political attitudes can serve a value-expressive function ("I do not like Senator Y because he is dishonest") or an instrumental function ("I like Senator Y because he is trying to lower my taxes"). Which of these functions is served can depend on whether value relevance or outcome relevance is more salient. Political candidates whose apparent values conflict with those of their potential constituents would benefit from focusing their campaign on issues relevant to the instrumental function, whereas candidates whose policy agendas may conflict with those of their potential constituencies could benefit from focusing their campaigns on issues relevant to the value-expressive function. As noted in the following, however, application of these theoretical considerations to the world outside of the laboratory can lead to a number of complications.

APPLIED CONSIDERATIONS REGARDING INVOLVEMENT

The results reviewed in this chapter underscore the conclusion that it is important to consider involvement in order to understand message-based persuasion. It is not unusual in message-based persuasion settings for would-be persuaders to misjudge the type of involvement that is facilitated or the attitude functions involved. In fact, this problem even occurs in published persuasion research. In a study testing the utility of the elaboration likelihood model in getting school officials to accept the recommendations of psychoeducational reports, Andrews and Gutkin (1994) manipulated involvement by telling participants, who were students training to be teachers, that they would have to summarize the recommendations of the report in a presentation in front of an educational psychology professor. These researchers were surprised that they did not find differences in persuasion based on either argument quality or source credibility. However, these results are much less surprising if one interprets their manipulation as tapping impression-relevant involvement rather than outcome-relevant involvement. As drawn out earlier in the chapter, outcome-relevant involvement often leads to an increase in unbiased systematic processing, whereas impression-relevant involvement generally leads participants to adopt socially adaptive, often middle-of-the-road, positions. The participants in this study were most likely motivated to convey competence and strength to the professor. Although this goal has the potential to motivate more systematic processing, a more effective tactic to induce change is to increase the salience of what is best for the child. For example, emphasizing that the teacher's judgment has important implications for the success or failure in dealing with the relevant child will likely be more effective. Andrews and Gutkin's manipulation of involvement likely focused participants' attention on their social selves rather than the subject of the message.

Researchers and practitioners may be able to take a lesson from the difficulties confronted in manipulating involvement over the course of this research. Although direct manipulations of involvement have become the cleanest way to test causal relationships and get a handle on the effects of involvement, the instances in which involvement can be manipulated in applied settings may be limited. The attitude issues that researchers and practitioners in applied settings handle may carry with them types of involvement that are relatively unchangeable. For example, parents who wish to convince their teenagers to avoid using alcohol or to practice sexual abstinence or safer sex may be most comfortable when their children approach their message with a high level of outcome-relevant involvement. However, when considering the postmessage effects of this type of situation, they must take into account the impression-relevant involvement that may be inherent in teenage social settings. If parents take this issue into account, and focus their discussion so that both types of involvement are considered, their chances for success should increase. Based on research indicating that functionally relevant messages are more persuasive (e.g., DeBono, 1987), parents should address both instrumental and social-adjustive aspects of the issue.

Individuals in other applied persuasion settings can also take a lesson from this research. There has been research demonstrating that outcome-relevant involvement can moderate the way in which people process stereotype disconfirming information (Johnston & Coolen, 1995). In a series of experiments, Johnston and Coolen found that under low involvement, stereotype-based judgments were influenced by source credibility. Essentially, the message was enhanced by a high credibility source. Under high involvement, however, message cues influenced stereotypic judgments, whereas source cues did not. These results have some very provocative implications. There are a number of situations in which people encounter stereotype disconfirming information; however, it is often not processed deeply or as disconfirming. The implications of this research are that if involvement is increased, stereotype disconfirming information may be processed at a deeper level and be more effective at reducing prejudice.

Practitioners who wish to take advantage of involvement should be wary, however. For example, politicians who may be inclined to appeal to potential voters' values are taking a risk (see Garst & Bodenhausen, 1996). Assuming they are successful in activating a high level of value-relevant involvement, they run the risk of failing to persuade those who do not perceive their values as the same, especially if they are presenting a counterattitudinal message. They may fare better if they focus on the outcome relevance of their particular race. Although demonstrations of how their values match the voters' values better than their opponents' values may be effective at wooing some voters, emphasis on how the voters will gain more (or lose less) by electing them rather than their opponents may be more successful. Focusing participants' election-relevant thinking on the consequences of the election may be the best tactic. Similarly, individuals making use of these principles to market products should be aware of the type of involvement. Advertisements that appear in low involvement settings should include a larger dose of heuristic and peripheral cues, rather than expecting much message processing from their targets. Marketing attempts to induce involvement generally are most effective when aiming for outcome-relevant involvement. When the targets are focused on what they have to gain or lose through the product, they will be most likely to pay attention to the message and evaluate the product on those grounds. Along the same lines, social marketing practitioners who design messages intended to prevent risky sexual behavior face problems regarding attitude functions and involvement. In order to facilitate behavior change, outcome-relevant involvement appears to be the ideal motivational state. However, people who have previously engaged in risky behavior may be inclined to process the message defensively. Compounding this difficulty, impression-relevant involvement may be inherent in most risky sexual situations.

CONCLUSION

Research on involvement has certainly progressed a great deal since its inception. It has grown from a single construct helping to explain resistance to persuasion to multiple constructs that moderate the effects of a persuasive message. It has also been invaluable in helping researchers understand what mediates a person's reaction to a message. However, it is clear from reviewing this literature that there are still a number of avenues that need to be explored in future research.

The research on involvement should serve as a tremendous asset for individuals who seek a better understanding of the variables that influence message processing and persuasion. Understanding that (a) outcome-relevant involvement generally leads to relatively objective, unbiased message processing, (b) value-relevant involvement leads to biased or reduced message processing, and (c) impression-relevant involvement leads to social information processing should help researchers and practitioners both to understand better how to motivate the type of processing that best suits their needs and to understand why persuasion attempts often fail. It is essential to understand the motivation that accompanies the attitude issue and the context in which the message and response are delivered. Understanding these variables, as well as the specific functions that an attitude may serve, is invaluable in understanding this process.

ACKNOWLEDGMENT

The preparation of this manuscript was facilitated by National Institutes of Health grant K21-MH01377 to Blair T. Johnson.

REFERENCES

Abelson, R. P. (1988). Conviction. *American Psychologist, 43*, 267–275.

Andrews, L. W., & Gutkin, T. B. (1994). Influencing attitudes regarding special class placement using a psychoeducational report: An investigation of the elaboration likelihood model. *Journal of School Psychology, 32*, 321–337.

Apsler, R., & Sears, D. O. (1968). Warning, personal involvement, and attitude change. *Journal of Personality and Social Psychology, 9*, 162–166.

Areni, C. S., & Lutz, R. J. (1988). The role of argument quality in the elaboration likelihood model. *Advances in Consumer Research, 15*, 172–175.

Axsom, D., Yates, S., & Chaiken, S. (1987). Audience response as a heuristic cue in persuasion. *Journal of Personality and Social Psychology, 53*, 30–40.

Boninger, D. S., Krosnick, J. A., & Berent, M. K. (1995). The origins of attitude importance: Self-interest, social identification, and value-relevance. *Journal of Personality and Social Psychology, 68*, 61–80.

Burnkrant, R. E., & Howard, D. J. (1984). Effects of the use of introductory rhetorical questions versus statements on information processing. *Journal of Personality and Social Psychology, 47*, 1218–1230.

Chaiken, S. (1987). The heuristic model of persuasion. In M. P. Zanna, J. M. Olson, & C. P. Herman (Eds.), *Social influence: The Ontario symposium* (Vol. 5, pp. 3–39). Hillsdale, NJ: Lawrence Erlbaum Associates.

Chaiken, S., Liberman, A., & Eagly, A. H. (1989). Heuristic and systematic information processing within and beyond the persuasion context. In J. S. Uleman & J. A. Bargh (Eds.) *Unintended thought* (pp. 212–252). New York: Guilford Press.

Chen, S., Shechter, D., & Chaiken, S. (1996). Getting at the truth or getting along: Accuracy versus impression-motivated heuristic and systematic processing. *Journal of Personality and Social Psychology, 71*, 262–275.

Cialdini, R. B., Green, B. L., & Rusch, A. J. (1992). When tactical pronouncements of change become real change: The case of reciprocal persuasion. *Journal of Personality and Social Psychology, 63,* 30–40.

Cialdini, R. B., Levy, A., Herman, C. P., Kozlowski, L. T., & Petty, R. E. (1976). Elastic shifts of opinion: Determinants of direction and durability. *Journal of Personality and Social Psychology, 34,* 663–672.

Cialdini, R. B., & Petty, R. E. (1981). Anticipatory opinion effects. In R. E. Petty, T. M. Ostrom, & T. C. Brock (Eds.), *Cognitive responses in persuasion* (pp. 217–235). Hillsdale, NJ: Lawrence Erlbaum Associates.

Davies, M. F. (1993). Dogmatism and the persistence of discredited beliefs. *Personality and Social Psychology Bulletin, 19,* 692–699.

DeBono, K. G. (1987). Investigating the social-adjustive and value-expressive functions of attitudes: Implications for persuasion processes. *Journal of Personality and Social Psychology, 52,* 279–287.

DeBono, K. G., & Klein, C. (1993). Source expertise and persuasion: The role of recipient dogmatism. *Personality and Social Psychology Bulletin, 19,* 167–173.

Eagly, A. H., & Chaiken, S. (1993). *The psychology of attitudes.* Fort Worth, TX: Harcourt Brace Jovanovich.

Eagly, A. H., & Chaiken, S. (1995). Attitude strength, attitude structure, and resistance to change. In R. E. Petty & J. A. Krosnick (Eds.), *Attitude strength: Antecedents and consequences* (pp. 413–432). Mahwah, NJ: Lawrence Erlbaum Associates.

Festinger, L. (1957). *A theory of cognitive dissonance.* Evanston, IL: Row, Peterson.

Fishbein, M., & Ajzen, I. (1974). Attitudes toward objects as predictors of single and multiple behavioral criteria. *Psychological Review, 81,* 59–74.

Fishbein, M., & Ajzen, I. (1975). *Belief, attitude, intention, and behavior: An introduction to theory and research.* Reading, MA: Addison–Wesley.

Fishbein, M., & Ajzen, I. (1981). Acceptance, yielding, and impact: Cognitive processes in persuasion. In R. E. Petty, T. M. Ostrom, & T. C. Brock (Eds.), *Cognitive responses in persuasion* (pp. 339–359). Hillsdale, NJ: Lawrence Erlbaum Associates.

Garst, J., & Bodenhausen, G. V. (1996). "Family values" and political persuasion: Impact of kin-related rhetoric on reactions to political campaigns. *Journal of Applied Social Psychology, 26,* 1119–1137.

Greenwald, A. G. (1968). Cognitive learning, cognitive response to persuasion, and attitude change. In A. G. Greenwald, T. C. Brock, & T. M. Ostrom (Eds.), *Psychological foundations of attitudes* (pp. 147–170). San Diego, CA: Academic Press.

Greenwald, A. G. (1982). Ego task analysis: An integration of research on ego-involvement and self-awareness. In A. H. Hastorf and A. M. Isen (Eds.), *Cognitive social psychology* (pp. 109–147). New York: Elsevier/North-Holland.

Hovland, C. I., Harvey, O. J., & Sherif, M. (1957). Assimilation and contrast effects in relation to communication and attitude change. *Journal of Abnormal and Social Psychology, 55,* 244–252.

Hunter, J. E., Levine, R. L., & Sayers, S. E. (1976). Attitude change in hierarchical belief systems and its relationship to persuasibility, dogmatism, and rigidity. *Human Communication Research, 3,* 3–28.

Janis, I. L., & King, B. T. (1954). The influence of role playing on opinion change. *Journal of Abnormal and Social Psychology, 49,* 211–218.

Johnson, B. T. (1994). Effects of outcome-relevant involvement and prior information on persuasion. *Journal of Experimental Social Psychology, 30,* 556–579.

Johnson, B. T., & Eagly, A. H. (1989). The effects of involvement on persuasion: A meta-analysis. *Psychological Bulletin, 106,* 290–314.

Johnson, B. T., & Eagly, A. H. (1990). Involvement and persuasion: Types, traditions, and the evidence. *Psychological Bulletin, 107,* 375–384.

Johnson, B. T., Levin, K. D., & Killeya, L. A. (1997). [The good, the bad, and the likely: A closer look at argument quality]. Unpublished raw data. Syracuse University, Syracuse, NY.

Johnson, B. T., Lin, H. Y., Symons, C. S., Campbell, L. A., & Ekstein, G. (1995). Initial beliefs and attitudinal latitudes as factors in persuasion. *Personality and Social Psychology Bulletin, 21,* 502–511.

Johnson, B. T., & Nichols, D. R. (1997). [The effects of dogmatism and value-relevant involvement on persuasion]. Unpublished raw data. Syracuse University, Syracuse, NY.

Johnson, B. T., Symons, C. S., & Newman, B. C. (1991). The ephemeral nature of impression-relevant involvement. *In Proceedings of the Society for Consumer Psychology*, pp. 21–28. Annual convention of the American Psychological Association, San Francisco, CA.

Johnson, H. H., & Scileppi, J. A. (1969). Effects of ego-involvement conditions on attitude change to high and low credibility communicators. *Journal of Personality and Social Psychology, 13*, 31–36.

Johnston, L., & Coolen, P. (1995). A dual processing approach to stereotype change. *Personality and Social Psychology Bulletin, 21*, 660–673.

Katz, D. (1960). The functional approach to the study of attitudes. *Public Opinion Quarterly, 24*, 163–204.

Killeya, L. A., & Johnson, B. T. (1998)..Experimental induction of biased systematic processing: The directed thought technique. *Personality and Social Psychology Bulletin, 24*, 17–33.

Krakauer, J. (1997). *Into thin air*. New York: Villard.

Kristiansen, C. M., & Hotte, A. M. (1996). Morality and the self: Implications for the when and how of value-attitude-behavior relations. In C. Seligman, J. M. Olson, & M. P. Zanna (Eds.), *The psychology of values: The Ontario symposium* (Vol. 8, pp. 77–105). Hillsdale, NJ: Lawrence Erlbaum Associates.

Krosnick, J. A. (1988). The role of attitude importance in social evaluation: A study of policy preferences, presidential candidate evaluations, and voting behavior. *Journal of Personality and Social Psychology, 55*, 196–210.

Kunda, Z. (1990). The case for motivated reasoning. *Psychological Bulletin, 108*, 480-498.

Leippe, M. R. (1991). A self-image analysis of persuasion and attitude involvement. In R. C. Curtis (Ed.), *The relational self: Theoretical convergences in psychoanalysis and social psychology*. New York: Guilford Press.

Leippe, M. R., & Elkin, R. A. (1987). When motives clash: Issue involvement and response involvement as determinants of persuasion. *Journal of Personality and Social Psychology, 52*, 269–278.

Levin, K. D., Johnson, B. T., & Turco, R. M. (1997). [The effects of argument quality on persuasion: A meta-analysis]. Unpublished raw data. Syracuse University, Syracuse, NY.

Liberman, A., & Chaiken, S. (1992). Defensive processing of personally relevant health messages. *Personality and Social Psychology Bulletin, 18*, 669–679.

Liberman, A., & Chaiken, S. (1996). The direct effect of personal relevance on attitudes. *Personality and Social Psychology Bulletin, 22*, 269–279.

Maheswaran, D., & Chaiken, S. (1991). Promoting systematic processing in low-motivation settings: Effect of incongruent information in processing and judgment. *Journal of Personality and Social Psychology, 61*, 13–25.

Maio, G. R., & Olson, J. M. (1995). Involvement and persuasion: Evidence for different types of involvement. *Canadian Journal of Behavioural Science, 27*, 64–78.

Marsh, K. L., Hart-O'Rourke, D. M., & Julka, D. L. (1997). The persuasive effects of verbal and nonverbal information in a context of value relevance. *Personality and Social Psychology Bulletin, 23*, 563–579.

Nichols, D. R., & Johnson, B. T. (1997). *Exploring a forgotten manipulation of value-relevant involvement: Ostrom and Brock's (1968, 1969) value-bonding technique*. Unpublished manuscript.

Ostrom, T. M., & Brock, T. C. (1968). A cognitive model of attitudinal involvement. In R. P. Abelson, E. Aronson, W. J. McGuire, T. M. Newcomb, M. J. Rosenberg, & P. H. Tannenbaum (Eds.), *Theories of cognitive consistency: A sourcebook* (pp. 373–383). Chicago: Rand- McNally.

Ostrom, T. M., & Brock, T. C. (1969). Cognitive bonding to central values and resistance to a communication advocating change in policy orientation. *Journal of Experimental Research in Personality, 4*, 42–50.

Maio, G. R., & Olson, J. M. (1994). Value-attitude Functions. *British Journal of Social Psychology, 33*, 301–312.

Petty, R. E., & Cacioppo, J. T. (1979). Issue involvement can increase or decrease persuasion by enhancing message-relevant cognitive responses. *Journal of Personality and Social Psychology, 37*, 1915–1926.

Petty, R. E., & Cacioppo, J. T. (1981). Issue involvement as a moderator of the effects on attitude of advertising content and context. In K. B. Monroe (Ed.), *Advances in consumer research* (Vol. 8, pp. 20–24). Ann Arbor, MI: Association for Consumer Research.

Petty, R. E., & Cacioppo, J. T. (1984). The effects of involvement on responses to argument quantity and quality: Central and peripheral routes to persuasion. *Journal of Personality and Social Psychology, 46*, 69–81.

Petty, R. E., & Cacioppo, J. T. (1986). *Communication and persuasion: Central and peripheral routes to attitude change.* New York: Springer-Verlag.

Petty, R. E., & Cacioppo, J. T. (1990). Involvement and persuasion: Tradition versus integration. *Psychological Bulletin, 107*, 367–374.

Petty, R. E., Cacioppo, J. T., & Goldman, R. (1981). Personal involvement as a determinant of argument-based persuasion. *Journal of Personality and Social Psychology, 41*, 847–855.

Petty, R. E., Cacioppo, J. T., & Heesacker, M. (1981). Effects of rhetorical questions on persuasion: A cognitive response analysis. *Journal of Personality and Social Psychology, 40*, 432–440.

Petty, R. E., & Krosnick, J. A. (Eds.). (1995). *Attitude strength: Antecedents and consequences.* Mahwah, NJ: Lawrence Erlbaum Associates.

Poiesz, T. B. C., & de Bont, C. J. P. M. (1995). Do we need involvement to understand consumer behavior? *Advances in Consumer Research, 22*, 448–452.

Rhine, R. J., & Severance, L. J. (1970). Ego-involvement, discrepancy, source credibility, and attitude change. *Journal of Personality and Social Psychology, 16*, 175–190.

Rokeach, M. (1960). *The open and closed mind.* New York: Basic Books.

Rokeach, M. (1968). *Beliefs, attitudes, and values: A theory of organization and change.* San Francisco: Jossey-Bass.

Rokeach, M. (1973). *The nature of human values.* New York: Free Press.

Rokeach, M., & Fruchter, B. (1956). A factorial study of dogmatism and related concepts. *Journal of Abnormal and Social Psychology, 53*, 356–360.

Schul, A., & Knapp, J. R. (1984). On attitude change: Issue-involvement and demand characteristics. *Psychological Reports, 55*, 547–553.

Shavitt, S. (1989). Operationalizing functional theories of attitude. In A. R. Pratkanis, S. J. Breckler, & A. G. Greenwald (Eds.), *Attitude Structure and Function* (pp. 311–337). Hillsdale, NJ: Lawrence Erlbaum Associates.

Sherif, C. W., Kelly, M., Rodgers, H. L., Sarup, G., & Tittler, B. I. (1973). Personal involvement, social judgment, and action. *Journal of Personality and Social Psychology, 27*, 311–328.

Sherif, C. W., Sherif, M., & Nebergall, R. E. (1965). *Attitude and attitude change: The social judgment–involvement approach.* Philadelphia: Saunders.

Sherif, M., & Cantril, H. (1947). *The psychology of ego-involvements: Social attitudes and identifications.* New York: Wiley.

Sherif, M., & Hovland, C. I. (1961). *Social judgment: Assimilation and contrast effects in communication and attitude change.* New Haven, CT: Yale University Press.

Sivacek, J., & Crano, W. D. (1982). Vested interest as a moderator of attitude–behavior consistency. *Journal of Personality and Social Psychology, 43*, 210–221.

Slater, M. D., & Rouner, D. (1996). Value-affirmative and value-protective processing of alcohol education messages that include statistical evidence or anecdotes. *Communication Research, 23*, 210–235.

Smith, M. B., Bruner, J. S., & White, R. W. (1956). *Opinions and personality.* New York: Wiley.

Snyder, M. (1987). *Public appearances/private realities: The psychology of self-monitoring.* New York: Freeman.

Snyder, M., & DeBono, K. G. (1987). A functional approach to attitudes and persuasion. In M. P. Zanna, J. M. Olson, & C. P. Herman (Eds.), *Social influence: The Ontario symposium* (Vol. 5, pp. 107–125). Hillsdale, NJ: Lawrence Erlbaum Associates.

Sorrentino, R. M., Bobocel, D. R., Gitta, M. Z., Olson, J. M., & Hewitt, E. C. (1988). Uncertainty orientation and persuasion: Individual differences in the effects of personal relevance on social judgments. *Journal of Personality and Social Psychology, 55,* 357–371.

Taylor, S. E., & Fiske, S. T. (1978). Salience, attention, and attribution: Top of the head phenomena. In L. Berkowitz (Ed.), *Advances in experimental social psychology* (Vol. 11, pp. 249–288). New York: Academic Press.

Tetlock, P. E. (1989). Structure and function in political belief systems. In A. R. Pratkanis, S. J. Breckler, & A. G. Greenwald (Eds.), *Attitude structure and function* (pp. 129–152). Hillsdale, NJ: Lawrence Erlbaum Associates.

Troldahl, V. C., & Powell, F. A. (1965). A short-form dogmatism scale for use in field studies. *Social Forces, 44,* 211–214.

Zimbardo, P. G. (1960). Involvement and communication discrepancy as determinants of opinion conformity. *Journal of Abnormal and Social Psychology, 60,* 86–94.

Zuwerink, J. R., & Devine, P. G. (1996). Attitude importance and resistance to persuasion: It's not just the thought that counts. *Journal of Personality and Social Psychology, 70,* 931–944.

7

Attitude Functions and Consumer Psychology: Understanding Perceptions of Product Quality

Kenneth G. DeBono
Union College

The rekindling of interest in questions concerning attitude functions that social psychology has witnessed in the past decade or so (e.g., Pratkanis, Breckler, & Greenwald, 1989) has spawned numerous theoretical and practical advances in our knowledge of the attitude construct. Theory and research, for example, in areas such as persuasion (e.g., DeBono, 1987; DeBono & Harnish, 1988; Murray, Haddock, & Zanna, 1996; Shavitt, 1990; Spivey, Monson, & Locander, 1983), attitude–behavior relations (e.g., Maio & Olson, 1994, 1995), consumer behavior (e.g., DeBono & Packer, 1991; DeBono & Telesca, 1990; Johar & Sirgy, 1991; Korgaonkar, Lund, & Price, 1985; Shavitt, Lowrey, & Han, 1992), and the psychology of stigmatized groups (e.g., Herek, 1986a, 1986b, 1987; Kristiansen, 1990; Leone & Wingate, 1991; Wyman & Snyder, 1997) have benefited greatly from renewed attempts to understand the many and diverse differences in why we evaluate. Interestingly, these increased efforts toward understanding why we evaluate have also led researchers to a new, but related, set of questions: those concerning how we evaluate (DeBono & Rubin, 1995).

Consider, as an example, two attitude functions that have received a good deal of attention in recent years, the social-adjustive function and the value-expressive function (Bazzini & Shaffer, 1995; DeBono, 1987; Herek, 1986a, 1986b; Kristensian & Zanna, 1991; Maio & Olson, 1994, 1995; Murray, Haddock, & Zanna, 1996). In theory, attitudes that serve a social-adjustive function allow an individual to fit into and interact smoothly with important reference groups. They allow individuals to project images appropriate for particular social settings and particular social groups (Smith, Bruner, & White, 1956). In contrast, attitudes that serve a value-expressive function (Katz, 1960) allow individuals to express their sense of self—their underlying values and dispositions. Such attitudes allow individuals to achieve some degree of consistency between publicly expressed attitudes and privately held values and beliefs.

These two functions illustrate quite clearly two very different reasons that we evaluate. They suggest that sometimes we evaluate out of a concern for social appropriateness and at other times we evaluate out of a concern with expressing our true sense of self. These two motivations, however, also have implications for how we evaluate. If an individual's motivation is to hold socially correct attitudes, for example, the ways in which he or she evaluates a particular attitude object will likely be quite different than if the individual's goal is to hold attitudes and beliefs that are consistent with his or her sense of self. As an example, consider an individual's evaluation of a candidate for political office. If an individual's motivation for evaluation is social adjustive, this individual may decide whether the candidate is desirable and worthy of a vote on the basis of his or her perceptions of what important others (e.g., parents, friends) believe and feel. If important others indicate that they believe that this political candidate is good or desirable, the individual may use that information as a basis for arriving at his or her own understanding of the desirableness of this candidate. That is, in pursuit of the goal of maintaining socially desirable attitudes, an individual may decide what is good and what is bad on the basis of what others believe is good and bad.

In contrast, if an individual has the goals of holding attitudes that correctly express his or her sense of self, the ways in which that individual is likely to decide whether an attitude object is good or bad are likely to be quite different. Rather than relying on feedback from others, in this case, an individual may attempt to gauge the degree of consistency between the attributes of the attitude object and his or her own values, and decide the desirableness of the object on the extent of this consistency. In the evaluation of our hypothetical political candidate, people who are ardent conservatives and whose attitudes serve a value-expressive function may care little about what parents, loved ones, or peers believe. Rather, they may base their evaluation of the candidate on the extent to which they believe that candidate embodies the conservative ideals that they themselves hold dear.

The extent to which differences in why we evaluate lead to differences in how we evaluate has been the central research question that my students and I have pursued in the past few years. Our research, admittedly, has been quite narrowly defined. We have investigated the implications of but two functions (social-adjustive and value-expressive) in but one domain (the evaluation of consumer products). Nevertheless, the results we have achieved strongly suggest that differences in attitude functions can lead to important differences in evaluation strategies.

A problem that has historically plagued research addressing attitude functions concerns how, properly, to operationalize particular functions (Keisler, Collins, & Miller, 1969). Although functions can surely be defined through and influenced by particular situations in which individuals find themselves, and by the particular attitude objects under consideration (Shavitt, 1990), we have elected to operationalize attitude functions through a personality construct, that of self-monitoring (Snyder, 1974, 1979, 1987). Numerous studies indicate that the self-monitoring construct appears to reliably identify individuals whose attitudes serve either predominantly social-adjustive or value-expressive functions (Bazzini & Shaffer, 1995; DeBono, 1987; Kristiansen & Zanna, 1991). As such, it represents a valuable vehicle for examining questions related to attitude functions.

High self-monitors, as identified by their relatively high scores on the self-monitoring scale (Snyder & Gangestad, 1986), typically try to be the kind of person called for in each situation in which they find themselves. They tend to be concerned about the image they project to others in social situations, and they are generally adept at adjusting their self-presentations to fit differing social and interpersonal considerations of appropriateness. As a consequence of this orientation, high self-monitors often display marked situation-to-situation shifts in the images they project to others. Moreover, research on the motivations that underlie attitudes of high self-monitors has suggested that their attitudes serve primarily a social-adjustive function. In particular, high self-monitors appear to be especially responsive to information targeted at social adjustive concerns (DeBono, 1987; DeBono & Edmonds, 1989). For example, research indicates that when high self-monitors are presented with information indicating that their current attitudes are at odds with those of important references groups, they will change their attitudes in the direction of the consensus (cf. Snyder, 1987).

In contrast, low self-monitors characteristically do not attempt to mold their behavior to fit situation-specific considerations of appropriateness. Rather, they appear more concerned with maintaining a relatively high degree of congruence between their attitudes, values and dispositions, and overt behaviors. As a consequence, they tend to rely on their own attitudes, feelings, and dispositions when making decisions or behavioral choices, and they typically display a high degree of consistency between their private attitudes and public behaviors. Research on the functional bases of low self-monitors' attitudes suggests that their attitudes may be primarily value expressive in nature (Kristiansen & Zanna, 1988). Low self-monitors are very responsive to information that concerns the relationship between their values and their current attitudes. Research indicates that, if informed that a current attitude is not consistent with a professed value, but that an alternative attitude is, low self-monitors will change their attitudes in the direction of the more value-consistent attitude. Interestingly, high self-monitors are not responsive to this kind of value-congruence information nor are low self-monitors especially responsive to social adjustive type messages previously discussed (cf. Snyder, 1987).

One arena in which the different functional orientations of high and low self-monitors manifest themselves quite strikingly is that of consumer psychology. Research on the psychology of advertising, for example, has consistently indicated that high and low self-monitors, on a cognitive, affective, and behavioral level, are differentially responsive to different advertising strategies (DeBono & Packer, 1991, Shavitt et al., 1992; Snyder & DeBono, 1985). High self-monitors tend to be particularly influenced by advertisements that can be classified as "soft-sell" (Fox, 1984) advertisements. These are advertisements that highlight the image associated with using a product, or the image that one can project by owning or using a particular product. Compared to low self-monitors, high self-monitors evaluate such advertisements more favorably, are willing to pay more for products so advertised, and express an increased willingness to sample a product when its advertisement stresses product image (Snyder & DeBono). In addition, high self-monitors tend to judge a product's quality higher if it is advertised with an image orientation (DeBono & Packer).

Low self-monitors, on the other hand, tend to be influenced by advertisements that stress the performance of the product, in particular, the extent to which the product operates as products of that type should. Such "hard-sell" (Fox, 1984) advertisements often highlight the durability of a product; the high quality of the materials or ingredients in the product; or, in cases of things to eat and drink, the good taste of that product. Unlike their high self-monitoring counterparts, low self-monitors think more highly of these types of advertisements, are willing to pay more for products so advertised, and are more likely to try a product that is marketed with a hard-sell approach (Snyder & DeBono, 1985). In addition, low self-monitors rate the quality of products advertised with a quality orientation more favorably than they would if these same products were advertised with more of an image orientation (DeBono & Packer, 1991). It appears, then, that low self-monitors' concerns with the consistency between what they purport to be (e.g., defined through their values) and what they actually do is paralleled by a concern with the consistency between what a product purports to be and what it actually does.

In our recent research, we have extended these findings beyond the differential effects of advertising strategies on the evaluations of high and low self-monitors by focusing our attention on the more basic evaluative strategies that high and low self-monitors use to decide whether a product is good. We reasoned that, given their general social adjustive concerns, and given their particular responsiveness to the "image" aspects of products, high self-monitors would likely evaluate the quality of a product by the extent to which that product possesses attributes that could be used for image-enhancing purposes. Consumer psychologists have identified a number of such image-enhancing attributes, which are defined as ones that are distinct from the product itself, but are strongly associated or identified with the product and, as a consequence, can be and are used when evaluating the product (Erickson, Johansson, & Chao, 1984). Often these image variables contain some information about the image a consumer can attain or project by using or possessing a particular product. Examples include, among others, the product's country of origin, celebrity endorsements, and brand name.

In contrast, we reasoned that, given their overriding concerns with consistency between a product and its performance, low self-monitors would adopt distinctly different strategies for evaluating consumer products. We expected that a product's actual performance would primarily influence the evaluations of low self-monitors. We reasoned that, regardless of the presence or absence of any image variables, if a product performs as products of that type should, low self-monitors would favorably evaluate that product. If the product fails to perform adequately, however, we expected low self-monitors to render less favorable evaluations.

To address these predictions we performed a series of studies, all of which have the same basic design. We asked students to evaluate different products for which we varied the actual performance of the product and the presence of some image-related cue. The particular image cues that we manipulated across our different studies were the product's country of origin, the attractiveness of the product's packaging, the attractiveness of the spokesperson endorsing the product, the store from which the product was purchased, the price of the product, and, finally, feedback from others. In all cases, our predictions essentially were the same. After subjects learned about and then actually sampled a product, we expected that the evaluations of high self-monitors would be driven by the presence or absence of an image cue, but that the evaluations of low self-monitors would be determined by the actual performance of the product.

IT'S MADE WHERE?

All of the television commercials in a recent series for a national brand of salsa present the same basic scenario: people sample a salsa and react quite negatively to it. Someone then reads the label and exclaims loudly, "It's made in New York City," following which the others laugh derisively. The message the advertisers are trying to convey is quite clear. They are suggesting to the audience that where a product is made is predictive of its quality and should be taken into account when evaluating that product. And indeed, there is evidence that, in general, people do take a product's place of origin into account when they judge a product's quality (Harris, Garner, Sprick, & Carroll, 1994; Hastak & Hong, 1991; Hong & Wyer, 1989; Lim, Darley, & Summers, 1994). To the extent, however, that a product's place of origin represents one of these so-called image variables, Karen Rubin and I hypothesized that it is high self-monitors who might be particularly likely to use a product's place of origin when evaluating that product's quality (especially when the place of origin is image enhancing). Low self-monitors, we speculated, would rely more on the actual performance of the product (DeBono & Rubin, 1995).

To examine these notions, we had students sample and evaluate different cheeses. Before we conducted the study, however, we did a number of pretests. In one pretest, we had students sample and rate the taste of various cheeses. From this pretest, we were able to identify a cheese that most everyone rated as tasting quite good (a cheddar) and a cheese that most everyone rated as not tasting very good (an Edam loaf). In a second pretest, we had students imagine that they were giving a party and that they wanted to impress the people they invited. We then asked them how impressed they thought their guests would be with cheeses made in various countries. Our subjects indicated that they thought guests would be most impressed with a cheese imported from France and least impressed with a cheese made in Kansas. We then used these two places of origin as our image manipulation.

In the main study, we told subjects that we were interested in people's reactions to typical consumer products and that, in this session, they would be tasting and evaluating a sample of cheese. Before we allowed subjects to taste the cheese (which was either the pleasant tasting cheddar or the less pleasant tasting Edam loaf), however, we gave them some general information about the cheese. All subjects received the same information, except for the cheese's purported place of origin. Some were told that the cheese was imported from Strasbourg, France, and others were told that the cheese was made in Mulberry, Kansas. After they sampled the cheese, we asked subjects to evaluate its overall quality and taste. The results are presented in Fig. 7.1.

As is seen, our hypotheses were confirmed. High and low self-monitors appeared to employ quite different strategies when evaluating the cheese. For high self-monitors, the cheese's country of origin was of particular importance. They evaluated the cheese believed to be from France more highly than the cheese believed to be from Kansas, regardless of the cheese's actual taste. In fact, the type of cheese sampled did not emerge as a significant predictor of high self-monitors' judgments (i.e., there was no main effect for type of cheese).

In contrast, low self-monitors' evaluations relied more on the product's performance. They evaluated the pleasant tasting cheese more favorably

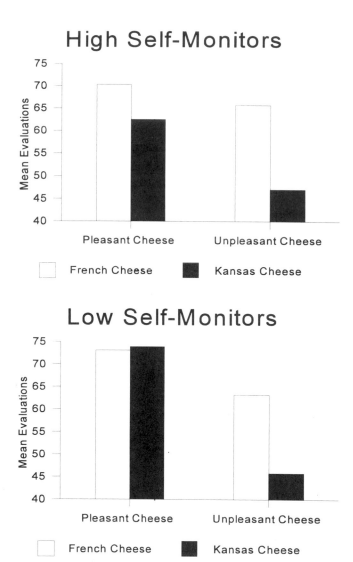

FIG. 7.1. Mean evaluations of cheese samples.

than the less pleasant tasting cheese regardless of its purported country of origin. And, unlike for high self-monitors, country of origin was not a significant predictor of low self-monitors' evaluations. For high self-monitors, then, the extent to which the product could be used for image-enhancing purposes appeared to be a paramount concern when deciding the cheese's quality; for low self-monitors, the consistency between the product type and its performance appeared to be a much more important consideration.

PRETTY PLEASES, PART I

A television commercial for a popular instant coffee attempts to convince the viewer of the quality of this coffee by showing consumers' reactions when this instant coffee was, unbeknownst to the consumer, substituted for the regular fare at a posh restaurant. In the advertisement, we are shown the coffee being served to customers in an elegant silver coffee service by a well-dressed waiter. We then see the customers commenting quite favorably on the taste of the coffee and reacting with surprise when they learn that it is an instant coffee and not one freshly brewed with the finest coffee beans. The message the audience is asked to believe is that this instant coffee tastes just as good as, if not better than, freshly brewed. Now, this may well be the case, but, even if we grant that the commercial depicts actual customers' genuine reactions, another possibility presents itself. Perhaps it wasn't the actual taste of the coffee that influenced the customers' reactions. Perhaps the favorable reactions had something to do with the posh setting and the elegant way in which the product was presented to the customers (in the very fancy silver coffee service). Indeed, there is a body of evidence that suggests that, in general, a product's appearance and packaging can and does influence evaluative reactions to that product (e.g., Dawar & Parker, 1994).

In thinking about these possibilities, it occurred to me Amy Leavitt, Jennifer Backus, and me (DeBono, Leavitt, & Backus, 1997) that, in a scenario such as this, both product packaging and product performance probably influence consumer's reactions, but that it might be the high self-monitoring consumers who are primarily influenced by the packaging of a product and it might be the low self-monitoring consumers who, once again, are more influenced by the product's actual performance. That is, those consumers who are attuned to and concerned with the image that they may be projecting to others through product choice might elect to use a product's packaging as an indication of the product's worth, whereas those who are more concerned with product type–product performance consistency might be more likely to rely on the actual performance of the product. We attempted to address these hypotheses in two studies. In the first study, we initially had students, in a pretest, rate four containers for each of three different products (i.e., four coffee containers, four chocolate packages, and four bottled water containers) in terms of how attractive the container/package was. For each of the three products, then, we knew which was the most attractive container, the second most attractive, and so on. In the main part of the study, we presented subjects with four samples of the three products. Each sample was believed to have come from one of the four containers, but in reality, the samples were a constant. That is, it was the identical brand in each of the four containers (e.g., even though subjects thought they were sampling four different brands of chocolate, one from each container, in reality, the brand of chocolate in each container was the same. The only thing that varied was the attractiveness of the container). After each sampling , we asked subjects to rate the products' taste and quality. The results were in line with our predictions. For high self-monitors, the attractiveness of the product's container predicted their evaluations. For all three products, the more attractive the container was the more favorably high self-monitors rated the quality and taste of the sample. For low self-monitors, although within each product type there was variability in their ratings across the four samples, this variability was not accounted for by the attractiveness of the sample's container. For low self-monitors, product packaging was not a significant predictor of evaluations.

In our second study, we had male and female students sample either a pretested pleasant smelling cologne (for males)/perfume (for females) or a pretested less pleasant smelling cologne/perfume that they believed came from either a pretested attractive bottle or a pretested unattractive bottle. After subjects smelled their particular cologne/perfume, we asked them to rate its smell and its quality. The results are presented in Fig. 7.2. As is seen, consistent with our first study and consistent with expectations, high and low self-monitors appeared to rely on different cues to evaluate quality of the scent. For high self-monitors, only the attractiveness of the scent's bottle emerged as a significant and strong predictor of their evaluative reactions. Regardless of the actual aroma, high self-monitors rated the cologne/perfume that they believed came from the attractive bottle more favorably than the one they believed came from the less attractive bottle. In contrast, the evaluations of low self-monitors were predicted only by the actual fragrance of the scent. They evaluated the pleasant smelling cologne/perfume more favorably than the less pleasant smelling cologne/perfume, regardless of the attractiveness of the con-

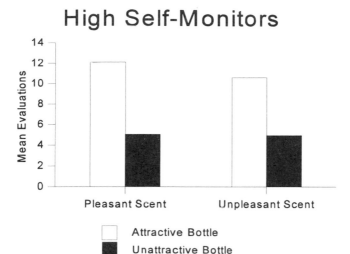

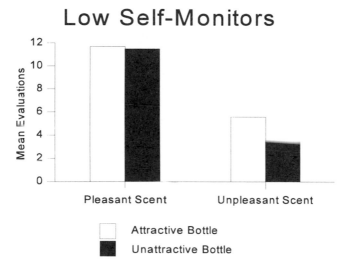

FIG. 7.2. Mean perfume evaluations.

tainer from which it came. Again, it appears that the different motivations that underlie the beliefs and attitudes of high and low self-monitors lead them to adopt different strategies for evaluating objects in their environments.

PRETTY PLEASES, PART II

A staple of Western advertising and marketing is the use of physically attractive spokespeople and/or models. Our airwaves and magazines are flooded with advertisements that invariably depict unusually attractive people using, enjoying, and, of course, extolling the virtues of products ranging from soft drinks and household cleaners to expensive jewelry and automobiles. And, indeed, evidence suggests that such strategies have some success. That is, research indicates that, in general, people seem to react more positively to advertisements, and the products advertised, when the spokespeople and models are physically attractive (Caballero & Pride, 1984; Caballero & Solomon, 1984; Joseph, 1982; Parekh & Kanekar, 1994).

Our previous research and understanding of the social-adjustive and value-expressive functions, and on the relations between these functions, differences in self-monitoring, and consumer behavior, led Dennis Ruggeri, Ainslee Foster, and me (DeBono, Ruggeri, & Foster, 1997) to speculate that the use of attractive spokespeople may have more of an influence on high self-monitors than on low self-monitors. One rationale for the use of physically attractive individuals in advertising and marketing is the belief that attractive spokespeople/models present to consumers a desirable image that they (the consumers) may attain by using or possessing a particular product. By associating themselves with a product endorsed by an attractive other, consumers not only may feel better about themselves, but may also anticipate a favorable reaction from those in their social environs. To the extent that this is one of the mechanisms by which attractive spokespeople/models favorably influence individuals' reactions to products, we reasoned that marketing strategies that employ attractive spokespeople/models should be particularly effective with consumers who are acutely concerned with presenting desirable images and eliciting favorable reactions from others in their social surroundings (i.e., individuals with heightened social adjustive motivations).

To the extent that the self-monitoring construct appears to successfully identify individuals with such social-adjustive concerns, we hypothesized that high self-monitors would react more favorably to products endorsed by physically attractive people than to products endorsed by less attractive people. In contrast, given low self-monitors' apparent concern with the consistency between product type and product performance, we hypothesized that spokesperson attractiveness would not be as strong an influence on product evaluations. Rather, as in previous research, we believed that the evaluations of low self-monitors would be driven primarily by product performance. To test these ideas, we asked subjects to help us collect some data on a new brand of chocolate that was going to be introduced to the area and that would be targeted for a college-aged population. In particular, we told participants that we wanted them to react to a sample advertisement for this new product and then taste and evaluate a sample of the chocolate. All participants were then exposed to an advertisement that consisted of a facial photo of a woman, below which was written a description of the chocolate as well as the woman's supposed endorsement of the product. The advertisement presented was the same for all participants save one feature, the attractiveness of the model. For some she was a pretested very physically attractive woman and for others she was significantly less attractive. It should be noted that in this latter condition, the model was not unattractive. She was believable as a model in an advertisement. She was, however, statistically less attractive than the other model.

We then gave participants a sample of the supposed new chocolate. In reality, some received a pretested very pleasant tasting chocolate and others received a pretested much less pleasant tasting chocolate. Participants were then asked to complete a questionnaire that inquired not only about their reactions to the advertisement, but also about their perceptions of the chocolate in terms of its taste and quality. The results of these latter questions are depicted graphically in Fig. 7.3.

As is evident, our basic hypotheses were supported. High self-monitors evaluated the chocolate associated with the attractive spokesperson more favorably than that associated with the less attractive spokesperson, regardless of the actual taste of the chocolate. The actual taste of the chocolate was not a significant predictor of their evaluations.

In contrast, the actual taste of the product was apparently more influential with low self-monitors. They evaluated the pleasant tasting chocolate more favorably than the less pleasant tasting chocolate regardless of the model's attractiveness. Consistent with our previous findings, the results of this study provide additional support for the notion that the differences in the motivations underlying people's beliefs and attitudes appear to lead to differences in how people arrive at final evaluations.

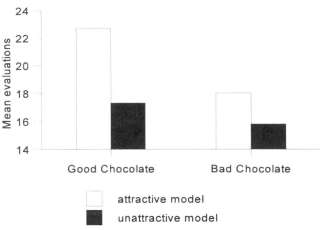

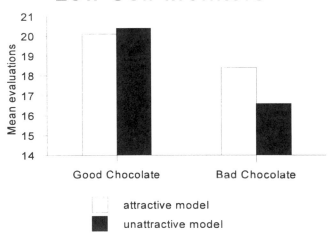

FIG. 7.3. Mean evaluations of chocolate samples.

WHERE DID YOU BUY THAT?

I once heard the following joke that circulated among the faculty at a very expensive college whose students tended to be quite image conscious: Q: "What are the three little words that (this college's) students are likely to never hear?" A: "Attention K-Mart shoppers." Although humorous, this witticism also appears to contain a grain of truth. It suggests that people see a relationship between the image projected by a particular store and the quality of the products that are likely to be found in that store, a suggestion that has been documented in studies examining the relations between store image and perceptions of product quality (Baugh & Davis, 1989; Jacoby & Mazursky, 1984; Szybillo & Jacoby, 1974). Jeremy Pflaum and I (DeBono & Pflaum, 1997) did some pretesting and also confirmed this relationship, at least in the case of colognes. We asked students to rate the image projected by the colognes that are likely to be found in various large U.S. department stores (e.g., Sears). There was surprising consensus. Most students agreed that the colognes in certain stores projected quite desirable images (with Saks Fifth Avenue projecting the most desirable) and that the colognes that could be purchased in certain other stores projected quite undesirable images (with K-Mart projecting the least desirable).

Armed with this knowledge, we then proceeded to investigate the extent to which the image projected by a store is used by individuals when they evaluate products from that store. In particular, we speculated that those individuals who are particularly concerned about their social image (i.e., high self-monitors) might be more likely to rely on the image projected by a store when they evaluate products from that store than would individuals with less pressing social adjustive concerns (i.e., low self-monitors). As before, we suspected that low self-monitors would be less concerned with where a product was purchased than with how it performs. To test these notions, we invited subjects to participate in a study on scent perception. As part of this study, students were asked to sample and evaluate a cologne (the brand name of which was not given). Some participants were given a pretested pleasant smelling cologne to sample and others were given a pretested less pleasant smelling cologne. Before sampling the cologne, however, students were given a generic description of the cologne. Included in this description was a mention of the store from which we purportedly purchased the cologne. Some subjects were led to believe that the cologne was purchased at Saks Fifth Avenue, whereas others were told that it was from K-Mart. After they sampled the cologne, we asked subjects to indicate the extent to which they would consider purchasing the cologne if the occasion arose.

The results are presented in Fig. 7.4. As is seen, for high self-monitors, the store from which the product came was particularly important.

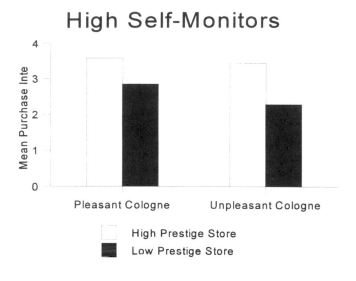

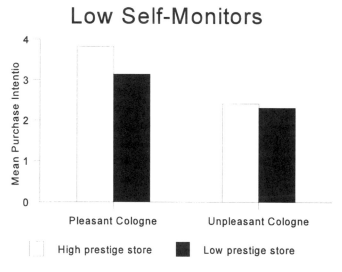

FIG. 7.4. Mean evaluation of cologne samples.

Regardless of the cologne's actual fragrance, high self-monitors expressed more of a willingness to purchase the cologne when they believed it was purchased at Saks Fifth Avenue than when they believed it came from K-Mart. For low self-monitors, actual fragrance made a difference. They were more likely to indicate a willingness to purchase the pleasant smelling cologne rather than the less pleasant smelling cologne irrespective of where they thought it was purchased. Different motivations again appear to precipitate different strategies of evaluation.

HOW MUCH DID IT COST?

The effect that a product's price has on consumer's evaluations of that product has received a good deal of attention from consumer psychologists. And the conclusions from that research are quite clear. Consumers frequently use the price of a product when they evaluate the quality of that product, generally evaluating more expensive products more favorably (Chang & Wildt, 1994; Dodds, Monroe, & Grewal, 1991; Rao & Monroe, 1989; Valenzi & Andrews, 1971). But what are the mechanisms by which product price might influence consumer perceptions? At least two possibilities present themselves. On the one hand, product price may serve the role of a so-called image variable. That is, individuals may look favorably on a product with an expensive price tag because they believe that such a product might allow them to project a desirable image to others and may elicit favorable reactions from others. On the other hand, consumers may believe that a strong association exists between the price of a product and its likely performance. Expensive products, for example, may be made of superior materials (which are more costly), which, in turn, will likely improve product reliability, endurance, performance, and so on.

Given these two possibilities, Sarah Burman and I found ourselves in the interesting position of believing that product price should be a factor in the product evaluations of both those individuals with social-adjustive concerns and those with more value-expressive orientations. For those with social-adjustive concerns, we reasoned, product price might likely serve the role of an image variable. Such individuals might gravitate toward more expensive products for the purpose of image enhancement, in the belief that more expensive products have the potential to project a more desirable image. In contrast, it occurred to us that those individuals who are more concerned with product performance may also gravitate toward more expensive products, in the belief that the relatively high price of the product might be due, in part, to the high quality of material used in producing the product.

Although we are still actively examining these possibilities, we have completed one study that produced promising results (DeBono & Burman, 1997). If those individuals with social adjustive concerns, high self-monitors, use the price of a product as an indication of product quality primarily on the basis of the image-enhancing potential of a product, they should evaluate a relatively expensive product more favorably than a less expensive product irrespective of that product's actual performance. For those individuals who are more concerned with consistency between the product and its performance, low self-monitors, we hypothesized that although the price of a product might play a role in influencing their product evaluations, their evaluations should, unlike those of their high self-monitoring counterparts, be affected by the extent to which the product performs as products of that type should.

In this study, we used a cola soft drink as our focus product. Before conducting our main study, we conducted a couple pretests. In the first pretest, we asked subjects to give what they would consider a relatively expensive price for a 2-liter bottle of soda and then what they would consider a relatively inexpensive price. The mean relatively expensive price for 2 liters of soda was $2.35, and the mean relatively inexpensive price was $.99. These, then, became the product prices we used in the main study. In the second pretest, we had subjects take a blind taste test in which they sampled many different colas (ranging from national brands to local supermarket brands) and rated their tastes. Subjects in this pretest, of course, never knew what specific brand they were tasting. The ratings revealed that our subjects thought that Coke/Diet Coke had the best taste and that a local supermarket brand had the least desirable taste. These two colas, then, became our stimulus products.

In the main study, we told subjects that a new cola product was going to be marketed in this area and that we were doing some preliminary testing. In particular, we wanted them to sample this new product and then give us their evaluations. Before allowing them to sample the soda, however, we gave them some background information about the product. All subjects received the same information with one exception. Some were told that the manufacturer's suggested retail price for this product was $.99 and others were told that the suggested retail price was $2.35. Subjects were then given a sample of either Coke or the supermarket brand (subjects were, of course, unaware of the actual brand they were drinking) and were asked, on a questionnaire, to rate their perceptions of the product's taste and quality. Our results are presented in Fig. 7.5.

As the graphs indicate, our suspicions were generally confirmed. For high self-monitors, the price of the product was the only factor that was

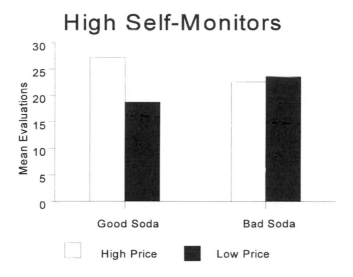

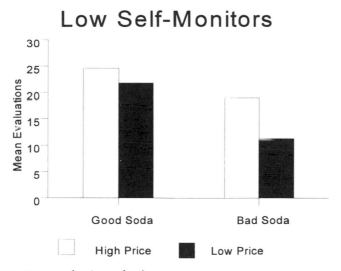

FIG. 7.5. Mean evaluations of soda.

significantly related to their evaluations. In general, they thought more highly of the more expensive cola than they did of the less expensive one (i.e., there was a trend toward a main effect for price), but price actually only made a difference in their evaluations of the better tasting cola. Coke, but not the supermarket brand, was more favorably evaluated when it was associated with the relatively expensive price than when associated with the relatively inexpensive price.

The results for low self-monitors were equally complex. They also were apparently swayed by the price of the product, more favorably evaluating the sodas with the more expensive price tags. Unlike with high self-monitors, however, the actual taste of the product was a significant predictor of low self-monitors' evaluations. They preferred the better tasting Coke to the less pleasant tasting supermarket brand regardless of its supposed price.

YOU LOOK MARVELOUS

In all of the preceding studies, the image variable manipulated was either one that is inherent to the product itself (e.g., country of origin) or one that is typically associated with consumer products (e.g., packaging, price). There are, however, other mechanisms by which a consumer can judge the extent to which a product might have image-enhancing potential. One such mechanism might be positive feedback or compliments from others. Having someone comment that a new piece of jewelry looks terrific on us or that a new tie is a perfect complement for our sport coat can certainly be taken as evidence that we are creating a positive social impression and projecting a desirable image to others. Indeed, research on the effects of compliments in areas as diverse as worker satisfaction (Yukl & Tracey, 1992) and interpersonal attraction (Aronson & Linder, 1965; Sigall and Aronson, 1969) suggests that compliments are effective because of the social approval they bring to the person at the receiving end of them.

Given this possibility, Sharon Krim and I conjectured that, in terms of the perception of product quality, compliments from others may be particularly effective on those consumers with social-adjustive needs (DeBono & Krim, 1997). If a product is associated with positive feedback from others, such individuals may use that information as an indication of the quality of that product. In particular, they may regard such products as ones of high quality. Such feedback from others should be of less importance to those consumers with more value-expressive concerns. As before, they should be more influenced by product–performance consistency. To test these notions, we invited high and low self-monitoring women to participate in a study on scent perception. We told them that we were interested in reactions to a variety of odors and that in this session they would be asked to smell and evaluate a sample of perfume. Subjects were then asked to spray on a small amount of either a pretested pleasant smelling perfume or a pretested less pleasant smelling perfume. After the perfume was applied, the experimenter told some of the women, "That smells good on you." Other women were given no feedback at all. We then asked our subjects, via an anonymous questionnaire, to rate the quality and smell of the perfume. The results are presented in Fig. 7.6.

The results indicate general support for the hypotheses. As is seen, for the high self-monitoring women, the presence or absence of the positive feedback from the experimenter was the only significant influence on their evaluations. They evaluated the perfumes associated with the compliment more favorably than the ones not associated with the compliment regardless of their actual fragrances. Compliments also played a significant role in the evaluations of low self-monitoring women. They also evaluated the perfumes associated with the compliment more favorably than the ones not so associated. Unlike those of high self-monitors, however, the evaluations of low self-monitors were also significantly predicted by the actual fragrance of the perfume. Regardless of the presence or the absence of the compliment, low self-monitors evaluated the pleasant smelling perfume more favorably than the less pleasant smelling perfume.

GENERAL CONCLUSIONS

The results of our research program appear to paint a consistent picture. In a variety of settings, using a variety of manipulations and a variety of products, we have been able to demonstrate the possible influence that attitude functions have for the way in which different individuals go about the business of evaluating objects in their environment. In every study, there was evidence that individuals who likely evaluate based on social-adjustive concerns use different criteria to judge the quality of everyday products than do those who evaluate with a concern for the consistency between what a product is and how it performs. For those with social-adjustive concerns, as operationalized by the self-monitoring construct, the potential a product has to enhance or promote a desirable image appears to be of prime importance when these individuals judge the merits of a product. Be it where the product was made, who was

High self-monitors

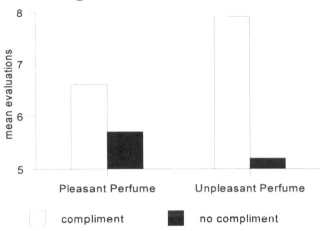

Low Self-Monitors

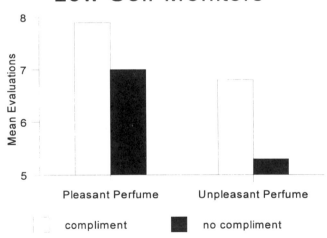

FIG. 7.6. Mean evaluations of perfume samples.

promoting it, or what store it came from, high self-monitoring individuals used the image cues we provided much more so than they used a product's performance in their evaluations. In general, products that could be construed as image enhancing were perceived as good; those not so construed were perceived as less desirable.

In contrast, for those with a more-value expressive orientation, which appears to be manifested as a concern for the consistency between pretense and performance (as applied to both their own lives as well as to the objects in their environment), product performance was a particularly important factor in their product evaluations. Although they were not immune to the effects of some of our image cues, in each study the overall product evaluations of low self-monitors appeared to be influenced by how well the product performed. In general, the better a product performed, the more highly low self-monitors evaluated it.

Although it remains to be seen whether research on other attitude functions, or on the social-adjustive and value-expressive functions operationalized differently, will produce similar results, to the extent that we have successfully demonstrated that different motivations for why we evaluate can lead to different strategies in how we evaluate, we believe that our results might add to a perspective from which to conceptualize attitudes and attitude functions that has been forwarded by Fazio and colleagues (Fazio,1989; Fazio, Blascovich, & Driscoll, 1992). They suggest and provide evidence that the primary function of all attitudes is what earlier theorists called an object appraisal (Smith et al., 1956) or knowledge (Katz, 1960) function. That is, they suggest, all attitudes exist to give us a quick and efficient means to evaluate what is good and bad in our environment and to inform us of what we should approach and what we should avoid. Attitudes in general, they argue, make it easier for us to navigate our complex social worlds and allow us to make decisions with relatively little cognitive resources. They further argue that the other functions that have been proposed for attitudes (e.g., social-adjustive) "have more to do with the content and direction of attitudes than with the general utility of simply holding an attitude, regardless of its valence" (Fazio, Blascovich, & Driscoll, 1992, p. 389).

We believe that our results can be interpreted as consistent with their conceptualization. If we grant that the primary function of attitudes is to give us immediate knowledge of whether an object in our environment is good or bad, then perhaps the other functions proposed for attitudes more accurately represent the strategies that individuals use to ascertain whether an attitude object is good or bad and more accurately indicate the types of information consulted in arriving at these judgments. That is, the other proposed attitude functions may more accurately describe how individuals arrive at their appraisals and evaluations of attitude objects than why individuals appraise and evaluate (see also Bazzini & Shaffer, 1995).

In our own research, although we believe that suggesting that the attitudes of high self-monitors generally serve a social-adjustive function and that the attitudes of low self-monitors generally serve a value-expressive function is consistent with the original spirit, and explication of functional theories, we also recognize that the ultimate goal for high and low self-monitors, be it when considering their position on capital punishment or, as in our research, when considering everyday products, is likely the same: to arrive at a global assessment of the objects in their environment. To the extent that the primary motivation, or function, underlying evaluation is "knowledge" or "object appraisal," then perhaps, as we have demonstrated, what meaningfully differs among people, and what terms like social-adjustive function and value-expressive function more accurately indicate, are the various decision rules that different individuals employ to arrive at global assessments of the objects, issues, and people in their social environments.

ACKNOWLEDGMENTS

I thank Deborah Loffredo for her help in searching the literature and Jim Olson for his helpful comments on an earlier version of this chapter. Portions of the research reported were funded by Faculty Research Grants and Internal Education Fund grants from Union College. Correspondence should be addressed to Ken DeBono, Department of Psychology, Union College, Schenectady, NY 12308. E-mail: debonok@union.edu.

REFERENCES

Aronson, E., & Linder, D. (1965). Gain and loss of esteem as determinants of interpersonal attraction. *Journal of Experimental Social Psychology, 1*, 156–171.

Baugh, D. F., & Davis, L. (1989). The effect of store image on consumers' perceptions of designer and private label clothing. *Clothing and Textiles Research Journal, 7*, 15–21.

Bazzini, D. G., & Shaffer, D. R. (1995). Investigating the social adjustive and value expressive functions of well-grounded attitudes: Implications for change and for subsequent behavior. *Motivation and Emotion, 19*, 279–305.

Caballero, M. J., & Pride, W. M. (1984). Selected effects of salesperson sex and attractiveness in direct mail advertisements. *Journal of Marketing, 48*, 94–100.

Caballero, M. J., & Solomon, P. J. (1984). Effects of model attractiveness of sales response. *Journal of Advertising, 13*, 17–23.

Chang, T. Z., & Wildt, A. (1994). Price, product information, and purchase intentions: An empirical investigation. *Journal of the Academy of Marketing Science, 22*, 16–27.

Dawar, N., & Parker, P. (1994). Marketing universals: Consumers' use of brand name, price, physical appearance, and retailer reputation as signals of product quality. *Journal of Marketing, 58*, 81–95.

DeBono, K. G. (1987). Investigating the social adjustive and value expressive functions of attitudes: Implications for persuasion processes. *Journal of Personality and Social Psychology, 52*, 279–287.

DeBono, K. G., & Burman, S. (1997). Unpublished raw data.

DeBono, K. G., & Edmonds, A. (1989). Cognitive dissonance and self-monitoring: A matter of context? *Motivation and Emotion, 13*, 259–270.

DeBono, K. G., & Harnish, R. J. (1988). Source expertise, source attractiveness, and the processing of persuasive information: A functional approach. *Journal of Personality and Social Psychology, 55*, 541–546.

DeBono, K. G., & Krim S. (1997). Compliments and perceptions of product quality: An individual difference perspective. *Journal of Applied Social Psychology, 27*, 1359–1366.

DeBono, K. G., Leavitt, A., & Backus, J. (1997). *Product packaging and perceptions of product quality.* Unpublished manuscript.

DeBono, K. G., & Packer, M. (1991). The effects of advertising strategy on perceptions of product quality. *Personality and Social Psychology Bulletin, 17*, 194–200.

DeBono, K. G., & Pflaum, J. (1997). Unpublished raw data.

DeBono, K. G., & Rubin, K. (1995). Country of origin and perceptions of product quality: An individual difference perspective. *Basic and Applied Social Psychology, 17*, 239–247.

DeBono, K. G., Ruggeri, D., & Foster, A. (1997). Unpublished raw data.

DeBono, K. G., & Telesca, C. (1990). The influence of source physical attractiveness on advertising effectiveness: A functional perspective. *Journal of Applied Social Psychology, 20*, 1383–1395.

Dodds, W. B., Monroe, K. B., & Grewal, D. (1991). Effects of price, brand, and store information on buyers' product evaluations. *Journal of Marketing Research, 28*, 307–319.

Erickson, G. M., Johansson, J. K., & Chao, P. (1984). Image variables in multi-attribute product evaluations: Country of origin effects. *Journal of Consumer Research, 11*, 694–699.

Fazio, R. H. (1989). On the power and functionality of attitudes: The role of attitude accessibility. In A. R. Pratkanis, S. J. Breckler, & A. G. Greenwald (Eds.), *Attitude structure and function* (pp. 153–179). Hillsdale, NJ: Lawrence Erlbaum Associates.

Fazio, R. H., Blascovich, J., & Driscoll, D. M. (1992). On the functional value of attitudes: The influence of accessible attitudes on the ease and quality of decision-making. *Personality and Social Psychology Bulletin, 18*, 388–401.

Fox, S. (1984). *The mirror makers.* New York: Morrow.

Harris, R. J., Garner, E. B., Sprick, S. J., & Carroll, C. (1994). Effects of foreign product names and country of origin attributions on advertisement evaluations. *Psychology and Marketing, 11*, 129–144.

Hastak, M., & Hong, S. (1991). Country of origin effects on product quality judgments: An information integration perspective. *Psychology and Marketing, 8*, 129–143.

Herek, G. M. (1986a). The instrumentality of attitudes: Toward a neofunctional theory. *Journal of Social Issues, 42*, 99–114.

Herek, G. M. (1986b). The social psychology of homophobia: Toward a practical theory. *Review of Law and Social Change, 14*, 923–934.

Herek, G. M. (1987). Can functions be measured? A new perspective to the functional approach to attitudes. *Social Psychology Quarterly, 50*, 285–303.

Hong, S., & Wyer, R. S. (1989). Effects of country of origin and product attribute information on product evaluation: An information processing perspective. *Journal of Consumer Research, 16*, 175–187.

Jacoby, J., & Mazursky, D. (1984). Linking brand and retail images: Do the potential risks outweigh the potential benefits? *Journal of Retailing, 60,* 105–122.

Johar, J. S., & Sirgy, M. J. (1991). Value-expressive versus utilitarian advertising appeals: When and why to use which appeal. *Journal of Advertising, 20,* 23–33.

Joseph, W. B. (1982). The credibility of physically attractive communicators: A review. *Journal of Advertising, 11,* 15–24.

Katz, D. (1960). The functional approach to the study of attitudes. *Public Opinion Quarterly, 24,* 163–204.

Keisler, C. A., Collins, B. E., & Miller, N. (1969). *Attitude change: A critical analysis of theoretical perspectives.* New York: Wiley.

Korgaonkar, P. K., Lund, D., & Price, B. (1985). A structural equations approach toward examination of store attitude and store patronage. *Journal of Retailing, 61,* 39–60.

Kristiansen, C. M. (1990). The symbolic/value expressive function of outgroup attitudes among homosexuals. *Journal of Social Psychology, 130,* 61–69.

Kristiansen, C. M., & Zanna, M. P. (1988). Justifying attitudes by appealing to values: A function perspective. *British Journal of Social Psychology, 27,* 247–256.

Kristiansen, C. M., & Zanna, M. P. (1991). Value relevance and the value-attitude relation: Value expressiveness versus halo effects. *Basic and Applied Social Psychology, 12,* 471–483.

Leone, C., & Wingate, C. (1991). A functional approach to understanding attitudes toward AIDS victims. *Journal of Social Psychology, 131,* 761–768.

Lim, J. S., Darley, W. K., & Summers, J. O. (1994). An assessment of country of origin effects under alternative presentation formats. *Journal of the Academy of Marketing Science, 22,* 274–282.

Maio, G. R., & Olson, J. M. (1994). Value–attitude–behaviour relations: The moderating role of attitude functions. *British Journal of Social Psychology, 33,* 301–312.

Maio, G. R., & Olson, J. M. (1995). Relations between values, attitudes, and behavioral intentions: The moderating role of attitude function. *Journal of Experimental Social Psychology, 31,* 266–285.

Murray, S. L., Haddock, G., & Zanna, M. P. (1996). On creating value-expressive attitudes: An experimental approach. In C. Seligman, J. M. Olson & M. P. Zanna (Eds.), *The psychology of values: The Ontario symposium* (Vol. 8, pp 107–133). Mahwah, NJ: Lawrence Erlbaum Associates.

Parekh, H., & Kanekar, S. (1994). The physical attractiveness stereotype in a consumer-related situation. *Journal of Social Psychology, 134,* 297–300.

Pratkanis, A, R., Breckler, S. J., Greenwald, A. G. (Eds.). (1989). *Attitude structure and function.* Hillsdale, NJ: Lawrence Erlbaum Associates.

Rao, A. R., & Monroe, K. B. (1989). The effect of price, brand name, and store name on buyers' perceptions of product quality: An integrative review. *Journal of Marketing Research, 26,* 351–357.

Shavitt, S. (1990). The role of attitude objects in attitude functions. *Journal of Experimental Social Psychology, 26,* 124–148

Shavitt, S., Lowrey, T. M., & Han, S. (1992). Attitude functions in advertising: The interactive role of products and self-monitoring. *Journal of Consumer Psychology, 1, 337–364.*

Sigall, H., & Aronson, E. (1969). Liking for an evaluator as a function of her physical attractiveness and nature of evaluations. *Journal of Experimental Social Psychology, 5,* 93–100.

Smith, W. B., Bruner, S. J., & White, R. W. (1956). *Opinions and personality.* New York: Wiley.

Snyder, M. (1974). The self-monitoring of expressive behavior. *Journal of Personality and Social Psychology, 30,* 526–537.

Snyder, M. (1979). Self-monitoring processes. In L. Berkowitz (Ed.), *Advances in experimental social psychology* (Vol. 12). New York: Academic Press.

Snyder, M. (1987). *Public appearances/private realities: The psychology of self-monitoring.* New York: Freeman.

Snyder, M., & DeBono, K. G. (1985). Appeals to image and claims about quality: Understanding the psychology of advertising. *Journal of Personality and Social Psychology, 49,* 586–597.

Snyder, M., & Gangestad, S. (1986). On the nature of self-monitoring: Matters of assessment, matters of validity. *Journal of Personality and Social Psychology, 51*, 125–139.

Spivey, W. A., Monson, J. M., & Locander, W. B. (1983). Improving the effectiveness of persuasive communications: Matching message with functional profile. *Journal of Business Research, 11*, 257–269.

Szybillo, G. J., & Jacoby, J. (1974). Intrinsic versus extrinsic cues as determinants of perceived product quality. *Journal of Applied Psychology, 59*, 74–78.

Valenzi, E. R., & Andrews, I. R. (1971). Effects of price information on product quality ratings. *Journal of Applied Psychology, 55*, 87–91.

Wyman, M. A., & Snyder, M. (1997). Attitudes toward "gays in the military": A functional perspective. *Journal of Applied Social Psychology, 27*, 306–329.

Yukl, G., & Tracy, J. B. (1992). Consequences of influence tactics used with subordinates, peers, and the boss. *Journal of Applied Psychology, 77*, 525–535.

8

Opinions and Personality: On the Psychological Functions of Attitudes and Other Valued Possessions

Deborah A. Prentice
Kevin M. Carlsmith
Princeton University

In the study of personality, researchers have often had difficulty generating empirical support for propositions that seem, on the face of them, obviously true. Such has been the case, for example, in research on the relation of opinions to personality. Most researchers and laypeople alike would agree that personality is expressed, at least to some extent, in the opinions an individual holds. That is, we tend to view attitudes as significant expressions of the self: We assume that we have learned something about a person when we know his or her attitudes and assume further that these attitudes should relate, in some lawful way, to other aspects of the person. At a general level, these claims are uncontroversial. But when we move to more specific research questions about *how* personality is manifested in people's opinions, *which* other aspects of the person should be consistent with his or her attitudes, and what the *source*

223

of any observed consistency might be, answers are much more difficult to come by. Theories that have addressed these questions about the relationship of opinions to personality have proven very difficult to test, and empirical evidence of consistency between attitudes and other aspects of the person has been elusive.

In this chapter, we report a line of research designed to uncover evidence of consistency across the possessions that an individual values. By possessions, we mean not just material objects—a favorite sweatshirt, a lucky charm, or a valuable piece of jewelry, for example. We mean all of the things, mental and physical, animate and inanimate—and including, of course, opinions—that a person can call his or her own.[1] The idea that personality is expressed through a person's possessions can be traced to James (1890), who argued that

> man's Self is the sum total of all that he CAN call his, not only his body and his psychic powers, but his clothes and his house, his wife and children, his ancestors and friends, his reputation and works, his lands, and yacht and bank-account. (pp. 291–292)

Similar ideas have served as a starting point for a number of investigations since then, notably, for our purposes, those of Csikszentmihalyi and Rochberg-Halton (1981) in the domain of material objects and Smith, Bruner, and White (1956) in the domain of opinions. Our goal is to extend these investigations to address the question of whether individuals value similar things, or perhaps have similar ways of valuing things, across domains.

As to the source of this similarity, we consider two potential candidates: the psychological needs or, as we refer to them, functions that possessions serve for the individual, and the kinds of attachment individuals form to their possessions. In other words, we seek consistency in *why*

---

[1]We refer throughout this chapter to people's *possessions*; alternatively, we might have opted, in line with philosophers and political theorists, to use the term *property*. We decided on possessions rather than property because the natural language connotations of the term *possessions* are more apt for our purposes. Both possessions and property define a class of things one calls one's own. But the term *property* implies ownership—even exclusive ownership—which works well for material objects and perhaps even for some kinds of relationships, but not for attitudes and values. We think of the value of property to each individual as decreasing the more individuals hold it (as in co-ownership of a house); in contrast, in at least some cases, attitudes, values, and relationships increase in their value to each individual the more individuals hold them. One's property is defined more formally and less experientially than one's possessions; it is the experiencing of having things in which we are interested here. Therefore, possessions better captures our meaning, and we use it throughout the chapter to refer to all things, mental and physical, that one considers one's own.

and *how* people value things. Each of these perspectives on personality has a rich tradition of theory and empirical research behind it, far too rich to review in a single chapter. Therefore, we limit our review to the literature most relevant to the study of attitudes because attitudes are central both to our own research interests and to the present volume. We begin with the functional approach.

CONSISTENCY IN PSYCHOLOGICAL FUNCTION

Early Theories of Attitude Functions

The functional approach to attitudes originated in two places at more or less the same time. In 1956, Smith, Bruner, and White published *Opinions and Personality*, in which they reported on intensive case studies of 10 men. Their focus was on understanding the ways in which each respondent's attitude toward Russia fit into his overall personality structure (see also Smith, 1947). Their theoretical assumptions are well captured in the following passage:

> A person's behavior is marked by a certain self-consistency or congruency. Expressive movement, speech, intensity of striving, style of thinking, "temperament"—all of these things and many others seem to constitute a congruent pattern which we think of as typical of the individual.... Opinions, like any other form of complex behavior, are involved in such a pattern of consistency. They reflect the man's style of operating.... A man's opinions reflect the deeper-lying pattern of his life—who he has become by virtue of facing a particular kind of world with a particular kind of constitution. (Smith et al., 1956, pp. 37–38)

Then in 1960, Katz published an article in *Public Opinion Quarterly*, in which he offered the functional approach as a means of resolving various theoretical tensions in the study of attitudes. Katz's treatment of the functional approach was theoretical, rather than empirical; his primary interest was in how attitude functions might serve as moderators of the processes of attitude formation, arousal, and change.

It has become customary in discussions of the origins of the functional approach to emphasize the similarities in these two early treatments, and, indeed, there are many. Both were concerned with the question of why people hold the opinions they do, and both sought the answer to this question in the psychological functions an attitude can serve for the individual. Both identified a finite number of functions that attitudes might serve, and their lists of functions overlapped considerably. Smith et al. (1956) focused on the adjustive functions of opinion—the ways in which opinions help people deal with inner demands (the *externalization* function), social demands (the *social-adjustment* function), and reality demands (the *object-appraisal* function). Katz (1960) also proposed that attitudes were useful in dealing with inner demands (the *ego-defense* function) and reality demands (variously termed the *instrumental, utili-tarian,* and *adjustment* function); in addition, he distinguished those attitudes that serve as a means of expressing values important to the self-concept (the *value-expressive* function) and those that enable people to find structure and meaning in the world (the *knowledge* function). Moreover, this characterization of the functions proposed by each research team understates their common ground. Smith et al. acknowledged that opinions are often expressive of one's important values and can provide cognitive clarity; these functions of attitudes were both subsumed under their *object appraisal* function. And Katz, for his part, certainly appreciated that opinions exist in a social environment. He saw the social-adjustment function of attitudes not as a separate and distinct category but instead as cutting across the four primary motivations he identified, with the form of social adjustment dependent on the particular relation of the group to the individual.

Even though the functional theories of Smith et al. (1956) and Katz (1960) shared some striking similarities (all the more striking in light of the fact that the approaches were developed independently), they also were characterized by several important differences. These differences stemmed, for the most part, from the divergent interests of their authors. Katz was a student of public opinion, with strong roots in the social and behavioral sciences more generally. He was the author of a book on *Public Opinion and Propaganda* and approached the study of attitudes with a particular interest in the processes of attitude change. In his explication of the functional approach to attitudes, he devoted considerable attention to the determinants of attitude arousal and attitude change, detailing the conditions necessary to arouse and to change attitudes serving each of his four functions. The primary challenge for the functional approach, according to Katz, was to find ways of targeting the needs that various attitudes satisfy.

Smith, Bruner, and White were part of an interdisciplinary team of clinical and social psychologists and social anthropologists at Harvard University, whose goal was to understand attitudes as an integral part of personality. In the preface of *Opinions and Personality*, they described their study as "one of a long series of investigations at the Harvard Psychological Clinic in which normal personality has been brought under close scrutiny through case studies carried out by groups of investigators" (Smith et al., 1956, p. v). They acknowledged their indebtedness to Henry Murray, the pioneer of the intensive case study method, and to Gordon Allport, who, in their words, "has long been concerned with attitudes as an integral and important aspect of personality" (p. vi). Thus, whereas Katz's functional approach used personality in the service of understanding attitudes, Smith et al.'s functional approach used attitudes in the service of understanding personality.

These differences in orientation had a number of implications for the nature of the functional approach that each research team developed. First, although both teams recognized that an attitude might serve primarily one or multiple functions, they differed in which they took to be the prototypical case. Katz (1960) focused on attitudes that served a single function. Given the goals of his theory, this focus is not surprising: Because he was interested in the prospects for changing attitudes by undermining their functional basis, Katz naturally began with the simplest case, in which there was only one function to attack. A successful strategy for changing an attitude that serves a single function could presumably be adapted to attitudes that serve multiple functions (at least in theory). Smith et al. (1956), in contrast, conceptualized attitudes as equilibrium points within the motivational force field that constitutes personality. More specifically, they viewed each attitude as determined by the strength of an individual's inner, social, and reality needs at a given point in time, combined with the potential of the attitude in question to satisfy those needs. Attitude change occurs when there is a shift in the relative importance of different needs, in the relevance of the attitude to satisfying those needs, or in both. Thus it made no sense, in their formulation, to conceptualize an attitude as serving only a single function. As they put it, "The Psychologists' act of isolating certain motives and holding them up for examination is an artifical one. For strivings, like a set of simultaneous equations, must be viewed as inextricably interdependent" (p. 144).

The two research teams also differed in the extent to which they looked beyond the identified functions to other sources of individual differences in attitudes. Smith et al. (1956) did not restrict the basis for consistency to the functions that attitudes serve for individuals; instead, they considered many ways in which attitudes are expressive of an individual's personality. For example, they analyzed the ways in which a respondent's attitudes toward Russia were generally expressive of his intellectual capacity, his level of impulsivity, and the degree of optimism with which he viewed the world. They related each respondent's attitude to various aspects of his cognitive style, including his facility at abstraction, his cognitive flexibility, and his insight into other viewpoints. In short, they went beyond an analysis of the adjustive functions of opinion to examine all of the aspects of the person that might relate systematically to his attitudes. Katz (1960), in contrast, was less interested in the multiple correlates of attitudes. He focused his analysis more narrowly on their causes, which he saw as residing in the functions they served for their holders.

Recent Revival

In recent years, research on the functions of attitudes has followed up on Katz's (1960) project by integrating the functional approach into information-processing models of attitude formation and change. The most sustained research activity has centered on the matching hypothesis: The idea that people will be more persuaded by arguments that address the functional basis for their attitudes than by equally strong arguments that address a different function. The majority of studies that have tested the matching hypothesis have used the self-monitoring scale (Snyder, 1974) to identify individuals whose attitudes are likely to serve a social-adjustment function (i.e., the high self-monitors) and individuals whose attitudes are likely to serve a value-expressive function (i.e., the low self-monitors). These two groups are then compared on their receptivity to appeals that target the social-adjustment and value-expressive functions. Research that uses this paradigm has demonstrated that individuals are more persuaded by appeals that match, in content, source, or likely outcome, the functional basis of their attitudes (DeBono, 1987; DeBono & Harnish, 1988; Snyder & DeBono, 1985) and that this effect appears to be driven by the greater scrutiny given to functionally relevant appeals (DeBono & Packer, 1991; DeBono & Telesca, 1990; Lavine & Snyder, 1996; Petty & Wegener). Additional research has indicated that the functional matching effect is quite robust, occurring across different types of functions, issues, and contexts (see Bazzini & Shaffer, 1996; Clary, Snyder, Ridge, Miene, & Haugen, 1994; Shavitt, 1990; Shavitt, Lowrey & Han, 1992, for various extensions).

Much less attention has been paid of late to the broader questions about opinions and personality that motivated Smith et al.'s (1956) inquiry. However, a similar kind of investigation, focusing not on attitudes but on material possessions, was reported by Csikszentmihalyi and Rochberg-Halton (1981). These investigators conducted extensive interviews with respondents about their neighborhoods, their homes, and, in particular, the things in their homes that are special to them. They also collected information on respondents' personalities; goals and aspirations; family dynamics; role models; and professional, political, and recreational activities. A content analysis of respondents' descriptions of their favorite possessions revealed a lot about these individuals: their past experiences, central values, means of enjoyment, important relationships, and so on. Moreover, their possessions related in systematic ways to other aspects of their personalities and lives. Csikszentmihalyi and Rochberg-Halton's analysis and interpretation of these data reinforced a number of Smith et al.'s (1956) claims about the ways in which personality is expressed and revealed. At a general level, both investigations suggested that an analysis of the things that are important to people—their personal convictions and most cherished material possessions—can provide a valuable window through which to view their lives. At a more specific level, both investigations suggested that a focus on the psychological functions of these important objects and attitudes might prove especially revealing.

Empirical Research

Our own research on the functions of attitudes took these observations as a starting point. We sought, as Smith, Csikszentmihalyi, and their colleagues did, to learn something about the psychology of individuals through an analysis of the things they believe and value. But, compared to these earlier investigations, ours was considerably more circumscribed. We focused on three domains of a person's life—favorite possessions, attitudes, and values—and analyzed the psychological functions these objects serve for the person. Our primary hypothesis was that these functions would be consistent within individuals.

Dimensions of Possession Value. Our research began with an exploratory study of the sources of value in people's favorite material possessions. The goal of this study was to identify the psychological functions that material possessions can serve. Previous research suggested that we would find evidence for a distinction between objects that serve a self-expressive function and those that serve an instrumental function (see Csikszentmihalyi and Rochberg-Halton, 1981). We hoped to validate this distinction, which is prominent in discussions of attitudes and personality as well.

We asked a sample of undergraduates to list their five favorite material possessions (not including a car, if they had one) and to explain why they value those particular objects. Students told us about their stereo, their walkman, the ring that had been passed down through the generations, the photograph taken at their family reunion, their books, their pearls, their Bible, their credit cards, their model airplane collection, and the artwork they had done themselves. In total they listed 70 distinctly different objects to which they attached special significance.

To elucidate the psychological structure that underlay these valued objects, we gave another sample of undergraduates the 70 possessions typed on cards and asked them to sort the cards into piles, in which all of the cards in a pile describe possessions that are similar in their source of value. We used these pile sorts to create 1-0 incidence matrices that represented the pairwise similarity of the items in the stimulus set, summed these matrices across participants, and then submitted the final matrix to a nonparametric multidimensional scaling procedure. The results indicated that a four-dimensional solution provided a good representation of the stimulus array. We interpreted the dimensions first subjectively, by contrasting the possessions loading at the extremes of each, and then validated those interpretations empirically (see Prentice, 1987, for details of these procedures.)

The results confirmed the importance of the self-expressive–instrumental distinction. The first and primary dimension of the scaling solution arrayed possessions along a continuum, from those for which primary value resided in their symbolic meaning (e.g., photographs, family heirlooms, and a diary) to those for which primary value resided in the direct benefits they provided (e.g., a stereo, a computer, and a bicycle). This distinction maps extremely well onto Csikszentmihalyi and Rochberg-Halton's (1981) distinction between possessions as symbols of kinship ties and continuity versus as a means of enjoyment; it also echoes Katz's (1960) distinction between the value-expressive and utilitarian functions of attitudes, and of Spence and Helmreich's (1980) distinction between expressive and instrumental personality types.

The remaining three dimensions of the scaling solution also reflected individuals' use of possessions to express aspects of their personalities: The second dimension contrasted recreational and practical possessions, the third dimension contrasted cultured and everyday possessions, and the fourth dimension contrasted common and elite possessions. But our primary interest was in the first dimension because it held the promise of characterizing beliefs and attitudes as well.

Dimensions of Belief Value.   Next, we conducted a similar exploratory analysis of the dimensions of value in people's cherished beliefs, to examine whether the self-expressive–instrumental distinction is also evident in this domain. The same individuals who told us about their five favorite material possessions were asked to list their five most cherished beliefs and to explain why those beliefs were important to them. Students found it more difficult to generate their favorite beliefs than they had their favorite objects, and there was considerable idiosyncrasy in what they listed. But all were eventually able to give five responses, from which we deleted statements that were meaningless or redundant to create a master list of 79 distinctly different belief statements.

To elucidate the psychological structure that underlay these valued beliefs, we gave another sample of undergraduates the 79 belief statements typed on cards and asked them to sort the cards into piles, in which all of the cards in a pile describe beliefs that are "conceptually similar—in other words, beliefs that a single individual could hold simultaneously and consistently." We used these pile sorts to create 1–0 incidence matrices that represented the pairwise similarity of the items in the stimulus set, summed these matrices across participants, and then submitted the final matrix to a nonparametric multidimensional scaling procedure. The results indicated that a three-dimensional solution provided a good representation of the stimulus array.[2] Interpretation of the dimensions relied primarily on the superimposition on the scaling solution of the results of a hierarchical clustering analysis of the belief statements.

The first and primary dimension yielded a contrast between symbolic beliefs at one pole and instrumental beliefs at the other. Symbolic beliefs are those that state, in general terms, how the world is or ought to be. Statements that loaded at this pole include, "All people are basically the same and should be treated equally," "It is important to have close family relations," and

---

[2] The three-dimensional solution accounted for 75% of the variance, with a stress of .18.

"People should be open-minded about others." Instrumental beliefs are those that have direct applicability to everday existence—in other words, beliefs that can guide action. Statements that loaded at this pole include, "One should not room with one's best friends," "The only person anyone can count on is him or herself," and "It is important to be organized and to keep records." The second dimension distinguished a personal view from a world view. Beliefs that express a personal view describe the way individuals should lead their lives, including such statements as, "It is beneficial to participate in athletics," "It is important to take opportunities that arise," and "People should always have something that interests them besides work." Beliefs that express a world view describe states of or ideals for the nation and world in general, including such statements as, "The environment is the primary determinant of all events," "Hunger is the most important world problem today," and "People are more moral than institutions." The third dimension reflected the classic left–right ideological distinction. Statements at the left pole included, "Students should not worry about grades in school," "People should live together before they get married," and "People should be free to make their own decisions and to do what they want with their lives." Statements at the right pole included, "Abortion is wrong," "Young people should be thrifty," and "People should assimilate with the culture in which they live."

Thus, our first two studies supported the notion that people think about material possessions and beliefs in similar ways. The distinction between beliefs used to express symbols, ideals, and personal values and beliefs designed to guide action provided a parallel to the self-expressive–instrumental continuum we found in favorite objects. In addition, these analogous dimensions reflected the primary evaluations made by participants in both scaling studies. Thus, the data suggested that people use both beliefs and objects to understand and manipulate the environment, in the instrumental case, and to understand and express their important values, in the self-expressive case.

Consistency in the Functions Served by Objects and Attitudes. Of course, we were not simply interested in demonstrating a parallel structure across domains; we wanted to know whether physical and mental possessions served the same function for their holders. To examine individual consistency in function across domains, we used the strategy that has been popular among recent researchers of the functional approach: We tested for matching between the predominant function served by material possessions and receptivity to functionally oriented persuasive appeals. The logic of this strategy was as follows: If people have functional orientations that characterize their interactions with both material possessions and attitudes, then we should be able to diagnose that orientation in one domain (in this case, the material possession domain) and measure it in another. Thus, we divided people in functional groupings on the basis of their favorite material possessions and then tested their responses to a manipulation of attitude function.

We wrote two versions of a persuasive message about each of six unfamiliar (but real) social issues. All messages began with a brief description of the issue, followed by a proposed course of action and four arguments in support of that course of action. The two versions of each message differed in the course of action proposed and the nature of the arguments that supported it. In one version, the proposal was symbolically toned and was supported by arguments that expressed the important social values and ideals that the plan would uphold. In the other version, the proposal was instrumentally toned and was supported by arguments that described the direct and instrumental benefits of the plan. The students who had contributed their favorite material possessions to our first scaling study read messages about all six issues, three in the symbolic version and three in the instrumental version, and rated their favorability toward the course of action proposed in each (see Prentice, 1987, for details of the materials and procedure).

We expected to find an interaction between possession function and appeal type: Students who valued self-expressive objects should be more persuaded by symbolic appeals than by instrumental appeals, whereas students who valued instrumental objects should show the opposite pattern. We divided students into those whose favorite objects were primarily self-expressive and those whose favorite objects were primarily instrumental and compared the responses of these two groups to the two types of appeals.[3] The results revealed the predicted interaction, but the effect was driven entirely by students with a self-expressive orientation.

---

[3]We divided students into possession groups by averaging the weights of their five favorite possessions on the first dimension of the scaling solution and then assigning those with negative averages to one group and those with positive averages to the other. (A median split would have produced the same groupings.) It is important to note that there was little consistency in the functions served by the five possessions listed by each individual. The average first dimension weights were normally distributed with a mean around zero. Thus, the groupings represent a tendency to favor one or the other type of material possession, rather than a clear and consistent preference for one over the other.

That is, students who listed self-expressive possessions as their favorites were more persuaded by symbolic than by instrumental appeals, whereas students who listed instrumental possessions were equally persuaded by the two types of appeals.[4] Thus, we have evidence for consistency across domains only in the self-expressive function.

The Role of Values. We were also interested in the relation of values to material possession and attitude functions. Previous functional theories suggested two different forms this relation might take. First, according to Katz's (1960) functional theory, values should relate to objects and attitudes only for those individuals with a self-expressive orientation. Katz distinguished sharply between attitudes that serve a value-expressive function (similar to our self-expressive function) and those that serve an instrumental or utilitarian function, and argued that values should predict the former but not the latter. Alternatively, according to Smith et al.'s (1956) functional theory, values, material possessions, and attitudes all reflect the individual's major interests and ongoing concerns. Therefore, if those interests and concerns focus on self-exploration and self-expression, then the individual's favorite objects, attitudes, and values should all be symbolic or self-expressive. If those interests and concerns focus on obtaining immediate benefits (in the form of pleasure, enjoyment, or resources) from the environment, then the individual's favorite objects, attitudes, and values should all be instrumental.

To test these two hypotheses about the relation of values to material possessions and attitudes, we asked our sample of students to divide up Rokeach's (1968) 36 values into six piles of approximately 6 values each, ranging from their least important values to their most important values. We translated these pile sorts into ratings of each value on a 6-point scale, and averaged each participants' ratings of the 6 most symbolic values (a world at peace, a world of beauty, family security, national security, mature love, and self-respect) and their ratings of the 6 most instrumental values (being ambitious, capable, courageous, imaginative, intellectual, and logical).[5] We then tested for an interaction between the type of

---

[4]Students responded consistently to the three appeals of each type. The hypothesized interaction was significant when using both subjects and appeals as random factors in the analysis.

[5]The six symbolic and six instrumental values were selected on the basis of independent ratings of all 36 values by 10 psychology graduate students. Although the symbolic–instrumental distinction shares quite a bit in common with Rokeach's (1968) distinction between instrumental and terminal values, the two are not similar enough for us to have used his classification of values.

material possessions they tended to value (self-expressive or instrumental) and their endorsement of these two types of values. The analysis revealed the predicted interaction between possession function and value type, which was again driven entirely by students with a self-expressive orientation. Students who favored self-expressive possessions rated symbolic values as significantly more important to them than instrumental values, whereas students who favored instrumental possessions rated the two types of values as equally important. Moreover, it was those students who favored self-expressive possessions, endorsed symbolic values, and rejected instrumental values who showed the greatest preference for symbolic over instrumental appeals (see Prentice, 1987, for details of these analyses). Thus, we again find impressive evidence for consistency in function across domains, but only in the self-expressive function.

These findings support Katz's (1960) view that attitude functions moderate the relation between values and attitudes. Additional evidence on this point has been provided in recent investigations by Maio and Olson (1994, 1995). In several studies, these researchers measured or manipulated whether attitudes served a value-expressive or utilitarian function and then examined the relation of these attitudes to values. The results indicated that values relate systematically to attitudes only when those attitudes serve a value-expressive function. In their studies, utilitarian attitudes showed no relation to values (though see Maio & Olson, 1996, for some preliminary evidence to the contrary).

Gender Differences.   One final aspect of the data from these studies deserves mention. There was a strong relation between gender and functional orientation across two of the three domains. In the domain of material possessions, 18 of the 24 students classified as favoring self-expressive objects were women, whereas only 8 of the 24 students classified as favoring instrumental objects were women.[6] In the domain of attitudes, there was a significant difference in the way men and women responded to the two types of appeals: Women were significantly more persuaded by symbolic than by instrumental appeals, whereas men were equally persuaded by both.[7] The first of these findings has considerable precedent

---

[6]A chi-square analysis revealed a significant association between gender and possession group, χ^2 = 8.66, p .005.

[7]An analysis of variance revealed a significant Sex × Appeal type interaction, $F(1,46)$ = 6.59, p .02. The means for women were 3.81 and 2.82 for symbolic and instrumental appeals, respectively; the comparable means for men were 3.41 and 3.45.

in the research literature: Numerous studies have shown that women and men value very different types of material possessions, with women favoring symbolic objects and men favoring instrumental objects (see Dittmar, 1992, for a review). The link between gender and attitude functions is less well documented. Early studies of attitude functions used only men as respondents (e.g., Smith et al., 1956). More recent studies have included women in their samples, but most have ignored gender in their analyses. Those that have included it have found no relation of gender to the self-expressive and instrumental functions (e.g., Herek, 1987). Yet, researchers in other traditions have argued that instrumentality and expressiveness are, in fact, central dimensions on which males and females differ (see Spence & Helmreich, 1980). Our results indicate that those gender differences (or at least the difference in expressiveness) may be manifested in both the material possessions men and women value and the attitudes they hold. More research on gender and functional orientation is needed.

It is interesting to note that the values domain provided no evidence for a link between gender and functional orientation. Again we see that, although it is possible to identify symbolic and instrumental values that people hold, these values do not function, so to speak, in the same way that material possessions and attitudes do.

Unresolved Issues

There are at least three issues that remain unresolved in our research on the functions of possessions. One pertains to the nature of the instrumental orientation. In our studies, we found no evidence of consistency in instrumentality across domains. We offer three potential explanations for this (null) result. First, it is possible that the objects we called instrumental were, in fact, defined by some other quality: their monetary value, salience in the environment, or social significance, for example. (Recall that the instrumental label was one we imposed on one pole of the first dimension of a multidimensional scaling solution, to distinguish it from the symbolic or self-expressive pole at the opposite end. The objects that we labeled instrumental were certainly not symbolic, but they may not have been valued especially for their instrumentality; see Prentice, 1987, Study 2.) In this case, people who valued those objects would not be defined by their instrumentality and would not be expected to hold instrumental attitudes or values. Second, it is possible that the problem was not our measure of possession function, but rather our measure of attitude function. Specifically, the unfamiliar issues we used in our research may not have been sufficiently self-relevant to evoke any instrumental concerns. If this were the case, the two types of messages we created would not have differed in their appeal to individuals with an instrumental orientation—which is exactly what we found. Finally, it is possible that the instrumental orientation simply is not consistent across domains. Instrumentality is inherently opportunistic and situationally responsive; indeed, this quality may define the category of people who are *least* likely to show measurable consistency among their valued possessions. And the fact that many previous investigations, using very different methods and measures, have also failed to turn up consistency in instrumentality suggests that this last explanation is most likely true.

A second unresolved issue concerns the claim that material possessions, attitudes, and possibly even values can serve multiple functions for an individual. Although researchers, ourselves included, have paid lip service to the idea that an attitude can serve multiple functions simultaneously, they have designed their empirical studies in ways that do not allow for this possibility. In our own research, we have emphasized the opposite point—that each individual has a single functional orientation that extends not only across their attitudes toward different issues but also across possessions in different domains. And we have demonstrated that some individuals do seem to have a dominant functional orientation that characterizes their attachments to many of their possessions. That said, we also believe that possessions often serve multiple functions simultaneously, and we plan to expand our empirical approach to explore this possibility.

Finally, our research leaves unresolved many lingering issues in functional theory. Perhaps the most pressing of these issues concerns the psychological status of attitude functions. Early theorists equated functions with psychological needs; that is, an attitude served a function to the extent that it helped an individual deal with inner demands, social demands, and/or reality demands (Smith et al., 1956). More recent researchers—again, ourselves included—have adopted this definition of attitude functions with very little critical scrutiny. They too have defined functions in terms of needs, but without elaborating a conception of needs. Until recently, this omission has probably done more good than harm, for it liberated the study of attitude functions from the theoretical and methodological constraints imposed on it by an overly rigid interpretation of psychological needs. But in more recent research, as we have begun to move beyond simple demonstrations of the matching hypothesis, the need for a more developed functional theory has become apparent.

Consider, for example, two different conceptions of the psychological needs that attitudes (and other valued possessions) might fill. One conception relies on the analogy between psychological needs and biological needs. According to this model, possessions are to the psyche what food and drink are to the body—a way of restoring it (at least temporarily) to an equilibrium state. What predictions follow from this model? We might expect a person to be most likely to adopt an attitude that meets a particular need when deprived of other ways to meet that need. We might expect a change in circumstance to produce a change in the strength of certain needs and therefore a change in the value attached to particular kinds of objects and attitudes. We might expect different possessions to serve different functions, so that all of an individual's needs are met. Or we might expect different types of possessions to serve different functions: An individual might use her attitudes to fill her instrumental needs and her material possessions to fill her self-expressive needs, for example. Alternatively, for a person who has only one dominant need, we might expect all of his or her possessions to serve the same function, but for each additional possession to have diminishing marginal psychological utility. All of these predictions follow from a concept of psychological needs as analogous to biological needs.

An alternative conception uses not biological needs but cognitive sets or schemas as the model. Here, the need served by a possession is not controlled by a homeostatic mechanism, as in the biological model, but is chronic, ongoing—to be managed, not satisfied. According to this model, each individual derives certain benefits from his or her valued possessions and seeks out things that can provide those benefits. Needs, in this sense, are akin to values or preferences in that they determine which features of an object or attitude will make it especially attractive to an individual. How would the predictions of this model differ from those of the biological model? The primary difference would be in the predictions regarding consistency across possessions. The cognitive model suggests that most possessions, within and across domains, serve the same function or set of functions, because individuals select them using similar criteria—those defined by their functional schema or set (see Abelson, 1986; Abelson & Prentice, 1989 for examples of this kind of analysis in the belief domain).

It is important to note that both of these conceptions of psychological needs were present—and not clearly distinguished—in early functional theories of attitudes. The assumptions of the biological model were best exemplified by the ego-defense function, whereas the assumptions of the cognitive model most apparent in the object-appraisal function (Smith et al., 1956) and the knowledge function (Katz, 1960). In our own research, we have implicitly adopted a cognitive model, as have most other researchers in the modern era. However, the language we all use to describe the functions of attitudes and material possessions, as well as many of our predictions, still echoes the biological model. The point here is not that the biological model is invalid—indeed, we believe that it may very well have limited applicability in some domains—but that research in this area will benefit from greater theoretical and conceptual clarity with regard to the psychological mechanisms that underlie functionality.

CONSISTENCY IN ATTACHMENT STYLE

In recent years, research on individual differences in attitudes has examined differences not only in why people hold the attitudes they do, but also in how they hold the attitudes they do. In particular, attitude strength has proven to be an important moderator of attitude change and attitude–behavior relations, just as attitude functions have been (see Petty & Krosnick, 1995, for a review of the literature on attitude strength). Researchers in this area have adopted two strategies for defining attitude strength. Some have defined it in terms of its consequences; that is, a strong attitude is one that persists over time, withstands exposure to counterattitudinal messages, has an impact on information processing and judgment, and guides behavior. Others have defined it in terms of its presumed antecedents; that is, a strong attitude is one that has an extensive knowledge base, high perceived importance, high ego relevance, and so on. To our knowledge, no researchers have drawn on theories of personality and individual differences in their conceptualizations of attitude strength.

Given our interest in characterizing individuals, personality theory served as a natural starting point for our investigation of the extent to which the form and quality of people's attachments to their possessions are consistent across domains. More specifically, we drew on attachment theory, with its well-developed account of individual differences in the bonds people form to their significant others. We begin by reviewing the main tenets of attachment theory and then examine the extent to which it applies beyond the interpersonal domain.

Attachment Theory

Attachment theory originated in Bowlby's (1979) work with British children who were orphaned during World War II. Bowlby was prompted by his observations of these children, as well as his interest in ethology and control system theories, to develop a theory of interpersonal relations that accorded a central role to the bond formed between infants and caregivers (Reis & Patrick, 1996). According to Bowlby, human infants are born with an innate need to seek and maintain proximity with caregivers; this need gives rise to an elaborate and highly adaptive attachment system that governs the infant–caregiver relationship. The quality and security of this initial relationship with a caregiver, in turn, serve as the foundation for all of the attachments the individual forms in later life. The infant–caregiver relationship exerts its influence on later relationships through *internal working models*—mental representations—of self and attachment figures that are formed during childhood. These internal working models both summarize past relational experience and direct future interactions.

Although Bowlby himself was not especially interested in exploring individual differences in the attachment bond, this topic has occupied many researchers since. Notably, Ainsworth, Blehar, Waters, and Wall (1978), focused on individual differences in the quality of the attachment relationship and on the connection of these so-called attachment styles with caregiving. They identified three general types of attachment style: *secure attachment*, in which caregivers are available, sensitive, and responsive; *anxious avoidance*, in which caregivers are distant, cold, or unavailable; and *anxious ambivalence*, in which caregivers are inconsistently and unpredictably responsive or unresponsive. These attachment styles show remarkable stability across the lifespan and across generations. For example, longitudinal studies have demonstrated substantial consistency in attachment style through childhood, across several-year spans in adulthood, and across generations within families (see Reis & Patrick, 1996, for a review). This temporal stability has been attributed to the impact of internal working models, which structure information processing, social motivation, and interpersonal behavior in ways that elicit confirmatory feedback and experiences with relationship partners.

This concept of internal working models also serves as the basis for our predictions about consistency in attachments across domains. Specifically, we posit that the internal working models developed out of the infant–caregiver relationship serve as a blueprint not just for interpersonal attachments but also for attachments to other things, including those inanimate and incorporeal. Of course, it is easy to identify differences between the animate and inanimate domains. Perhaps the most obvious of these is that creatures in the animate domain act and react, providing feedback that, as we have noted, serves to sustain and perpetuate attachment styles. Objects in the inanimate domain do not provide this kind of confirmatory feedback. Nevertheless, we maintain that, although internal working models of attachment may be created and perpetuated in the interpersonal domain, they exert (unidirectional) influence in the inanimate domain. We believe that this influence is triggered by affect: The experience of feeling a strong attachment or commitment to something, whether it is a person, an object, an issue, or a cause, primes one's representation of emotional attachments, that is, one's internal working models. The contents of that representation—the thoughts and feelings it evokes and expectations it generates—then shape one's interactions with the object of attachment.

Empirical Research

We have just begun to test some of these ideas about individual consistency in attachment styles across domains. In our research thus far, we have examined attachments to two kinds of targets: persons and material possessions (Carlsmith, 1996). Our decision to start with these two domains was based simply on pragmatic considerations: Attachment theory was developed in the interpersonal domain and the extension to the domain of material objects was straightforward. Thus, we do not yet have data on attachments to attitudes, although we do offer number of ideas about whether and how attachment might operate in the attitude domain at the end of this section.

Attachment Measure. We began our empirical work by developing a scale to measure attachment to a particular individual or material possession. The 35 scale items were adapted from prior research on attachment in the person and possession domains. Approximately half the questions were taken from Hazan and Shaver's (1987) descriptions of secure, avoidant, and anxious ambivalent adult attachment relationships. These questions (phrased here for the material possession domain) included, "I often worry that this possession will not remain close to me," "I am somewhat uncomfortable about how strong my feelings are toward this possession," and "I am comfortable depending on this possession." The remaining half were based on the dimensions of possession value identified by Dittmar (1988) and Prentice (1987). These questions (again, phrased for the material possession domain) included, "This object is primarily recreational in nature," "The value of this object comes from what it does or what it allows me to do"; and "This object truly says something about who I am."

We asked a sample of undergraduates to identify their three most cherished or important people and their three most cherished or important material possessions, and to write a free-format paragraph that explained each of their choices. Then we asked them to complete our 35-item attachment measure for each of the six targets. (Note that they answered the same 35 questions about each target, with the term "person" used to designate a significant other, and the terms "possession" or "object" used interchangeably to refer to a favorite material possession.) We submitted these data (treating each person's three people and three objects as independent observations) to two factor analyses, one for the person domain and one for the object domain. Both analyses yielded five-factor solutions; a varimax rotation was used to facilitate the substantive interpretation of the factors (see Carlsmith, 1996, for details of the analyses).

In the solution for the person data, the first factor represented a secure attachment style. Items that loaded on this factor included, "This person makes my life easier" and "My relationship with this person provides a 'window into the real me.'" The second factor represented an anxious ambivalent attachment style. Items that loaded on this factor included, "I find this person is reluctant to get as close as I would like" and "I often worry that this person will not want to stay with me." The third factor represented an avoidant attachment style. Items that loaded on this factor included, "I am nervous when this person gets too close" and "I am somewhat uncomfortable being close to this person." The fourth factor represented relationship stability. Items that loaded on this factor included, "I do not worry about being abandoned by this person" and "Throughout the changes in my life, this person will remain important and stable in my life." The fifth factor represented a casual relationship. Items that loaded on this factor included, "It would be relatively easy to replace this person in my life" and "I have no particularly important memories or experiences associated with this person." Thus, the first three factors captured the three traditional attachment styles, and the last two reflected other important qualities of relationships (stability and level of intimacy).

In the solution for the material possessions data, the first factor represented objects as means of recreation. Items that loaded on this factor included, "This object is primarily recreational in nature" and "I could probably place a dollar value on this object." The second factor represented objects as positive symbols. Items that loaded on this factor included, "This object truly says something about who I am" and "This particular object has far more value to me than it would to others." The third factor represented a conflicted attachment to an object. Items that loaded on this factor included, "I am nervous that this possession may become too important to me" and "Sometimes my desire to keep this possession with me creates problems." The fourth factor represented objects as dependable. Items that loaded on this factor included, "I know that this possession will be there when I need it" and "I do not worry about losing this possession." The fifth factor represented objects as useful. Items that loaded on this factor included, "Without this object, I would be unable to do certain things, or unable to do them as well" and "This object makes my life easier."

Taken together, these two factor analyses suggest there is a considerable degree of similarity in the structure of attachments to people and to material possessions. With only a small amount of license, we can interpret the secure attachment style as corresponding to an attachment to objects as positive symbols, the anxious ambivalent and avoidant attachment styles as corresponding to a conflicted attachment to objects, the stability of a relationship as corresponding to the dependability of an object, and a casual attachment to people as corresponding to a use of objects for recreation (although, admittedly, this last interpretation may require more than a little license). Of course, this parallel structure may result, in large part, from our use of the same measure of attachment across domains. Still, the fact that we obtained interpretable factor structures for both the person and object datasets suggests, at the very least, that it made sense to our participants to think about their attachments to people and to material possessions in similar ways.

Consistency in Attachments to People and Objects.   Of course, we were not simply interested in demonstrating a parallel structure across domains; we wanted to know whether a given individual formed similar attachments to people and to material possessions. We tested for correspondence across domains in two ways. First, we calculated scores for each participant on each of the five person factors and five object factors (averaging across the three targets within each domain), and correlated those scores across domains.[8] The results revealed moderate relationships between the factors that we hypothesized would correspond: The secure relationships factor was positively correlated with symbolic possession attachment; the two insecure relationship factors (anxious ambivalent and avoidant) were positively correlated with conflicted possession attachment; and the stable relationships factor was positively correlated with dependable possession attachment. Only the correlation between the casual relationship factor and attachment to possessions for recreation failed to reach significance. Although this analysis was fraught with methodological difficulties,[9] the results were encouraging.

A second test of cross-domain correspondence was facilitated by some additional data we collected from our participants. After completing the measures of their attachments to their favorite persons and material possessions, participants completed a number of standard personality inventories, including the Adult Attachment Scale (Collins & Read, 1990) and the Bem Sex-Role Inventory (Bem, 1974). The Adult Attachment Scale is an 18-item measure that yields three subscales: Close, Depend, and Anxiety. These subscales correspond quite closely to the three traditional attachment styles, and thus provided an independent index of attachment that we could correlate with our person and possession attachment factors.[10] Not surprisingly, the three subscales correlated in

---

[8]To determine whether it was appropriate to average across targets, we first calculated separate factor scores for the three targets rated by each respondent and a computed coefficient alpha for each of the 10 factors. These alphas ranged from .82 to .50, with an average of .67—a magnitude we deemed sufficient to justify averaging across each respondents' three person and possession targets.

[9]Two of these difficulties are that the correlations between the person and object factor scores might have been inflated by positive within-set intercorrelations among the factors and by shared method variance. To account for these possibilities, we tested the significance of each of our predicted correlations against a null hypothesis of .05 (the average correlation between factors in the noncorresponding cells of the correlation matrix), rather than 0. The pattern of significant and nonsignificant results was unchanged.

[10]In fact, the measures are not as independent as we would like them to be. The Adult Attachment Scale is a self-report instrument whose items are extremely similar to those we included on the person attachment scale, although they are phrased in terms of relationships in general rather than in terms of a particular relationship (e.g., "I find it difficult to allow myself to depend on others," "People are never there when you need them," "I often worry that my partner does not really love me," etc.). Thus, the problem of shared method variance afflicts this analysis as well.

predictable ways with the factors from the person attachment measure. More significant (in the nonstatistical sense) were the correlations with the factors from the possession attachment measure. The Close scale was positively correlated with the symbolic and dependable possession factors and negatively correlated with the conflicted and recreation factors. The Depend scale (which assesses discomfort with dependence) was positively correlated with the conflicted factor, as was the Anxiety scale. These results again provide encouraging evidence for consistency in attachment style across domains.

Gender Differences. Finally, we again found gender differences in attachments across domains. On the person attachment measure, women scored lower on the distancing factor; on the possession attachment measure, they scored higher on the symbolic factor and lower on the conflicted and recreation factors. These results are perfectly in line with our own previous studies and with previous work on gender differences in attachment styles (see Reis & Patrick, 1996). Interestingly, the Femininity subscale of the Bem Sex-Role Inventory turned up a consistent and much stronger pattern of results. On the person attachment measure, Femininity was positively correlated with secure attachment and relationship stability and negatively correlated with anxious ambivalent and avoidant attachments. On the possession attachment measure, it was positively correlated with symbolic and dependable attachments, and negatively correlated with conflicted and recreational attachments to objects. The fact that men and women showed these parallel differences in their attachments to people and objects lends further support to our analysis.

Are People Attached to Their Attitudes?

Our initial foray into the study of attachment styles has demonstrated that people have emotional attachments not just to their significant others but also to their favorite objects. Moreover, it appears that a given individual may have a particular style of attachment that characterizes his or her relationships with both people and material possessions. But the question of whether this analysis is applicable to the mental domain remains unaddressed. Are people really attached, in the same sense, to their beliefs and attitudes? Do they miss attitudes they no longer hold, feel conflicted about their attachments to certain attitudes, and find some attitudes more useful and more dependable than others?

We know of no empirical studies that have addressed these questions directly, although some suggestive evidence was provided by Abelson (1988). He and his colleagues conducted several surveys to assess people's conviction on various sociopolitical issues. Several of the survey items tapped into a construct that they labeled "emotional commitment." These items included, "My beliefs express the real me," "I can't imagine ever changing my mind," "My beliefs are based on the moral sense of the way things should be," and "I think my view is absolutely correct." The claim that people have emotional commitments to their beliefs and attitudes has much in common with the idea of attachment, especially in the central role it accords to affect. Although most other theories of attitude strength have focused on its cognitive components, they do not preclude the existence of an emotional component as well.

In summary, the literature contains some hint that people may form attachments to their attitudes that look at least something like the attachments that characterize interpersonal relations. In our future research, we plan to validate this claim empirically and to test for correspondence in attachment style across the interpersonal, physical, and mental domains. We suspect that the three traditional attachment styles may well show some degree of consistency, although capturing that consistency empirically may require more methodological ingenuity than we have shown to date.

CONCLUSIONS

Our research on the functions of attitudes and other valued possessions has demonstrated a number of ways in which things, mental and physical, animate and inanimate, reveal the person. We have shown that individuals are consistent in the sources of benefit they derive from their attitudes and material possessions, and in the style in which they attach to significant people and objects in their lives. An individual's valued possessions reflect the workings of functional and relational schemas that direct his or her thoughts, emotions, and behaviors across many different domains. We have not probed directly the nature of these schemas but instead have inferred their properties by documenting their observable manifestations. This is a time-honored strategy in personality research and provides a nice complement to the more recent focus on direct assessments of mediating processes.

Although we have framed our research as an investigation of individual consistency, our findings speak to the psychology of attitudes as well. In particular, they reinforce the importance of understanding the basis of an attitude in order to predict or change it. They suggest new directions in the study of the quality and form of people's convictions. And, more generally, they highlight the insights that can be gained by considering attitudes in the context of the total person. Opinions and personality are not just related to one another; they are part of one another. Research on both sides will benefit from an understanding of their interdependence.

REFERENCES

Abelson, R. P. (1986). Beliefs are like possessions. *Journal for the Theory of Social Behaviour, 16*, 223–250.

Abelson, R. P. (1988). Conviction. *American Psychologist, 43*, 267–275.

Abelson, R. P., & Prentice, D. A. (1989). Beliefs as possessions: A functional perspective. In A. R. Pratkanis, S. J. Breckler, & A. G. Greenwald (Eds.), *Attitude structure and function* (pp. 361–381). Hillsdale, NJ: Lawrence Erlbaum Associates.

Ainsworth, M. D. S., Blehar, M. C., Waters, E., & Wall, S. (1978). *Patterns of attachment: Assessed in the strange situation and at home.* Hillsdale, NJ: Lawrence Erlbaum Associates.

Bazzini, D. G., & Shaffer, D. R. (1995). Investigating the social-adjustive and value-expressive functions of well-grounded attitudes: Implications for change and for subsequent behavior. *Motivation and Emotion, 19*, 279–305.

Bem, S. L. (1974). The measurement of psychological androgyny. *Journal of Consulting and Clinical Psychology, 42*, 155–162.

Bowlby, J. (1979). *The making and breaking of affectional bonds.* London: Tavistock.

Carlsmith, K. M. (1996). *Objectifying the person, personifying the object: A study of persons and possessions.* Unpublished manuscript, University of New Hampshire.

Clary, E. G., Snyder, M., Ridge, R., Miene, P. K., & Haugen, J. A. (1994). Matching message to motives in persuasion: A function approach to promoting volunteerism. *Journal of Applied Social Psychology, 24*, 1129–1149.

Collins, N. L., & Read, S. J. (1990). Adult attachment, working models, and relationships quality in dating couples. *Journal of Personality and Social Psychology, 58*, 644–663.

Csikszentmihalyi, M., & Rochberg-Halton, E. (1981). *The meaning of things: Domestic symbols and the self.* Cambridge: Cambridge University Press.

DeBono, K. G. (1987). Investigating the social-adjustive and value-expressive functions of attitudes: Implications for persuasion processes. *Journal of Personality and Social Psychology, 52*, 279–287.

DeBono, K. G., & Harnish, R. J. (1988). Source expertise, source attractiveness, and the processing of persuasive information: A functional approach. *Journal of Personality and Social Psychology, 55*, 541–546.

DeBono, K. G., & Packer, M. (1991). The effects of advertising appeal on perceptions of product quality. *Personality and Social Psychology Bulletin, 17*, 194–200.

DeBono, K. G., & Telesca, C. (1990). The influence of source physical attractiveness on advertising effectiveness: A functional perspective. *Journal of Applied Social Psychology, 20*, 1383–1395.

Dittmar, H. (1988). Gender identity-related meanings of personal possessions. *British Journal of Social Psychology, 28*, 159–171.

Dittmar, H. (1992). *The social psychology of material possessions: To have is to be.* Hemel Hempstead: Harvester Wheatsheaf and New York: St. Martin's Press.

Hazan, C., & Shaver, P. R. (1987). Romantic love conceptualized as an attachment process. *Journal of Personality and Social Psychology, 52,* 511–524.

Herek, G. M. (1987). Can functions be measured? A new perspective on the functional approach to attitudes. *Social Psychology Quarterly, 50,* 285–303.

James, W. (1890). *The principles of psychology.* New York: Holt.

Katz, D. (1960). The functional approach to the study of attitudes. *Public Opinion Quarterly, 24,* 163–204.

Lavine, H., & Snyder, M. (1996). Cognitive processing and the functional matching effect in persuasion: The mediating role of subjective perceptions of message quality. *Journal of Experimental Social Psychology, 32,* 580–604.

Maio, G. R., & Olson, J. M. (1994). Value-attitude-behaviour relations: The moderating role of attitude functions. *British Journal of Social Psychology, 33,* 301–312.

Maio, G. R., & Olson, J. M. (1995). Relations between values, attitudes, and behavioral intentions: The moderating role of attitude functions. *Journal of Experimental Social Psychology, 31,* 266–285.

Maio, G. R., & Olson, J. M. (1996, August). *Effects of value-expressive attitudes on value associations.* Paper presented at the annual meeting of the American Psychological Association, Toronto, Canada.

Petty, R. E., & Krosnick, J. A. (Eds.). (1995). *Attitude strength: Antecedents and consequences.* Mahwah, NJ: Lawrence Erlbaum Associates.

Petty, R. E., & Wegener, D. T. (1998). Matching versus mismatching attitude functions: Implications for scrutiny of persuasive messages. *Personality and Social Psychology Bulletin, 24,* 227–240.

Prentice, D. A. (1987). Psychological correspondence of possessions, attitudes, and values. *Journal of Personality and Social Psychology, 53,* 993–1003.

Reis, H. T., & Patrick, B. C. (1996). Attachment and intimacy: Component processes. In E. T. Higgins & A. W. Kruglanski (Eds.), *Social psychology: Handbook of basic principles* (pp. 523–563). New York: Guilford Press.

Rokeach. M. (1968). *Beliefs, attitudes, and values: A theory of organization and change.* San Francisco: Jossey-Bass.

Shavitt, S. (1990). The role of attitude objects in attitude functions. *Journal of Experimental Social Psychology, 26,* 124–148.

Shavitt, S., Lowrey, T. M., & Han, S. (1992). Attitude functions in advertising: The interactive role of products and self-monitoring. *Journal of Consumer Psychology, 1,* 337–364.

Smith, M. B. (1947). The personal setting of public opinions: A study of attitudes toward Russia. *Public Opinion Quarterly, 11,* 507–523.

Smith, M. B., Bruner, J. S., & White, R. W. (1956). *Opinions and personality.* New York: Wiley.

Snyder, M. (1974). The self-monitoring of expressive behavior. *Journal of Personality and Social Psychology, 30,* 526–537.

Snyder, M., & DeBono, K. G. (1985). Appeals to image and claims about quality: Understanding the psychology of advertising. *Journal of Personality and Social Psychology, 49,* 586–597.

Spence, J. T., & Helmreich, R. L. (1980). Masculine instrumentality and feminine expressiveness: Their relationships with sex role attitudes and behaviors. *Psychology of Women Quarterly, 5,* 147–163.

9

What *is* a "Value-Expressive" Attitude?

Gregory R. Maio
Cardiff University

James M. Olson
University of Western Ontario

Some people claim that they favor capital punishment because they value law and order; they support affirmative action programs as a means of promoting equality; they support recycling programs because they value the environment; they go to war to defend freedom; and they frown on cheating because it is dishonest. All of these assertions refer to *values* (e.g., equality, freedom), which are abstract ideas that people consider to be important guiding principles in their life (Rokeach, 1973; Schwartz, 1996). More important, all of the assertions illustrate the hypothesis that values influence attitudes, such as attitudes toward capital punishment, recycling, and war.

This idea that attitudes can express values is a prominent hypothesis in research on attitude functions. Such research examines the psychological functions that attitudes fulfill and suggests that some attitudes serve to express values (see Eagly & Chaiken, 1993; Olson & Zanna, 1993). These value-expressive attitudes are frequently distinguished from attitudes that express other motivations (e.g., the motivation to promote one's own welfare; Herek, 1986; Katz, 1960; Prentice, 1987; Shavitt, 1990), and research has discovered several important characteristics of value-expressive attitudes. For example, value-expressive attitudes are especially resistant to attack (Johnson & Eagly, 1989; Maio & Olson, 1995a; Ostrom & Brock, 1968). In addition, value-expressive attitudes elicit high degrees of commitment to relevant behaviors that are performed under adversity (e.g., volunteerism; Lydon & Zanna, 1990; Murray, Haddock, & Zanna, 1996; see also Lavallee & Campbell, 1993). Also, contemplation of the relevance of values to attitudes increases the structural balance between attitudes (Lavine, Thomsen, & Gonzales, 1997). Overall, value-expressive attitudes appear to be strong (Boninger, Krosnick, & Berent, 1995).

Nonetheless, value expressive attitudes have been defined and operationalized in many different ways. As a result, it is sometimes unclear which attitudes should be considered value-expressive and which should not. This chapter presents theory and evidence that help to clarify this construct.

BACKGROUND: ATTITUDE FUNCTIONS

The value-expressive attitude function was described in Katz's (1960) well-known theory of attitude function. This theory indicates that attitudes can serve one or some combination of four attitude functions: the knowledge, ego-defensive, utilitarian, and value-expressive functions. The knowledge function exists in all attitudes, because all attitudes help to simplify interaction with the environment by classifying objects according to their positive and negative implications for the individual. The other three functions are less broad. The ego-defensive function exists in attitudes that protect the self from internal conflict. The utilitarian function exists in attitudes that maximize rewards and minimize punishments obtained from the environment. The value-expressive function exists in attitudes that express central values and the self-concept.[1]

The value-expressive attitude function is perhaps best illustrated by contrasting it with the utilitarian attitude function. On the one hand, the value-expressive function exists when people adopt particular attitudes as

---

[1]The knowledge and ego-defensive functions are similar to two attitude functions (object appraisal and externalization) that were proposed by Smith, Bruner, and White (1956).

a means of being consistent with specific values. For example, if people are asked to indicate their attitude toward donating to a charity, they might think about the importance of helping others. Their subsequently expressed attitude toward donating might therefore reflect this value. On the other hand, when asked to indicate their attitude toward donating, people might simply consider whether they can afford to donate, rather than some abstract social value. When people conduct such a utilitarian cost–benefit analysis, their subsequently expressed attitude may be said to serve a utilitarian attitude function.

This comparison suggests an important feature of value-expressive attitudes. Because value-expressive attitudes are formed to express specific values, these attitudes should be predicted by the extent to which people consider the values to be important. For example, people who consider the value of helpfulness to be important should be more favorable toward donating than people who consider helpfulness to be unimportant, but only if their attitudes toward donating are used to express this value. If their attitudes being used to express other concerns (e.g., utilitarian motives), the perceived importance of helpfulness should not predict attitudes toward donating. Put simply, value-attitude relations should exist only or most strongly for value-expressive attitudes.

STUDY 1: CORRELATIONAL EVIDENCE SUPPORTING THE MODERATING ROLE OF ATTITUDE FUNCTION

This hypothesis provided a useful starting point in our attempt to make concrete the notion of the value-expressive attitude function. We first tested the hypothesis in a study that examined value-attitude relations for both value-expressive attitudes and utilitarian attitudes (Maio & Olson, 1994). In this study, the focal attitude topic was a dance to support the construction of an enclosed smoking area in a university student center. This attitude topic was chosen because the smoking issue was related to several values (e.g., freedom, health), whereas buying a ticket to a dance was related to outcomes (e.g., pleasure from having a good time, displeasure from spending money). Thus, this issue seemed capable of eliciting attitudes that fulfilled either or both value-expressive and utilitarian functions.

Before being asked to consider this issue, the participants were falsely told that they would be taking part in several studies, dealing with different topics. In the first study, participants were asked to complete a value survey that included four values related to the smoking issue: freedom, individualism, collective well-being, and health. Next, after completing a filler study, participants took part in a third study, wherein they rated their attitudes toward the smoking area dance using semantic differential scales and completed a thought-listing measure of attitude function (e.g., Shavitt, 1990). The thought-listing measure asked participants to report their thoughts pertaining to their attitudes, which were subsequently coded according to the functions that they represented. For example, some participants gave mostly value-expressive reasons, such as the belief that smoking threatens their freedom to breathe clean air. Other participants focused on utilitarian concerns, including the cost of a ticket or the likelihood of having a good time at the dance. Not surprisingly, some participants mentioned both value-expressive and utilitarian concerns in approximately equal proportions. These participants were coded as possessing a mixed attitude function.

Within each of these three groups, we examined the correlations between participants' ratings of the importance of the four relevant values (freedom, individualism, collective well-being, and health) and their attitudes toward attending the smoking area dance. Results indicated that significant value–attitude correlations occurred only among participants whose thoughts had been coded as revealing value-expressive attitudes; within these individuals, those who considered freedom and individualism to be more important were less favorable toward attending the smoking area dance than those who considered these values to be less important, $r = -.55, p < .01$, and $r = -.47, p < .01$, respectively. These correlations probably reflect the fact that more than 90% of our participants were nonsmokers. It seems likely that these participants saw the enclosed smoking area as an infringement on their breathing space, and this infringement particularly bothered those who possessed value-expressive attitudes and who happened to consider freedom and individualism to be important.

To further examine value–attitude relations, we extended the analyses to the multivariate level. In these analyses, we regressed participants' attitude ratings on their ratings of the importance of the four values, which were entered simultaneously in the regression equation. Consistent with the findings at the univariate level, participants with value-expressive attitudes exhibited a significant multivariate relation between their values and attitudes, $R^2 = .41, p < .04$, but participants with utilitarian or mixed attitudes did not, $R^2 < .13$, *ns*. Overall, then, value–attitude relations were observed only for participants who, on the thought-listing measure, had given value-relevant reasons for their attitudes.

STUDY 2: EXPERIMENTAL EVIDENCE

The results of Study 1 provided initial evidence that significant value–attitude relations are a unique property of value-expressive attitudes. There were several issues, however, that needed to be addressed in a second study (Maio & Olson, 1995b).

First, we employed a manipulation of attitude function instead of a measure of attitude function. In the previous study, participants might have deduced their reasons for their attitudes from their degree of value–attitude correspondence by using self-inference processes (see Olson, 1990, 1992). That is, participants might have been aware of the extent of their value–attitude correspondence while completing the thought-listing measure, and those who noticed strong value–attitude consistency may have been inclined to write many value-relevant reasons. By manipulating attitude function in our second study, we could be confident that attitude functions were affecting value–attitude relations and not vice versa.

Second, we examined the patterns of relations between an attitude and a wide range of values, rather than the relation between a particular attitude and four specifically relevant values. Possible patterns were derived from Schwartz's (1992, 1996) model of value associations. In his cross-cultural research, Schwartz asked people to rate the importance of different values, and the relations between values were plotted using multidimensional scaling. Schwartz predicted and found that values can be grouped into four broad domains: conservation, openness to change, self-enhancement, and self-transcendence (see Fig. 9.1). Conservation values emphasize the preservation of the status quo (e.g., conformity, tradition). In contrast, openness values involve following intellectual and emotional interests in uncertain directions (e.g., creativity, freedom). Self-enhancement values emphasize following self-interests (e.g., social power, wealth), whereas self-transcendence values emphasize promoting the welfare of others (e.g., helpfulness, honesty).

As shown in Fig. 9.1, conservation values are negatively related to openness values. That is, people who consider conservation values to be

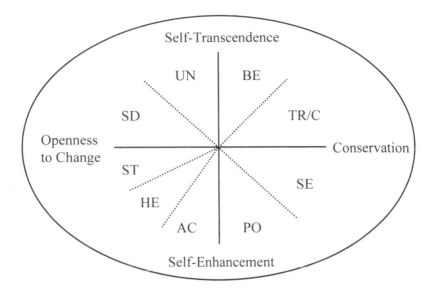

FIG. 9.1. SD = self-direction values (e.g., creativity, freedom, independent); ST = stimulation values (e.g., daring, exciting life, varied life); HE = hedonism values (e.g., enjoying life, pleasure); AC = achievement values (e.g., ambitious, influential, successful); PO = power values (e.g., authority, social power, social recognition); SE = security values (e.g., national security, reciprocation of favours, sense of belonging); TR = tradition, self-discipline; BE = benevolence values (e.g., altruism, forgiving, helpful, honest); UN = universalism values (e.g., broadminded, equality, protecting environment).

important tend to consider openness values to be unimportant. Similarly, self-enhancement values are negatively related to self-transcendence values. Conservation and openness values are orthogonal, or unrelated, to self-enhancement and self-transcendence values.

According to Schwartz (1992, 1996), these connections between value domains enable predictions about patterns of relations between values and other variables. For example, self-transcendence values may be positively related to attitudes toward donating to a charity. If so, there should also be a negative relation between self-enhancement values and attitudes toward donating, because self-enhancement values are negatively related to self-transcendence values. In this example, no predictions would be made for the conservation and openness domains, because these domains are orthogonal to the self-transcendence and self-enhancement domains.

Schwartz (1992, 1996) has, in fact, found such patterns in the relations between values and many other variables, including age, education, interpersonal cooperation, readiness for out-group social contact, and voting behavior. We hypothesized, however, that in the domain of value–attitude relations, the expected pattern of value–attitude relations might occur when attitudes serve a value-expressive function, but not when attitudes serve other functions.

Using an experimental approach, our second study (Maio & Olson, 1995b) tested this hypothesis. Participants were told that they would be participating in three different studies. In the first study, participants rated the importance of values in all four of Schwartz's value domains, using a shortened version of Schwartz's (1992) value survey. In the second study, participants completed a manipulation of the functions of their attitudes toward donating to cancer research. Participants then completed the third study, which measured their attitudes toward donating to cancer research, by using several semantic differential scales.

The experimental manipulation made salient either value-expressive or utilitarian concerns prior to attitude expression, similar to past research (e.g., Young, Thomsen, Borgida, Sullivan, & Aldrich, 1991). Value-expressive or utilitarian reasons for donating were made salient through posters that were presented to participants. Participants in the value-expressive attitude condition read a poster that made salient a value-expressive reason for donating to cancer research: donating would help others. In contrast, participants in the utilitarian attitude condition read a poster that made salient a utilitarian reason for donating: donations might eventually benefit the donor by increasing the likelihood of finding a cure that would help the donor, if the donor gets cancer. Participants were asked to rate these posters, ostensibly as a means of pretesting the posters for widespread use.

We assessed the effectiveness of this manipulation in a separate pilot sample of participants by using a thought-listing measure. In this sample, participants' attitudes were, in fact, more value expressive in the value-expressive attitude condition (i.e., after reading the value-relevant poster) than in the utilitarian attitude condition (i.e., after reading the utilitarian poster).

The effects of this manipulation on value–attitude relations in the main sample were interesting. To examine value–attitude relations, we calculated semipartial correlations between participants' attitudes toward donating and their mean ratings of the four types of values. As recommended

by Schwartz (1992), these semipartial correlations controlled for participants' mean ratings of all of the values in the survey. Results indicated
that, in the value-expressive attitude condition, attitudes correlated negatively with self-enhancement values, $sr = -.32$, $p < .001$, and positively
with self-transcendence values, $sr = .36$, $p < .001$, but not with openness
values, $sr = .15$, ns, or conservation values, $sr = .04$, ns. In contrast, in the
utilitarian attitude condition, none of the value domains correlated
significantly with attitudes ($p > .05$). Thus, a reliable pattern of value-attitude relations was detected in the value-expressive attitude condition,
but not in the utilitarian attitude condition. These results were consistent
with those obtained in Study 1.

The inclusion of the Schwartz (1992) values in this study raised an
interesting question, however, because Schwartz's self-enhancement values (e.g., achievement, power) are distinctly utilitarian in nature. One
might expect that such utilitarian values should predict utilitarian attitudes. In other words, in the experimental condition where a cure for
cancer was shown to serve participants' interests, one might expect that
those who considered self-enhancement values to be important should
have been more favorable toward donating to cancer research than those
who considered self-enhancement values to be unimportant. Yet, this
finding was not obtained. If this finding were to occur, it would challenge
the distinction between value-expressive and utilitarian attitudes, because
values would seem to predict both types of attitudes.

There is an important limitation to our findings, however. It is possible
that no value-attitude relations were discovered in the utilitarian attitude
condition because we did not elicit purely utilitarian attitudes. That is,
although the utilitarian poster persuaded participants that donating to
cancer research could promote utilitarian goals, it might not have eliminated the more common value-expressive motivation to donate. In other
words, our informing participants about how donating to cancer research
might help themselves may not have eliminated their general awareness
that donating to cancer research also helps others. Participants in the
utilitarian condition might have been favorable toward donating because
it would help others and themselves, which means that attitudes in this
condition might have served utilitarian and value-expressive attitude
functions simultaneously.

In fact, the data from our separate pilot sample enabled us to examine
this possibility. As indicated above, pilot participants in the value-expressive attitude condition were more likely to possess value-expressive

attitudes than were pilot participants in the utilitarian attitude condition. This finding provided important support for our manipulation. Nonetheless, examination of the responses of pilot participants in the utilitarian condition showed that they tended to express both value-expressive and utilitarian concerns. Thus, this experiment could not rule out the possibility that a different pattern of results would occur for utilitarian attitudes that were relevant only to utilitarian concerns.

STUDY 3: VALUE–ATTITUDE RELATIONS FOR A PURELY UTILITARIAN ATTITUDE

The results of Studies 1 and 2 revealed significant value–attitude relations for attitudes that serve a value-expressive function. Nonetheless, neither study could eliminate the possibility that such value–attitude relations might also occur for utilitarian (self-enhancement) values and utilitarian attitudes. In Study 1, only one of the four focal values in the study was utilitarian in nature (health), and, as previously indicated, purely utilitarian attitudes were rare in Study 2. Consequently, we designed a third study that focused exclusively on the relation between utilitarian values and utilitarian attitudes.

In this study, we selected an attitude topic that was relevant only to utilitarian goals, thereby ensuring that participants' attitudes would serve a utilitarian function. Specifically, after completing the values measure that was employed in our second study, participants read a poster describing a festival that was ostensibly being planned by the university and then indicated their attitudes toward attending the festival. The poster indicated that the festival would present a wide variety of music and live performances and that the festival would occur immediately before exams. Thus, students could weigh the costs and benefits of studying rather than having fun. In other words, both positive and negative utilitarian outcomes were relevant.

Because attending the festival would disrupt studying, it seemed likely that participants who considered self-enhancement values (e.g., achievement, success) to be important would be less favorable toward attending the festival than participants who considered these values to be unimportant. Indeed, participants' attitudes toward the festival correlated negatively with their previously expressed self-enhancement values, $sr = -.40$, $p < .002$. In other words, students who considered personal achievement and success to be important were less favorable to disrupting their studying by attending the festival than were students who considered these values to be less important. It is not surprising that participants' attitudes toward attending the festival also correlated positively with their self-transcendence values, $sr = .33$, $p < .01$, because these values are negatively related to self-enhancement values. Attitudes did not correlate significantly with conservation values, $sr = -.08$, $p < .10$, or openness values, $sr = .22$, ns.[2]

The findings that utilitarian attitudes were related to self-enhancement values and to the opposing, self-transcendence values indicate that significant value–attitude relations can occur when an attitude is relevant only to utilitarian goals. Thus, utilitarian attitudes can be predicted by values that promote or conflict with utilitarian goals.

A NEW APPROACH: GOAL-EXPRESSIVE ATTITUDES

At first glance, the results of Study 3 might appear inconsistent with the results of Studies 1 and 2, which did not obtain value–attitude relations for utilitarian attitudes. As previously mentioned, however, only Study 3 included utilitarian values and purely utilitarian attitudes. Consequently, we are inclined to view these studies as providing different parts of the solution to the question that guided these studies: Do value–attitude relations exist only for value-expressive attitudes?

In combination, the results of Studies 1, 2, and 3 suggest an interesting answer. In Study 1, values predicted attitudes when participants cited values as relevant to their attitudes. Similarly, in Study 2, values predicted attitudes when the attitudes were made relevant to specific values (in the value-expressive attitude condition). Again, in Study 3, relevant values predicted attitudes, even though the attitude topic and values were utilitarian in nature. Overall, it is clear that value–attitude relations occur for value-expressive attitudes and utilitarian attitudes, with utilitarian attitudes being predicted by utilitarian values.

The finding that utilitarian attitudes can express values is intriguing, because it suggests the possibility that attitudes serving a variety of

---

[2]We also examined the relationship between participants' attitudes toward attending the festival and their ratings of hedonism values (enjoying life, pleasure). Schwartz (1992, 1996) regards hedonism values as a distinct type of value, because hedonism values are similar to both self-enhancement and openness values. Results indicated no significant relations between participants' attitudes and their ratings of the hedonism values, $sr = -.06$, ns.

motivations might be labeled "value expressive." This possibility is further supported by Schwartz's (1992, 1996) model of values. As previously indicated, his model describes how values express universal motivations: self-enhancement, self-transcendence, conservation, and openness. He also predicted and found that these broad categories can be divided into 10 smaller motivational domains. The self-enhancement category can be subdivided into values that maximize power and values that promote achievement; the self-transcendence category includes values that promote benevolence and values that promote universalism; the openness category includes values that promote self-direction and values that promote stimulation; and the conservation category includes values that promote tradition, values that promote conformity, and values that promote security. In addition, there are values that promote hedonism (enjoying life, pleasure), which do not fall into any particular higher order domain.

Because values reflect these different motivations, value-expressive attitudes might potentially derive from any of the motivations. For example, as in Study 2, an individual might be favorable toward donating to a particular charity because the person holds values that emphasize benevolence. Similarly, as in Study 3, an individual might be favorable toward studying for exams because the person holds values that emphasize achievement. Such attitudes that express different values might be said to express different motivations. That is, attitudes that express different values might fulfill different functions.

Nevertheless, when Katz (1960) first defined the value-expressive attitude function, he explicitly distinguished between values and social-adjustive or utilitarian motivations, stating that value-expressive attitudes do not promote the achievement of "social recognition or monetary rewards" (p. 173). Thus, it is important to distinguish his perspective from the current one, which acknowledges that recent theorists have identified values (e.g., social recognition, wealth) that promote such motivations or goals (Rokeach, 1973; Schwartz, 1992).

To differentiate our new perspective from Katz's (1960) approach, we introduce the notion of a goal-expressive attitude: Goal-expressive attitudes are directed and energized by goals that are important and relevant to an individual and are derived from values. Goal-expressive attitudes encompass what Katz referred to as value-expressive and utilitarian functions, both of which refer to attitudes that reflect important motivations or goals. When people form attitudes that express any of the values identified by Schwartz (1992), these attitudes reflect specific motivational goals associated with the values. In contrast, when none of Schwartz's values is relevant to an attitude, other attitude functions prove to be especially relevant (e.g., ego defense, knowledge).[3]

It is important to note that the notion of goal-expressive attitudes helps highlight the idea that attitudes can express a variety of motivational goals that are derived from values. Thus, the capacity of attitudes and values to reflect diverse motivations is emphasized. In addition, our emphasis on the role played by important and relevant goals is consistent with findings that the importance and relevance of values to attitudes are important factors in predicting attitudes and their resistance to persuasion (Kristiansen & Zanna, 1988, 1994; Maio & Olson, 1995a; see also Mellema & Bassili, 1995; Ostrom & Brock, 1968).

STUDY 4: DO DIFFERENT VALUES ELICIT DISTINCT MOTIVATIONS?

We designed an experiment to examine an important implication of our conceptualization of goal-expressive attitudes: If values elicit different, important motivational goals, then making salient a particular value should also make salient the goal that is derived from the value. For example, making salient the value of helpfulness should cause people to want to be benevolent. This motivation could be expressed in subsequent attitudes toward behaviors and issues that are relevant to this value (e.g., donating to a charity).

To test whether motivations can be elicited in this manner, Study 4 utilized a rationale that is frequently described in theories of attitude function (Katz, 1960; Smith, Bruner, & White, 1956). According to these theories, attitude function should moderate the impact of persuasive messages on attitudes. In particular, a persuasive message should elicit more attitude change when the message targets the motivation that underlies people's attitudes than when it targets an irrelevant motivation. Thus, if values elicit distinct motivations, priming a value should elicit the corresponding motivation, and this motivation should affect partici-

---

[3]Unlike Katz's (1960) description of value-expressive attitudes, our conceptualization of goal-expressive attitudes does not include reference to self-identity. Although values can serve as a source of self-identity, values are not unique in this capacity (Herek, 1986; Pratkanis & Greenwald, 1989; Prentice, 1987; Shavitt, 1990). Consequently, our perspective emphasizes values alone.

pants' receptiveness toward different persuasive messages. Specifically, people should be more persuaded by a message that highlights the ability of an attitude object to promote a salient value or motivation than by a message that highlights a different value or motivation.

The procedure was straightforward. Participants were told that they would be participating in several different studies. Following some "studies" unrelated to the present concerns, the experimenter conducted a "study" that made salient either the value of enjoying life or the value of success. The value of enjoying life was made salient by presenting participants with a survey of students' attitudes toward enjoying life. Similarly, the value of success was made salient by asking participants to complete a survey of students' attitudes toward success. The instructions and items for these surveys were similar, except for their differential focus on enjoying life versus success. Theoretically, making salient the value of enjoying life should elicit a pleasure-seeking motivation (hedonism goals), whereas making salient the value of success should elicit an achievement motivation (performance goals).

The "enjoying life survey" can be used to illustrate the value salience manipulation. First, the experimenter stated that psychologists believe it is important for students to perform many fun activities in order to buffer the stresses of student life. He then stated that he was attempting to measure the extent to which students consider this value to be important. The survey contained many questions that induced contemplation of the value. For example, participants were asked to rate the value's importance, using a 9-point scale from -1 (*not at all important*) to 7 (*extremely important*). In addition, they rated their overall evaluations of the value, using semantic differential scales (bad–good, negative–positive), and they described their reasons for considering the value to be important or unimportant. Also, participants were asked to read a list of statements that describe enjoyable behaviors (e.g., "I go out at least once a week with my friends") and to check each statement that was true for them. Finally, participants were asked to rate the extent to which they could enjoy life to a greater degree and the extent to which it is important for them to enjoy life.

After completing this manipulation, participants were told that the next study was an administrative study of students' attitudes toward the university's proposed tuition fee increases. The experimenter stated that the administration was proposing to raise tuition fees over the next five years. He indicated that a finance subcommittee had put together a proposal that might use the increased fees in a manner that would provide more benefits to students. Participants were asked to read the finance subcommittee's summary of this proposal.

The summary indicated either that part of the funds raised from the increased fees would be used to provide a new student travel fund or that part of the fees would provide a new study skills program. The travel fund was described as an initiative that would give students substantial discounts on travel to foreign countries. According to the summary, a small commitment of money was all that was needed to enable a major travel agency to offer significant discounts, based on large-group rates. It was argued that this program would give students an opportunity to take a break from studying, while at the same time providing an educational experience. In contrast, the study skills program was described as a series of 1-day seminars that would train students in easy-to-learn strategies for improving reading skills, comprehension, memory, and essay writing. The summary indicated that such seminars increase students' grades by 10% to 20%, helping students to obtain jobs. In summary, the difference between the two messages was that the travel fund promoted enjoying life, whereas the study skills program promoted success.

After reading the persuasive message appropriate to their experimental condition, participants rated their attitudes toward the university's tuition fee increases by using several semantic differential scales. We expected that participants for whom the value of enjoying life was made salient would be more persuaded by the message that included travel opportunities than by the message that included a study skills program. Similarly, we expected that participants for whom the value of success was made salient would be more persuaded by the message that included the study skills program than by the message that included travel opportunities.[4]

To test these predictions, a 2 (Value salience: enjoying life vs. success) × 2 (Persuasive message: student travel vs. study skills) between-subjects ANOVA was conducted on attitudes toward the proposed tuition fee increases. Results indicated a main effect of the persuasive message, $F(1, 79) = 6.45, p < .02$, such that participants were less unfavorable toward the fee increase proposal that included the study skills program ($M = -.18$) than toward the proposal that included the travel opportunities ($M = -.78$).

---

[4]To reduce demand, participants were given instructions that emphasized anonymity. For example, the experimenter stated that he would not see the data booklets, because a research assistant would collect the booklets and enter the data directly into computer files. Participants were told to put their questionnaires in a covered box that was designated for the research assistant.

This main effect was qualified by the two-way interaction, $F(1, 79) = 4.58, p < .04$. Examination of this interaction revealed that, as expected, participants for whom the value of success was made salient were more favorable toward the proposal that included the study skills program ($M = .25$) than toward the proposal that included travel opportunities ($M = -.86$), $t(79) = 3.31, p < .001$. Also, participants for whom the value of success was made salient were more favorable toward the study skills program ($M = .25$) than were participants for whom the value of enjoying life was made salient ($M = -.61$), $t(79) = 2.56, p < .01$. In contrast, participants for whom the value of enjoying life was made salient were not differentially favorable toward the proposal that included the study skills program ($M = -.61$) and the proposal that included travel opportunities ($M = -.70$), $t(79) = 0.27$, ns. Also, participants for whom enjoying life was made salient were not more or less favorable toward the proposal that included travel opportunities ($M = -.70$) than were participants for whom success was made salient ($M = -.86$), $t(79) = -0.47$, ns.

These results supported the hypothesis that different values elicit distinct motivations. When the value of success was made salient, participants were more favorable toward a fee increase proposal that promoted this value than toward a proposal that promoted enjoying life. Presumably, participants became more motivated to attain success after this value was made salient. Consequently, they were more favorable toward the proposal that fulfilled this motivation than toward the proposal that fulfilled a different, nonsalient motivation (enjoying life).

It is interesting that making salient the value of enjoying life did not affect participants' attitudes toward the proposal. Perhaps this value was not as important to participants as was the value of success. In fact, participants' responses to the final question within the value salience manipulation (described earlier) showed that the value of enjoying life was rated as less important ($M = 6.31$) than the value of success ($M = 7.10$), $F(1, 82) = 5.76, p < .02$. Consequently, participants may have been less motivated to form attitudes that promote the enjoyment of life.

Nevertheless, it is important that different motivations were elicited by seemingly similar values. The values of success and enjoying life both reflect utilitarian motivations (i.e., concern with maximizing rewards and minimizing punishments obtained from the environment). Yet, this study shows that these values can produce disparate effects on attitudes, consistent with the hypothesis that different values reflect distinct motivations and, thus, distinct attitude functions.

MANIPULATING ATTITUDE FUNCTION:
MOTIVATIONS VERSUS BELIEFS

The use of values to elicit motivations might help to resolve a nagging ambiguity in research on attitude function, by unconfounding motivations and beliefs. Past research has been criticized for not adequately distinguishing the motivations that underlie attitudes from the beliefs that underlie attitudes (see Eagly & Chaiken, 1998). This situation has arisen because manipulations of attitude functions often give participants different reasons for holding particular attitudes. Such manipulations might implant specific beliefs about attitude objects, in addition to making salient a particular motivation. For example, our second study informed participants either that donating to cancer research would help themselves or that donating would help others, and we assumed that this manipulation made salient a utilitarian motivation or a value-expressive motivation, respectively. Nonetheless, participants who were told that donating to cancer research helps themselves may have come to believe that donating promotes their own interest, and this belief might not have been held before the manipulation. Consequently, this new belief might provide an alternative explanation for the results of this study or participants' new belief might have reduced the value–attitude correlations in the utilitarian condition; a utilitarian motivation might not have been responsible for the reduced value-attitude relations.

To some extent, it is difficult to avoid affecting beliefs in manipulations of attitude function, because an attitude may fail to express a motivation if people do not believe that the motivation is relevant to the attitude object. Thus, highlighting of this relevance helps ensure that the desired motivation is expressed by the target attitude. Nonetheless, pure manipulations of attitude function would attempt to elicit particular motivations, without affecting beliefs about an attitude object. The manipulation of value salience has this characteristic because it inspires the pursuit of specific values, without explicitly connecting the values to an attitude object.

This aspect of the manipulation of value salience can be further illustrated by describing some additional evidence obtained in our fourth study. Near the end of the lab session, we asked participants to take part in a study of students' attitudes toward consumer objects. In this study, participants were asked to rank order 16 different attitude objects according to the objects' desirability. Eight of these objects were useful for school studies (e.g., a computer, daily planner), whereas the other 8 objects were directly enjoyable (e.g., a hi-fi stereo, a trip to Paris). Thus, 8 objects promoted success, whereas 8 objects promoted enjoying life.

We wished to examine participants' relative rankings of these objects. Consequently, we subtracted participants' mean rankings of the "success" objects from their mean rankings of the "enjoying life" objects. Using this procedure, higher scores implied more favorability toward the "success" objects.

It was expected that the participants' relative rankings of the "success" and "enjoying life" objects would vary depending on which values had been made salient beforehand. For some participants, the value of success had been the focus of both the value salience manipulation and the persuasive message. For other participants, the value of enjoying life had been emphasized in both the value salience manipulation and the persuasive message. These two groups provided the strongest test of the hypothesis that participants would prefer objects that promoted their salient motivation. As expected, participants who had been exposed to the value of success in both the salience manipulation and the persuasive message ranked the success items more favorably ($M = 0.07$) than did participants who had been exposed to the value of enjoying life in both the salience manipulation and the persuasive message ($M = -1.93$), $t(39) = 2.04$, $p < .05$.

Importantly, the value salience manipulation and the persuasive message made no reference to the consumer items. Thus, value salience affected attitudes toward a variety of objects that were not mentioned in connection with the values, which shows that the values reflect powerful, general motivations. This finding is consistent with the results that would be expected for any general motivation. For example, if people are hungry, they are favorable toward eating many different things. Just as people desire many foods when they are hungry, they should be favorable toward many success-promoting objects (e.g., a computer, a day planner) when they crave success.

CONCLUSIONS

The goal of this chapter was to examine the notion of the value-expressive attitude function. We began by examining value–attitude relations for value-expressive attitudes and utilitarian attitudes. Results across Studies

1, 2, and 3 indicated that significant value–attitude relations can occur for value-expressive attitudes (Studies 1 and 2) but also for utilitarian attitudes (Study 3). Thus, it became apparent that attitudes serving a utilitarian motivation might also be labeled "value expressive."

Based on these findings and on recent models of values (e.g., Schwartz, 1996; see also Feather, 1995, and Maio & Olson, 1998), we introduced the concept of goal-expressive attitudes. These attitudes express important and relevant goals that are derived from values. To test this new perspective, we investigated whether manipulation of the salience of different values would elicit qualitatively different motivational goals. Study 4 demonstrated support for this hypothesis by finding that different values can elicit distinct motivations, which cause people to adopt attitudes that satisfy these motivations. Further, this experiment showed that two values (enjoying life and success) that seem to reflect the same attitude function (a utilitarian function) can actually elicit distinct motivations.

These results suggest that the concept of goal-expressive attitudes might have practical and theoretical benefit. From a practical point-of-view, the use of values to elicit different motivations provides a simple and powerful way to affect attitude function. This approach is powerful because it is not confined to manipulating people's beliefs about a particular attitude object. Instead, it taps motivations that can affect people's attitudes toward many different objects, such as the success-promoting objects in Study 4.

In addition, the concept of goal-expressive attitudes suggests a new way to measure attitude function. Future research might attempt to measure attitude function by discovering which values people perceive as important and relevant to their attitudes. Presumably, the important and relevant values will reflect at least some of the motivations that are served by the attitude.

From a theoretical perspective, the notion of goal-expressive attitudes can be used as a vehicle for facilitating greater integration of attitude function research with other research in psychology. This integration is made possible because values can be used to elicit numerous motivations that have been studied in psychology, but not in prior attitude function research. For example, values can be used to elicit a benevolence motivation, which has been the focus of abundant research on altruism and helping (Batson, 1987; Batson, Kobrynowicz, Dinnerstein, Kampf, & Wilson, 1997). Values can also be used to elicit an achievement motivation, which is another important construct in psychology (Elliot &

Church, 1997; Spangler, 1992). There is a need for research on attitude function to incorporate the wide range of motivations that have been examined in other areas of psychology (see chap. 15, this volume), and the use of values to elicit motivational goals is one approach that can promote this integration.[5]

In addition, this perspective allows attitude function to vary across attitude objects, situations, and individuals. Different attitude objects are relevant to different values. In addition, some situations make particular values salient and more likely to affect attitudes. Also, there are individual differences in the values that people consider important.

Finally, this perspective suggests new hypotheses for study. For example, future research might test whether attitudes that express different motivational goals differ in attitude strength. Perhaps goal-expressive attitudes that promote benevolence are more or less stable and predictive of behavior than are goal-expressive attitudes that promote conservation. In addition, attitudes that express many values across several different motivational domains might be stronger than attitudes that express many values within only one motivational domain. Such possibilities remain to be explored.

ACKNOWLEDGMENTS

Most of the research reported in this chapter was conducted while the first author was supported by a doctoral fellowship from the Social Sciences and Humanities Research Council of Canada (SSHRC). The research was also funded by a grant from SSHRC to the second author.

REFERENCES

Batson, C. D. (1987). Prosocial motivation: Is it ever truly altruistic? In L. Berkowitz (Ed.), *Advances in experimental social psychology* (Vol. 20, pp. 65–122). San Diego, CA: Academic Press.

Batson, C. D., Kobrynowicz, D., Dinnerstein, J. L., Kampf, H. C., & Wilson, A. D. (1997). In a very different voice: Unmasking moral hypocrisy. *Journal of Personality and Social Psychology, 72,* 1335–1348.

Boninger, D. S., Krosnick, J. A., & Berent, M. K. (1995). Origins of attitude importance: Self-interest, social identification, and value relevance. *Journal of Personality and Social Psychology, 68,* 61–80.

---

[5]This approach might not be feasible when no values are expressed directly by attitudes, i.e., when people do not perceive a link between an attitude and specific values (see chap. 15, this volume).

Eagly, A., Chaiken, S. (1998). Attitude structure and function. In D. T. Gilbert, S. T. Fiske, & G. Lindzey (Eds.), *The handbook of social psychology*. (4th Ed.) (Vol. 1). Boston, MA: McGraw-Hill.

Elliot, A. J., & Church, M. A. (1997). A hierarchical model of approach and avoidance achievement motivation. *Journal of Personality and Social Psychology, 72*, 218–232.

Feather, N. T. (1995). Values, valences, and choice: The influence of values on the perceived attractiveness and choice of alternatives. *Journal of Personality and Social Psychology, 68*, 1135–1151.

Herek, G. M. (1986). The instrumentality of attitudes: Toward a neofunctional theory. *Journal of Social Issues, 42*(2), 99–114.

Johnson, B. T., & Eagly, A. H. (1989). Effects of involvement on persuasion: A meta-analysis. *Psychological Bulletin, 106*, 290–314.

Katz, D. (1960). The functional approach to the study of attitudes. *Public Opinion Quarterly, 24*, 163–204.

Kristiansen, C. M., & Zanna, M. P. (1988). Justifying attitudes by appealing to values: A functional perspective. *British Journal of Social Psychology, 27*, 247–256.

Kristiansen, C. M., & Zanna, M. P. (1994). The rhetorical use of values to justify social and intergroup attitudes. *Journal of Social Issues, 50*, 47–65.

Lavallee, L. F., & Campbell, J. D. (1993, August). *Attitude–behaviour correspondence: The role of self-interest and social values.* Paper presented at the American Psychological Association, Toronto, Canada.

Lavine, H., Thomsen, C. J., & Gonzalez, M. H. (1997). The development of interattitudinal consistency: The shared-consequences model. *Journal of Personality and Social Psychology, 72*, 735–749.

Lydon, J. E., & Zanna, M. P. (1990). Commitment in the face of adversity: A value-affirmation approach. *Journal of Personality and Social Psychology, 58*, 1040–1047.

Maio, G. R., & Olson, J. M. (1994). Value–attitude–behaviour relations: The moderating role of attitude functions. *British Journal of Social Psychology, 33*, 301–312.

Maio, G. R., & Olson, J. M. (1995a). Involvement and persuasion: Evidence for different types of involvement. *Canadian Journal of Behavioural Science, 27*, 64–78.

Maio, G. R., & Olson, J. M. (1995b). Relations between values, attitudes, and behavioral intentions: The moderating role of attitude function. *Journal of Experimental Social Psychology, 31*, 266–285.

Maio, G. R., & Olson, J. M. (1998). Values as truisms: Evidence and Implication. *Journal of Personality and Social Psychology, 74*, 294–311.

Mellema, A., & Bassili, J. N. (1995). On the relationship between attitudes and values: Exploring the moderating effects of self-monitoring and self-monitoring schematicity. *Personality and Social Psychology Bulletin, 21*, 885–892.

Murray, S. H., Haddock, G., & Zanna, M. P. (1996). On creating value-expressive attitudes: An experimental approach. In C. Seligman, J. M. Olson, & M. P. Zanna (Eds.), *The psychology of values: The Ontario symposium* (Vol. 8, pp. 107–133). Mahwah, NJ: Lawrence Erlbaum Associates.

Olson, J. M. (1990). Self-Inference processes in emotion. In J. M. Olson & M. P. Zanna (Eds.), *Self-inference processes: The Ontario symposium*, (Vol. 6, pp. 17–41). Hillsdale, NJ: Lawrence Erlbaum Associates.

Olson, J. M. (1992). Self-perception of humor: Evidence for discounting and augmentation effects. *Journal of Personality and Social Psychology, 62*, 369–377.

Olson, J. M., & Zanna, M. P. (1993). Attitudes and attitude change. *Annual Review of Psychology, 44*, 117–154.

Ostrom, T. M., & Brock, T. C. (1968). A cognitive model of attitudinal involvement: In R. P. Abelson, E. Aronson, W. J. McGuire, T. M. Newcomb, M. J. Rosenberg, & P. H. Tannenbaum (Eds.), *Theories of cognitive consistency: A sourcebook* (pp. 373–383). Chicago: Rand-McNally.

Pratkanis, A. R., & Greenwald, A. G. (1989). A sociocognitive model of attitude structure and function. In L. Berkowitz (Ed.), *Advances in experimental social psychology* (Vol. 22, pp. 245–285). Mahwah, NJ: Lawrence Erlbaum Associates.

Prentice, D. A. (1987). Psychological correspondence of possessions, attitudes, and values. *Journal of Personality and Social Psychology, 53*, 993–1003.

Rokeach, M. (1973). *The nature of human values*. New York: Free Press.

Schwartz, S. H. (1992). Universals in the content and structure of values: Theoretical advances and empirical tests in 20 countries. In M. P. Zanna (Ed.), *Advances in experimental social psychology* (Vol. 25, 1–65). San Diego, CA: Academic Press.

Schwartz, S. H. (1996). Value priorities and behavior: Applying a theory of integrated value systems. In C. Seligman, J. Olson, & M. P. Zanna (Eds.), *The psychology of values: The Ontario symposium* (Vol. 8, pp. 1–24). Mahwah, NJ: Lawrence Erlbaum Associates.

Shavitt, S. (1990). The role of attitude objects in attitude functions. *Journal of Experimental Social Psychology, 26*, 124–148.

Smith, M. B., Bruner, J. S., & White, R. W. (1956). *Opinions and personality*. New York: Wiley.

Spangler, W. D. (1992). Validity of questionnaire and TAT measures of need for achievement—2 metaanalyses. *Psychological Bulletin, 112*, 140–154.

Young, J., Thomsen, C. J., Borgida, E., Sullivan, J., & Aldrich, J. H. (1991). When self-interest makes a difference: The role of construct accessibility in political reasoning. *Journal of Experimental Social Psychology, 27*, 271–296.

10

A Motivational Approach to Experimental Tests of Attitude Functions Theory

Kerry L. Marsh
University of Connecticut

Deana L. Julka
University of Portland

Since the mid-1980s, social psychologists have exhibited a renewed interest in attitude functions. This renewal of interest is a testament that the question, "What are attitudes good for?" is an enduring one for social psychologists. The rebirth of interest in attitude functions reflects a more general renewal of pragmatism in social psychology, demonstrated by concerns with the functionality of various social cognitions and behaviors (e.g., Kowalski, 1996; Roese, 1994; Roese & Olson, 1995). Buss (1996), for instance, made a strong case that understanding functionality is critical to advancing the understanding of any psychological phenomenon.

In the area of attitude functions, Snyder and DeBono (1985; DeBono, 1987) helped reinvigorate attitude functions research with their first studies focusing on the attitude functions of high and low self-monitors.

Shavitt (1989, 1990; Shavitt & Fazio, 1991) broadened the focus to include the inherent functionality of attitude objects. Another significant spur to interest in the functionality of attitudes has been attitude accessibility research that demonstrates the benefits of having a readily available response (i.e., an accessible attitude) when one encounters an attitude object (Fazio, Blascovich, & Driscoll, 1992). From this perspective, the most basic and universal function all attitudes serve is merely to ease the process of making judgments (Fazio, 1989). The primacy of the cognitive utility of attitudes is an implicit assumption that underlies nearly all recent experimental attempts to manipulate the functional basis of attitudes. A broad theme, then, in current attitude functions experimentation and theorizing is that of conceptualizing attitude functionality in terms of cognitive processes.

On the other hand, the intriguing early attempts to test attitude functions theory had a distinctly motivational flavor that is missing from most current conceptualizations of attitude functions. In his attitude experiments that examined individuals who differed in "other-directed-ness" and "ego-defensiveness," McClintock (1958; Katz, McClintock, & Sarnoff, 1957) explicitly interpreted attitude change in his studies as a response to specific motivational forces. Sarnoff's (1960) approach was the most thoroughly motivational in nature, suggesting that individuals form attitudes in order to reduce the tension of particular motives. In this early research, there is clearly an understanding of motivational forces that press individuals to reject certain persuasive attempts or be vulnerable to others. The functional nature of attitudes was not just a shorthand for the cognitive contents of various aspects of an attitude or its cognitive utility, but functions were viewed as motives having a directing, causal tension that impacted persuasion.

In the current chapter, we describe our program of research that attempts to bring the notion of motivation back into conceptualizations of attitude function and yet offer rigorously experimental tests of attitude functions theory. In doing so, we eliminate the methodological problems that confounded early research on the motivational perspective to attitude functions theory. These experiments test the idea that a persuasive message that matches an individual's need will be more persuasive than an unmatched message. In this chapter, we describe the limited past experimental research that has been done and summarize our own program of research. We first begin with an elaboration of motivational and cognitive perspectives on attitude functions.

MOTIVATIONAL AROUSAL VERSUS COGNITIVE
ACCESSIBILITY PERSPECTIVES

The key question of this chapter is that of whether the term "attitude function" is to be given merely a pragmatic meaning or whether there may be some merit to considering the potential motivational nature of attitude functions. Here we mean motivation in the classic, textbook sense (e.g., Atkinson, 1964; Jones, 1955; Lewin, 1961; Mook, 1987; Weiner, 1992), as having causal, directing effects on cognition and behavior. In the area of persuasion, for example, motives influence the kinds of persuasion contexts an individual chose to expose him- or herself to, and serve to direct and sustain cognitive processing and behavior. These motives should have effects analogous to motives such as hunger. For instance, once hunger needs have been met, the seeking of food is diminished. Similarly, a reduction in persuadability is expected once a given need is met. Thus, an adolescent who experiences feelings of social rejection might alleviate some affiliation need by more readily accepting attitude positions that the speaker argues are popularly held by her peers. If affiliation needs were minimal, however, such a persuasive attempt would be less effective.

Researchers have recognized some fundamental categories of attitude functions. These are the need for individuals to express their values (value-expressive function), to organize and make sense of their world (knowledge function), to defend themselves against threat (ego-defensive function), to affiliate and be viewed positively by others (social-adjustive function) or to experience more basic hedonic rewards (utilitarian function; Katz, 1960; Smith, Bruner, & White, 1956; Snyder & DeBono, 1989). In current experimental research, however, the need-based quality of these attitude functions has been de-emphasized. If one truly considers attitude functions as motivational forces rather than as convenient taxonomic categories for the sorting of attitudes, one concludes that an unmet need (i.e., a stimulated attitude function) can serve as a pressure that makes an individual more susceptible to a given persuasive attempt. From this perspective, attitude functions are best conceptualized in terms of process—in terms of the way they energize individuals to embrace or repel persuasive attempts. This motivational arousal perspective suggests that if an attitude function is aroused in an individual (i.e., the person is experiencing the tension of an unmet need), that individual will be more persuaded by an appeal that successfully addresses that need than by an appeal that does not. We refer to this prediction as the *motivational matching hypothesis*.

Take, for instance, someone forced to experience some situation that undermines the ability to express and assert his or her values. For example, a liberal thinker forced to listen to a television show with a conservative host should experience a deprivation in the current ability to meet that need to express and assert one's values. The situation is distressing and tension inducing, and leads to attempts to reassert his or her own values. As a result, the individual actively seeks means of reexpressing those values (yelling back at the television, directing comments to another viewer). More important to our argument, the individual has an increased vulnerability to persuasive attempts that enable him or her to meet this need (by expression of values). Suppose, for example, that the viewer is interrupted by a knock at the door by a person collecting signatures for a local ordinance change. It is our contention that the viewer will be more persuaded by the activist if the activist appeals to the viewer's personal values rather than to the positive economic or efficiency consequences of the ordinance change.

On the other hand, from the more cognitive or pragmatic perspective on defining attitude functions, this matching effect is also expected, but the mediating mechanisms are predicted to be somewhat different. According to what we term the *cognitive accessibility matching hypothesis*, if the respondent had merely been engaged in a task that led to thoughts about values (i.e., did not pose a threat to the expression of values), the values appeal of the activist would still be more effective than an appeal to practical rewards. From this perspective, however, a persuasive attempt should be successful if it merely matches the functional content of an individual's current attitude or if it matches the most recently primed category of general content. By "content" we mean here the types of information, thoughts, feelings, and beliefs that pertain to each of the attitude function categories.

This hypothesis is derived from attitude function work by Fazio (1989) and Shavitt and Fazio (1991), as well as from research on attitude accessibility. When one repeatedly expresses one's attitude about some object, this is said to strengthen the "object-evaluation association"; that is, one's evaluation of that object can be accessed quickly when one is exposed to the object (Powell & Fazio, 1984). Fazio et al. (1992) suggested that such accessible attitudes increase the speed and quality of decision making. Moreover, they found that participants who formed and rehearsed attitudes toward an object displayed a smaller increase in blood pressure (an indicant of effort) than did control participants. These findings emphasize the importance and power of accessible knowledge structures (i.e., attitudes) in affecting one's subsequent judgments and actions. Perhaps, in addition, increasing the accessibility of broad categories of content (i.e., attitude functions) similarly eases the process of forming, accessing, and changing attitudes in line with those categories. Thus, individuals exposed to situations that merely lead them to think about their values more readily form or change attitudes when they are subsequently exposed to a message that appeals to values. In other words, induction of a prior need state is unnecessary.[1]

Thus, current social cognitive perspectives on attitude functions focus less on energizing processes, and more on the structure and contents of attitudes. The content of attitudes that serve certain functions can be primed or made accessible by leading people to think about certain kinds of content. In contrast, from a motivational perspective, attitude functions are the driving force of an individual's inner needs and cognitions, acting in response to the behavior and messages of others; they determine how an individual acts on and is influenced by the circumstances of the external world. Both approaches predict matching effects—that an experimental manipulation that primes an attitude function or arouses a particular need leads to greater susceptibility to persuasive messages that match the manipulated function. But if the motivational matching hypothesis is correct, experimental manipulations that arouse motivation should lead to stronger matching effects than do experimental manipulations that merely prime a function.

Recent experimental research has provided some evidence of matching effects, but the methodologies do not allow one to distinguish between cognitive accessibility and motivational interpretations of the results. Specifically, this research has demonstrated that priming procedures can lead participants to form attitudes based on that function (Maio & Olson, 1995; Young, Thomsen, Borgida, Sullivan, & Aldrich, 1991) and that, after individuals have been primed to form attitudes in a given function, persuasion and behavior processes reveal matching effects. Research by Shavitt and her colleagues provides such evidence (Shavitt & Fazio, 1991; Shavitt, Swan, Lowrey, & Wänke, 1994). In these studies, a social-image

---

[1]Of course, the prediction of matching effects assumes that the persuasive message contains strong arguments. In the case of weak arguments, increased accessibility of constructs presumably leads to greater rejection of the persuasive message.

function was primed by asking participants to rate a variety of different objects for how useful they were in making a good impression on others. Other participants were asked to focus on the sensory qualities of a wide range of events or to focus on qualities such as taste (Shavitt & Fazio; Shavitt et al., 1994). For example, in one study, an attitude function was primed, and participants then predicted their likelihood of engaging in various behaviors that pertain to a specific object (7-Up or Perrier water). When the natural functionality of the object (e.g., image for Perrier) matched the priming manipulation, correlations between attitudes and behavioral predictions were higher than when the function of the specific object and the general prime did not match (Shavitt & Fazio).

Additional evidence for matching effects has involved experimental manipulation of the value-expressive and social-adjustive functions (Murray, Haddock, & Zanna, 1996). The manipulation of a given function combined three procedures. Participants engaged in a task in which they linked values (or social groups) to their attitudes on a variety of different issues. In addition, participants were induced to believe that the holding of attitudes that served the particular manipulated function was more desirable, and they were led to believe that their own attitudes were typically based on that function. The study indicated strong support for the matching hypothesis. Individuals who had experienced the value-expressive manipulation were more persuaded by a value-based message than by a social appeal; the opposite effect was obtained for the social-adjustive manipulation (Murray et al., 1996). Clearly, the results might be explained by the cognitive accessibility perspective because the procedures should have heightened the accessibility of value-based or social-based constructs. On the other hand, other aspects of the procedure might also engage some arousal of motivation. For instance, the procedure seems likely to motivate individuals to actively attempt to make their attitudes reflect a given attitude function. Perhaps the procedure even arouses a sense of deprivation because, as individuals focus on their attitudes, the ways in which their attitudes might fail to meet this function become salient.

These several studies, then, have established that different functional contents of one's attitudes can be primed, and that individuals can be induced to express their attitude and behavior in a way that is congruent with the attitude function prime. These studies, however, have not examined whether these results are merely a consequence of increase in accessibility of the functional content of attitudes and behavior, or whether some arousal of need might be involved. Accessibility may play some role in formation or change in attitudes congruent with primed categories, but if the original motivational implications of attitude functions theory are correct, inducement of a motivational state should enhance matching effects beyond mere priming. In the following section, we describe how we tested this hypothesis.

EXPERIMENTAL TESTS OF THE MOTIVATIONAL MATCHING HYPOTHESIS

Our approach has been to test the matching hypothesis using a procedure that extends beyond mere priming of a function category of thought. Participants in experimental conditions are exposed to a single motivational induction designed to thwart participants' abilities to satisfy a particular psychological need normally served by their attitudes. Others participants are exposed to the same situation but with a difference in the level of induced arousal of the need. These milder attitude function manipulations are designed to involve only mild arousal or mere priming of the attitude function. After manipulation of an attitude function, participants are exposed to persuasive appeals that match or do not match this manipulated attitude function (Julka & Marsh, 1993, 1996, 1998a; Marsh & Julka, 1998; Marsh & Thielen, 1993). In the current chapter, we focus on experiments in which we manipulated the value-expressive or knowledge function because we explored the social-adjustive function less often (e.g., Marsh & Thielen).

Motivational manipulations of the value-expressive function are designed to make individuals feel that they are not living up to their personal values on some particular issue, to create a sense of frustrated ability to express their personal values and opinions, or to undermine the sense that their values and beliefs are valid. Our milder versions of these manipulations are designed merely to arouse a general concern with values, a tendency to reflect on those values without inducing feelings of inadequacy in expression of those values. The mild value-expressive manipulations are thus somewhat analogous to value-priming procedures (Maio & Olson, 1995), in that they should involve less of a state of value-expressive deprivation. The consequence of stronger arousal of a value-expressive function is that participants should be more vulnerable to appeals that address values of personal importance to them than to messages that do not address their values.

Experimental inductions of the knowledge function are designed to create a sense of confusion and uncertainty, or to create what has been described as an inability to construct a mental model of a situation (Kofta, 1993). Situations that induce this confusion should cause individuals to attend to factually based information in order to relieve their need to make sense of the world. For example, in the area of research on control motivation, control deprivation manipulations in which participants try to solve apparently unsolvable problems (e.g., T. S. Pittman & D'Agostino, 1985, 1989; T. S. Pittman & N. L. Pittman, 1980) may involve arousal of the knowledge function. In addition, manipulations that are designed to induce a need for closure (e.g., time pressure in a group decision-making task, Kruglanski, 1989; Kruglanski & Freund, 1983) involve arousal of the knowledge function. In contrast, mild manipulations of the knowledge function should merely engage thought about information, without inducing a state of confusion. The consequences of stronger arousal of a knowledge function are that individuals should be motivated to engage in relatively accurate and thorough, elaborative processing of subsequent information, or be motivated to take in information that offers them a quick and simplified view of the world. Our knowledge persuasive messages are designed such that the messages should appeal to participants who seek quick, simple answers as well as those who seek complete, thorough answers.

The typical research paradigm involves a 2 × 2 × 2 experimental design in which participants are randomly assigned to experience a mild or strong motivational induction of the value-expressive or knowledge function, and receive one or more persuasive messages or advertisements that appeal to one of these functions. In designing these studies, we have relied on some assumptions about the processes involved in arousal and alleviation of need states.

Arousal of General Need States

When inducing specific needs, we assume that an induced need can have an impact on persuasion regardless of the original, specific topic of need arousal. That is, the specific attitude object or topic in which the function was induced does not have to be the specific focus of the persuasive message in order to find matching effects. Researchers who use priming manipulations often rely on similar implicit assumptions (e.g., Shavitt et al., 1994). However, this is different from the implicit assumptions of early attitude function theories. For example, when Katz (1960) explained the conditions for changing a given attitude, he stated that the current attitudinal position can be made inadequate for meeting its original function. He discussed how undermining the functional basis of a specific attitude was an alternative to inducing general need states.

One reason for examining the effects of nonspecific motivational arousal was practical. Our earliest efforts to manipulate attitude function involved having individuals think about a series of questions (value based or factually based) regarding their attitude. Participants were then exposed to a counterattitudinal message on the same attitude topic; the message either did or did not match the manipulated function. In that study, we found a slight (although nonsignificant) tendency for more persuasion under nonmatching conditions (Marsh, 1986). It became clear that one practical problem with keeping the topic the same in both the induction and the matching steps was that if the attitude object remains the same, unmatching conditions may offer more new information for persuasion. Thus, individuals who focused first on values and then on facts about the same issue are given more new sources of information about the issue than individuals in the matching conditions. Another disadvantage of keeping the domain the same in the arousal and alleviation of needs is that demand characteristics are more likely in such a situation. Thus, in our current program of research we explore whether general states of motivational arousal can be used to induce formation and change of specific attitudes. Our program of research suggests that they can.

Alleviation of the Need State

Once a state of deprivation is created, an individual should be more vulnerable to persuasive attempts (on a variety of topics) that appeal to this general need. By yielding to the message, the state of deprivation should presumably be diminished. Despite our assumption that domain specificity is unnecessary, it is still important to be sensitive to the persuasion context. It is not sufficient for the message to match the aroused need, but acceptance of the specific message content must alleviate the need. For instance, if in the process of arousing a knowledge function, it happens that students are made to feel stupid, then a specific persuasive message that argues for requiring a senior thesis will be ineffective, regardless of its match to the induced function (Julka & Marsh, 1993). Similarly, yielding to advertisements is unlikely to occur if some function induction causes a participant to feel undesirably gullible.

Ethnocentrism Scale and Confusing Script Study

A recent study (Julka & Marsh, 1998a) illustrated the promise and problems inherent in testing the motivational matching hypothesis. Participants were randomly assigned to receive a strong or mild induction of the value-expressive or knowledge function. Afterward, participants rated their preference for a series of pairs of advertisements. Each pair contained one ad pretested to contain value-based information; the other relied on factual information. The dependent measure was participants' liking for the different types of ads.

Value-Expressive Conditions.

Participants were exposed to materials that were designed to weakly or strongly induce a value-expressive function. Participants in these conditions were told that we were interested in their evaluation of some scales that we had developed and that, to best evaluate the scales, participants should complete them as though they were respondents. They were told that we were not interested in their own responses, but rather in their later evaluations of the scales.

In the strong value-expressive condition, participants received the Thielen–Marsh Ethnocentrism Scale (Marsh & Thielen, 1993). The scale was designed to arouse a feeling that participants are not quite living up to their values opposing racism and sexism and discrimination, values found to be important in our population. The first page contains questions that ask students to provide some personal information (e.g., "describe your personal ethnic identity," and "I have dated an...Hispanic, African-American, Asian, Caucasian"). The next six questions deal with the individual's specific behaviors toward members of other groups. For example, participants are asked whether they have ever laughed at racial or ethnic jokes, or whether they would be frightened if they were walking alone at night and were approached by a group of individuals of another race. The next section involves indicating their agreement with a series of four belief statements based on items from earlier prejudice scales (e.g., Adorno, Levinson, Frenkel-Brunswik, & Sanford, 1950). For example, one item states that "the minority problem is so general and deep that democratic methods can never solve it." The final set of questions are social distance items for which participants indicate how comfortable they feel with various situations such as, "If a brother/sister/member of my family married a person of another race, I would feel...." Participants were then told that for them to get a true feel for the entire scale, they should score their own responses to the scale items. They were told that we are interested only in their feedback on the scale and on the scoring procedures, and not in their actual score. The four scoring categories were paragraphs headed by the titles "superiorly living up to values," "adequately living up to your values," "falling short of values," and "falling terribly short of values." The wording of the questionnaire items was designed to constrain participants' responses such that participants fell into a category of "adequately living up to your values." Participants were instructed at the end of the procedure to discard their questionnaires in order to confirm for participants that the experimenter was not interested in their particular scores.

In the mild value-expressive condition, participants read the Ethnocentrism Scale but did not complete it. Instead, they read through the questionnaire, they were asked to think about how they would respond to the questions and then decide which questions on the scale they personally felt were better for assessing values related to ethnocentrism. Participants did not view the scoring categories. In general, these procedures should induce participants to think about their personal values regarding sexism, racism, and discrimination, but the discrepancy between their responses and their personal values should not be highly salient.

As in other studies, we pretested the manipulations by content analyzing participants' responses to an open-ended question that asked them to report their current feelings and thoughts. The coding categories included whether participants indicated a focus on values, indicated feeling bad about themselves, and expressed affective reactions. Pretesting indicated that both manipulations induced a moderate focus on values, but participants in the strong condition expressed more affective intensity and more bad feelings about the self.[2] These results may seem somewhat surprising, because the label of the scoring category in the strong condition ("adequately living up to your values") is positive. However, pretesting indicated that the strong manipulation used in this study did evoke a feeling of not living up to one's values. In part, this is probably because the scoring of the scale was only a minor, final part of the manipulation. Much of the effectiveness of the manipulation involved the active process

---

[2]Relying on content analysis of participants' spontaneous remarks has its limitations. In our research, as in others' research (e.g., Ennis & Zanna, chap. 14, this volume), underreporting of functions is common. To address this problem, we recently developed a set of Likert-type items for general use in assessing motivational inductions of various attitude functions. This validation scale is available from the authors (Marsh & Julka, 1998).

of completing each item. The completion of items on which one is repeatedly aware that one's response is less than ideal was a critical part of the process. Apparently, in this population, students had high standards for how they felt they should respond to items and should score on such a scale.

Knowledge Manipulations. For these manipulations, participants were told that we were interested in their reactions to several psychological experiments. We indicated that we wanted to know how interesting they found each study and that we wanted their feedback on the discussion of these experiments in general. Participants then listened to a 4-minute audiotape in which the methods, results, and conclusions of three classic experiments on bystander intervention were described. In the mild version of the manipulation, participants simply heard the facts of each experiment, presented in a logical sequence. In the strong version of the manipulation, the script had identical content except that many sentences of the script were read out of order. For instance, following a description of the methods of an experiment in which an experimenter falls while trying to retrieve a book, the next sentence described the results of the "smoke-filled room" experiment. Immediately following that sentence the speaker described the methodological variations used in the "drunk/victim on a subway" experiment.

Results. The results are summarized in Fig. 10.1. They provide clear evidence that motivational manipulations can successfully be used to test the attitude functions matching hypothesis. Preference for value-expressive advertisements was stronger for those exposed to value-expressive manipulations than for those who received knowledge manipulations. The opposite was true for the knowledge advertisements. Strength of the motivational manipulation, however, did not affect the results. Contrary to expectations, matching effects were equally strong with both mild and strong manipulations. Thus, these matching effects could be readily explained by a cognitive accessibility perspective.

Degree of Motivational Arousal

One critical limitation of the study, however, was that the mild and strong manipulations were quite similar. One possibility is that our mild manipulations were engaging some degree of motivational arousal. In fact,

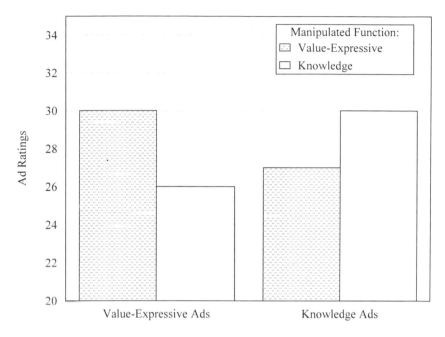

FIG. 10.1. Preferences for value-expressive and knowledge ads for participants exposed to value-expressive and knowledge manipulations.

to keep our mild and strong manipulations comparable, our mild procedures have been considerably different from priming manipulations used by other researchers (e.g., Shavitt & Fazio, 1991; Shavitt et al., 1994; Young et al., 1991). It may be the case that there is some minimal threshold of arousal needed to induce matching effects, but beyond this threshold stronger arousal has only limited effects. Thus, a more definitive test of the hypothesis would use mild manipulations that more purely prime a function, compared to manipulations that clearly engage a motivational state. In what follows, we discuss a recent study that provides such a test.

One other question regarding strength of a motivational manipulation involves what occurs with more extreme inductions of a function. Presumably, the stronger a manipulation is, the greater a need it evokes, and the more matching effects are strengthened. However, an alternative prediction is that manipulations of attitude functions that are too extreme may lead to defensive reactions and result in a reduction of any matching effects. In the following section, this issue is also addressed.

Use of Intense Inductions of Attitude Functions.   One study in particular illustrates the consequences of intense arousal of attitude functions (Julka & Marsh, 1993). The manipulations in the study involved making participants feel as though they lacked some important knowledge pertaining to a wide range of topics including science, art, literature, history, and politics. Afterward, participants read a factually based or values-based persuasive message. (Participants in the control conditions responded to the message before receiving a manipulation.) In the experimental conditions, participants first completed an Aesthetic Awareness Scale, in which they saw a series of color pictures of famous works of art (e.g., An American Gothic, the Mona Lisa, the Notre Dame Cathedral in Paris) and were asked to identify the name, artist, and other details of the work. Afterward, participants completed a scale in which they identified areas of knowledge about which they felt informed. The experimenter used this scale to justify having participants then complete the Cultural Literacy Scale, described as involving areas of knowledge with which they were familiar. The Cultural Literacy Scale contained short questions selected from Hirsch's (1988) book on information that every member of our culture ought to know. The items were ones that pilot participants did not perform well on, but were questions that sounded to us and our pilot participants very familiar—items that people feel they ought to know. In the more difficult version of these scales, the distracter answers on some questions made the test more difficult. For example, if the question concerned when the U. S. Civil War started, the difficult version contained answers that covered a narrow ranges of years, whereas the easier version covered a broad range of years.

Participants then self-scored their responses to both the Aesthetic Awareness and Cultural Literacy Scales. In the easier version of the scales, the scoring categories were designed such that participants fell into a category of having "adequate knowledge." In the harder version, participants fell into the category, "falling short of required knowledge." Regardless of our design of the scales, however, participants in all conditions expressed strong negative reactions after the procedure. As we intended, participants reported feeling that they did not have sufficient knowledge; these feelings were also strongest with the more difficult version. However, even in the easier version, participants showed substantial evidence of feeling threatened and defensive. Substantial negative affect was reported, and participants also showed tendencies to justify their lack of knowledge and question the validity of the procedure. Indeed, the unexpectedly negative nature of the responses became apparent to the experimenter during the procedure. Occasional outbursts and cursing was heard from participants' rooms, and participants often expressed frustration and annoyance when the experimenter brought the scoring procedure into the room. Thus, contrary to our intentions, in the course of evoking a sense of not being able to retrieve and make sense of important factual information, we also threatened participants' perceptions of themselves as intellectually competent and broadly knowledgeable members of society. The defensiveness of participants' responses suggested that such strong manipulations of an attitude function are qualitatively different than are manipulations that engage more moderate arousal.

In fact, no matching effects occurred in this study. In contrast to control subjects who had a definite preference for knowledge messages over value-based messages, in individuals exposed to knowledge manipulations, this tendency was somewhat reduced. A similar reduction of matching effects occurred in studies with extreme inductions of the value-expressive function (Marsh & Thielen, 1993). In that study, we compared the effects of the Ethnocentrism Scale, described earlier, with the effects of a more negatively worded and more harshly scored version of the scale. To intensify the manipulations, participants also completed an Imagery Scale, in which they colored various objects and answered some questions involving visual images. Self-scoring of the scale later revealed to participants that their responses were ethnocentric and biased. For instance, their scores were decreased by using their own skin color to determine how to color in "a nude colored bandaid" and the "typical American family," and by designating the familiar Mercator map of the world as correct.

Afterward, participants rated pairs of advertisements that appealed to a value-expressive or social-adjustive need. Again, the results of this study suggested that intense manipulation of the attitude function led to reduced tendencies to display matching effects in attitude formation. In general, our results involving more intense manipulations suggest that these manipulations evoke states that are perhaps better labeled "ego defensive" rather than "value-expressive" or "knowledge". For instance, any experimental induction that offers a significant threat to self-esteem is likely to evoke ego-defensive concerns. Manipulations of an ego-defensive function should engage a tendency toward avoidance, rejection, psychological "flight," or defensive avoidance unless an appeal specifically alleviates the concerns (e.g., as in the case of effective fear appeals, Rogers, 1983).

Use of Purer Manipulations of Priming and Moderate Motivational Arousal. An adequate test of the motivational matching hypothesis, then, seems to require avoidance of overly intense manipulations because these seem to induce defensiveness and rejection of messages. But an adequate test may require arousal levels that differ more extensively than in the Ethnocentrism and Script Confusion Study. In a recent replication and extension of that study (Julka & Marsh, 1998b), comparable manipulations were used, but the mild versions of the manipulations were purer at merely priming the function. In the experimental conditions, participants received a value-expressive or knowledge manipulation. Participants' attitudes toward organ donation were then assessed after they read either a strong value-based or factually based persuasive message about the topic.

In the strong value-expressive condition, the previously described Ethnocentrism Scale was used. However, the mild condition involved a somewhat different procedure. Participants in this condition read a list of 10 values related to issues of ethnocentrism selected from Rokeach (1973) (e.g., acceptance, equality, freedom, giving others a fair go, courage, politeness) and ranked them in order of their personal importance. Next, participants rated how personally important each value is to them on 9-point scales. Finally, participants rated how relevant each of the related behaviors (e.g., acceptance of others, giving others a fair chance) is in measuring values related to ethnocentrism, racism, and equality. The instructions emphasized that we were not interested in what kinds of behaviors they engage in, but rather in their opinion about each value and behavior. The Value Ranking Procedure was designed to have participants think about their values without actually arousing a feeling that they were failing to live up to their values.

Validation of the value-expressive manipulations indicated that both versions induced substantial focus on values (Julka, 1998; Julka & Marsh, 1998b). Participants in the strong condition expressed much more negative affect than did individuals in the mild condition. In the strong condition, one-quarter of the participants also spontaneously expressed feeling disappointed in themselves; participants in the mild condition spontaneously expressed more positive affect and response to the scale. In general, validation of these manipulations revealed more substantial differences between the manipulations than in the Ethnocentrism and Script Confusion Study.

Participants exposed to a knowledge manipulation were told that we were interested in how people communicate information while teaching, and the effectiveness of these methods. To that end, they read directions to a game and then taught another participant how to play the game. Participants in the strong version of the knowledge manipulation were presented with a deck of cards, a cribbage board, and poorly written and confusing (although correct) instructions on how to play cribbage. Students were given 10 minutes to read the instructions. In the mild version of this knowledge manipulation, students read clearly written instructions to a simplified version of the game cribbage, referred to as "cribbit." (The cribbit instructions eliminate half of the normal cribbage procedure that was difficult to describe simply.) Validation of the procedures revealed some evidence of confusion and lack of understanding. Moreover, these effects were significantly more pronounced in the strong condition (Julka, 1998; Julka & Marsh, 1998b).

In this study, the results replicated the matching effects found previously—individuals who received a matching message showed more attitude change than if the organ donation message did not match. Most important, the three-way interaction predicted by the motivational matching hypothesis (manipulated function by strength of manipulation by message type) was found. Matching effects were stronger when individuals received a stronger manipulation than when the function was merely primed. Presumably, one important factor in detecting the effects was the greater disparity between mild and strong manipulations. In addition, we assessed attitude change by using pretest attitudes assessed from a mass prescreening session earlier in the semester. Thus, statistical power was greater.

CONCLUSIONS FROM TESTS
OF THE MOTIVATIONAL MATCHING HYPOTHESIS

One contribution of the research testing the motivational matching hypothesis is the successful development of manipulations for arousing attitude functions, especially the value-expressive and knowledge functions. This was a particularly challenging task for a number of reasons. There was scant prior evidence about the motivational nature of various attitude functions. In addition, the naturally occurring boundaries between arousal of many of these attitude functions is inherently nebulous and inconstant. Indeed, focusing on the value-expressive and knowledge manipulations may be easier than trying to distinguish between other functions.

For example, manipulations of the social-adjustive function may be inherently more difficult to separate from value-expressive manipulations. In some situations, in fact, researchers have used categorizations that combine these functions (e.g., Shavitt, 1990). Another problem in defining this functional category is whether to manipulate the function as a desire for union, similarity, and belonging with others, or whether to manipulate the function in terms of the upward drive to achieve status and power and to be perceived as more desirable to others than the average person. For the former need, similarity and union is the desired endstate; for the latter need, a superior uniqueness is the desired state. Manipulations of this function might be considered along a continuum in which the endpoint involving desire for acceptance and similarity is most closely linked with value-expressive concerns (sharing values with like-minded family and friends). Toward the other endpoint, social-adjustive concerns probably blend into the utilitarian desire for other rewards highly valued by society such as wealth and other pragmatic rewards.

Thus, this experimental paradigm may be somewhat more challenging to use with needs that are more closely linked such as the social-adjustive and value-expressive functions. But on the basis of our studies, which manipulate the value-expressive and knowledge functions, a number of general conclusions about attitude functions seem justified.

Messages that Match a Manipulated Function are More Effective

Our research has provided strong support for the matching hypothesis. Arousal of a need can lead to increased susceptibility to persuasive attempts, even when the attitude issue involved in the persuasive message is entirely unrelated to the topic involved in attitude function arousal. These effects have been found by using experimental manipulations of both the value-expressive and knowledge functions, and replicated with different manipulations of each function. Moreover, we have found evidence for matching effects when examining attitude formation in an ad preference task and when assessing attitude change after exposure to a persuasive message.

Intense Arousal of a Function Induces Defensive Reactions

In some of our studies, we inadvertently made people feel quite stupid, disappointed in themselves, and rejected. The manipulations were highly involving and engaged considerable reactions from our participants. But in every case in which the induction of attitude function was too extreme, we found no matching effects. Rather, the results suggested that too extreme arousal of a state of deprivation (e.g., extreme arousal of value-expressive function) leads to a reduction in tendencies to yield to messages that appeal to the manipulated function. This inverse U-shape function resulting from motivational arousal is commonly found in motivation research. For example, consider how organisms respond to control threats (i.e., arousal of control needs). Mild control loss leads to reactance and increased susceptibility to opportunities to regain control, but too extreme arousal of control concerns leads to expectations of uncontrollability, learned helplessness, depression, and a reduction in attempts to regain control (Wortman & Brehm, 1975).

Thus, intense arousal of an attitude function may lead to defensiveness and greater difficulty in obtaining attitudinal effects. This is the same pattern found by early researchers in their attempts to specifically target ego-defensive attitudes. In these early studies, counterattitudinal messages were the least effective for individuals categorized as highest in ego defensiveness (Katz et al., 1957; McClintock, 1958). Only moderate levels of ego defense led to successful matching effects; in some cases, even moderate levels led to less persuasion than low levels (Katz, Sarnoff, & McClintock, 1956). Clearly, finding a way to match persuasive attempts to induced ego-defensive functions is a more difficult task.

Induction of Motivational States Often Involves Negative Affect

Arousal of needs is a messy business. Richly engaging procedures that are successful at making an individual feel confused, feel that one is not living up to one's values, or feel socially undesirable can often lead to negative emotions. The consequence of this is that in our experiments, control participants who are exposed to no experimental inductions typically have more positive ratings of the persuasive messages than do participants exposed to experimental inductions. As many current theories of affect predict (e.g., Bower, 1981; Forgas, 1995), individuals may use their negative state as a cue to how they feel about the messages; alternatively, negative affect may lead to increased retrieval of negative information from memory. However, experimental participants subsequently exposed to matching messages do demonstrate more susceptibility to the messages; thus experimental participants in matching conditions have scores either no different from, or slightly higher than, those of control participants. Even mood theories that predict a "mood by processing" interaction cannot account for why mere negative affect would lead to increased susceptibility to messages that specifically appeal to certain functional content. For example, negative mood can lead to increased vigilance of processing (e.g., Bless, Bohner, Schwarz, & Strack, 1990; Forgas, 1995), but this cannot explain matching effects, because our persuasive arguments in unmatching messages are pretested to be as cogent as those in our matching messages. Thus, the negative affect involved in many (although not all) of our manipulations does not provide a plausible alternative hypothesis for matching effects.

Inductions Lead to Increased Specific Needs, Not to General Arousal of Self-Affirmation Concerns

For each of our studies, we can contrast the predictions of the motivational matching hypothesis with those of self-affirmation theory (Steele, 1988). Self-affirmation theory suggests that when a specific concern about the self is aroused, individuals should demonstrate subsequent attempts to reaffirm their self-concept. The self-system is viewed as highly flexible, such that a threat to one aspect of the self can be alleviated by affirmation of some other important dimension of the self-system. From this reasoning, arousal of a need should lead to increased susceptibility to any persuasive attempt that allowed self-affirmation; matching of the specific induced need is unnecessary. In our studies we have tested self-affirmation theory predictions by using milder and stronger inductions. Self-affirmation theory would lead to the prediction of a main effect for strength of induction—stronger arousal of functions (i.e., stronger threat to the self-system) should lead to more persuasion. This should occur regardless of the persuasive message received, because each of our messages appeals to some important need of the self-system (to affirm one's values, or to be able to understand and organize the world). Our experiments generally offer support not for self-affirmation predictions, but for matching effects. But because our experiments were not specifically designed to test the self-affirmation hypothesis, the lack of support might be due to differences between self-affirmation procedures and our own. More recently, even in a close replication of self-affirmation procedures, we found no support for self-affirmation theory over attitude functions theory (Julka, 1998).

Motivational Inductions Lead to Stronger
Matching Effects Than Priming Manipulations

An explicit assumption of our program of research is that motivational arousal energizes people in a way that mere priming cannot. Should persuasion be thought of as a process of dispassionately responding to environmental cues that prime responses by triggering access to stored past experience? Alternatively, is there some utility for considering the underlying motivational forces that invigorate these processes? Results from many of our studies have been adequately explainable by a cognitive accessibility perspective. In these, mild procedures were as effective as strong inductions at inducing matching effects. But in one study, we found motivational matching effects (Julka & Marsh, 1998b). Presumably the reasons for detecting this effect in the most recent study is the increase in statistical power and the strengthened discrimination between mild and strong manipulations.

There may be another method that is especially appropriate for exploring the potential advantages of motivational manipulations over priming ones—namely, the use of additional dependent measures. Perhaps the advantage of a motivational manipulation is especially apparent on delayed attitude measures relative to immediate measures of attitude. On such measures, individuals in motivational matching conditions might subsequently display behavior more congruent with their expressed attitudes than do individuals in priming matching conditions. For instance, motivational inductions might lead individuals not only to express positive attitudes after reading a persuasive message, but also to take active steps to affirm their attitude once leaving the laboratory. In contrast, there may be circumstances in which exposure to a matched message after a priming manipulation might result in superficial attitudinal effects that appear similar to those in the motivational matching conditions. However, participants in primed matching conditions might demonstrate considerably less invigoration of attitude-related behavior. Once the experiment ended, behavioral effects might be more limited.

It is possible that satisfaction of an aroused need is better served by active behavior than by submission to a persuasive message. For example, given a choice of different activities, individuals who have a function aroused might be more inclined to choose activities that match that function than are individuals who merely have a function primed. Thus, individuals who experience an arousal of value-expressive concerns might be more willing to engage in tasks that allow them to express their values in an active way (e.g., helping others). In addition, they might have an increased preference to watch a documentary that appeals to their values. Similarly, individuals who experience an arousal of a knowledge need might be more interested in watching a program that presents factual information, or they might be more interested in engaging in a problem-solving task that allows them the opportunity to put order and coherence to some information. Mere priming of a function might not have as much of an energizing effect on behavior.

In fact, this is perhaps the greatest promise of the motivational approach. The last great advance in attitude research was recognizing the recipient of a persuasive message as an active thinker rather than as merely a passive processor of information (e.g., Chaiken, Liberman, & Eagly, 1989; Petty & Cacioppo, 1986). Perhaps it is now time to more fully explore the message recipient as an executor of action.

REFERENCES

Adorno, T. W., Levinson, D. J., Frenkel-Brunswik, E., & Sanford, R. N. (1950). *The authoritarian personality*. New York: Harper & Row.

Atkinson, J. W. (1964). *An introduction to motivation*. Princeton, NJ: Van Nostrand.

Bless, H., Bohner, G., Schwarz, N., & Strack, F. (1990). Mood and persuasion: A cognitive response analysis. *Personality and Social Psychology Bulletin, 16*, 331–345.

Bower, G. H. (1981). Mood and memory. *American Psychologist, 36*, 129–148.

Buss, D. M. (1996). The evolutionary psychology of human social strategies. In E. T. Higgins & A. W. Kruglanski (Eds.), *Social psychology: Handbook of basic principles* (pp. 3–38). New York: Guilford Press.

Chaiken, S., Liberman, A., & Eagly, A. H. (1989). Heuristic and systematic processing within and beyond the persuasion context. In J. S. Uleman & J. A. Bargh (Eds.), *Unintended thought* (pp. 212–252). New York: Guilford Press.

DeBono, K. G. (1987). Investigating the social-adjustive and value-expressive functions of attitudes: Implications for persuasion processes. *Journal of Personality and Social Psychology, 52*, 279–287.

Fazio, R. H. (1989). On the power of functionality of attitudes: The role of attitude accessibility. In A. R. Pratkanis, S. J. Breckler, & A. G. Greenwald (Eds.), *Attitude structure and function*, (pp. 153–180). Hillsdale, NJ: Lawrence Erlbaum Associates.

Fazio, R. H., Blascovich, J., & Driscoll, D. M. (1992). On the functional value of attitudes: The influence of accessible attitudes on the case of quality of decision making. *Personality and Social Psychology Bulletin, 18*, 388–401.

Forgas, J. P. (1995). Emotion in social judgments: Review and a new affect infusion model (AIM). *Psychological Bulletin, 19*, 39–66.

Hirsch, E. D. (1988). *Cultural literacy: What every American needs to know*. Boston: Houghton Mifflin.

Jones, M. R. (Ed.). (1955). *Nebraska symposium on motivation* (Vol. 3). Lincoln: University of Nebraska.

Julka, D. L. (1998). *Increasing organ donor participation: A functional approach*. Unpublished dissertation, University of Notre Dame, Notre Dame, IN.

Julka, D. L., & Marsh, K. L. (1993). [Attitude functions and the matching hypothesis: Are messages which match an aroused need for information more effective?]. Unpublished raw data.

Julka, D. L., & Marsh, K. L. (1996, June). *Validating situational manipulations of the functional bases of individuals' attitudes*. Poster presented at the Eighth Annual American Psychological Society Convention, San Francisco.

Julka, D. L., & Marsh, K. L. (1998a). *Matching messages to induced needs: An experimental test of attitude functions theory*. Manuscript submitted for publication.

Julka, D. L., & Marsh, K. L. (1998b). *The persuasive advantage of motivational manipulations of attitude functions over primed attitude functions*. Manuscript in preparation.

Katz, D. (1960). The functional approach to the study of attitudes. *Public Opinion Quarterly*, *24*, 163–204.

Katz, D., McClintock, C., & Sarnoff, D. (1957). The measurement of ego-defense as related to attitude change. *Journal of Personality*, *25*, 465–474.

Katz, D., Sarnoff, D., & McClintock, C. (1956). Ego-defense and attitude change. *Human Relationships*, *9*, 27–46.

Kofta, M. (1993). Uncertainty, mental models, and learned helplessness: An anatomy of control loss. In G. Weary, F. Gleicher, & K. L. Marsh (Eds.), *Control motivation and social cognition* (pp. 122–153). New York: Springer-Verlag.

Kowalski, R. M. (1996). Complaints and complaining: Functions, antecedents, and consequences. *Psychological Bulletin*, *119*, 179–196.

Kruglanski, A. W. (1989). *Lay epistemics and human knowledge*. New York: Plenum Press.

Kruglanski, A. W., & Freund, T. (1983). The freezing and unfreezing of lay inferences: Effects of impressional primacy, ethnic stereotyping, and numerical anchoring. *Journal of Experimental Social Psychology*, *19*, 448–468.

Lewin, K. (1961). Intention, will and need. In T. Shipley (Ed.), *Classics in psychology* (pp. 1234–1289). New York: Philosophical Library.

Maio, G. R., & Olson, J. M. (1995). Relations between values, attitudes, and behavioral intentions: The moderating role of attitude functions. *Journal of Experimental Social Psychology*, *31*, 266–285.

Marsh, K. L. (1986). *Functional attitude theories revisited: An ecological perspective on attitude change*. Unpublished master's thesis, Texas A & M University, College Station.

Marsh, K. L., & Julka, D. L. (1998). *Development of a measure for validating situational inductions of attitude functions*. Manuscript in preparation.

Marsh, K. L., & Thielen, M. (1993, June). *Enhancing advertisement effectiveness: Matching ads to aroused or salient attitude functions*. Poster presented at the Fifth Annual Convention of the American Psychological Society Convention, Chicago.

McClintock, C. (1958). Personality syndromes and attitude change. *Journal of Personality*, *26*, 479–493.

Mook, D. G. (1987). *Motivation*. New York: Norton.

Murray, S. L., Haddock, G., & Zanna, M. P. (1996). On creating value-expressive attitudes: An experimental approach. In C. Seligman, J. M. Olson, & M. P. Zanna (Eds.), *The psychology of values: The Ontario symposium* (Vol. 8, pp. 107–133). Mahwah, NJ: Lawrence Erlbaum Associates.

Petty, R. E., & Cacioppo, J. T. (1986). The Elaboration Likelihood Model of persuasion. In L. Berkowitz (Ed.), *Advances in experimental social psychology* (Vol. 19, pp. 123–205). New York: Academic Press.

Pittman, T. S., & D'Agostino, P. R. (1985). Motivation and attribution: The effects of control deprivation on subsequent information processing. In G. Weary & J. Harvey (Eds.), *Attribution: Basic issues and applications* (pp. 117–141). New York: Academic Press.

Pittman, T. S., & D'Agostino, P. R. (1989). Motivation and cognition: Control deprivation and the nature of subsequent information processing. *Journal of Experimental Social Psychology*, *25*, 465–480.

Pittman, T. S., & Pittman, N. L. (1980). Deprivation of control and the attribution process. *Journal of Personality and Social Psychology, 39*, 377–389.

Powell, M. C., & Fazio, R. H. (1984). Attitude accessibility as a function of repeated attitudinal expression. *Personality and Social Psychology Bulletin, 10*, 139–148.

Roese, N. J. (1994). The functional basis of counterfactual thinking. *Journal of Personality and Social Psychology, 66*, 805–818.

Roese, N. J., & Olson, J M. (1995). Functions of counterfactual thinking. In N. J. Roese & J. M. Olson (Eds.), *What might have been: The social psychology of counterfactual thinking* (pp. 169–198). Mahwah, NJ: Lawrence Elbaum Associates.

Rogers, R. W. (1983). Cognitive and physiological processes in fear appeals and attitude change: A revised theory of protection motivation. In J. T. Cacioppo & R. E. Petty (Eds.), *Social psychophysiology: A sourcebook* (pp. 153–176). New York: Guilford Press.

Rokeach, M. (1973). *The nature of human values.* New York: Free Press.

Sarnoff, D. (1960). Reaction formation and cynicism. *Journal of Personality, 28*, 129–143.

Shavitt, S. (1989). Operationalizing functional theories of attitude. In A. R. Pratkanis, S. J. Breckler, & A. G. Greenwald (Eds.), *Attitude structure and function* (pp. 311–338). Hillsdale, NJ: Lawrence Erlbaum Associates.

Shavitt, S. (1990). The role of attitude objects in attitude functions. *Journal of Experimental Social Psychology, 26*, 124–148

Shavitt, S., & Fazio, R. H. (1991). Effects of attribute salience on the consistency between attitudes and behavior predictions. *Personality and Social Psychology Bulletin, 17*, 507–516.

Shavitt, S., Swan, S., Lowrey, T. M., & Wänke, M. (1994). The interaction of endorser attractiveness and involvement in persuasion depends on the goal that guides message processing. *Journal of Consumer Psychology, 3*, 137–162.

Smith, M. B., Bruner, J. S., & White, R. W. (1956). *Opinions and personality.* New York: Wiley.

Snyder, M., & DeBono, K. G. (1985). Appeals to image and claims about quality: Understanding the psychology of advertising. *Journal of Personality and Social Psychology, 49*, 586–597.

Snyder, M., & DeBono, K. G. (1989). Understanding the functions of attitudes: Lessons from personality and social behavior. In A. R. Pratkanis, S. J. Breckler, & A. G. Greenwald (Eds.), *Attitude structure and function* (pp. 339–359). Hillsdale, NJ: Lawrence Erlbaum Associates.

Steele, C. M. (1988). The psychology of self-affirmation: Sustaining the integrity of the self. In L. Berkowitz (Ed.), *Advances in experimental social psychology* (Vol. 21, pp. 261–302). San Diego, CA: Academic Press.

Weiner, B. (1992). *Human motivation: Metaphors, theories, and research.* Newbury Park, CA: Sage.

Wortman, C. B., & Brehm, J. W. (1975). Responses to uncontrollable outcomes: An integration of reactance theory and the learned helplessness model. In L. Berkowitz (Ed.), *Advances in experimental social psychology* (Vol. 8, pp. 277–336). New York: Academic Press.

Young, J., Thomsen, C. J., Borgida, E., Sullivan, J. L., & Aldrich, J. H. (1991). When self-interest makes a difference: The role of construct accessibility in political reasoning. *Journal of Experimental Social Psychology, 27*, 271–296.

11

Attitudes Toward Persons With HIV/AIDS: Linking a Functional Approach With Underlying Process

Glenn D. Reeder
John B. Pryor
Illinois State University

On November 7, 1991, Earvin "Magic" Johnson shocked the world with his announcement that he had contracted HIV (the virus that causes AIDS). The three-time Most Valuable Player of the National Basketball Association (NBA) retired from the game. After cameo appearances in the 1992 NBA All-Star Game and with the U.S. Dream Team at the Barcelona Olympics, he tried to make a comeback in fall 1992. But the fears of some outspoken NBA players forced him back into retirement. In 1996, Magic was invited to rejoin his old team, the Los Angeles Lakers. Magic agreed, in part, because the response from his fellow players was decidedly more positive this time around. Yet, there were still pockets of resistance among the players—and among the general public. After years of research and AIDS education from the U.S. Centers for Disease Control and Prevention (CDC), what could be the basis for this resistance?

Our attempt to answer this question begins with the functional approach to attitudes (Katz, 1960; Smith, Bruner, & White, 1956). The functional approach maintains that attitude formation and change are best understood by examining the reasons people hold an attitude (i.e., the functions it serves). Although the early theorists in this area never reached consensus, at least four functions were identified: an adaptation function, a value-expressive function, an ego-defensive function, and a knowledge organization function. More recent conceptualizations have tended to place the adaptation and knowledge concerns together as serving an *instrumental* function, and value expression and ego defense together as serving a *symbolic* function (Herek, 1986; Sears & Kinder, 1985; Shavitt, 1990).

Can these functions help us to understand attitudes about Magic Johnson? An instrumental function seems to be involved to the extent that people are concerned about scratches, open wounds, and physical contact on the basketball court. According to the CDC, when adequate precautions are taken, the AIDS virus need not be a danger in sports. Despite these assurances, people may still fear the possibility of contagion in this setting.

A more symbolic function also may be at work. In the United States and Western Europe, many people think of AIDS as a symbol for a negatively evaluated group—homosexuals. To the extent that people object to homosexuality, they may also oppose any type of interaction with persons who have contracted the virus. When Magic Johnson announced that he had contracted the virus, he attributed it to years of unprotected sexual intercourse with numerous female admirers. The media did not question his heterosexuality, and as a consequence, few people regard him as homosexual. Nevertheless, Magic is associated with a virus that has come to symbolize homosexuality. Might this symbolic connection to homosexuality influence people's reactions to Magic's return to the NBA? The research that follows examines this possibility.

In March and April 1996, shortly after Magic had rejoined the Los Angeles Lakers, Pryor and Reeder (1996) asked 122 college men and 78 college women how they felt about Magic Johnson's continuing to play basketball in the NBA. Not surprisingly, there was a range of opinion on the issue. We included additional measures to assess the importance of instrumental and symbolic factors as they predicted these opinions. Instrumental concerns were assessed by the following question: "Are other NBA players likely to contract HIV by playing with Magic Johnson?" After a series of unrelated questionnaires, we also inserted a widely used measure of attitudes toward homosexuality (Larsen, Reed, & Hoffman, 1980). Because attitudes toward homosexuality appear to have no direct bearing on the issue of Magic's return to the NBA, we viewed this measure as tapping a symbolic function.

The results indicated that both beliefs about the transmission of the virus and attitudes toward homosexuality were significantly correlated with participants' opinions about Magic Johnson ($r = -.50$ and .31, respectively, for women and $r = -.49$ and .27, respectively, for men). Specifically, people who believed that NBA players were at risk for contracting the virus from Magic and/or who held negative attitudes toward homosexuals tended to oppose Magic's return to the NBA. Hierarchical multiple regression analyses were conducted to determine the independent contributions of these two predictors. Table 11.1 shows that attitudes toward homosexuality significantly boosted the Multiple R in the analysis of the women's data after beliefs about transmission were entered first into the equation. In addition, beliefs about transmission significantly boosted the Multiple R following the entry of attitudes about homosexuality. A similar pattern holds for the men's data. Apparently, instrumental concerns (beliefs about transmission) *and* symbolic concerns (attitudes toward homosexuality) made significant, and independent, contributions to opinions about Magic's return to the NBA.

TABLE 11.1

Beliefs about HIV Transmission and Attitudes toward Homosexuality as Predictors of Attitudes about Magic Johnson.

Predictors	Data for Women Participants	
	Multiple R	F for R square change
Transmission beliefs entered first		
Step 1: Transmission beliefs	.50	
Step 2: Homosexuality attitudes	.55	$F(2,75) = 5.16, p < .03$
Homosexuality attitudes entered first		
Step 1: Homosexuality attitudes	.31	
Step 2: Transmission beliefs	.55	$F(2,75) = 21.15, p < .01$
Predictors	Data for Male Participants	
	Multiple R	F for R square change
Transmission beliefs entered first		
Step 1: Transmission beliefs	.48	
Step 2: Homosexuality attitudes	.51	$F(2,117) = 5.34, p < .03$
Homosexuality attitudes entered first		
Step 1: Homosexuality attitudes	.31	
Step 2: Transmission beliefs	.55	$F(2,117) = 30.86, p < .01$

These findings extend earlier work indicating that instrumental and symbolic factors predict prejudice directed at children who have contracted HIV (Pryor, Reeder, Vinacco, & Kott,1989). Participants in these studies rated their feelings about having their children interact with a grammar school child who had contracted HIV from a blood transfusion. The participants' attitudes toward homosexuality and their beliefs about the pros and cons of the interaction (including the likelihood of contracting the virus from casual contact) were examined as predictors of their reactions to the child with HIV. Because of the child's age, concerns about homosexuality were conceptualized as serving a symbolic function, whereas the perceived pros and cons of the interaction were viewed as serving an instrumental function. Multiple regression analyses revealed that instrumental and symbolic factors were both important: People who were most worried about transmission of the virus and/or who held negative attitudes about homosexuals tended to reject the child with HIV.

This work supports the functional approach to attitudes by demonstrating that multiple factors underlie attitudes toward persons with AIDS (PWAs). Clearly, our participants were concerned about more than the issue of transmitting the virus. Attitudes toward homosexuality also contributed to their reactions to PWAs. This occurred despite the fact that the PWAs in these studies (Magic Johnson and grammar school children) could not be construed as homosexuals. In this context, feelings toward homosexuality appear to make a symbolic (and seemingly irrational) contribution.

Although the unique insights of the functional theorists (Katz, 1960; Smith et al., 1956) laid the groundwork for these studies, questions about the underlying theoretical mechanisms remain unanswered. How are attitude functions related to cognitive representation? How do aspects of this representation affect the processing of information as attitudes are formed? The early functional theorists provided little insight into these questions. Yet issues of representation and process are currently the driving force in social cognition research (Bargh, 1997; Carlston & Smith, 1996). This chapter makes an effort to connect the functional approach with the mainstream of social cognition theory. The broad aim is to sketch a process model that explains how multiple functions interact to shape attitudes. Although the contextual focus of this analysis is on people's reactions to PWAs, we believe the basic tenets of the model are applicable to other types of attitudes as well.

In an attempt to link functions with underlying process, we began with the observation that different attitude functions imply different types of thinking. The impact of symbolic concerns in the research previously described seems to be based on *associations*. That is, even though people tend to think of Magic Johnson as a heterosexual, they may associate him with AIDS, which is a "gay disease" in the eyes of some people. Little conscious thought or effortful processing seems to be involved in such associative thinking. In contrast, thinking about instrumental factors appears to involve a deeper level of processing. Consider, for example, what happens when people envision various possible interaction scenarios (involving scratches and physical contact on the basketball court), and combine those scenarios with what they know about the transmissibility of the virus. This type of thinking seems both conscious and effortful. Consequently, in our model, symbolic factors are identified with associative thinking, whereas instrumental factors are identified with a more controlled type of thinking (Bargh, 1997). This model is described in what follows.

OVERVIEW OF A TWO-STAGE MODEL

We view reactions to PWAs as occurring in two sequential stages. The first stage reflects associative processing, and its hallmark is an immediate (often negative) evaluative reaction. Research in social cognition suggests that evaluative reactions, of at least a primitive sort, tend to occur within the first second of exposure to evaluatively laden constructs (Bargh, Chaiken, Govender, & Pratto, 1992; Zajonc, 1980). Thus, when encountering a particular PWA for the first time, whether at work, in a social setting, or in the newspaper, perceivers may experience an initial, relatively spontaneous evaluative reaction. The evaluative tone, or valence, of this initial response is dictated largely by the nature of the associations that the perceiver attaches to HIV/AIDS. For instance, Fig. 11.1 displays a schematic representation of constructs that might have been activated in the mind of a person thinking about Magic Johnson's return to the NBA. The constructs are represented as interconnected nodes within an associative network (Anderson, 1983; Kunda & Thagard, 1996). Constructs that are directly observed (such as *Magic Johnson* and *AIDS* in the figure) receive strong activation that is then likely to spread to related associates (Kunda & Thagard; Read & Miller, 1993). In this example, the observation that Magic has the AIDS virus leads to the activation of associates such as *contagiousness* and *gays*.

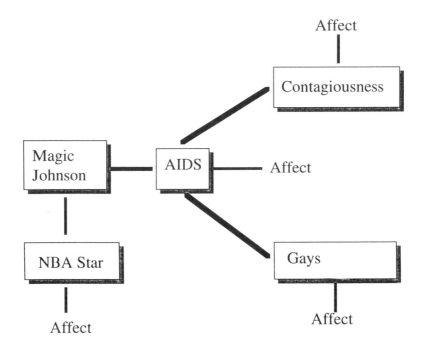

FIG. 11.1. Associative network pertaining to reactions to Magic Johnson.

Associative connections in the network need not derive from any factual or semantic basis (Bargh, Raymond, Pryor, & Strack, 1995). Rather, associations between nodes in the network primarily reflect the idiosyncratic learning history of the perceiver and may appear quite arbitrary (Kelly, 1955). People who first learned about AIDS as a contagious, gay disease, as many U.S. adults did in the 1980s, may still harbor such associates (Herek & Glunt, 1993; Pryor & Reeder, 1993; Shilts, 1987). The fact that the majority of those who have died of AIDS in the United States are gay men helps to perpetuate this association. New facts may be acquired, such as that HIV/AIDS cannot be contracted via casual contact and that approximately half of new infections occur in nonhomosexual populations. But new information must build on an earlier foundation of associations and may not reconstruct the basic nature of those associations (Epstein, Lipson, Holstein, & Huh, 1992; Lord, Ross, & Lepper, 1979). The model assumes that these "primitive" associations may continue to be accessed in the presence of a PWA. Thus, even though people tend not to view Magic Johnson as *gay*, his presence leads to the activation of the *gay* construct.

As shown in Fig. 11.1, constructs in the network are accompanied by an evaluative (or affective) reaction. When a given construct in the network receives activation, the evaluative reaction is accessed as well. In this sense, affect can be treated much the same as other types of material that are stored in memory, such as representations of a target person's behaviors, attributes, and traits (Bargh, 1997; Bower, 1981; Carlston & Smith, 1996). In general, the evaluation of any new stimulus is a function of the constructs that are currently active during the processing of the stimulus (Tesser & Martin, 1996). It follows that if the *AIDS* construct is linked with negative affect, initial reactions to a PWA will tend to be negative as well. It is important to note that negative affect at this point derives from associations in the network, rather than from a reasoned consideration of the perceiver's factual knowledge.

The mental activity just described is associative in nature and involves relatively automatic (as opposed to more controlled) processing (Bargh, 1997). That is, little conscious effort or awareness is involved, and processing is assumed to be relatively efficient (largely unaffected by concurrent demands). Processing may stop at this point in certain circumstances. If so, reactions to the target person tend to be based mainly on the associative process. In other circumstances, associative processing merely sets the stage for more thoughtful and deliberative processing. Research across many areas of cognition supports the existence of two systems of reasoning, with the first being associative in nature and the second being rule based (Sloman, 1996). For example, in the area of dispositional inference (Gilbert & Malone, 1995; Reeder, 1993), perceivers' first inclination is to make a relatively spontaneous trait judgment about a target person ("She is acting anxious, therefore she must be an anxious person"). At a subsequent adjustment stage, however, perceivers may consider situational factors that could have shaped the target's behavior ("The experimenter asked her a lot of embarrassing questions") and adjust their inferences accordingly ("Maybe she is not so anxious after all"). Similarly, when making attitudinal judgments about racial issues, perceivers tend to have a relatively automatic (often negative) evaluative reaction to a person of another race (Devine, 1989; Fazio, Jackson, Dunton, & Williams, 1995). This initial reaction may then be offset or adjusted by subsequent processing of a more controlled nature (Fazio, 1990).

Figure 11.2 portrays some of the factors that determine whether there is a transition from associative processing to an adjustment stage. These factors include time, resources, and motivation. For example, when perceivers are in a hurry, or when their cognitive resources are depleted by being forced to memorize an eight-digit number, their dispositional

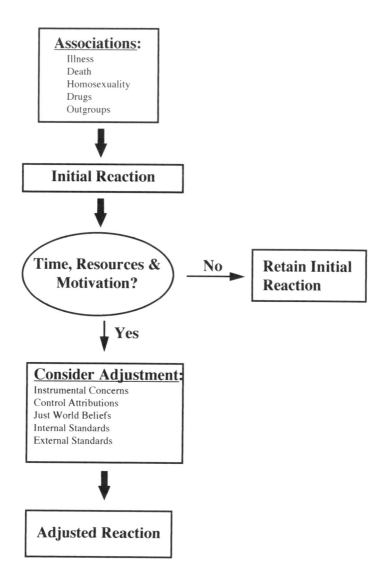

FIG. 11.2. Two-stage model of reactions to persons with AIDS.

inferences about a target person tend not to be adjusted for situational factors (Fletcher, Reeder, & Bull, 1990; Gilbert & Malone, 1995; Reeder, 1997). Finally, the level of motivation to make an adjustment is also important. Perceivers are more likely to engage in extensive processing when they take a personal interest in the target person (Brewer, 1988; Fiske & Neuberg, 1990), are concerned about the accuracy of their initial reaction (Kruglanski & Webster, 1996), and are motivated to avoid prejudicial responses (Dunton & Fazio, 1997).

At the adjustment stage, the perceiver may consciously consider a variety of factors that are perceived as relevant to responding to the PWA. As shown in Fig. 11.2, such rule-based thinking may involve weighing the pros and cons (instrumental concerns) of interacting with a PWA (Pryor et al., 1989), analyzing the causes of the PWA's illness (Weiner, 1995), consulting general beliefs about the nature of justice in the world (Lerner & Miller, 1978), bringing to mind internal standards or goals related to egalitarianism and empathy (Devine, 1989; Montieth, 1993), and monitoring how other persons may construe public responses (Dunton & Fazio, 1997). The model assumes that this adjustment stage begins with the output of the earlier associative stage. Thus, if the initial reaction is negative, the perceiver might consider the factors previously noted in order to determine whether an adjustment in the positive direction is warranted.

In summary, the perspective outlined in Fig. 11.2 is an attempt to identify the psychological processes that underlie the broad types of concerns identified by functional theories. Thus, processing at the associative stage reflects the kind of thinking that underlies symbolic functions, whereas processing at the adjustment stage (e.g., calculating pros and cons and making causal attributions) has clear parallels with instrumental functions. Moreover, the model focuses attention on the need to better understand how the processes of association and adjustment interact with each another. The next two sections examine the associative and adjustment stages in greater detail.

ASSOCIATIVE PROCESSING

The distinction between associative thought and true reasoning is traceable to James (1890) and is echoed in terms such as intuitive versus rational, primary process versus secondary process, and autistic thinking versus realistic thinking. Table 11.2 compares these two styles of thinking across a variety of dimensions (Epstein et al., 1992; Sloman, 1996). The table notes some potentially unique aspects of associative thought as it pertains to reacting to a PWA. That is, associative thought about PWAs may be especially focused on evaluation, often of a negative sort.

The Power of Simple Associations

Cialdini (1993) reported that television weather forecasters are often reviled for simply reporting bad weather. Like the imperial messengers of old Persia, who were celebrated when they arrived with good news and slain when the news was bad, weather forecasters tend to be viewed in same light as the news they bring. More generally, any innocent association with good or bad things can shape the impression process (Clore & Byrne, 1974). Thus, impressions of a stranger are more positive as a result of watching a happy movie, whereas impressions tend toward the negative after one has watched a sad movie (Gouaux, 1971) or when one is placed in an overheated room (Griffitt, 1970).

The fact that associations are formed with such ease may help explain why many people *overrespond* to the threat of HIV disease. In their national sample, Herek and Capitanio (1993) report that some percentage of Americans believe that HIV can be contracted from kissing a person on the cheek (19%), from sharing a drinking glass (47%), or from being bitten by a mosquito (50%). Can these overreactions be attributed to a

TABLE 11.2

Characteristics of Processing at Different Stages

Associative Processing	Processing at Adjustment
Associative relations	Logical, causal relations
Operations based on similarity	Rule-based operations
Automatic, parallel processing	Controlled, sequential processing
Personal, experiential	Shared, cultural knowledge
Emotional	Rational
Intuitive	Deliberative, strategic
Pleasure seeking	Meeting standards
Preconscious	Awareness of processing
Changes slowly with repetitive, intense experience	Changes quickly
Evaluative	Multiple meanings, ascription of purpose
Avoidance oriented	Approach oriented

web of associations that link AIDS with misfortune, illness, and immorality? At least in part, the research summarized in what follows suggests an affirmative answer to this question.

Rozin, Markwith, and McCauley (1994) asked their respondents a series of questions about a photo of an attractive man wearing a sweater. The respondents first indicated how favorable they felt toward wearing a new sweater of this sort. They then indicated how they would feel about wearing the sweater after it had been worn by the man shown in the picture, but thoroughly laundered. In all cases reported here, the favorability ratings were made on a scale from 0 (*something you would dislike extremely*) to +100 (*something that you would like extremely*). Respondents were somewhat less favorable to wearing a used sweater than a new one, even if the man who had worn it was described as perfectly healthy (20 points lower). But ratings dropped further for subsequent descriptions that indicated that the man had lost his leg in an accident (33 points lower), was homosexual (42 points lower), had committed murder (57 points lower), had contracted AIDS from a blood transfusion (58 points lower), was homosexual and had AIDS (60 points lower), or had tuberculosis (61 points lower). Rozin et al. (1994) used multiple regression to predict the reactions to the AIDS/transfusion sweater. Ratings of the accident victim, tuberculosis patient, and person who had committed murder were entered (simultaneously) into the equation. All of these ratings made a significant contribution, which suggests that associations related to misfortune (accidents), illness (tuberculosis), and moral taint (murder) predict feelings toward a PWA.

The aversion shown to a sweater that was previously worn by someone who was sick (with AIDS or tuberculosis) might conceivably represent an actual fear of biological contamination. But the fact that negative reactions follow from *association* with misfortune (loss of a leg) or moral taint (homosexuality and murder) seems to argue that biological contamination is not the only issue.

Associative reactions can be at odds with the laws of cause and effect. For example, Rozin, Markwith, and Nemeroff (1992) demonstrated a type of association they called "backward contagion." Respondents first indicated their feelings about staying in a Holiday Inn hotel in San Francisco. On a follow-up questionnaire item, they were significantly less favorable to the same hotel when it was said to have been scheduled for conversion to a hospital for AIDS patients the *next year*. Thus, the association here is to an event in the distant future, something which could not possibly affect the condition of the hotel during their stay.

The apparent irrationality of reactions to HIV disease is also evident in survey data. A national survey conducted by Blendon and Donelan (1988) found that only 10% of parents in the United States believe that their children could contract AIDS by sitting in a classroom with a PWA, yet 33% of these parents would try to withdraw their children from such a classroom because of their own anxiety. At a more basic level, Nemeroff's (1995) analysis suggests that associations to the source of an illness (e.g., self, stranger, friend, lover, or disliked peer) are crucial to understanding the threat posed by the illness. She examined people's drawings of germs and found that their perceptions varied, depending on the source. Germs emanating from a lover were depicted as less threatening and were thought to cause less severe illness than germs emanating from a disliked peer. The aversion evident in these findings cannot be based on a reasoned analysis of the mechanisms of disease transmission, but such aversion is consistent with associative thinking.

In the minds of many people living in the United States and western Europe, there is a strong association between PWAs and homosexuality. Consequently, people who are opposed to homosexuality may reject PWAs, even when the PWAs are not homosexual. In one of the studies reported by Pryor et al. (1989), college students in a lower level psychology course were asked by a substitute instructor to fill out a series of questionnaires on the first day of class. Among the questionnaires was a measure of their beliefs concerning the acceptability of homosexuality (Larsen et al., 1980). The students were then informed that their instructor was absent due to an accident that had occurred over the summer. They were further informed that, as a result of the accident, the instructor had received a blood transfusion and had contracted HIV. Although the instructor was fully able to teach the class, the psychology department wanted to find out how students felt about transferring to another section of the course. The students then responded to a 7-point scale that assessed their feelings about transferring. Attitudes toward homosexuality were found to be strongly correlated with a desire to transfer out of the class ($r = .65$), such that the students who were most opposed to homosexuality were the most eager to transfer. It bears repeating that attitudes toward homosexuality played this role despite the fact that the instructor was said to have contracted the virus from a blood transfusion.

These studies suggest that the relationship between attitudes toward homosexuality and aversion to PWAs is quite robust (Herek & Glunt, 1993; see Pryor, Reeder, & Landau, 1999). In the United States and western Europe, the association between homosexuality and HIV is traceable to news and media accounts of the 1980s. These accounts linked the virus to homosexuals living in population centers such as New York and San Francisco, who succumbed to a rare form of pneumonia (caused by *Pneumocystis carinii*) and Kaposi's sarcoma (a skin cancer). In contrast, the associations formed to HIV may be quite different among people living in other cultures (Farmer, 1990; Goldin, 1994). In Africa, for example, the disease has been linked to heterosexual contact with migratory workers or to those who break sexual taboos. The physical manifestations of the disease in Africa often lead to a wasting syndrome, referred to as "slim disease." Some African cultures have attributed this condition to the power of witches, who are believed to eat the life souls of their victims (Goldin). These cultural differences may have important implications for disease prevention strategies and are deserving of further study (Goldin).

The Automaticity of Associative Processing

Conventional wisdom suggests that our impressions of a target person are based on a process whereby we consciously weigh the person's good and bad points. Indeed, until about 20 years ago, many social psychologists believed that our evaluations followed from a careful adding up, or averaging, of the target's attributes (Anderson, 1981). Recent findings, however, point to a more spontaneous and automatic form of evaluation (Bargh, 1997; Tesser & Martin, 1996). In an early statement of this position, Zajonc (1980) proposed that evaluations occur quickly, before perceivers have time for conscious processing. In his view, "preferences need no inferences," by which he meant that we may come to like (or dislike) a thing before we even consciously recognize it. Evidence has accumulated in support of this "evaluation primacy" proposal. For example, Smith and Miller (1983) presented sentences of the form "Andy slips an extra $50 into his wife's purse" and asked research participants to answer questions about the event. They found that participants were quicker to answer a question about liking ("Do you like the actor?") than they were to answer questions about the cause of the event ("Was the action caused by something about the person?"). This finding supports a key assumption of our model. That is, the evaluation from associative thinking precedes other types of cognition, including causal attributions.

Devine (1989) extended this work by suggesting that preconscious processing can take the form of prejudice. But there is controversy over whether individual differences occur at the preconscious stage. Devine's dissociation model points to a separation between a person's knowledge of cultural stereotypes about racial issues and the same person's personal beliefs about racial issues. In her model, stereotypical knowledge is activated preconsciously, and it exerts an automatic effect on evaluations made of a target person of another race. Because cultural stereotypes are broadly shared, this automatic effect of stereotypical knowledge is said to operate similarly for those who hold prejudiced personal beliefs and for those who do not. In Devine's view, then, almost everyone is prejudiced at a preconscious level.

In contrast to Devine's view, Fazio and his colleagues (Dunton & Fazio, 1997; Fazio et al., 1995) observed substantial individual differences in the automatic activation of evaluative beliefs concerning race. They presented White participants with photos of White and Black faces at brief durations (315 ms). Each face was followed by the presentation of a positive or negative adjective, and participants were instructed to press a key labeled "good" or a key labeled "bad" to indicate their judgment of the meaning of the adjective. Fazio et al. (1995) assumed that photos of Black faces would automatically activate (or prime) negative affect among some White participants. The presence of this negative affect should then facilitate response time to negative adjectives (but not to positive adjectives). In general, White participants did show the predicted priming effect, which indicates prejudice at a nonconscious level. Yet Fazio et al. also found that the priming effect was stronger among some participants than among others. Of greater interest, these individual differences on the priming measure predicted nonverbal behavior toward a Black experimenter in a separate part of the study. That is, participants who showed evidence of prejudice on the priming measure tended to behave in a less friendly manner toward the Black experimenter.

Our theoretical model of reactions to a PWA makes predictions that are similar to those made by Fazio and his colleagues: Negative affect directed toward PWAs derives, at least in part, from preconscious processing, and such processing should show evidence of individual differences. In this case, however, the negative affect is thought to derive from associations that involve the construct of homosexuality. Pryor and Reeder (1993) tested the idea that preconscious activation of the construct of homosexuality could lead to the kind of contamination reactions discussed in earlier sections of this chapter (Pryor et al., 1989; Rozin et al., 1994). The research utilized a subliminal priming procedure, which was adapted from earlier work by Bargh and Pietromonaco (1982). Words associated with the stereotype of homosexuality (e.g., swishy) were flashed on a computer screen for brief periods of time (100 ms), and participants were asked to monitor the location of these flashes on the screen. A control condition was included in which the words flashed on the screen were primarily of a neutral nature. In both conditions, a subsequent recognition task indicated that participants could not discriminate the words that had appeared on the screen from words that had not appeared.

Immediately following the priming procedure, all participants engaged in an impression task. They were asked to evaluate a prospective roommate, who was said to be infected with a noncontagious disease called supproxiosis. When the priming task had activated the stereotype of homosexuality, participants who held antihomosexual attitudes tended to reject the prospective roommate. In contrast, this relationship was absent in the neutral word priming condition. In other words, when mainly neutral words were primed, those who were prejudiced against homosexuality were no more negative toward the roommate than were those who were less prejudiced. Taken as a whole, the results are consistent with the idea that preconscious priming of the homosexual stereotype led to negative affect—but only among participants who tended to be prejudiced against homosexuals. Like people in an overheated room who tended to dislike a stranger (Griffitt, 1970), our participants who experienced negative affect tended to reject the roommate.

This finding suggests a possible alternative interpretation of the correlation between attitudes toward homosexuality and reactions to PWAs, which we have observed in several studies (Pryor et al., 1989; Pryor & Reeder, 1996). Our preferred interpretation of this correlation is that when persons who are prejudiced against homosexuals encounter a PWA, negative affect toward homosexuals is automatically activated. Unless there is an adjustment for this negative affect, it then colors the reaction to the PWA. An alternative interpretation of the correlation is that there is a third variable that accounts for both attitudes toward homosexuality and reactions to PWAs. For example, people who are authoritarian might react negatively to anyone who appears to violate the norm, including homosexuals and PWAs (Larsen, Elder, Bader, & Dougard, 1990). Two pieces of evidence can be marshaled against this "third variable" explanation. First, in the study described in the preceding paragraph (Pryor & Reeder, 1993), we varied the activation level of attitudes toward homosexuals. When these attitudes were activated (at a subconscious level), persons who were opposed to homosexuality tended to reject a person infected with a novel disease. Thus, the study provides relatively direct evidence that negative attitudes toward homosexuality can taint reactions to a person who is merely associated with that affect. Second, Pryor, Reeder, and McManus (1991) found that the correlation between attitudes toward homosexuality and reactions to nonhomosexual PWAs remained significant even when authoritarianism (Berkowitz & Wolkon, 1964) was controlled in the statistical analysis. In summary, although the personality construct of authoritarianism is related to reactions to PWAs (Larsen et al., 1990), this construct alone cannot explain the powerful relationship between attitudes toward homosexuals and reactions to PWAs.

Negativity in Associative Thinking

Because our focus is on prejudice directed toward PWAs, we have focused mainly on negative associative processing. Although both positive and negative evaluative meaning can be extracted automatically (Fazio, Sanbonmatsu, Powell, & Kardes, 1986), negative stimuli may receive preferential processing at this stage. Pratto and John (1991), for example, found evidence for *automatic vigilance* toward negative social information. Their research utilized a variation of the Stroop (1935) color interference paradigm. Participants were shown positive adjectives (e.g., honest, outgoing) and negative adjectives (e.g., sadistic, wicked) printed in different colors. Pratto and John predicted that negative adjectives would draw greater attention and, as a result, color processing would be disrupted for these adjectives. The results supported this assumption: Relative to positive adjectives, participants were slower to name the color in which a negative adjective was printed.

Such automatic vigilance is consistent with a broader psychological tendency called the negativity effect (Peeters & Czapinski, 1990; Reeder & Brewer, 1979; Skowronski & Carlston, 1989). In studies of decision making, for example, people exhibit loss aversion, assigning relatively greater weight to potential negative events, as opposed to potential positive events (Kahneman & Tversky, 1984). In studies of impression formation, people tend to place greater emphasis on a target person's bad behaviors than on the target's good behaviors (Skowronski & Carlston). Peeters and his colleagues (Peeters, 1971; Peeters & Czapinski, 1990) maintain that an emphasis on the negative is functional for the perceiver.

Perceivers live in a world where negative events (such as eating a poisonous plant) can have a strong, and irreversible, impact on them. In contrast, positive events (e.g., eating an especially delicious fruit) tend to affect us in a less dramatic and less permanent way. Thus, it would be adaptive for the perceiver to develop protective mechanisms to counter the threat posed by negative stimuli. Automatic vigilance to negative social information is certainly consistent with this functional perspective.

Taylor (1991) has taken the argument a step further by proposing that people's reactions to negative events follow a temporal pattern. Negative events first evoke strong and rapid responses, such as the fight–flight response described by Cannon (1932). This mobilization phase is then followed by a minimization phase that tends to damp down and minimize the impact of the negative event. In the case of reactions to a PWA, Taylor's perspective implies that initial fears in the perceiver may be reexamined at the minimization phase. This line of reasoning is reflected in Fig. 11.2 and Table 11.2 of our model. In particular, the model assumes that associative reactions to a PWA tend to be avoidance oriented. In contrast, at least in some circumstances, controlled processing at the adjustment stage tends to be approach oriented. The next section examines the adjustment stage in greater detail.

PROCESSING AT THE ADJUSTMENT STAGE

Clearly, not all thinking about PWAs is reflexive, or automatic. Thinking that is conscious, rule based, and systematic occurs at the adjustment stage in our model. Tallying up of the pros and cons of interacting with a PWA seems to epitomize this type of processing, which fits Katz's (1960) definition of an adjustment (or instrumental) function. Two other functions also seem to imply a relatively deep level of thinking. For example, the knowledge function is based on a need to find structure and meaning in the world (Katz). This type of thinking can be identified with causal attribution, whereby people wonder about the sources of a PWA's infection and assign responsibility accordingly. The value-expressive function can also involve active, effortful thinking, particularly as it pertains to meeting standards. For instance, people often try to manage their emotions and behavior in order to avoid prejudice. These efforts may be based on a need to meet internal, personal standards of fairness and equality, or based on external concerns about wanting to avoid the appearance of prejudice. In the following sections, we review effortful processing related to adaptation, causal attribution, and meeting standards.

Adaptation

Thinking often involves an attempt to better one's position in the world by seeking rewards and avoiding punishments (Herek, 1986; Katz, 1960). Pryor et al. (1989) studied the impact of the perceived pros and cons of interacting with a PWA. Following the prescriptions of an expectancy-value model of attitude (Ajzen & Fishbein, 1980), they measured both the perceived likelihood of various consequences occurring in the interaction (e.g., living in fear of AIDS) and evaluations of these consequences. Not surprisingly, people who perceived little danger from casual contact with PWAs were more willing to work alongside a PWA or to allow their children to attend school with another child who had AIDS (Pryor et al., 1989).

Although such instrumental thinking differs in important respects from associative thinking, it may not be completely independent of associative reactions. Pryor et al. (1991) examined the persuasive impact of an HIV/AIDS educational film on college students' attitudes toward interaction with PWAs. The film presented factual information in an effort to dispel misconceptions about the possibility of HIV infection from casual contact. The instrumental considerations addressed in the film led to a more positive view of interaction with PWAs among viewers who did not hold negative attitudes toward homosexuals. In contrast, the film had little impact on viewers who were relatively prejudiced against homosexuals. This occurred despite the fact that attitudes were assessed toward *nonhomosexual* PWAs.

In accord with a functional analysis, Pryor et al. (1991) suggested that the film had directly addressed the instrumental concerns of those who were not opposed to homosexuality (Herek, 1986). But the film did not address the more symbolic concerns of those who were opposed to homosexuality. Our current conceptualization of these issues aims to identify the psychological mechanisms that underlie the instrumental and symbolic functions of attitudes. Symbolic concerns about AIDS are represented in terms of the web of associations and accompanying affect which is linked to AIDS. Accordingly, the film about PWAs is expected to lead to considerable negative affect among people opposed to homosexuality. The presence of this negative affect could bias viewers toward a negative evaluation of the instrumental arguments in the film. This transfer of affect could be due to simple classical conditioning (Griffitt, 1970). A more cognitive tendency, involving the interpretation (misattribution) of affect, could also be at work (Schwarz, Bless, & Bohner, 1991). As noted earlier, negative affect to PWAs may be activated automatically, and film viewers may not be aware of its origin. Consequently, that negative affect could be misattributed to the instrumental arguments presented in the film, leading to the rejection of those arguments.

Indeed, there was evidence in the Pryor et al. (1991) study that watching of the AIDS film led viewers to hold a more polarized set of instrumental beliefs. After either watching the control film or the AIDS film, viewers provided likelihood ratings and evaluations of several potential consequences of interacting with an HIV-infected co-worker (e.g., helping a sick person). Following the control film, viewers who were relatively prohomosexual versus antihomosexual did not differ significantly in their ratings of these consequences. But following the AIDS film, the two groups did differ: Antihomosexual viewers tended to rate helping a sick person as less positive and less likely. In contrast, prohomosexual viewers tended to rate helping a sick person as more positive and more likely. This pattern is consistent with the idea that affect from associative thinking can bias thinking that is more instrumental in nature.

Causal Thinking and Judging Responsibility

Early functional theories of attitude proposed that people have a need to acquire knowledge about the physical and social environment. Attribution researchers extended this insight by proposing that people operate like "naive scientists" who try to understand the causes of events in order to increase their sense of control (Heider, 1958; Kelley, 1973). More recent metaphors have characterized social perceivers as "naive lawyers" (Fincham & Jaspers, 1980), or even as "god-like" (Weiner, 1995) because they assume the right to assess responsibility and lay blame. Weiner (1995) suggests that people wonder, "How did this happen?" when they are confronted with a stigmatized individual. The perceiver aims to determine whether the stigma is *controllable*. According to Weiner, when the cause is uncontrollable (such as old age that leads to Alzheimer's disease), attributions of responsibility are reduced. The predicted result is that feelings of concern (or pity) then increase, along with greater intentions to help.

Weiner, Perry, and Magnusson (1988) collected ratings of perceived responsibility, affective reactions (sympathy and anger), and reports of intended action for a variety of different stigmas. Stigmas such as Alzheimer's disease, cancer, and paraplegia received low ratings of responsibility, whereas others such as AIDS and drug addiction received high ratings. As predicted, persons who were held responsible for their stigmatizing condition tended to be rejected. For example, relative to persons with cancer, PWAs received higher ratings of responsibility, blame, and anger, and *lower* ratings of intentions to help. It appears, therefore, that PWAs (as a group) are perceived as responsible for their own fate. This causal assessment by perceivers is accompanied by an unfortunate set of emotional reactions and behavioral predilections. Also, in general support of Weiner's (1995) perspective, negative reactions to PWAs are moderated by the perceived cause of the infection: Attributions of responsibility and feelings of anger were diminished when the cause was apparently uncontrollable (receiving a blood transfusion), as opposed to controllable (not using a condom when having sex).

Given the pattern of causal attributions just described, it should come as no surprise that PWAs who are homosexual tend to be blamed more than those who are heterosexual (Collins, 1994; St. Lawrence, Husfeldt, Kelly, Hood, & Smith, 1990). This bias against homosexual PWAs is present even when the transmission of the disease occurred via a blood transfusion, rather than via sex (see Weiner, 1993). These findings suggest that attributions of blame are hardly evenhanded and may be influenced by antigay sentiment. Like instrumental thinking, perhaps attributions of responsibility can be biased by negative affect from associative thinking. Evidence in support of this general notion has been reported by Keltner, Ellsworth, and Edwards (1993). These authors induced a state of anger in some of their study participants by asking them to imagine being treated unfairly. Subsequently, when told about an awkward social situation, these angry participants placed more blame for the mishap on other people (as opposed to making a situational attribution). Thus, feelings of anger that are irrelevant to a social decision (but reflect associative thinking) can bias attributions of responsibility (see also Quigley & Tedeschi, 1996).

Responsibility attributions also play a role in Lerner's "just world" hypothesis (Lerner & Miller, 1978). According to this hypothesis, people tend to think of the world as a just place, where people get what they deserve. A belief in a just world serves the function of enabling the individual to view the social and physical environment as stable and orderly. In addition to allowing for long-term planning, the belief shields the individual from dealing with the frightening possibility that he or she could be unjustly victimized. The just world hypothesis implies, of course, that a person afflicted with a terminal illness such as AIDS must have done something to deserve it. Although Lerner maintains that just world thinking is an integral part of Western culture, individual differences are also apparent (Rubin & Peplau, 1975). Indeed, those who express most agreement with items on the Just World Scale are most prone to rejecting PWAs (Connors & Heaven, 1990).

Causal thinking of a just world sort seems to reinforce negative associative thinking about PWAs. But another type of causal thinking may have the opposite effect. In a study of persuasion, Slusher and Anderson (1996) examined the impact of arguing that AIDS is not transmissible by casual contact. They determined that such arguments were more effective when the latter included causal evidence regarding the mechanisms of HIV transmission. Arguments that relied on statistical evidence, in contrast, were found to be less effective. It appears, therefore, that causal thinking can be a double-edged sword. Causal thinking that implies low responsibility for HIV infection, or that describes the mechanisms of disease transmission, can help overcome prejudice. But other types of causal reasoning can actually reinforce prejudice.

Meeting Standards

According to Katz's (1960) description of the value-expression function, people gain satisfaction from expression of attitudes that reflect their cherished beliefs or self-image. In essence, people attempt to meet standards that they have set for themselves. Out of feelings of egalitarianism, for example, a person may bend over backward to try to be fair with certain ethnic groups. Under the category of "meeting standards," we also include people's efforts to meet external standards, which reflect their concerns about how others view their actions. Although external standards might also be identified with an adaptation function, we place them here because the psychological processes involved appear similar to those for internal standards (Dunton & Fazio, 1997). That is, when attempting to meet either internal or external standards, people monitor their behavior for signs of prejudice and take action to counteract any prejudice they uncover.

Devine and her colleagues have provided evidence for this monitoring process (Devine, 1989; Monteith, 1993). They have drawn a sharp distinction between stereotypes and personal beliefs. Stereotypes are prejudicial beliefs that are acquired as part of socialization in our culture. For instance, while growing up, an individual may have heard negative comments directed toward homosexuals. As a result, the individual may acquire a negative sterotype of gays and this stereotype may be automatically activated when the individual is in the company of a homosexual. Such automatic activation can occur even when the sterotype is in conflict with the individual's personal beliefs (which may be more accepting of homosexuality). Thus, the individual may feel uncomfortable sitting next to a gay male on a bus, but believe that the reaction was inappropriate. In order to respond in a less prejudiced manner, the individual needs to become aware of a discrepancy between automatic (stereotypical) reactions and personal beliefs. Such awareness may then initiate a self-regulatory cycle that includes heightened self-focus, negative self-directed affect, slowed reactions, and less prejudicial responses. In a test of this model, Monteith induced heterosexual participants to believe that they had discriminated against a gay law school applicant because of his sexual orientation. Subsequently, low prejudiced participants (but not high prejudiced participants) experienced heightened self-focus and negative self-directed affect. In a second study, participants were again led to believe that they had behaved in a prejudicial manner. This manipulation led low prejudiced participants to respond more slowly and to give unfavorable ratings to gay-related jokes. Thus, Monteith's findings are consistent with the notion that a process involving conscious, rule-based adherence to standards may be invoked following evidence that one has acted in a prejudicial manner.

Fazio and his colleagues provided more direct evidence that people are often motivated to overcome *automatically* activated feelings of prejudice (Dunton & Fazio, 1997; Fazio et al., 1995). As described earlier, these researchers obtained estimates of automatically activated racial attitudes by presenting photos of Black and White students as primes in an adjective judgment task. In addition to measuring automatically activated attitudes, Dunton and Fazio included two other measures. The first assessed racial attitudes from participants' self-reports—an index of conscious, controlled responding. The second measure assessed participants' motivations to control their prejudicial reactions. The results indicated that automatically activated prejudice was not always reflected in participants' self-reports of racial attitudes. Instead, self-reports were moderated by *motivations to control prejudice*: Individuals with high motivation to control prejudice expressed relatively positive attitudes toward Blacks, even when their automatic reactions were in the negative range. In contrast, participants with low motivation showed greater consistency between their self-reports and automatically activated attitudes.

The research of Devine and Fazio supports our assumption that conscious, controlled thinking at the adjustment stage may overcome negative reactions at the associative stage. But adjustment cannot be taken for granted. Only people who are motivated to appear unprejudiced (to themselves or to others) engage in such a corrective process.

A TEST OF THE TWO-STAGE MODEL

A central assumption of the model depicted in Fig. 11.2 is that reactions to a PWA tend to follow a systematic progression. At the associative stage, automatic responses are dictated by the web of negative associations linked to HIV/AIDS. Rule-based thinking at the adjustment stage sometimes leads to a "damping down" of this negative affect (Taylor, 1991). In this sense, the model resonates with the increasing emphasis social psychologists are placing on the dynamic qualities of behavior (Vallacher, Nowak, & Kaufman, 1994). To date, however, social psychological research has not explicitly tracked prejudicial reactions over the course of time.

Figure 11.2 suggests that *time* is a requirement for adjustment. People's initial feelings about a PWA, which reflect associative processing, may not be diagnostic of their ultimate reactions and behavior. In the first empirical test of this idea, Reeder, Pryor, and Smith (1997) asked college students to indicate how attracted they were to a variety of potential lunch partners, including a girl with AIDS. Half of the participants were required to render their judgment about the lunch partner immediately (within 5 seconds). In contrast, the remaining participants were asked to wait 15 seconds before providing their response.

Does it matter whether people are rushed, or have plenty of time, when they rate their attraction to a stranger? Apparently, it depends on the characteristics of the stranger. For example, initial reactions to having lunch with a drug addict or criminal were unfavorable and remained so following a delay. In contrast, responses to a girl with AIDS showed a temporal pattern: Participants who responded after a delay were more favorable to the girl than were those who responded immediately. Supporting data indicate that participants perceived the girl with AIDS as having relatively low responsibility for her infection. This attribution of low responsibility may have played some role in prompting a more positive reaction to the child PWA at the adjustment stage (Weiner, 1995). In summary, the pattern of data is consistent with a temporal sequence to HIV/AIDS stigma. That is, in some circumstances, people tend to adjust their initially negative reactions to a PWA.

CONCLUSION

Research on the functional approach to attitudes languished for many years. This period of neglect was due, in part, to the growth of social cognition and its emphasis on mental process. Without a bridge to cognitive process, research on functions was difficult to integrate with the mainstream. This chapter represents a step toward identifying the cognitive mechanisms that underlie attitude functions. We proposed that the impact of symbolic factors in attitude research occurs via associations. Essentially, a symbol is a stimulus that evokes a collection of associations. Associative thinking is relatively automatic and preconscious. We also proposed that other functions, such as adjustment, knowledge, and value expression, tend to involve a more controlled, conscious type of thinking, which is addressed at the adjustment stage of our model.

There are at least three issues that complicate the picture we have drawn. First, given that each function has been defined as multifaceted by prior theory, some functions may be identified with more than one psychological process. In this chapter, we have identified a value-expressive function with a need to meet standards. As such, it relates to the adjustment stage of our model, where controlled processing occurs. Yet, value expression can also be implicated when people respond to a symbol by experiencing an automatic emotional reaction. Thus, some people become angry over AIDS-related issues because AIDS symbolizes homosexuality. Clearly, their values are at work. Perhaps the difference between meeting standards and responding to symbols lies in whether values are expressed directly or indirectly. Meeting standards seems to involve a more direct, and more effortful, expression of values than does responding to issues in terms of symbols.

A second complexity relates to our view of the adjustment stage as a moderating influence on reactions to PWAs. Although we suggested that reactions tend to shift in the positive direction at adjustment, there are other possibilities. We reviewed evidence, for example, that associative reactions can bias both the consideration of instrumental factors and attributions of responsibility. In fact, research in social cognition suggests that initial perceptions of a target issue can polarize following the introduction of mixed evidence (Lord et al., 1979) or even following mere thought on the issue (Tesser, 1978). Thus, the moderation of attitudes toward PWAs at the adjustment stage is not assured in all cases. An important variable to consider in this light is perceivers' motivation to control their prejudices (Dunton & Fazio, 1997; Monteith, 1993). Adjustments seem most likely among those who feel guilty about rejecting PWAs or who wish to avoid the disapproval of other persons.

A related complexity is that perceivers may hold two incompatible reactions at the same time, corresponding to input from the two different types of thinking (Sloman, 1996). For instance, after careful consideration of instrumental concerns, parents may believe that their children are perfectly safe attending a school classroom where there is an HIV-infected child. Yet, due to the impact of associative thinking, parents may simultaneously feel opposed to their child attending this class. Parents' ultimate decisions may represent some compromise between these two ways of thinking (Epstein et al., 1992).

Much remains to be learned before social psychologists can succeed in turning the tide of prejudice away from PWAs such as Magic Johnson. But given the power and pervasiveness of associative thinking, it is now apparent that AIDS educational programs need to go beyond the presentation of factual information (Pryor et al., 1991; Rozin et al., 1994). To counteract negative associative thinking directly, the two-stage model implies that a new form of conditioning needs to take place. It follows that getting to know a PWA in an informal, relaxed setting may be a potent antidote for prejudice because it might inspire associations with positive affect. Indeed, research indicates that contact with a PWA is predictive of more positive attitudes (Pryor et al., 1999). The model also implies that negative associative thinking can be counteracted at the adjustment phase. Ideally, public service announcements and other types of persuasive appeals should encourage the general public to internalize positive attitudes toward PWAs and should include strategies to motivate the public to meet those attitudinal standards.

REFERENCES

Ajzen, I., & Fishbein, M. (1980). *Understanding attitudes and predicting social behaviors*. Englewood Cliffs, NJ: Prentice Hall.

Anderson, J. R. (1983). *The architecture of cognition*. Cambridge, MA: Harvard University Press.

Anderson, N. H. (1981). *Foundations of information integration theory*. New York: Academic Press.

Bargh, J. A. (1997). The automaticity of everyday life. In R. S. Wyer, Jr. (Ed.), *Advances in social cognition*, (Vol. 10, pp. 3–48). Mahwah. NJ: Lawrence Erlbaum Associates.

Bargh, J. A., Chaiken, S., Govender, R., & Pratto, F. (1992). The generality of the automatic attitude activation effect. *Journal of Personality and Social Psychology, 62*, 893–912.

Bargh, J. A., & Pietromonaco, P. (1982). Automatic information processing and social perception: The influence of trait information presented outside of cognitive awareness on impression formation. *Journal of Personality and Social Psychology, 43*, 437–449.

Bargh, J. A., Raymond, P., Pryor, J., & Strack, F. (1995). Attractiveness of the underling: An automatic power–sex association and its consequences for sexual harassment and aggression. *Journal of Personality and Social Psychology, 68*, 768–781.

Berkowitz, N. H., & Wolkon, G. H. (1964). A forced choice form of the F scale—free of acquiescent response set. *Sociometry, 27*, 54–65.

Blendon, R. J., & Donelan, K. (1988). Discrimination against persons with AIDS: The public's perspective. *The New England Journal of Medicine, 319*, 1022–1026.

Bower, G. H. (1981). Emotional mood and memory. *American Psychologist, 36*, 129–148.

Brewer, M. B. (1988). A dual process model of impression formation. In T. K. Srull & R. S. Wyer, Jr. (Eds.), *Advances in social cognition* (Vol. 1, pp. 1–36). Hillsdale, NJ: Lawrence Erlbaum Associates.

Cannon, W. B. (1932). *The wisdom of the body*. New York: Norton.

Carlston, D. E., & Smith, E. R. (1996). Principles of mental representation. In E. T. Higgins & A. W. Kruglanski (Eds.), *Social psychology: Handbook of basic principles* (pp. 184–210). New York: Guilford Press.

Cialdini, R. B. (1993). *Influence: Science and practice*. New York: HarperCollins.

Clore, G. L., & Byrne, D. (1974). A reinforcement-affect model of attraction. In T. L. Huston (Ed.), *Foundations of interpersonal attraction* (pp. 143–170). New York: Academic Press.

Collins, R. L. (1994). Social support provision to HIV-infected gay men. *Journal of Applied Social Psychology, 24*, 1848–1869.

Connors, J., & Heaven, P. (1990). Belief in a just world and attitudes toward AIDS sufferers. *Journal of Social Psychology, 130*, 559–560.

Devine, P. G. (1989). Stereotypes and prejudice: Their automatic and controlled components. *Journal of Personality and Social Psychology, 56*, 5–18.

Dunton, B. C., & Fazio, R. H. (1997). An individual difference measure of motivation to control prejudiced reactions. *Personality and Social Psychology Bulletin, 23*, 316–326.

Epstein, S., Lipson, A., Holstein, C., & Huh, E. (1992). Irrational reactions to negative outcomes: Evidence for two conceptual systems. *Journal of Personality and Social Psychology, 62*, 328–339.

Farmer, P. (1990). Sending sickness: Sorcery, politics and changing concepts of AIDS in rural Haiti. *Medical Anthropology Quarterly, 68*, 6–27.

Fazio, R. H. (1990). Multiple processes by which attitudes guide behaviors: The MODE model as an integrated framework. In M. P. Zanna (Ed.), *Advances in Experimental Social Psychology* (Vol. 23, pp. 75–108). New York: Academic Press.

Fazio, R. H., Jackson, J. R., Dunton, B. C., & Williams, C. J. (1995). Variability in automatic activation as an unobtrusive measure of racial attitudes: A bona fide pipeline? *Journal of Personality and Social Psychology, 69*, 1013–1027.

Fazio, R. H., Sanbonmatsu, D. M., Powell, M. C., & Kardes, F. R. (1986). On the automatic activation of attitudes. *Journal of Personality and Social Psychology, 50*, 229–238.

Fincham, F. D., & Jaspers, J. M. (1980). Attribution of responsibility: From man the scientist to man as lawyer. In L. Berkowitz (Ed.), *Advances in experimental social psychology*, (Vol. 13, pp. 82–139). New York: Academic Press.

Fiske, S. T., & Neuberg, S. L. (1990). A continuum of impression formation, from category-based to individuating processes: Influences of information and motivation on attention and interpretation. In M. P. Zanna (Ed.), *Advances in experimental social psychology* (Vol. 23, pp. 1–74). New York: Academic Press.

Fletcher, G. J. O., Reeder, G. D., & Bull, V. (1990). Bias and accuracy in attitude attribution: The role of attributional complexity. *Journal of Experimental Social Psychology, 26*, 275–288.

Gilbert, D. T., & Malone, P. S. (1995). The correspondence bias. *Psychological Bulletin, 117*, 21–38.

Goldin, C. S. (1994). Stigmatization and AIDS: Critical issues in public health. *Social Science and Medicine, 39*, 1359–1366.

Gouaux, C. (1971). Induced affective states and interpersonal attraction. *Journal of Personality and Social Psychology, 20*, 37–43.

Griffitt, W. (1970) Environmental effects on interpersonal behavior: Ambient effective temperature and attraction. *Journal of Personality and Social Psychology, 15*, 240–244.

Heider, F. (1958). *The psychology of interpersonal relations*. New York: Wiley.

Herek, G. M. (1986). The instrumentality of attitudes: Toward a neofunctional theory. *Journal of Social Issues, 42*, 99–114.

Herek, G. M., & Capitanio, J. P. (1993). Public Reactions to AIDS in the United States: A second decade of stigma. *American Journal of Public Health, 83*, 574–577.

Herek, G. M., & Glunt, E. K. (1993). Public attitudes toward AIDS-related issues in the United States. In J. B. Pryor & G. D. Reeder (Eds.), *The social psychology of HIV infection* (pp. 229–261). Hillsdale, NJ: Lawrence Erlbaum Associates.

James, W. (1890). *The principles of psychology*. New York: Holt.

Kahneman, D., & Tversky, A. (1984). Choices, values, and frames. *American Psychologist, 39*, 341–350.

Katz, D. (1960). The functional approach to the study of attitudes. *Public Opinion Quarterly, 24*, 163–204.

Kelley, H. H. (1973). The process of causal attribution. *American Psychologist, 28*, 107–128.

Kelly, G. A. (1955). *The psychology of personal constructs*. New York: Norton.

Keltner, D., Ellsworth, P. C., & Edwards, K. (1993). Beyond simple pessimism: Effects of sadness and anger on social perception. *Journal of Personality and Social Psychology, 64*, 740–752.

Kruglanski, A. W., & Webster, D. M. (1996). Motivated closing of the mind: "Seizing" and "freezing." *Psychological Review, 103*, 263–283.

Kunda, Z., & Thagard, P. (1996). Forming impressions from stereotypes, traits and behaviors: A parallel-constraint-satisfaction theory. *Psychological Review, 103*, 284–308.

Larsen, K. S., Elder, R., Bader, M., & Dougard, C. (1990). Authoritariansim and attitudes toward AIDS victims. *Journal of Psychology, 130*, 77–80.

Larsen, K. S., Reed, M., & Hoffman, S. (1980). Attitudes of heterosexuals toward homosexuality: A Likert-type scale and construct validity. *Journal of Sex Research, 16*, 245–257.

Lerner, M., & Miller, D. (1978). Just world research and the attribution process: Looking back and looking ahead. *Psychological Bulletin, 85*, 1030–1051.

Lord, C. G., Ross, L., & Lepper, M. (1979). Biased assimilation and attitude polarization: The effects of prior theories on subsequently considered evidence. *Journal of Personality and Social Psychology, 37*, 2098–2109.

Monteith, M. J. (1993). Self-regulation of prejudiced responses: Implications for progress in prejudice-reduction efforts. *Journal of Personality and Social Psychology, 65*, 469–485.

Nemeroff, C. J. (1995). Magical thinking about illness virulence: Conceptions of germs from "safe" versus "dangerous" others. *Health Psychology, 14*, 147–151.

Peeters, G. (1971). The positive–negative asymmetry: On cognitive consistency and positivity bias. *European Journal of Social Psychology, 1*, 455–474.

Peeters, G., & Czapinski, J. (1990). Positive-negative asymmetry in evaluations: The distinction between affective and informational negativity effects. In W. Stroebe & M Hewstone (Eds.), *European Review of Social Psychology* (Vol. 1, pp. 33-60). Chichester, England: Wiley.

Pratto, F., & John, O. P. (1991). Automatic vigilance: The attention-grabbing power of negative social information. *Journal of Personality and Social Psychology, 61*, 380-391.

Pryor, J. B., & Reeder, G. D. (1993). Collective and individual representations of HIV/AIDS stigma. In J. B. Pryor & G. D. Reeder (Eds.), *The social psychology of HIV infection* (pp. 263-286). Hillsdale, NJ: Lawrence Erlbaum Associates.

Pryor, J. B., & Reeder, G. D. (1996, August). *Symbolic and Instrumental functions of attitudes: A social cognitive account.* Paper presented at the meeting of the American Psychological Association, Toronto.

Pryor, J. B., Reeder, G. D., & Landau, S. (1999). A social-psychological analysis of HIV-related stigma. *American Behavioral Scientist, 42*, 1193-1211.

Pryor, J. B., Reeder, G. D., & McManus, J. A. (1991). Fear and loathing in the workplace: Reactions to AIDS-infected co-workers. *Personality and Social Psychology Bulletin, 17*, 133-139.

Pryor, J. B., Reeder, G. D., Vinacco, R., Jr., & Kott, T. L. (1989). The instrumental and symbolic functions of attitudes toward persons with AIDS. *Journal of Applied Social Psychology, 19*, 377-404.

Quigley, B. M., & Tedeschi, J. T. (1996). Mediating effects of blame attributions on feeling of anger. *Personality and Social Psychology Bulletin, 22*, 1280-1288.

Read, S. J., & Miller, L. C. (1993). Rapist or "regular guy": Explanatory coherence in the construction of mental models of others. *Personality and Social Psychological Bulletin, 19*, 526-540.

Reeder, G.D. (1993). Trait-behavior relations in dispositional inference. *Personality and Social Psychology Bulletin, 19*, 586-593.

Reeder, G. D. (1997). Dispositional inferences of ability: Content and process. *Journal of Experimental Social Psychology, 33*, 171-189.

Reeder G. D., & Brewer, M. B. (1979). A schematic model of dispositional attribution in interpersonal perception. *Psychological Review, 86*, 61-79.

Reeder, G. D., Pryor, J. B., & Smith, E. (1997). [The dynamics of HIV/AIDS stigma]. Unpublished raw data.

Rozin, P., Markwith, M., & McCauley, C. (1994). Sensitivity to indirect contacts with other persons: AIDS aversion as a composite of aversion to strangers, infection, moral taint, and misfortune. *Journal of Abnormal Psychology, 103*, 494-504.

Rozin, P., Markwith, M., & Nemeroff, C. (1992) Magical contagion beliefs and fear of AIDS. *Journal of Applied Social Psychology, 22*, 1081-1092.

Rubin, Z., & Peplau, A. (1975). Who believes in a just world? *Journal of Social Issues, 31*, 65-89.

Schwarz, N., Bless, H., & Bohner, G. (1991). Mood and persuasion: Affective states influence the processing of persuasive communications. In M. P. Zanna (Ed.), *Advances in experimental social psychology* (Vol. 24, pp. 161-199). San Diego, CA: Academic Press.

Sears, D. O., & Kinder, D. R. (1985). Whites' opposition to busing: On conceptualizing and operationalizing group conflict. *Journal of Personality and Social Psychology, 48*, 1141-1147.

Shavitt, S. (1990). The role of attitude objects in attitude functions. *Journal of Experimental Social Psychology, 26*, 124-148.

Shilts, R. (1987). *And the band played on: Politics, people and the AIDS epidemic.* New York: St. Martin's Press.

Skowronski, J. J., & Carlston, D. E. (1989). Negativity and extremity biases in impression formation. A review of explanations. *Psychological Bulletin, 105*, 131-142.

Sloman, S. A. (1996). The empirical case for two systems of reasoning. *Psychological Bulletin, 119*, 3-22.

Slusher, M. P., & Anderson, C. A. (1996) Using causal persuasive arguments to change beliefs and teach new information: The mediating role of explanation availability and evaluation bias in the acceptance of knowledge. *Journal of Educational Psychology, 88*, 110-122.

Smith, E. R., & Miller, F. D. (1983). Mediation among attributional inferences and comprehension processes: Initial findings and a general method. *Journal of Personality and Social Psychology, 44,* 492–505.

Smith, M. B., Bruner, J. S., & White, R. W. (1956). *Opinions and personality.* New York: Wiley.

St. Lawrence, J. S, Husfeldt, B. A., Kelly, J. A., Hood, H. V., & Smith, S. (1990). The stigma of AIDS: Fear of disease and prejudice toward gay men. *Journal of Homosexuality, 19,* 85–101.

Stroop, J. R. (1935). Studies of interference in serial verbal reactions. *Journal of Experimental Psychology, 18,* 643–662.

Taylor, S. E. (1991). The asymmetrical effects of positive and negative events: The mobilization–minimization hypothesis. *Psychological Bulletin, 110,* 67–85.

Tesser, A. (1978). Self-generated attitude change. In L. Berkowitz (Ed.), *Advances in experimental social psychology* (Vol. 11, pp. 289–338), New York: Academic Press.

Tesser. A., & Martin, L. (1996). The psychology of evaluation. In E. T. Higgins & A. W. Kruglanski (Eds.), *Social psychology: Handbook of basic principles* (pp. 400–432). New York: Guilford Press.

Vallacher, R. R., Nowak, A., & Kaufman, J. (1994). Intrinsic dynamics of social judgment. *Journal of Personality and Social Psychology, 67,* 20–34.

Weiner, B. (1993). AIDS from an attributional perspective. In J. B. Pryor & G. D. Reeder (Eds.), *The social psychology of HIV infection* (pp. 287–302). Hillsdale, NJ: Lawrence Erlbaum Associates.

Weiner, B. (1995). *Judgments of responsibility: Foundation for a theory of social conduct.* New York: Guilford Press.

Weiner, B., Perry, R. P., & Magnusson, J. (1988). An attributional analysis of reactions to stigmas. *Journal of Personality and Social Psychology, 55,* 738–748.

Zajonc. R. B. (1980). Feeling and thinking: Preferences need no inferences. *American Psychologist, 35,* 151–175.

12

The Social Construction of Attitudes: Functional Consensus and Divergence in the U.S. Public's Reactions to AIDS

Gregory M. Herek
University of California, Davis

Since the earliest days of the AIDS epidemic in the United States, public reactions to the disease have been shaped by a variety of factors. AIDS has been regarded as a deadly and transmissible illness. At the same time, it has been widely perceived as a disease that disproportionately affects society's out-groups, especially gay men, nongay men who have sex with other men, and people who share needles for injecting drug use (Captanio & Herek, 1999; Herek, 1999; Herek & Capitanio, 1999).

Consequently, educating the public about AIDS has been a complicated challenge. It requires communicating information about how to avoid infection with HIV, including discussion of formerly taboo topics such as male–male anal intercourse and needle sharing. It also requires disseminating clear messages about how HIV is *not* transmitted so as to minimize AIDS-related stigma and discrimination against the communities most affected by the epidemic. In these tasks, health workers have long known that simply providing accurate information about HIV is not enough. AIDS education must also confront many emotion-laden issues, including heterosexuals' attitudes toward homosexuality and the stigma associated with illegal drug use. How best to accomplish this task—e.g., which messages should be presented to different audiences, how they should be presented—has not always been obvious.

Because these questions ultimately are about persuasive communication and behavior change, findings from social psychological research on attitudes are potentially relevant to the design of AIDS interventions. The functional approach to attitudes can be especially helpful in this arena. It posits that people hold and express particular attitudes because they derive psychological benefit from doing so and that the type of benefit varies among individuals (Katz, 1960, 1968; Katz & Stotland, 1959; Sarnoff & Katz, 1954; Smith, 1947, 1973; Smith, Bruner, & White, 1956). Within this framework, attitudes are understood according to the psychological needs they meet, that is, the functions they serve. Thus, a functional perspective assumes that different people have different motivations for their attitudes concerning AIDS, with the consequence that various persuasive messages are differentially effective in reaching them.

Although it potentially offers valuable insights into AIDS-related attitudes to health workers and policy makers, functionalism itself has a great deal to gain from its application to societal problems such as the AIDS epidemic. Confronting the complexities of public reactions to AIDS can lead functional theorists to new insights that will enrich the theory. Thus, applying the functional perspective to AIDS education is likely to be mutually beneficial to front-line AIDS educators and to academic social psychologists.

In the present chapter, I offer some observations about attitude functions based on my own research in the area of AIDS and stigma. In the first part of the chapter, I present a conceptual framework for thinking about how the functions served by attitudes can vary across domains and among the specific attitude objects that comprise those domains. As used here, *domain* refers to a closely related set of specific attitude objects (Herek, 1986). For example, the objects that comprise the AIDS domain include people with AIDS (PWAs) as a group, specific PWAs, AIDS-related public policies and laws, and HIV prevention behaviors.

I argue that some attitude objects are socially constructed in such a way that they elicit the same function from virtually all members of a population (a pattern labeled *functional consensus*), whereas others are constructed such that they elicit a variety of functions (*functional divergence*). When attitudes are functionally divergent, their relationships to other theoretically relevant variables differ across function-based population subgroups. When attitudes are functionally consensual, however, the population exhibits a fairly homogeneous pattern of relationships between those attitudes and other theoretically relevant variables.

In the second part of the chapter, I present data from a series of opinion surveys about AIDS conducted between 1990 and 1997 with national probability samples of U.S. adults. These data provide estimates of the proportions of the U.S. adult population whose attitudes in the AIDS domain generally are motivated by concerns about contagion or by symbolic associations between AIDS and societal outgroups. In addition, the data indicate that most of the specific attitude objects included in the surveys elicited functional divergence: Depending on the function served generally by their attitudes in the AIDS domain, respondents' specific AIDS attitudes were differentially correlated with their beliefs about HIV transmission and attitudes toward gay men. However, some specific AIDS attitudes elicited functional consensus: Regardless of which function their AIDS attitudes generally served at the domain level, most respondents' attitudes toward these specific aspects of AIDS manifested a similar pattern of relationships to their transmission beliefs and attitudes toward gay men.

ATTITUDE FUNCTIONS
AND THEIR SOURCES OF VARIATION

No consensus has emerged for a definitive catalog of attitude functions. However, most researchers in this tradition have agreed that attitudes variously help to organize perceptions of the environment in a way that maximizes rewards and minimizes punishments for the individual (labeled *utilitarian, proximal, object instrumental, object appraisal,* and *schematic* functions), mediate one's interpersonal relations (*social-adjustment, social-expressive,* and *social-identity* functions), express values important to one's self-concept (*ego-instrumental* and *value-expressive* functions), and protect the self from anxiety and threats to self esteem (*ego-defensive, externalization,* and *ego-enhancement* functions; Katz, 1960, 1968; Katz & Stotland, 1959; Smith, 1947; Smith, Bruner, & White, 1956; for more recent conceptualizations, see DeBono, 1987; Herek, 1986, 1987; Lutz, 1981; Pratkanis & Greenwald, 1989; Shavitt, 1989).

Empirical research based on the functional approach has usually focused on the importance of personality traits in determining which attitude functions prevail for any individual. Although it has yielded important insights into attitude functions, this approach can limit understanding of how and why attitude functions vary across situations and attitude domains. Therefore, I offer three propositions about functional variation.

Attitude Objects Are Socially Constructed

Attitude objects and domains vary in their potential for eliciting different attitude functions (Herek, 1986; Lutz, 1981; Shavitt, 1989). An adequate analysis of this variation requires that attitude objects and domains be understood within their social context. In other words, the meanings associated with attitude objects and domains are largely socially constructed (see generally Berger & Luckman, 1966; Gergen, 1985).

Even many qualities of an attitude object that appear at first glance to result entirely from its physical characteristics (e.g., taste, cost, and utility, to use some characteristics noted by Shavitt, 1989) can be constructed differently from one social group to another. For example, whether a particular food or beverage is perceived as tasting pleasant or unpleasant varies not only among individuals but also among social groups and entire cultures. Indeed, groups differ in their perceptions of which edible items are even appropriate for ingesting. Consider group differences in attitudes toward consumption of red meat, dogs, monkeys, pigs, insects, caffeinated drinks, and liquor. Similarly, an object's cost, as well as the very notion of whether it is an appropriate item for exchange, is determined socially. And perceptions of an object's utility, and even whether the object is thought of in utilitarian terms, are strongly influenced by social factors.

How an object is socially defined largely determines the attitude functions it is capable of eliciting. For example, depending on historical events and social context, a brightly colored rectangle of fabric may come to be socially defined as a piece of clothing, a national flag, or a work of art. Depending on how a group defines the object, attitudes toward it will serve quite different functions. Attitudes toward the fabric as clothing may be based on utilitarian concerns about its durability and cost, or social-expressive concerns about the status associated with wearing it (which might vary according to whether it is mass produced or a designer original). Attitudes toward the fabric as a flag are likely to evoke in-group and out-group attitudes, as well as value-expressive attitudes about patriotism and nationalism. Attitudes toward the fabric as a piece of art are likely to be based on factors such as the esthetic pleasure the viewer receives from it or the message that it is perceived to convey.

Even objects that seem as though they might be evaluated strictly in terms of physical characteristics or personal utility are subject to these social processes. Whereas Shavitt (1990) found that an air conditioner was regarded primarily in utilitarian terms in a middle-class college student sample, for example, attitudes toward the same object might be quite different in an extremely poor population or for environmental activists. In a poor community, attitudes toward air conditioners might serve functions related as much to social status and identity as to utilitarianism. Among some environmentalists, in contrast, attitudes toward air conditioners might serve primarily value-expressive or social-adjustment functions, reflecting the individual's strong identification with a group that bases its judgments of consumer items more on their environmental impact than on the personal comfort they provide.

As these examples illustrate, the meanings that attitude objects have for an individual are rooted in that individual's relationships with others and the larger society, and develop through social interactions, both direct (e.g., experiencing or discussing the attitude object with others) and indirect (e.g., observing portrayals of the object in mass media). Because constructions of an object can differ dramatically across social groups, the same object can elicit different attitude functions from one group to another.

In a Given Population, The Social Construction of Attitude Objects Can Create One or Many Functions

Within any group, an object can be socially constructed to have a single meaning (so that attitudes toward it serve the same function for all members) or many different meanings (so that attitudes toward it can serve multiple functions). The likelihood that an object has multiple meanings increases with the complexity of the group. In large, pluralistic societies such as the United States and Canada, attitude objects and domains are more likely to evoke multiple meanings than in small, homogeneous societies.

John Capitanio and I have proposed the terms *functional consensus* and *functional divergence* to differentiate between an attitude domain that elicits, respectively, one function or multiple functions within a particular population (Herek & Capitanio, 1998a). Functional divergence is possible when an attitude object has multiple social constructions, such that the function served by a person's attitudes toward the object is determined primarily by individual-level factors such as personal experiences or dispositional traits, or can be manipulated situationally by making salient a particular type of need or a particular set of evaluative criteria. Consider, for example, a White U.S. citizen's attitudes toward African Americans and a heterosexual person's attitudes toward lesbians. In both cases, the attitude domain (i.e., the social groups *African Americans* and *lesbians*) has been socially constructed in the larger society in such a way that its exemplars can potentially be perceived by the attitude holder along many dimensions: religious, political, social, experiential, and others. One White heterosexual, for example, might think about both African Americans and lesbians mainly in religious terms, believing that both groups consist of human beings who were created in God's image and who deserve love and compassion or, alternatively, that religious beliefs require embracing African Americans but rejecting lesbians. Another White heterosexual, in contrast, might evaluate African Americans primarily in social expressive terms ("My friends and family, whose approval and acceptance I want, all dislike Blacks; therefore, I dislike Blacks") but lesbians in experiential terms ("My neighbor is a lesbian and I like her; therefore, I have positive feeling about lesbians as a group").

If an entire population (or the vast majority) defines an attitude domain along the same dimension, however, only one type of attitude function is realistically available to most people in that group. This is the case with functional consensus. For example, attitudes toward the Christian Bible probably serve a value-expressive function for most citizens of the United States. People may hold varying degrees of positive or negative attitudes toward the Bible and its contents, but they most likely base their attitudes on value considerations rather than, for example, utilitarian ones.

Two points warrant emphasis here. First, functional consensus and divergence are group level phenomena. They represent patterns in a population. Second, because the social construction of attitude objects can be highly nuanced, functional consensus and divergence may differ among specific attitude objects within a domain. For example, whereas attitudes toward the American flag may elicit functional consensus in the

United States (because they serve a value-expressive function for most Americans), attitudes toward a constitutional amendment to prohibit flag burning might be functionally divergent. Some people may hold value-expressive attitudes toward the issue (e.g., individuals who base their attitudes on patriotism or allegiance to the First Amendment), whereas others might hold social-expressive attitudes (e.g., people who form their attitudes in reaction to the position taken by family members or important reference groups) or even utilitarian attitudes (e.g., the flag manufacturer who fears that the wording of the amendment would prohibit him from incinerating old flags that are no longer usable).

An Individual's Attitudes Toward Different Objects Can Serve Different Functions

Once it is recognized that the meanings attached to any object reflect that object's social construction, and that social constructions can result in functional consensus for some objects and functional divergence for others, it follows that the functions served by any individual's attitudes can differ across attitude objects and domains. For a simple illustration of this point, consider the case when two different attitude objects each elicit functional consensus in a particular population. If the first object is socially constructed such that it uniformly elicits a utilitarian function, whereas the second object elicits exclusively value-expressive attitudes, an individual from that population will most likely hold utilitarian attitudes toward the first object and value-expressive attitudes toward the second object.

Functional researchers have always assumed that one person can express attitudes that serve a variety of functions. In the earliest functional theories, intraindividual variation was assumed to result from the interaction of personal needs and situational cues. Katz's (1960) formulation, for example, assumed that all of the needs associated with the different functions are more or less present in all individuals but that their relative intensity differs among people, and that situations vary in their ability to arouse particular needs and hence engage particular attitude functions. Consistent with this formulation, laboratory experiments based on the functional approach have used a variety of situational manipulations for making one type of function more salient than others (e.g., Peak, 1960; Maio & Olson, 1995).

Researchers have also long recognized that many attitude objects and domains are likely to elicit multiple functions (e.g., DeBono, 1987; Herek,

1987; Maio & Olson, 1995; Pryor, Reeder, Vinacco, & Kott, 1989). As Shavitt (1989, 1990) explained, multifunctionalism is more likely for some attitude objects than for others. Her studies laid the groundwork for a better understanding of how the characteristics of attitude objects affect functions, especially with unifunctional objects, that is, objects that elicit one principal function in a particular population. Considered in tandem with studies of multifunctional attitude objects, her research also empirically established that some objects elicit one function whereas others are multifunctional. Thus, the functions served by an individual's attitudes can differ across attitude objects and domains. This conclusion has important implications for operationalizing attitude functions.

Operationalizing Attitude Functions

Characterizing their study as "a prolegomenon to measurement," M. Brewster Smith and his colleagues collected mainly qualitative interview data in their exploratory study of opinions (Smith et al., 1956, p. 4). In contrast, Daniel Katz's group at Michigan and most later functional researchers used standardized assessment methods that allowed for objective scoring and mass administration. Operationalization of attitude functions with objective measures has been a challenge and often a problem. One reason for this difficulty is the longstanding tension within the functional approach between two conceptualizations of attitudes: as relatively stable personality traits and as dynamic outcomes of a dialectic among characteristics of persons, objects, and situations. Reflecting that tension, functional researchers have used a variety of indirect and direct measurement strategies.

Indirect Measurement of Attitude Functions

The use of indirect measures of attitude functions dates back to the 1950s, when Michigan researchers employed global measures such as the F-scale, MMPI items, and special TAT cards (e.g., Katz, McClintock, & Sarnoff, 1957; Katz, Sarnoff, & McClintock, 1956). Their operationalizations reflected the view that attitudes are equivalent to personality syndromes (e.g., McClintock, 1958). Many contemporary researchers have found this conceptualization useful and have continued to impute attitude functions from global assessments of personality traits, especially the trait of self-monitoring (e.g., Bazzini & Shaffer, 1995; DeBono, 1987; DeBono & Snyder, 1989; Petty & Wegener, 1998; Snyder & DeBono, 1985, 1987, 1989).

Another indirect approach to measuring attitude functions derives from research on symbolic and instrumental attitudes (Abelson & Prentice, 1989; Herek, 1986; Pryor et al., 1989). Researchers in this area differentiate between attitudes based on the individual's self-interested, utilitarian concerns (*instrumental attitudes*) and those reflecting symbolic expressions of deep-seated values and prejudices (*symbolic attitudes*; for background and debate, see Bobo, 1983; Herek, 1986; Jelen & Wilcox, 1992; Kinder, 1986; Kinder & Sears, 1981; Sears, 1993; Sniderman & Tetlock, 1986).

The instrumental–symbolic dichotomy has been translated into functional terms in various ways. In my own work (Herek, 1986, 1987), I have described two broad categories of attitude functions: the *expressive* functions, which underlie symbolic attitudes, and the *evaluative* functions, which underlie instrumental attitudes (see also Abelson & Prentice, 1989; Herek, 1987; Herek & Capitanio, 1998a; Prentice, 1987). Expressive attitudes (i.e., those that serve functions such as value expression, social adjustment, ego defense, or ego enhancement) derive their affective content from personal needs that are met by the attitude's expression—needs broadly related to affirmation of identity, enhancement of self-esteem, strengthening of relations to an in-group, or distancing of oneself from out-groups. The attitude object serves primarily as a symbol (e.g., for values integral to the self concept). In contrast, evaluative attitudes (e.g., utilitarian, schematic, proximal, object instrumental) are based principally on appraisals of the attitude object in terms of its direct utility for the person rather than as a symbol. The attitude's affect derives from whether the object itself is a source of benefit or detriment.

Measurement strategies for instrumental and symbolic attitudes have typically focused on assessing, respectively, cost–benefit evaluations of the attitude object and attitudes toward other objects to which it is symbolically linked (e.g., Bishop, Alva, Cantu, & Rittiman, 1991; Jelen & Wilcox, 1992; Pryor & Reeder, 1993; Pryor et al., 1989; Schneider, Snyder-Joy, & Hopper, 1993). A particular attitude has been characterized as serving a symbolic or instrumental function to the extent that symbolic and instrumental variables explain significant portions of its variance.

An empirical example of this approach is Pryor et al.'s (1989) innovative program of research on the symbolic and instrumental functions of attitudes toward interacting with a person with AIDS. Pryor and his colleagues operationalized instrumental attitudes with a series of expectancy-value measures that focused on the possible outcomes of such interaction (e.g., the likelihood that one's child would become infected through interactions with a schoolmate with AIDS). Symbolic attitudes were operationalized in terms of heterosexuals' attitudes toward homosexuality, which reflects the fact that the American public's perceptions of the epidemic were shaped by the disproportionate impact of AIDS on gay and bisexual men in the United States (Herek, 1997). In a series of studies, both instrumental and symbolic measures consistently predicted significant and independent portions of the variance in AIDS attitudes (see also Pryor & Reeder, 1993; Pryor, Reeder, & McManus, 1991).

Indirect approaches to operationalizing attitude functions have important advantages. Research with personality measures—especially the self-monitoring scale—has enjoyed impressive success at predicting differential responses to persuasive messages. Moreover, as Snyder and DeBono (1987, 1989) explained with reference to the use of the self-monitoring scale in functional research, such measures permit "differences in attitudinal functions to be placed in the larger psychological context of the generalized interpersonal orientations associated with self-monitoring propensities, and in the larger theoretical framework provided by the entire network of evidence for the construct validity of self-monitoring" (Snyder & DeBono, 1987, p. 122). Functional research based on the symbolic–instrumental distinction has also made important theoretical and empirical contributions. It has successfully demonstrated the multiple sources of attitudes toward important social problems, such as the AIDS epidemic, and has contextualized the findings of functional research within the scientific literature on symbolic politics and expectancy-value approaches.

However, indirect measures do not yield information about the specific functions served by the attitudes under study. As previously noted, the functions served by an individual's attitudes can differ across attitude objects and domains. Personality-based approaches in particular do not permit assessment of these intraindividual differences in attitude functions. Instead, such approaches are based on the assumption that a person who manifests a particular trait (e.g., high or low self-monitoring) consistently holds attitudes that serve the same function in multiple domains. For example, a White heterosexual man's attitudes toward Blacks are presumed to serve the same function as his attitudes toward gay men, gun control, the Boston Celtics, Coca-Cola, and the Microsoft Corporation.

The strategy of using instrumental and symbolic variables as proxy measures of attitude functions is more specific than that of using personality variables. The former allows intraindividual variation in attitude functions to be reflected in varying expectancy-value judgments and responses to symbolically linked attitude objects. Nevertheless, this operational strategy does not establish whether a functional connection actually exists between the proxy attitudes and the attitude of interest. Simply because a heterosexual man has negative attitudes toward gay men, for example, does not mean that antigay attitudes are the primary motivation for his AIDS-related attitudes. It is necessary to know as well whether AIDS, as an attitude domain, activates those antigay sentiments and makes them sufficiently salient that his AIDS-related attitudes function to express them symbolically. The extent to which such direct activation occurs can be known only when attitude functions are measured directly.

Direct Measurement of Attitude Functions

The feasibility of directly assessing functions has been demonstrated for a variety of attitude domains with a variety of approaches. Functions have been reliably and validly ascertained from content analysis of respondents' verbal statements (Herek, 1987; Maio & Olson, 1994, 1995; Shavitt, 1990) and through objectively scored direct questions about respondents' reasons for their opinions (Abelson, 1988; Anderson & Kristiansen, 1990; Gastil, 1992; Herek, 1987; Herek & Glunt, 1993; Shavitt, 1990), behavioral intentions (Hooper, 1983), and behaviors (Omoto & Crain, 1995).

I have detailed a method for directly assessing attitude functions with a series of objectively scored items which I call the Attitude Functions Inventory, or AFI (Herek, 1987). The AFI method involves developing a set of statements describing the reasons why an individual holds her or his attitudes in a particular domain, with each statement keyed to a particular attitude function. Respondents indicate the extent to which each statement describes their own attitudes (for studies that utilize the AFI and similar methods, see Anderson & Kristiansen, 1990; Brandyberry & MacNair, 1996; Herek, 1987; Herek & Capitanio, 1998a; Herek & Glunt, 1993; Wyman & Snyder, 1997).

Direct measures of attitude functions can focus on a specific attitude or a general domain. The AFI has typically been used to measure attitude functions at the domain level. In the first study that used the AFI, for example, respondents indicated the extent to which various factors had influenced their general attitudes toward lesbians and gay men (Herek,

1987). In the surveys detailed later in this chapter, respondents were asked how much various considerations (worry about getting AIDS, religious beliefs, etc.) had "influenced your own opinions about AIDS." The AFI format could also be used to measure the functions of attitudes toward specific objects within a domain. For example, one set of AFI items could be worded to refer specifically to attitudes toward policies that mandate reporting of the names of people who test positive for HIV, and another set could refer to attitudes toward working closely in an office with a PWA. At the most specific level, a separate set of AFI items could be administered in reference to each item on an attitude scale.

It seems reasonable to assume, however, that attitudes toward most objects within a domain derive from the same motivation(s); that is, an individual's attitudes within a particular domain generally serve the same function (or functions) across most attitude objects comprising that domain. For example, individuals whose AIDS-related attitudes generally reflect instrumental concerns about contagion and infection (the domain level) are likely to manifest those same concerns in their specific AIDS attitudes toward mandatory HIV reporting policies or working with a PWA (the specific attitude level).

Use of the AFI to assess functions at the domain level, rather than the more specific level of the attitude object, has at least two advantages. First, separate assessment of the functions associated with responses to each item on an attitude scale would create a considerable burden for respondents and would limit the extent to which other questions could be asked in an interview or self-administered questionnaire. Such an approach would be especially cumbersome in field research and surveys with population-based samples, whose respondents often are reluctant to engage in repetitive tasks and in which the addition of a single question can have high monetary costs. Second, such an approach permits general categorization of respondents according to the function most likely to be served by their attitudes toward specific objects within the domain. The utility of such categorization is illustrated below.

Operationalizing Consensus and Divergence

When attitude domains differ in the number of functions they elicit within a specific population, this difference is manifested in the relative numbers of people in that population who hold attitudes that serve each available function. With functional consensus, everyone (or nearly everyone) manifests the same function in their attitudes within that domain; with functional divergence, different functions are served by the attitudes of sizable portions of the population.

Methodologically, identifying whether functional consensus or functional divergence prevails for a particular domain in a particular population is somewhat akin to taking a vote. Rather than the outcome being determined by a simple majority, however, it should be based on whether the vast majority of a population (e.g., 90% or more) manifests attitudes that serve the same function. In that case, the domain can be said to elicit functional consensus. However, if significant portions of the sample manifest each function or combinations of functions, it is a case of functional divergence.[1]

Thus, determination of whether a particular attitude domain is unifunctional or multifunctional within a particular population requires that individuals be somehow categorized according to the function served predominantly or exclusively by their attitudes, and then counted. If most or all of the respondents can be placed in a single group, the attitude is unifunctional; the group's attitudes are characterized by functional consensus. If a significant minority holds attitudes that serve a different function from that of the majority, the attitude is multifunctional; the group's attitudes are functionally divergent.

---

[1]This approach differs from a strategy of simply comparing mean scores for different functions for a particular attitude object. Mean differences across functions may be statistically significant even when a sizable minority of a sample holds attitudes serving a nondominant function or a mix of functions. In Shavitt's (1990) study, for example, groups of attitude objects were rated significantly higher on the function they had been hypothesized a priori to serve. Thus, the group of self-esteem maintenance objects elicited higher scores on that function than on the other function items. However, those objects also elicited relatively high scores for the other functions: $M = 4.05$ for self-esteem maintenance, 3.88 for social identity, and 3.59 for utilitarian, based on a 5-point scale (Shavitt, 1990, Table 1). In a similar fashion, the self-esteem maintenance objects elicited about the same number of self-esteem maintenance thoughts as social identity thoughts ($M = 1.32$ and 1.31, respectively; Shavitt, 1990, Table 2). Thus, although she demonstrated convincingly that certain attitude objects elicited one type of function more than others, it is not clear from her published report how many of the individual objects studied by Shavitt (1990) were truly unifunctional. However, some objects appear to have fit this description. For example, the group of objects predesignated as utilitarian elicited substantially more utilitarian thoughts ($M = 3.20$) than social identity or self-esteem maintenance thoughts ($M = 0.17$ and 0.29, respectively; Shavitt, 1990, Table 2). Interpretation of the characteristics of specific objects is made difficult by the fact that Shavitt's published paper collapsed scores across objects within each category. Her observation that the "ratings for each attitude object individually were also supportive for *most* of the objects" (Shavitt, 1990, p. 132, italics added) suggests that some objects may not have been unifunctional. Indeed, my own research conducted around the same time (Herek, 1987) suggested that at least one of the attitude objects that she used (*homosexuals*) was likely to be multifunctional.

A Note on Methodological Paradigms

Traditionally, theoretical frameworks based on the functional approach have been operationalized in attitude-change paradigms. Research in this tradition usually tests the hypothesis that function-relevant messages are more persuasive or more favorably received when they match the recipient's dominant attitude function or the function that has been made most salient by situational manipulations (e.g., Katz, 1960; Maio & Olson, 1995; Peak, 1960; Snyder & DeBono, 1989). Despite the theoretical power of this approach, as well as the empirical support it has often enjoyed, we functional researchers should take care not to put all of our conceptual eggs in the experimental attitude-change paradigm basket. Many psychological processes are implicated in the process of persuasive communication (for a discussion of some of the steps between presentation of a message and attitude change, see the communication–persuasion matrix presented by McGuire, 1985). Most functional research has focused only on the initial input step (message presentation) and the ultimate output (attitude change) without consideration of intervening psychological processes (for exceptions to this pattern, see DeBono & Harnish, 1988; DeBono & Telesca, 1990; Petty & Wegener, 1998). The development of functional theory may be hampered if we rely exclusively on the experimental attitude-change paradigm. Such reliance might lead us to ignore other behavior patterns that are predicted by functional theories and even, in some cases, to inappropriately reject functional hypotheses because of failures to obtain statistically significant levels of attitude change through experimental manipulations.

In the remainder of this chapter, I discuss research relevant to the model previously described. It is based not on laboratory experimentation, but on survey methods and the analytic strategies employed in past studies of symbolic politics. Using data from a series of national surveys that included AFI items, I begin by describing the distribution of functions for the general domain of AIDS attitudes in the sample (and, by implication, in the U.S. adult population at the time the surveys were conducted). Then I assess the adequacy of this description for attitudes toward a variety of specific AIDS-related objects by extending a model used in the symbolic politics literature. This model tests whether attitudes toward a particular object are instrumental or symbolic by using multiple regression to assess the relative power of instrumental versus symbolic variables in prediction of attitude scores.

I hypothesized that whether AIDS attitudes were functionally consensual or divergent would affect their relationship to instrumental and symbolic variables. If attitudes toward a specific attitude object within the domain of AIDS are functionally divergent, they should be predicted by an instrumental variable for persons whose AIDS attitudes generally (at the domain level) serve an evaluative function, but by a symbolic variable for persons whose attitudes generally (at the domain level) serve an expressive function. Consequently, the specific attitudes of those who are generally evaluative and those who are generally expressive will manifest quite different patterns of relationships to other key variables. If functional consensus prevails, whether a person has generally evaluative or generally expressive attitudes within the domain of AIDS will not matter; the specific attitudes of both groups should be predicted mainly by one type of variable (either the symbolic or the instrumental variable, depending on the social construction of the attitude object).

FUNCTIONAL CONSENSUS AND DIVERGENCE IN AIDS-RELATED ATTITUDES

My focus in the studies described in what follows is the attitude domain of AIDS, which includes the attitudes of non-HIV-infected individuals toward a wide range of phenomena, for example, persons with AIDS, behaviors related to AIDS (e.g., personal AIDS prevention, donation of time or money to AIDS charities, interaction with or avoidance PWAs), and AIDS-related public policies (e.g., treatment, prevention, and surveillance programs; nondiscrimination laws).

In the United States, Canada, and much of the world, stigma has been a dominant feature of social constructions of AIDS (Herek, 1999; Herek et al., 1998). AIDS-related stigma affects the quality of life for people infected with HIV, those at risk for infection, and those perceived to be at risk. People with HIV (or believed to be infected) have been fired from their jobs, driven from their homes, and even physically attacked. AIDS stigma also poses threats to the physical and psychological well-being of the loved ones of PWAs, their caregivers, and communities disproportionately affected by HIV. Fears of AIDS stigma and its attendant discrimination appear to deter people from seeking information and assistance for AIDS risk reduction, being tested for HIV, and, if they are HIV-positive, disclosing their serostatus to others. The latter may lead to social isolation and interfere with receiving needed medical and social services (for general discussions, see Herek, 1990; Herek & Glunt, 1988; Herek et al., 1998; Mann, Tarantola, & Netter, 1992; Pryor & Reeder, 1993). Because of the prevalence of AIDS stigma and its widespread impact, I selected various aspects of AIDS stigma for operationalization in the studies described here.

The 1991 and 1992 Surveys

The first set of data concerning functional divergence and consensus in AIDS-related attitudes comes from a two-wave telephone survey about AIDS. Because the data were drawn from a national probability sample, they provided an unusual opportunity to assess the extent to which various attitude objects within the domain of AIDS were functionally divergent or functionally consensual in the U.S. adult population.

Method

Sampling and Procedures.
The sampling methods and interview procedures for the survey have been described in detail elsewhere (Herek & Capitanio, 1993, 1997, 1998a). In brief, a two-stage random-digit dialing (RDD) method was used to obtain a sample of respondents from the universe of all English-speaking adults (at least 18 years of age) residing in households with telephones within the 48 contiguous states. They were interviewed on two separate occasions approximately 1 year apart. Interviews were conducted by the staff of the Survey Research Center at the University of California at Berkeley between September 1990 and February 1991 for Wave 1, and between November 1991 and February 1992 for Wave 2, using their computer-assisted telephone interviewing (CATI) system. Wave 1 interviews were completed with 538 individuals. Wave 2 reinterviews were completed with 382 (71%) of the original respondents. Of the 382 Wave 2 respondents, 366 had identified themselves as heterosexual at Wave 1 and are included in the analyses discussed here.

The Wave 1 sample was 46% male and 54% female. Described racially and ethnically, it was 81% White, 10% Black, 5% Hispanic, and 3% Asian. The mean age was 44 years; median annual household income was between $30,000 and $40,000; and the median level of educational attainment was some college or postsecondary technical school. The demographic characteristics of the Wave 2 sample were nearly identical to those of Wave 1, except that significantly more Asians and significantly fewer Whites were lost between Waves 1 and 2 than would be expected through random attrition. In addition, the highest income category (income greater than $70,000 annually) had a significantly lower attrition rate than did any of the other income categories. More detailed information about the sample is reported elsewhere (Herek & Capitanio, 1993, 1994, 1995, 1996, 1997).

Measures. As noted earlier, although a person's attitudes toward the various objects in a particular domain are likely to display some degree of consistency, they need not be uniform across all objects within that domain. In recognition of the importance of such complexities, four types of attitudes within the domain of AIDS were assessed: (a) *coercion and blame*, including support for quarantine and public labeling of PWAs, and the belief that PWAs deserve their illness; (b) *attitudes toward interacting with persons with AIDS* in various social situations; (c) *negative feelings* (fear, anger, and disgust) toward PWAs as a group (asked only at Wave 1) or toward a homosexual man with AIDS (asked only at Wave 2); and (d) *attitudes toward policies* that mandate HIV testing of immigrants and people "at high risk for getting AIDS" (asked only at Wave 2).

Three AFI items were used to directly assess respondents' attitude functions in the general domain of AIDS and to categorize respondents into functional groups. One item was used to assess the extent to which AIDS-related attitudes served an evaluative function for the individual. After reporting whether they were *very worried, somewhat worried, not too worried,* or *not at all worried* that they would get AIDS, respondents were asked, "How much has that [e.g., the fact that they were somewhat worried] influenced your feelings about AIDS and what should be done about it?" This question is referred to hereafter as the *personal worry* item. Two other items were used to assess the expressive function, one that asked how much the respondent's political values had influenced her or his "feelings about AIDS and what should be done about it" (the *political* item) and the other that asked about the influence of "your own personal religious or moral beliefs—your feelings about right and wrong" (the *religious* item). For all three AFI items, four response alternatives were provided (*a great deal, some, very little, no influence at all*).

Consistent with previous research in this area (Pryor et al., 1989), attitudes toward gay men were used as a symbolic auxiliary variable, and beliefs about HIV transmission were used as an instrumental auxiliary variable. Attitudes toward gay men were assessed with a three-item short form of the Attitudes Toward Gay Men (ATG) scale (Herek, 1994), and beliefs about the risk of HIV transmission through casual contact were measured with a four-item Casual Contact Transmission Beliefs (CCTB) scale. Higher scores on the scales indicated, respectively, more unfavorable attitudes toward gay men and greater overestimation of risk from casual social contact (see Herek & Capitanio, 1997, 1998a).

Functional Categorization. The responses to the three AFI items were used to identify respondents whose attitudes in the domain of AIDS generally served a single primary function and to categorize them into two groups: evaluatives (persons with attitudes motivated primarily by personal worry about getting HIV) and expressives (persons with attitudes motivated primarily by political or religious values). Respondents' general AIDS attitudes were categorized as serving primarily an evaluative function when their score for the *personal worry* item was greater (i.e., indicating stronger influence) than their score for either the *religious* or *political* items. They were categorized as primarily expressive if their score for either the *religious* or *political* items was greater than their score for the *personal worry* item.

Results

Functional Categorization. Forty-eight respondents (13%) were classified as evaluatives and 179 (49%) as expressives. The remainder scored equally high on both functions (30%) or reported that none of the three factors had exerted an influence on their attitudes about AIDS (8%). This overall pattern suggests that US attitudes in the general AIDS domain were functionally divergent, in that substantial portions of the sample manifested an evaluative or expressive function (either singly, or in combination). The fact that a near-majority of respondents was categorized as primarily expressive—with another 30% manifesting both an expressive and an evaluative function—suggested that AIDS domain attitudes were more strongly expressive than evaluative when the survey was conducted. (As explained in the following, however, findings from the 1997 survey suggested that more evaluatives might have been identified had additional items been included in the survey.)

Based on this pattern of functional divergence, it would be expected that the specific AIDS attitudes assessed in the survey are differentially predicted by an instrumental or symbolic variable, depending on the individual respondent's domain level dominant attitude function. Before examining the findings in this regard, it is appropriate to consider how functional divergence and consensus for a specific attitude could be reflected in the relationships among the key variables.

Operational Criteria for Functional Divergence and Consensus. If a specific attitude object (e.g., attitudes toward mandatory AIDS testing) in a particular population (in this case, adults in the United States) is characterized by functional divergence, we should observe different correlational patterns among subgroups of individuals, depending on which function their attitude serves. That is, the valence and intensity of attitudes should be influenced by different factors for people whose attitudes serve expressive functions than for people whose attitudes serve an evaluative function. Symbolic factors—for example, attitudes toward groups perceived to be closely associated with the epidemic, such as gay men—should be powerful predictors of attitudes for expressives, that is, people whose attitudes in the larger domain (i.e., AIDS) serve an expressive function. In contrast, utilitarian considerations—for example, beliefs about whether HIV is easily transmitted—should be more influential for evaluatives, people whose attitudes in the general domain of AIDS serve an evaluative function. If, on the other hand, attitudes toward a specific aspect of AIDS show functional consensus, the extent to which relevant symbolic and instrumental variables predict those attitudes should not differ between the evaluative and expressive groups.

The four rows of Table 12.1 describe regression analysis results expected for specific attitude objects associated with four different patterns of functional consensus and divergence. The first two columns display predicted patterns among respondents whose attitudes in the general domain serve an evaluative function; the middle two columns describe respondents whose attitudes in the general domain serve an expressive function.[2] For each pattern, the table indicates the extent to which symbolic independent variables (e.g., general attitudes toward groups associated with AIDS) and instrumental independent variables (e.g., beliefs about the risk of contracting AIDS) are expected to predict attitudes toward specific AIDS objects. A plus sign (+) indicates that the

---

[2]Many members of the population inevitably will have attitudes that serve a combination of experiential and expressive functions. With the exception of Pattern 4, discussed in the following, I focus here on the conceptually simpler cases of individuals whose attitudes in a particular domain serve more or less pure functions.

variable is expected to explain a relatively high proportion of the variance in attitudes toward the object (R^2 in a regression model), whereas a minus sign (–) means that the variable should explain a relatively low proportion of variance.

The first two rows of Table 12.1 describe the expected pattern when functional consensus prevails. For example, if attitudes toward interacting with PWAs were instrumental for most of the U.S. public, their valence and intensity would be substantially and significantly predicted by scores on an instrumental variable (e.g., beliefs about the likelihood of HIV being transmitted in casual social contact), whereas a symbolic variable (e.g., attitudes toward gay men) would not explain a great deal of variance in attitudes. This pattern of *instrumental consensus* is portrayed in Row 1 of Table 12.1. If attitudes about contact with PWAs instead represent a symbolic issue for most of the population, regardless of the domain level functions served by their general AIDS attitudes, symbolic variables would be the main predictor (Table 12.1, Row 2).

TABLE 12.1

Predicted Patterns of Variance Explained by Symbolic and Instrumental Variables for Functional Divergence and Functional Consensus

| | Function Group | | | | | |
| | *Evaluative* | | *Expressive* | | *Function Ratios* | |
PATTERN	*Symbolic Variable*	*Instrumental Variable*	*Symbolic Variable*	*Instrumental Variable*	*VFR*	*XFR*
Functional consensus: Instrumental	–	+	–	+	~1	~1
Functional consensus: Symbolic	+	–	+	–	~1	~1
Functional divergence: Simple case	–	+	+	–	>1	>1
Functional divergence: Special case	–	+	+	+	~1	>1

Note. + = relatively large proportion of R^2 predicted to be explained; – = relatively small proportion of R^2 predicted to be explained, or R^2 predicted to be not substantively significant; VFR = evaluative function ratio; XFR = expressive function ratio.

The third row of Table 12.1 represents a simple case of functional divergence: Expressives' attitudes are predicted largely by the symbolic variable and evaluatives' attitudes are predicted largely by the instrumental variable. Put another way, the symbolic variable accounts for a significant and substantial amount of variance in the attitudes of expressives (but not evaluatives), and the instrumental variable accounts for a significant and substantial amount of variance in the attitudes of evaluatives (but not expressives).

The case of AIDS—and, most likely, other transmissible diseases that have strong symbolic connotations in popular discourse—suggests a variation on the simple functional divergence pattern (see Row 4 of Table 12.1). Because practically all AIDS stigma, regardless of the psychological function it serves, is based to some extent on the characteristics of AIDS as a disease, most specific aspects of AIDS stigma might be significantly predicted by instrumental variables (e.g., casual contact beliefs) for both functions groups. For this pattern, the plus sign (+) in the instrumental variable column for both groups indicates that this variable should account for a significant proportion of variance for expressives as well as evaluatives. For the expressive group, a significant portion of additional variance in specific forms of AIDS stigma should be predicted by attitudes toward gay men, indicated by the plus sign (+) in the symbolic variable column.

Interpretation of the patterns described in the first four columns of Table 12.1 can be aided by comparing the relative proportion of variance explained by the symbolic and instrumental variables across groups (see the last two columns of Table 12.1). The *evaluative function ratio*, or VFR, summarizes the relative proportion of variance explained by the instrumental variable (in this case, casual contact beliefs) for evaluatives compared to expressives. It is computed as:

$$\text{VFR} = \frac{R_{VI}^2}{(R_{VI}^2 + R_{VS}^2)} \bigg/ \frac{R_{XI}^2}{(R_{XI}^2 + R_{XS}^2)}, \qquad (1)$$

where $R^2{}_{VI}$ is the proportion of variance in evaluatives' attitudes explained by the instrumental independent variable (beliefs about casual contact), $R^2{}_{VS}$ is the proportion of variance in evaluatives' attitudes explained by the symbolic independent variable (attitudes toward gay men), $R^2{}_{XI}$ is the proportion of variance in expressives' attitudes explained by the instrumental independent variable, and $R^2{}_{XS}$ is the proportion of variance in expressives' attitudes explained by the symbolic independent variable.

Values of VFR > 1 indicate that casual contact beliefs are a more powerful predictor of attitudes for evaluatives than for expressives. Values of VFR < 1 indicate that such beliefs are a less powerful predictor for evaluatives, and values of VFR $= 1$ indicate that the variable's predictive power is approximately the same for both function groups.

The *expressive function ratio* (XFR) is computed in a similar manner, except that it describes the relative proportion of variance explained by the symbolic variable (attitudes toward gay men) for the expressive group compared to the evaluative group:

$$\text{VFR} = \frac{R_{XS}^2}{(R_{XS}^2 + R_{XI}^2)} \bigg/ \frac{R_{VS}^2}{(R_{VS}^2 + R_{VI}^2)} \tag{2}$$

Examined in conjunction with the actual proportions of variance explained (i.e., the information in the first four columns of Table 12.1), the functional ratios assist in interpreting functional patterns. Instrumental functional consensus is indicated when (a) both ratios are approximately equal to 1, indicating that the predictive power of the instrumental and symbolic variables is similar for both groups, and (b) the proportion of variance explained by the instrumental variable (casual contact beliefs) is greater than the proportion explained by the symbolic variable (attitudes toward gay men). With symbolic functional consensus, both ratios again are equal to 1, but the proportion of variance explained by the symbolic variable is greater than that explained by the instrumental variable.

Simple functional divergence is indicated when (a) both ratios are substantially greater than 1, (b) the symbolic variable accounts for a substantial amount of variance in the attitudes of expressives (but not evaluatives), and (c) the instrumental variable accounts for a significant and substantial amount of variance in the attitudes of evaluatives (but not expressives). With the special case of functional divergence hypothesized for AIDS (Table 12.1, Row 4), the instrumental variable explains the attitudes of both function groups to a significant extent (and VFR is approximately equal to 1), but the symbolic variable is a significant predictor for expressives (and XFR is substantially greater than 1).

For the data presented in what follows, in addition to the use of ordinary least squares regression analyses to assess the substantive proportion of variance explained by symbolic and instrumental independent variables (with the patterns in Table 12.1 serving as a guide for interpretation), moderated regression analysis was used to test the extent to which the magnitude of the predictors (i.e., the unstandardized coefficients associated with each independent variable) was significantly different between expressives and evaluatives. Put differently, we tested whether the slope of the regression line for each independent variable differed significantly between evaluatives and expressives (Herek & Capitanio, 1998a).

This analysis required the construction of a set of multiplicative interaction terms, representing the product of a dummy-coded variable (indicative of the respondent's primary attitude function) and scores on each of the symbolic and instrumental variables. The interaction terms were entered into the regression equation on a second step, after the "main effects" variables (the instrumental and symbolic variables, as well as the dummy variable for function group) had been entered on the first step. In addition to consideration of statistical significance, the magnitude of statistically significant effects in this analysis can be evaluated by calculating the proportional reduction in error (PRE, the squared partial correlation) for each interaction term. The PRE is an indicator of whether inclusion of the interaction term substantially improves the explanatory power of the regression equation (McClelland & Judd, 1993).

Predictors of AIDS Stigma: Regression Analyses Within Function Groups.

Table 12.2 reports the results of a series of regression analyses for the evaluatives ($n = 43$ self-described heterosexuals who provided complete responses for all variables) and expressives ($n = 157$). ATG scores (the symbolic variable) and CCTB scores (the instrumental variable) were entered simultaneously. The results suggest three patterns.

First, coercion and blame (at both waves) and attitudes toward mandatory testing manifested patterns consistent with those previously described for the special case of functional divergence. CCTB scores explained the attitudes of both expressives and evaluatives, and VFR was approximately equal to 1, but ATG scores significantly predicted expressives' attitudes and XFR > 1.

Second, negative feelings toward PWAs were consistent with the pattern described earlier for simple functional divergence. Both XFR and VFR were greater than 1, and ATG scores accounted for a substantial portion of the variance in expressives' scores, whereas CCTB scores accounted for a substantial portion of the variance in evaluatives' scores.

TABLE 12.2

Function Ratios and Percentage of Variance (R^2) in AIDS Stigma Explained by
Symbolic and Instrumental Variables for Each Function Group (1991–1992 Surveys)

| | Function Group | | | | Function Ratios | |
| | Evaluative | | Expressive | | | |
Dependent Variable	ATG	CCTB	ATG	CCTB	VFR	XFR
Coercion and blame						
1991	4.9	19.1[**]	8.9[***]	11.9[***]	1.39	2.10
1992	0.0	15.3[**]	7.2[***]	22.9[***]	1.30	23.92
Interacting with PWA						
1991	1.8	21.8[**]	2.0[*]	30.9[***]	0.98	0.80
1992	4.2	25.1[***]	3.6[**]	19.3[***]	1.02	1.10
Negative feelings						
for PWA						
1991 (Generic)	2.4	12.9[*]	13.4[***]	4.0[**]	3.67	4.91
1992 (Homosexual)	2.5	18.4[**]	18.4[***]	6.9[***]	3.23	6.08
Mandatory testing						
index (1992 only)	0.0	10.4[*]	12.8[***]	12.4[***]	2.01	50.79

Note. $*p < .05$, $**p < .01$, $***p < .001$; $n = 43$ for evaluatives, 157 for expressives; ATG = attitudes toward gay men (symbolic variable); CCTB = casual contact transmission beliefs (instrumental variable); VFR = evaluative function ratio; XFR = expressive function ratio.

Third, attitudes toward interactions with a PWA fit the pattern for instrumental functional consensus. Both VFR and XFR were approximately 1, and the proportion of variance explained by CCTB scores was considerably greater than the proportion explained by ATG scores for both expressives and evaluatives.

Testing Interaction Effects: Moderated Regression Analyses Across Function Groups.   Table 12.3 reports results from the moderated regression analysis. Whereas Table 12.2 reports the reliability of transmission beliefs and attitudes toward gay men as predictors of AIDS stigma within each domain level function group, the results in Table 12.3 indicate the extent to which the magnitude of the predictors (i.e., the unstandardized coefficients associated with each independent variable) differs significantly between expressives and evaluatives. In all analyses, the interaction terms were entered into the equation only after their component variables (functional group, ATG scores, and CCTB scores) were entered. To simplify Table 12.3, and because our hypotheses focused on the interaction terms, results are presented only for the interactions.

TABLE 12.3

Comparison of Unstandardized Regression Coefficients for Interaction Terms
Between Expressives and Evaluatives

| | INTERACTION TERM | | | |
| | Function × ATG | | Function × CCTB | |
Dependent Variable	b	PRE	b	PRE
Coercion and blame				
1991	0.073	0.002	−0.000	0.000
1992	0.233*	0.021	0.130	0.014
Interacting with PWA				
1991	−0.000	0.000	0.035	0.006
1992	0.001	0.000	−0.003	0.000
Negative feelings for PWA				
1991 (Generic)	0.151	0.009	−0.058	0.003
1992 (Homosexual)	0.277*	0.023	−0.063	0.003
Mandatory testing				
index	0.259**	0.035	0.026	0.001

Note. $*p < .05$, $**p < .01$; $n = 43$ for evaluatives, 157 for expressives; n.s. = not significant ($p > .05$); PRE = proportional reduction in error (squared partial correlation); ATG = attitudes toward gay men (symbolic variable); CCTB = casual contact transmission beliefs (instrumental variable).

The dummy variable was coded so that positive regression coefficients in Table 12.3 indicate that the independent variable's predictive power is greater for the expressives than the evaluatives. Negative coefficients indicate that the independent variable's predictive power is greater for the evaluatives. Thus, the simple functional divergence hypothesis predicts that coefficients in the Function × ATG column are positive and statistically significant, whereas the coefficients in the Function × CCTB column are negative and statistically significant. Alternatively, the special case of functional divergence predicts that the Function × ATG interactions are positive and statistically significant, whereas the Function × CCTB interactions are near zero and nonsignificant. Functional consensus is indicated by nonsignificant, near-zero coefficients in both columns.

Table 12.3 shows that the regression coefficient for expressives' ATG scores was significantly greater than the coefficient for evaluatives' ATG scores for three outcome variables, all of them from the 1992 wave of data collection: feelings toward a homosexual man with AIDS, coercion and blame, and attitudes toward mandatory testing. The PRE associated with each of these interaction terms was greater than 2%, which indicates substantial improvement in the equation's explanatory power as a result of including the interaction term. In contrast, the differences for attitudes toward contact with PWAs were not significantly different at either wave. In light of the patterns in Table 12.2, we interpreted this finding as indicating functional consensus concerning personal interactions with PWAs.

For the remaining attitude measures—Wave 1 feelings toward a generic PWA and Wave 1 coercion and blame—Table 12.3 shows that the differences between expressives and evaluatives were not significant. However, because the Function × ATG coefficients for the Wave 2 counterparts to these variables were significant—along with the fact that the Table 12.2 patterns of explained variance are consistent with one of the functional divergence patterns—it is possible that the differences between expressives and evaluatives might have reached statistical significance with a larger sample.

In summary, the results were consistent with one of the patterns of functional divergence for measures of negative affect toward PWAs, coercion and blame, and support for mandatory testing. Attitudes toward interacting with PWAs, in contrast, were predicted mainly by transmission beliefs for expressives and evaluatives alike, a pattern that suggests functional consensus. The stability of these patterns was subsequently assessed in another national survey with a larger sample and somewhat refined measurement methods.

The 1997 Survey

The findings from the 1991 and 1992 surveys were limited in important respects. Although a national probability sample was used, the total number of respondents may not have been sufficient to overcome the problem of Type II error, which is common in moderated regression analyses with nonexperimental data (McClelland & Judd, 1993). As previously noted, a larger sample would have increased the statistical power of the analyses. In addition, the assessment of attitude functions was accomplished with only two expressive items and one evaluative item. The use of additional items would probably increase the accuracy of the analyses. These issues were subsequently addressed in a national survey completed in 1997.

Method

Sampling and Procedures. Following procedures similar to those employed in the earlier surveys, interviews were conducted by the staff of the Survey Research Center at the University of California at Berkeley between July 1996 and June 1997, using their CATI system. The median duration of the interview was 44 minutes.

As in the previous study, respondents were drawn from the universe of all English-speaking adults (at least 18 years of age) residing in households with telephones within the 48 contiguous states. Ten-digit telephone numbers were generated using list-assisted RDD (Casady & Lepkowski, 1993). This method resulted in 2,009 household phone numbers (56% of the 3,603 numbers initially generated by the procedure). Of these, interviews were completed with 1,309 (1,246 totally completed and 63 partially completed), yielding a final response rate of 65%. This sample was 45% male and 55% female. Described racially and ethnically, it was 79% White, 11% Black, 5% Hispanic, 2% Asian, and 1% Native American. The mean age was 44 years (SD = 16), the median annual household income was between $40,000 and $50,000, and the median level of educational attainment was some college or postsecondary technical school. Two thirds of respondents (68%) were currently employed.

An additional oversample of 403 individuals who described their own race or ethnicity as Black or African American was also recruited. Telephone numbers for the oversample were generated using the same RDD procedure, but were then cross-referenced with another list that identified telephone prefixes linked to census tracts with at least 15% Black households. This method yielded 3,230 telephone numbers, from which 638 (19.8%) were determined to be eligible household phone numbers. Interviews were completed with 403 (369 totally completed, 34 partially completed), for a response rate of 63%. The oversample was 40% male and 60% female, with a mean age of 41 years (SD = 14), a median household income between $20,000 and $30,000, and a median educational level of high school graduate. Nearly two thirds of respondents (63%) were currently employed.

The original purpose of oversampling Blacks in the survey was to permit more finely detailed statistical comparisons of response patterns across race (e.g., Herek & Capitanio, 1993, 1994, 1995). However, such comparisons are beyond the scope of the present chapter. For the analyses presented here, therefore, responses from the oversample were combined with those from the main sample. Cases were poststratified by sex and race to correspond to the U.S. adult population, based on U.S. census data.

Measures. The survey included most of the same items as the previous instrument to permit comparison across surveys. New items were added to assess additional facets of instrumental and symbolic stigma (Table 12.4). For instrumental stigma, in addition to the *personal worry* item, questions were included to assess the prominence of concerns about the *financial impact* of AIDS, the epidemic's impact on general *quality of*

TABLE 12.4

Items for Assessing Attitude Functions Associated With AIDS Stigma, 1997 Survey

"People's opinions about AIDS can be influenced by many different things. As I read each one of the following, please tell me how much it has influenced your own opinions about AIDS."

Evaluative Functions

1. How about the fact that you are [*very worried/somewhat worried/not too worried/not at all worried*] about getting AIDS or becoming infected with the AIDS virus? How much has that influenced your opinions about AIDS—a great deal, some, very little, or not at all?

2. How about the fact that you generally think of AIDS as affecting people [*in your own circle of family and friends/outside your own circle*]? (How much has that influenced your opinions about AIDS?)

3. How about the fact that you think it's [*very/somewhat/not too/not at all*] likely that the AIDS epidemic will affect you financially through higher taxes or health care costs? (How much has that influenced your opinions about AIDS?)

4. How about the fact that you think it's [*very/somewhat/not too/not at all*] likely that the AIDS epidemic will affect the general quality of your life in other ways? (How much has that influenced your opinions about AIDS?)

Expressive Functions

5. How about your political values? (How much have they influenced your opinions about AIDS—a great deal, some, very little, or not at all?)

6. How about your religious beliefs? (How much have they influenced your opinions about AIDS?)

7. How about your personal values about right and wrong? (How much have they influenced your opinions about AIDS?)

Note. Wording in brackets was inserted based on respondent's responses to related items administered earlier in the interview. Before item 1, for example, respondents were asked, "How worried are you about getting AIDS or becoming infected with the AIDS virus yourself? Would you say you are very worried, somewhat worried, not too worried, or not at all worried that you will get AIDS?" Responses to this item were inserted as indicated for item 1.

life, and the respondent's belief about whether the AIDS epidemic was likely to affect her or his *own social circle*. For symbolic stigma, the earlier *religious* item was separated into two items, one about religious influences and the other about the influence of personal values of *right and wrong*. The *political* item was retained.

The 1997 survey included the same sets of items to assess specific AIDS attitudes as in the previous surveys. These included three items related to coercion and blame (support for quarantine, support for public labeling of PWAs, blame for PWAs); attitudes toward interacting with PWAs (at a school, in the workplace, at a neighborhood grocery store); negative feelings (anger, disgust, fear) toward PWAs as a group;[3] and support for mandatory testing of certain groups (immigrants, "people at risk for getting AIDS"). In contrast to the previous surveys, the items concerning mandatory testing were not highly correlated and consequently could not be combined in a meaningful index. They are presented separately in the following.

Once again, respondents' attitudes toward gay men and beliefs about HIV transmission through casual contact were used as, respectively, symbolic and instrumental independent variables. In addition, a three-item index of attitudes toward injecting drug users (IDUs) was included in the survey as a possible alternative symbolic variable.[4]

Results

Functional Categorization. In preliminary analyses, I evaluated two different functional classification strategies. First, I replicated the classification procedure from the 1991 survey, described above. This categorization utilized only the function items that had been included in the 1991 survey (*personal worry, religious,* and *political*). Next, I classified respondents with an alternate method, which used the same general procedure but added the new function items (*financial impact, quality of life, own social circle,* and *right and wrong*).

The two methods produced an interesting difference in the distribution of domain level functions. The first method resulted in a pattern quite

---

[3]Feelings were assessed toward PWAs in general (as in the 1991 survey), rather than toward a homosexual man with AIDS (as in the 1992 survey).

[4]The scale consisted of three items, modeled after the ATG: "Injecting illegal drugs is just plain wrong," "I think people who inject illegal drugs are disgusting," and "People who inject illegal drugs are a threat to society" ($\alpha = .67$). Higher scores indicate more negative attitudes toward IDUs.

similar to that obtained in the 1991 survey. A substantial plurality (44%) manifested AIDS attitudes that served primarily an expressive function (compared to 49% in the previous survey). Another 27% (vs. 30% in the earlier survey) manifested a mix of expressive and evaluative functions, and only 14% (vs. 13% earlier) manifested primarily an evaluative function.

With the additional items permitting a richer operationalization, however, the alternate categorization method yielded a pattern in which a plurality (39%) manifested attitudes that serve multiple functions, with roughly comparable minorities manifesting expressive or evaluative functions (30% and 22%, respectively). For the analyses presented in what follows, I used the latter method (i.e., with the additional items) for categorizing respondents according to attitude function.

Predictors of AIDS Stigma: Regression Analyses Within Function Groups.   As before, I computed a series of regression equations to assess the extent to which the variance in different components of AIDS stigma was predicted for the evaluatives and expressives by a variable relevant to assessment of personal risk (i.e., knowledge about HIV transmission through various forms of casual contact) and a variable relevant to the symbolic aspects of AIDS stigma. For the latter, I conducted separate analyses using ATG scores and IDU attitude scores as symbolic independent variables. In most cases, the measure of attitudes toward gay men explained at least as much variance as the measure of IDU attitudes, and the patterns of results were highly similar for the two variables. Therefore, except in the one analysis in which IDU attitudes yielded noticeably different results (discussed later), I report results with ATG scores as the symbolic independent variable. As in the previous survey, all respondents included in the analysis were self-described heterosexuals who did not report that they were HIV positive. Cases with missing data were excluded from the analysis.

Table 12.5 displays the results of the separate regression analyses. Although the magnitudes of the values are somewhat different from those presented in Table 12.2, the relative predictive power of the variables was fairly consistent with those in the previous survey. As would be expected from the larger sample in the 1997 survey, variables that explained even relatively small proportions of variance were statistically significant.

The patterns of functional consensus and divergence were quite similar to those observed in the 1991 survey, which suggests that there exists a

TABLE 12.5

Percentage of Variance (R^2) in AIDS Stigma Explained by Symbolic and Instrumental Variables for Each Function Group (1997 Survey)

	Function Group				Function Ratios	
	Evaluative		Expressive			
Dependent Variable	ATG	CCTB	ATG	CCTB	VFR	XFR
Coercion and blame	3.3***	7.7***	13.7***	13.8***	1.39	1.66
Interacting with PWA	3.5***	6.1***	6.6***	13.5***	0.95	0.90
Negative feelings scale	2.6**	8.8***	13.2***	6.7***	2.29	2.91
Mandatory testing: Immigrants	3.5***	9.9***	2.5**	1.2*	2.28	2.59
Mandatory testing: "At risk" groups	2.9**	4.7***	4.8***	0.8*	4.33	2.25

Note. *$p < .05$, **$p < .01$, ***$p < .001$; $n = 311$ for evaluatives, 416 for expressives; ATG = attitudes toward gay men (symbolic variable); CCTB = casual contact transmission beliefs (instrumental variable); VFR = evaluative function ratio; XFR = expressive function ratio.

fair amount of stability in the social construction of attitudes toward specific aspects of AIDS. The measures of negative feelings and support for different types of mandatory testing generally corresponded to the pattern for simple divergence, whereas the measure of coercion and blame appeared to correspond to the special case of functional divergence. Attitudes toward contact with PWAs again matched the pattern for instrumental functional consensus.

Table 12.6 shows that the regression coefficient for expressives' ATG scores was significantly greater than the coefficient for evaluatives' ATG scores for negative feelings toward PWAs, coercion and blame, and support for mandatory testing of immigrants. The PRE associated with each of these interaction terms was relatively low, ranging from 0.5% to 1.4%, which indicates small-to-moderate improvement in the equation's explanatory power as a result of including the interaction term.

As shown in Table 12.6, the interaction terms associated with the item concerning mandatory testing of "at risk" groups were not significant. This analysis, however, was the only one in which use of IDU attitudes as the symbolic variable (rather than ATG scores) yielded substantially different results. With IDU attitudes in the moderated regression analysis, the IDU × Function interaction term was statistically significant ($b = 0.129$, $p < .001$, PRE = 0.017). IDU attitudes accounted for 11.1% of the variance in expressives' attitudes about testing people at risk, but only

TABLE 12.6

Results Of Moderated Regression Analysis for Expressive
and Evaluative Variables, 1997 Survey

	Interaction Term			
	Function × ATG		Function × CCTB	
Dependent Variable	b	PRE	b	PRE
Negative feelings				
scale	0.148***	0.014	−0.018	0.000
Interacting with PWA	0.014	0.001	0.019	0.002
Coercion and blame	0.132**	0.009	0.039	0.001
Mandatory testing:				
Immigrants	0.051*	0.005	−0.014	0.001
Mandatory testing:				
"At risk" groups	0.019	0.001	−0.041	0.004

Note. * $p < .05$, ** $p < .01$, *** $p < .001$; $n = 311$ for evaluatives, 416 for expressives; n.s. = not significant $(p > .05)$; PRE = proportional reduction in error (squared partial correlation); ATG = attitudes toward gay men (symbolic variable); CCTB = casual contact transmission beliefs (instrumental variable).

1.8% of the variance in evaluatives' attitudes. With the IDU variable, VFR = 5.18 and XFR = 4.05. Thus, attitudes toward mandatory testing of people at high risk for AIDS reflected functional divergence, but the key symbolic variable appears to have been attitudes toward injecting drug users rather than attitudes toward gay men.

DISCUSSION AND CONCLUSIONS

Work in the functional tradition has been dominated by an emphasis on personality characteristics, the use of indirect measures of attitude functions, and a nearly exclusive reliance on experimental attitude-change studies as a method for validation. In this chapter, I have tried to offer some alternative perspectives. Like Shavitt (1989, 1990), I have argued for the importance of considering the role of attitude objects and domains in the functional process. My analysis differs from hers somewhat in my emphasis on the meanings that come to be associated with attitude domains as a result of their social construction. Conceptualizing attitude objects as socially constructed highlights the importance of grounding an attitude domain within a specific social group, evaluating the extent to which patterns observed in that group can be reliably generalized to a larger population (see, e.g., Sudman, 1976), and explicitly recognizing the ways in which one group's social construction of an object might differ from that of others. Specific constructions are influenced by a host of factors, ranging from the importance and salience of the attitude object to the group, to group members' developmental stage in the life span, to the group's location on various continua related to broad cultural syndromes (see generally Alwin & Krosnick, 1991; Krosnick & Abelson, 1992; Sears, 1986; Triandis, 1996). Understanding the historical, cultural, and situational contexts in which data about attitude functions are collected is likely to enrich our interpretation of data and our theorizing.

In contrast to much recent empirical work in this area, I have argued for the importance of direct assessment of functions. Direct assessment should be regarded not as a competitor to indirect methods, but as a complement. Whereas indirect measures, such as the self-monitoring scale and the approach utilized in studies of instrumental and symbolic attitudes, have the advantage of helping functional researchers to link their observations with a broader body of knowledge about personality characteristics and political attitudes, direct measures permit an understanding of the functions served by attitudes within a specific domain. As previously noted, the same functions may not always be served by an individual's attitudes across domains. With direct measures, intraindividual differences in attitude functions can be studied. Such differences provide important insights into influences on behavior apart from personality and dispositional factors. These include situational, social, and cultural variables.

I have also suggested that in a particular population, attitude domains and their component objects can be socially constructed in a manner that elicits one or many functions. This notion, although not yet extensively studied, is not new (Shavitt, 1989, 1990; see also Herek, 1986). I hope, however, that the present chapter's conceptualization and operationalization of functional consensus and divergence helps to extend thinking in this area. A few of this chapter's empirical findings about consensus and divergence warrant brief comment here.

First, the importance of creating operational definitions of multiple facets of attitude functions is clear. Use of only three items (*personal worry, religious, political*) to classify respondents according to function resulted in quite similar proportions of evaluatives and expressives across the 1991 and 1997 surveys. When additional functional items were used in the 1997 survey, however, the proportion of evaluatives increased by roughly one half and the proportion of expressives dropped from 44% to 30%. This difference resulted mainly from previously unclassified respondents being recategorized as evaluative and from previously expressive respondents being reclassified as respondents having attitudes that served both functions. Fewer than 1% of respondents were reclassified from expressive to evaluative when the larger number of instrumental items was used; none were reclassified in the opposite direction. Thus, assessment of more facets of each type of function is likely to result in a more thorough (and presumably more accurate) categorization of respondents.

Second, the data supported the assumption that domain level functions are likely to hold for attitudes toward most of the specific objects that comprise the domain, at least in the AIDS domain. Response distributions for the AFI items suggested that AIDS attitudes were functionally divergent (especially in the 1997 survey, which included more functional items). Attitudes toward specific aspects of AIDS were similarly divergent, with the exception of attitudes toward interacting with PWAs. In this regard, the findings were quite consistent across the surveys, which suggests that the functional dynamics of AIDS-related attitudes in the United States have been fairly stable during the 1990s.

The finding about attitudes toward personal contact with a PWA appears to contradict the results reported by Pryor et al. (1989), which indicated a strong symbolic component to such attitudes. This inconsistency, however, may point to a difference between direct and indirect measurement strategies. Pryor et al. used an indirect method to assess functions, in contrast to the direct method employed with the present data set. When the present data were reanalyzed using regression analyses similar to those of Pryor's group (i.e., with attitudes toward gay men and beliefs about casual contact used to predict AIDS attitudes, but with no direct measure of attitude function included), both independent variables explained significant and unique portions of the variance; however, the instrumental variable (casual contact beliefs) explained considerably more variance (e.g., See Herek & Capitanio, 1997, Tables 2 and 6).[5]

One important implication of the distinction between consensus and divergence is that when everyone's attitudes toward a particular object

---

[5]Pryor et al. (1989) reported only the standardized regression coefficients (beta weights) for their analysis, so it was not possible to compare the amount of variance explained by each variable across studies. Even if they had reported additional regression data, however, comparisons between their study and the surveys described here would be problematic because of differences in the samples and measures, and the fact that Pryor and his colleagues collected their data several years earlier in the epidemic.

consistently serve one function, the functional approach may not be particularly useful in understanding or changing those attitudes. Rather, the principal utility of the functional approach lies in the insights it offers into attitudes that serve two or more functions in a particular population. Thus, the distinction between functional consensus and divergence can help to identify which attitude objects are most amenable to a functional analysis. Historically, the functional approach has been portrayed as applicable to all attitude domains. However, functionalism might be relevant principally to attitude objects that evoke functional divergence. That same subset of objects might also provide the most appropriate domains for a functional approach to attitude change, that is, one that stresses the importance of formulating different persuasive messages to appeal to attitudes with different functions.

What advice can this functional analysis offer to AIDS educators and those who seek to reduce AIDS stigma in the United States? A detailed discussion of the practical implications of the present research program is beyond the scope of this chapter, but a few observations can be made. First, the fact that the AIDS-related attitudes of more than two-thirds of the public serve expressive functions (primarily, or in combination with evaluative functions) points to the importance of direct confrontation of the symbolic linkages of AIDS to key social groups. To a great extent, the primary symbolic group continues to be the gay community. This is somewhat surprising because the proportion of new AIDS cases linked to male–male sexual activity has dropped considerably in recent years. In 1997, for example, only 35% of new AIDS cases in the United States were diagnosed among men who reported sex with other men, with another 4% among men who reported both homosexual sex and injecting drug use (Centers for Disease Control and Prevention, 1998). At the same time, injecting drug users are also strongly linked to symbolic AIDS attitudes. Indeed, public support for mandatory testing of people assumed to be at risk for AIDS appears to be more strongly linked to hostility toward injecting drug users than to hostility toward gay men.

Thus, efforts to reduce AIDS stigma must simultaneously strive to disentangle public reactions to AIDS from attitudes toward homosexuality and injecting drug use, while directly confronting societal hostility toward gay men and injecting drug users. The former task is complicated by the willingness of some groups in society to exploit popular fears and misconceptions about AIDS for political gain (e.g., Bailey, 1995). The latter task is made difficult by the fact that attitudes toward gay men and toward injecting drug users are clearly quite different from each other, and confronting them will require different strategies (for more general discussions, see Capitanio & Herek, 1999; Herek, 1991, 1992, 1994; Herek & Capitanio, 1995, 1996, 1999).

Second, almost as many adults in the United States have AIDS attitudes that serve an evaluative function as an expressive function (primarily, or in combination). These attitudes are motivated mainly by individuals' judgments about whether they are likely to become infected, or whether AIDS will affect people in their immediate social circle (25% and 23%, respectively, reported that their AIDS attitudes were influenced "a great deal" by these beliefs). As demonstrated here, when AIDS attitudes serve an evaluative function, they are shaped to a large extent by an individual's beliefs about how HIV is transmitted. Thus, AIDS educational programs must teach the public about the ways that HIV can and cannot be transmitted. The continuing need for this type of basic information is dramatized by the fact that substantial proportions of respondents to the 1997 survey—in some cases more than half—overestimated the risks of HIV infection through various types of casual social contact. Indeed, the proportion of the public harboring misinformation about HIV transmission appeared to increase from the 1991 survey (Herek & Capitanio, 1998b).

Finally, the fact that attitudes toward AIDS policies and general affective responses to PWAs are functionally divergent suggests that interventions seeking to affect these attitudes will be differentially effective depending on the dominant function served by the recipients' attitudes. Whether an intervention should focus primarily on symbolic or instrumental aspects of AIDS stigma will depend on its intended targets. Messages in these areas should be tailored to the intervention's audience. Attempts to break down reluctance to personal interaction with a PWA, in contrast, probably need to confront personal fears about contagion, regardless of the function served by the recipients' other AIDS attitudes.

ACKNOWLEDGMENTS

Preparation of this chapter was supported by grants from the National Institute of Mental Health (R01-MH55468 and K02-MH01455). I thank John Capitanio for his invaluable suggestions and advice for this chapter and throughout the survey projects, and Karen Garrett and Tom Piazza of the Survey Research Center, University of California, Berkeley.

REFERENCES

Abelson, R. P. (1988). Conviction. *American Psychologist, 43*, 267–275.

Abelson, R. P., & Prentice, D. A. (1989). Beliefs as possessions: A functional perspective. In A. Pratkanis, S. Breckler, & A. Greenwald (Eds.), *Attitude structure and function* (pp. 361–381). Hillsdale, NJ: Lawrence Erlbaum Associates.

Alwin, D. F., & Krosnick, J. A. (1991). Aging, cohorts, and the stability of sociopolitical orientations over the life span. *American Journal of Sociology, 97*, 169–195.

Anderson, D. S., & Kristiansen, C. (1990). Measuring attitude functions. *Journal of Social Psychology, 130*, 419–421.

Bailey, W. A. (1995). The importance of HIV prevention programming to the lesbian and gay community. In G. M. Herek & B. Greene (Eds.), *AIDS, identity, and community: The HIV epidemic and lesbians and gay men* (pp. 210–225). Thousand Oaks, CA: Sage.

Bazzini, D. G., & Shaffer, D. R. (1995). Investigating the social-adjustive and value-expressive functions of well-grounded attitudes: Implications for change and for subsequent behavior. *Motivation & Emotion, 19*, 279–305.

Berger, P. L., & Luckman, T. (1966). *The social construction of reality.* New York: Doubleday.

Bishop, G. D., Alva, A. L., Cantu, L., & Rittiman, T. K. (1991). Responses to persons with AIDS: Fear of contagion or stigma? *Journal of Applied Social Psychology, 21*, 1877–1888.

Bobo, L. (1983). Whites' opposition to busing: Symbolic racism or realistic group conflict? *Journal of Personality and Social Psychology, 45*, 1196–1210.

Brandyberry, L. J., & MacNair, R. R. (1996). The content and function of attitudes toward AIDS. *Journal of College Student Development, 37*, 335–346.

Capitanio, J. P., & Herek, G. M. (1999). AIDS-related stigma and attitudes toward injecting drug users among Black and White Americans. *American Behavioral Scientist, 42*, 1144–1157.

Casady, R. J., & Lepkowski, J. M. (1993). Stratified telephone survey designs. *Survey Methodology, 19*, 103–113.

Centers for Disease Control and Prevention. (1998). *HIV/AIDS Surveillance Report, 9* (2), 1–43.

DeBono, K. G. (1987). Investigating the social-adjustive and value-expressive functions of attitudes: Implications for persuasion processes. *Journal of Personality and Social Psychology, 52*, 279–287.

DeBono, K. G., & Harnish, R. J. (1988). Source expertise, source attractiveness, and the processing of persuasive information: A functional perspective. *Journal of Personality and Social Psychology, 55*, 541–546.

DeBono, K. G., & Snyder, M. (1989). Understanding consumer decision-making processes: The role of form and function in product evaluation. *Journal of Applied Social Psychology, 19*, 416–424.

DeBono, K. G., & Telesca, C. (1990). The influence of source physical attractiveness on advertising effectiveness: A functional perspective. *Journal of Applied Social Psychology, 20*, 1383–1395.

Gastil, J. (1992). Why we believe in democracy: Testing theories of attitude functions and democracy. *Journal of Applied Social Psychology, 22*, 423–450.

Gergen, K. J. (1985). The social constructionist movement in modern psychology. *American Psychologist, 40*, 266–275.

Herek, G. M. (1986). The instrumentality of attitudes: Toward a neofunctional theory. *Journal of Social Issues, 42*(2), 99–114.

Herek, G. M. (1987). Can functions be measured? A new perspective on the functional approach to attitudes. *Social Psychology Quarterly, 50*, 285–303.

Herek, G. M. (1990). Illness, stigma, and AIDS. In P. T. Costa, Jr., & G. R. VandenBos (Eds.), *Psychological aspects of serious illness: Chronic conditions, fatal diseases, and clinical care* (pp. 103–150). Washington, DC: American Psychological Association.

Herek, G. M. (1991). Stigma, prejudice, and violence against lesbians and gay men. In J. C. Gonsiorek, & J. D. Weinrich (Eds.), *Homosexuality: Research implications for public policy* (pp. 60–80). Thousand Oaks, CA: Sage.

Herek, G. M. (1992). Psychological heterosexism and anti-gay violence: The social psychology of bigotry and bashing. In G. M. Herek & K. T. Berrill (Eds.), *Hate crimes: Confronting violence against lesbians and gay men* (pp. 149–169). Thousand Oaks, CA: Sage.

Herek, G. M. (1994). Assessing attitudes toward lesbians and gay men: A review of empirical research with the ATLG scale. In B. Greene & G. M. Herek (Eds.) *Lesbian and gay psychology: Theory, research, and clinical applications* (pp. 206–228). Newbury Park, CA: Sage.

Herek, G. M. (1997). The HIV epidemic and public attitudes toward lesbians and gay men. In M. P. Levine, P. Nardi, & J. Gagnon (Eds.), *In changing times: Gay men and lesbians encounter HIV/AIDS* (pp. 191–218). Chicago: University of Chicago Press.

Herek, G. M. (1999). AIDS and stigma. *American Behavioral Scientist, 42,* 1102–1112.

Herek, G. M., & Capitanio, J. P. (1993). Public reactions to AIDS in the United States: A second decade of stigma. *American Journal of Public Health, 83,* 574–577.

Herek, G. M., & Capitanio, J. P. (1994). Conspiracies, contagion, and compassion: Trust and public reactions to AIDS. *AIDS Education and Prevention, 6,* 367–377.

Herek, G. M., & Capitanio, J. P. (1995). Black heterosexuals' attitudes toward lesbians and gay men in the United States. *The Journal of Sex Research, 32,* 95–105.

Herek, G. M., & Capitanio, J. P. (1996). "Some of my best friends": Intergroup contact, concealable stigma, and heterosexuals' attitudes toward gay men and lesbians. *Personality and Social Psychology Bulletin, 22,* 412–424.

Herek, G. M., & Capitanio, J. P. (1997). AIDS stigma and contact with persons with AIDS: The effects of personal and vicarious contact. *Journal of Applied Social Psychology, 27,* 1–36.

Herek, G. M., & Capitanio, J. P. (1998a). Symbolic prejudice or fear of infection? A functional analysis of AIDS-related stigma among heterosexual adults. *Basic and Applied Social Psychology, 20,* 230–241.

Herek, G. M., & Capitanio, J. P. (1998b). AIDS stigma and HIV-related beliefs in the United States: Results from a national telephone survey. *Conference record of the 12th World AIDS Conference.* Geneva, Switzerland.

Herek, G. M., & Capitanio, J. P. (1999). AIDS stigma and sexual prejudice. *American Behavioral Scientist, 42,* 1126–1143.

Herek, G. M., & Glunt, E. K. (1988). An epidemic of stigma: Public reactions to AIDS. *American Psychologist, 43,* 886–891.

Herek, G. M., & Glunt, E. K. (1993). Public attitudes toward AIDS-related issues in the United States. In J. B. Pryor & G. D. Reeder (Eds.), *The social psychology of HIV infection* (pp. 229–261). Hillsdale, NJ: Lawrence Erlbaum Associates.

Herek, G. M., Mitnick, L., Burris, S., Chesney, M., Devine, P., Fullilove, M. T., Fullilove, R., Gunther, H. C., Levi, J., Michaels, S., Novick, A., Pryor, J., Snyder, M., & Sweeney, T. (1998). AIDS and stigma: A conceptual framework and research agenda. *AIDS & Public Policy Journal, 13*(1), 36–47.

Hooper, M. (1983). The motivational bases of political behavior: A new concept and measurement procedure. *Public Opinion Quarterly, 47,* 497–515.

Jelen, T. G., & Wilcox, C. (1992). Symbolic and instrumental values as predictors of AIDS policies. *Social Science Quarterly, 73,* 736–749.

Katz, D. (1960). The functional approach to the study of attitudes. *Public Opinion Quarterly, 24,* 163–204.

Katz, D. (1968). Consistency for what? The functional approach. In R. P. Abelson et al. (Eds.), *Theories of cognitive consistency: A sourcebook* . Chicago: Rand–McNally.

Katz, D., McClintock, C., & Sarnoff, I. (1957). The measurement of ego defense as related to attitude change. *Journal of Personality, 25,* 465–474.

Katz, D., Sarnoff, I., & McClintock, C. (1956). Ego defense and attitude change. *Human Relations, 9,* 27–45.

Katz, D., & Stotland, E. (1959). A preliminary statement to a theory of attitude structure and change. In S. Koch (Ed.), *Psychology: A study of a science* (Vol. 3, pp. 423–475). New York: McGraw-Hill.

Kinder, D. R. (1986). The continuing American dilemma: White resistance to racial change 40 years after Myrdal. *Journal of Social Issues, 42* (2), 151–171.

Kinder, D. R., & Sears, D. O. (1981). Prejudice and politics: Symbolic racism versus racial threats to the good life. *Journal of Personality and Social Psychology, 40,* 414–431.

Krosnick, J. A., & Abelson, R. P. (1992). The case for measuring attitude strength in surveys. In J. M. Tanur (Ed.), *Questions about questions: Inquiries into the cognitive bases of surveys* (pp. 177–203). New York: Russell Sage Foundation.

Lutz, R. J. (1981). A reconceptualization of the functional approach to attitudes. *Research in Marketing, 5,* 165–210.

Maio, G. R., & Olson, J. M. (1994). Value–attitude–behaviour relations: The moderating role of attitude functions. *British Journal of Social Psychology, 33,* 301–312.

Maio, G. R., & Olson, J. M. (1995). Relations between values, attitudes, and behavioral intentions: The moderating role of attitude function. *Journal of Experimental Social Psychology, 31,* 266–285.

Mann, J., Tarantola, D., & Netter, T. (Eds.). (1992). *AIDS in the world.* Cambridge, MA: Harvard University Press.

McClelland, G. H., & Judd, C. M. (1993). Statistical difficulties of detecting interactions and moderator effects. *Psychological Bulletin, 114,* 376–390.

McClintock, C. G. (1958). Personality syndromes and attitude change. *Journal of Personality, 26,* 479–493.

McGuire, W. J. (1985). Attitudes and attitude change. In G. Lindzey, & E. Aronson (Eds.), *Handbook of social psychology* (3rd ed., pp. 233–346). New York: Random House.

Omoto, A., & Crain, A. L. (1995). AIDS volunteerism: Lesbian and gay community-based responses to HIV. In G. M. Herek & B. Greene (Eds.), *AIDS, identity, and community: The HIV epidemic and lesbians and gay men* (Vol. 2, pp. 187–209). Thousand Oaks, CA: Sage.

Peak, H. (1960). The effect of aroused motivation on attitudes. *Journal of Abnormal and Social Psychology, 61,* 463–468.

Petty, R. E., & Wegener, D. T. (1998). Matching versus mismatching attitude functions: Implications for scrutiny of persuasive messages. *Personality and Social Psychology Bulletin, 24,* 227–240.

Pratkanis, A. R., & Greenwald, A. G. (1989). A sociocognitive model of attitude structure and function. In L. Berkowitz (Ed.), *Advances in experimental social psychology* (Vol. 22, pp. 245–285). San Diego, CA: Academic Press.

Prentice, D. A. (1987). Psychological correspondence of possessions, attitudes, and values. *Journal of Personality and Social Psychology, 53,* 993–1003.

Pryor, J. B., & Reeder, G. D. (1993). Collective and individual representations of HIV/AIDS stigma. In J. B. Pryor & G. Reeder (Eds.), *The social psychology of HIV infection* (pp. 263–286). Hillsdale, NJ: Lawrence Erlbaum Associates.

Pryor, J. B., Reeder, G. D., & McManus, J. (1991). Fear and loathing in the workplace: Reactions to AIDS-infected co-workers. *Personality and Social Psychology Bulletin, 17,* 133–139.

Pryor, J. B., Reeder, G. D., Vinacco, R., & Kott, T. L. (1989). The instrumental and symbolic functions of attitudes toward persons with AIDS. *Journal of Applied Social Psychology, 19,* 377–404.

Sarnoff, I., & Katz, D. (1954). The motivational bases of attitude change. *Journal of Abnormal and Social Psychology, 49,* 115–124.

Schneider, A. L., Snyder-Joy, Z., & Hopper, M. (1993). Rational and symbolic models of attitudes toward AIDS policy. *Social Science Quarterly, 74,* 349–366.

Sears, D. O. (1986). College sophomores in the laboratory: Influences of a narrow data base on social psychology's view of human nature. *Journal of Personality and Social Psychology, 51,* 515–530.

Sears, D. O. (1993). Symbolic politics: A socio-psychological theory. In S. Iyengar & W. J. McGuire (Eds.), *Explorations in political psychology* (pp. 113–149). Durham, NC: Duke University Press.

Shavitt, S. (1989). Operationalizing functional theories of attitude. In A.R. Pratkanis, S. Breckler, & A. Greenwald (Eds.), *Attitude structure and function* (pp. 311–337). Hillsdale, NJ: Lawrence Erlbaum Associates.

Shavitt, S. (1990). The role of attitude objects in attitude functions. *Journal of Experimental Social Psychology, 26*, 124–148.

Smith, M. B. (1947). The personal setting of public opinions: A study of attitudes toward Russia. *Public Opinion Quarterly, 11*, 507–523.

Smith, M. B. (1973). Political attitudes. In J. N. Knutson (Ed.), *Handbook of political psychology* (pp. 57–82). San Francisco: Jossey-Bass.

Smith, M. B., Bruner, J. S., & White, R. W. (1956). *Opinions and personality.* New York: Wiley.

Sniderman, P. M., & Tetlock, P. E. (1986). Symbolic racism: Problems of motive attribution in political analysis. *Journal of Social Issues, 42*(2), 129–150.

Snyder, M., & DeBono, K. G. (1985). Appeals to image and claims about quality: Understanding the psychology of advertising. *Journal of Personality and Social Psychology, 49*, 586–597.

Snyder, M., & DeBono, K. G. (1987). A functional approach to attitudes and persuasion. In M. P. Zanna, J. M. Olson, & C. P. Herman (Eds.), *Social influence: The Ontario symposium* (Vol. 5, pp. 107–125). Hillsdale, NJ: Lawrence Erlbaum Associates.

Snyder, M., & DeBono, K.G. (1989). Understanding the functions of attitudes: Lessons from personality and social behavior. In A. Pratkanis, S. Breckler, & A. Greenwald (Eds.), *Attitude structure and function* (pp. 339–359). Hillsdale, NJ: Lawrence Erlbaum Associates.

Sudman, S. (1976). *Applied sampling.* New York: Academic Press.

Triandis, H. C. (1996). The psychological measurement of cultural syndromes. *American Psychologist, 51*, 407–415.

Wyman, M. A., & Snyder, M. (1997). Attitudes toward "gays in the military": A functional perspective. *Journal of Applied Social Psychology, 274*, 306–329.

13

The Functional Approach to Volunteerism

Mark Snyder
University of Minnesota

E. Gil Clary
College of St. Catherine

Arthur A. Stukas
University of Pittsburgh

Every year, millions of people volunteer substantial amounts of their time and energy to helping others in a committed and long-term way. Among other services, volunteers provide companionship to the lonely, tutoring to the illiterate, counseling to the troubled, and health care to the sick. The efforts of volunteers can be seen in activities as diverse as participating in a walk-a-thon, working weekends at a soup kitchen, and organizing a neighborhood group to help those in need. According to one estimate, 89.2 million adults in the United States engaged in some form of volunteerism during 1993, with 23.6 million of them giving 5 or more hours per week to their volunteer service, often doing so for periods of months and years at a time (Independent Sector, 1994). Moreover, volunteerism is not simply a phenomenon of the United States; in fact, it is an activity that can be found in many other parts of the world (Curtis, Grabb, & Baer, 1992).

A moment's reflection on volunteerism—with its effortful, sustained, and nonremunerative nature—raises a host of questions. Why do people decide to engage in helpful activities as volunteers? How do they choose one form of volunteer helping rather than another? What determines whether their experiences as volunteers are satisfying and whether they are effective as volunteers? And why do some people continue, for months and perhaps even years, to serve as volunteers? In efforts to understand the psychology of volunteerism, these questions can be regarded as variations on a more basic theme: What personal and social needs and goals, plans, and motives are served by individuals' involvement in sustained, planful action, in this case the sustained, planful helpfulness that is volunteerism? Answers to these questions have been provided by the application of functionalist theorizing and functionalist strategies of inquiry, which have sought to identify the psychological functions served by engaging in volunteerism, and to document the ways in which these psychological functions manifest themselves in the ongoing processes of volunteerism, influencing people's decisions to initiate volunteer activity, their satisfaction with their volunteer efforts, and their intentions to stay active and committed as volunteer helpers over extended periods of time.

In this chapter, we discuss the conceptual foundations of the functional approach to volunteerism, empirical investigations of the functions served by volunteerism, and linkages between functionalist theorizing in the domain of voluntary helping and in other attitudinal and behavioral domains. These considerations form something of a two-way street, with a functional approach contributing to an understanding of volunteerism as a form of sustained prosocial action and with this emerging understanding of the psychology of volunteerism contributing to the articulation of functionalist theorizing itself. Therefore, we first review theoretical and empirical research on the functional approach to volunteerism. Then, we explore some of the contributions of the functional approach to volunteerism to an understanding of the functional approach as a general perspective on human attitudes and behavior.

BACKGROUND AND RATIONALE
FOR A FUNCTIONAL APPROACH TO VOLUNTEERISM

In recent years, both the need for volunteerism and the profile of volunteerism have risen in the United States, in part due to action taken at the national level. For example, recent trends toward privatization of the delivery of human services previously offered by the government has created greater need for a community of volunteers to pick up the slack left by the government's departure. To ease the transition, government leaders have sought to increase awareness of the need for volunteers through presidential summits, the appointment of special task forces, and renewed attention to programs like Americorps, VISTA, and the Peace Corps. As a result of these calls to volunteer, the spotlight has fallen both on those who volunteer and on those who do not. Despite the many millions of people who volunteer, there are many who do not. In a 1991 survey, 49% of respondents had not volunteered in the previous 12 months and 27% had never volunteered (Independent Sector, 1992). Yet, in an earlier survey that found that 55% of respondents had not volunteered in the previous year, Americans agreed by a 3 to 1 margin that people should volunteer to make the world a better place (Independent Sector, 1988). Thus, the question that faces society is how to best mobilize the many individuals who believe volunteerism is a good thing but who do not engage in service. And, the question that faces social scientists is why it is that some people engage in prosocial action as volunteers and others do not.

The notion that one person would make personal sacrifices for another person, particularly a stranger, has long fascinated social scientists (e.g., Batson, 1991; Eisenberg, 1986; Latané & Darley, 1970; Piliavin, Dovidio, Gaertner, & Clark, 1981; Schroeder, Penner, Dovidio, & Piliavin, 1995; Staub, 1978). Although studies of helping are legion, the existing literature is largely concerned with the *spontaneous helping* that occurs in situations involving unexpected opportunities to help, which call for immediate decisions of whether to offer relatively brief acts of help (e.g., Bar-Tal, 1984; Benson et al., 1980; Piliavin & Charng, 1990). Volunteerism is a quite different form of helping, more prototypical of *planned helping,* which often "calls for considerably more planning, sorting out of priorities, and matching of personal capabilities and interests with type of intervention" (Benson et al., p. 89). Thus, volunteers often actively seek out opportunities to help others; may deliberate for considerable amounts of time about whether to volunteer, the extent to which they become involved, and the degree to which particular activities fit with their own personal needs; and may make a commitment to an ongoing helping relationship that may extend over a considerable period of time and that may entail considerable personal costs of time, energy, and opportunity (Clary & Snyder, 1991).

The defining features of volunteerism as voluntary, sustained, and ongoing helpfulness suggest that it may be useful to adopt a motivational perspective and to ask about the motivations that dispose individuals to seek out volunteer opportunities, to commit themselves to voluntary helping, and to sustain their involvement over extended periods of time. After all, the fundamental concerns of motivational inquiry are an understanding of the processes that move people to action—the processes that initiate, direct, and sustain action (Snyder & Cantor, 1998). These concerns are precisely the ones engaged by the questions, "Why do people volunteer?" and "What sustains voluntary helping?" These concerns can be addressed by employing the strategy of functional analysis, an approach that is concerned with the reasons and purposes, the plans and goals, that underlie and generate psychological phenomena, that is, the personal and social functions being served by a person's thoughts, feelings, and actions (Snyder, 1993).

In psychology, the themes of functionalism are reflected in diverse perspectives that emphasize the adaptive and purposeful strivings of people toward personal and social ends and goals. A core proposition of functionalist theorizing is that people can and do perform the same actions in the service of different psychological functions. Thus, for example, in the functional accounts of attitudes and persuasion offered separately by Smith, Bruner, and White (1956) and by Katz (1960), it is proposed that the same attitudes could serve different functions for different people and that attempts to change attitudes would succeed to the extent that they addressed the functions served by those attitudes. More recently, however, there has been a broadening of the domain of functionalist theorizing, with functions bearing clear familial resemblance to those proposed for attitudes appearing in analyses of diverse cognitive, affective, behavioral, and interpersonal processes (e.g., Cantor, 1994; Snyder, 1992, 1993; Snyder & Cantor, 1998).

In the tradition of such functionalist theorizing, a functional analysis may have the potential to reveal the motivational foundations of volunteer helping activity (see Clary & Snyder, 1991; Clary et al., 1998; Omoto & Snyder, 1995; Snyder & Omoto, 1992; Snyder, 1993). Specifically, the core propositions of a functional analysis of volunteerism are that acts of volunteerism that are similar on the surface may be supported by different underlying motivations, and that the functions served by volunteerism reveal themselves in the unfolding dynamics of the initiation and maintenance of voluntary helping behavior.

In accord with these propositions, past research (although not necessarily conducted from a functional perspective) on volunteers and their motivations certainly confirms that individuals may volunteer for very different reasons. Even a brief review of this literature demonstrates the variety of motives. For example, many researchers have reported that people claim that they volunteer because of deeply felt concern for those they are helping (Allen & Rushton, 1983; Anderson & Moore, 1978; Clary & Miller, 1986; Clary & Orenstein, 1991). Other researchers have pointed to additional motives. Gidron (1978) described volunteers who expected to receive benefits related to "self-development, learning, and variety in life." Rosenhan (1970) reported that the helpfulness of partially committed civil rights activists was guided by concerns over social rewards and punishments. Jenner (1982) described Junior League volunteers who perceived volunteering to be a means of preparing for a new career or of maintaining career-relevant skills. Frisch and Gerard (1981) found that some Red Cross volunteers reported that they volunteered to escape from negative feelings. Finally, Carlson, Charlin, and Miller (1988) and Jenner (1982) reported that some people use helping as a means of maintaining or enhancing positive affect or self-esteem.

To systematize the existing literature, and to approach it from an explicitly functional perspective, we (Clary & Snyder, 1991) found it heuristically useful to take the classic theories of attitudes offered by Katz (1960) and Smith et al. (1956) as a point of departure for considering the functions served by volunteerism. Although the labels vary, several functions are common to both Katz's and Smith et al.'s classifications. Some attitudes are thought to serve a knowledge (Katz's label) or object appraisal (Smith et al.'s label) function, bringing a sense of understanding to the world; other attitudes serve a value-expressive (in Katz's language) or quality of expressiveness (in Smith et al.'s language) function, helping people express deeply held values, dispositions, and convictions; and still other attitudes serve an ego-defensive (as Katz called it) or externalization (as Smith et al. called it) function, buffering people against undesirable or threatening truths about the self. In addition to these functions in common to the two classification systems, Katz proposed a utilitarian function by which attitudes reflect experiences with rewarding and punishing events, and Smith et al. proposed a social-adjustive function whereby attitudes help people fit in with important reference groups.

Part of the appeal of these earlier functional theories is the diversity of motivations that they could embrace. In this same spirit of inclusive theorizing, it has been suggested that the diverse functions identified in such theorizing have their counterparts in volunteers' motivations; however, refinement and articulation of the role of ego-related functions has suggested an important distinction between elimination of negative aspects associated with the ego and promotion of positive strivings associated with the ego, with the result being a set of six motivational functions served by volunteerism (for elaboration, see Clary et al., 1998).

One function volunteerism may serve is to allow individuals opportunities to express values related to altruistic and humanitarian concern for others. This "values" function finds its roots in Katz's (1960) value-expressive function and Smith et al.'s (1956) quality of expressiveness function, each of which proposed that some attitudes allow individuals to present their primary values to others. At the heart of the values function is the suggestion that volunteerism is influenced by values about other people's welfare. But, at the same time, not only is volunteerism guided by such values but also it helps individuals to remain true to their conception of self by affording them the opportunity to express deeply held values and convictions through action.

A second function of volunteerism may be to provide new learning experiences about different people, places, skills, or oneself; indeed, volunteer activities may be sought out in order to satisfy an intellectual curiosity about the world in general, the social world in particular, and the self. Additionally, volunteerism may offer a chance to gain greater understanding of one's own knowledge, skills, and abilities, particularly those that have been heretofore underutilized. This "understanding" function, too, has ties to the classic functional theories, specifically, Katz's (1960) knowledge function and Smith et al.'s (1956) object appraisal functions that described how attitudes allow people to apply a structure to their understanding of the world. The understanding function reflects not only the desire of volunteers to seek out new information that structures their world view, but also the need to demonstrate an understanding of the world by applying their skills and abilities to help those in need. That is, volunteerism can serve to extend one's understanding of the world and to reaffirm one's understanding of the world and one's place in it.

A third function that volunteerism may serve is to provide opportunities to engage in activities valued by important others. In groups where volunteerism is normative or there is strong social pressure to help, individuals may perform service in order to fit in and get along with their reference group. This "social" function is clearly related to Smith et al.'s (1956) social-adjustive function, by which attitudes allow people to fit into their social surroundings. At the same time, in this conceptualization of the social function, people are thought to help not only because they want to fit in with existing social groups, but also perhaps because they desire to expand their social circles or to join desirable new social groups.

A fourth function of volunteerism may be to provide individuals with career-related benefits. That is, volunteer activity is often seen as a way to acquire and develop new skills, forge professional contacts, enhance one's résumé, and prepare for a future career. This "career" function stems from the utilitarian function described by Katz (1960) as underlying attitudes that allow individuals to obtain rewards and avoid punishments. With the career function, this logic is extended to propose that volunteer activity may be expressly sought out as an instrumental activity that will further one's career; thus volunteerism becomes part of an attempt to strategically move oneself along in life.

A fifth function volunteerism may serve is to reduce guilt about being more fortunate than others and/or to provide the opportunity to address one's own personal problems. That is, through volunteerism, people may be better able to cope with inner conflicts, anxieties, and uncertainties concerning their personal worth and competence. Volunteerism may protect individuals from accepting the undesirable or threatening conclusions about the self that they might feel would be warranted in the absence of the good works of their volunteerism. This "protective" function is related to the earlier ego-defensive (Katz, 1960) and externalization (Smith et al., 1956) functions, which proposed that attitudes could protect the ego from negative features of the self. Although the ego-defensive and externalization attitudinal functions were often seen to be unconscious motivations, it is nevertheless quite possible that volunteerism may be explicitly chosen and deliberately used for protective purposes (although for some individuals these purposes may be relatively implicit).

Finally, a sixth function of volunteerism may be to allow individuals to enhance their own self-esteem with a focus on personal growth and development and the positive strivings of the ego. In accord with recent theorizing suggesting that positive and negative affect fall along separate dimensions (e.g., Watson, Clark, McIntyre, & Hamaker, 1992; Watson, Clark, & Tellegen, 1988), the enhancement function represents a distinct but complementary partner to the protective function, focusing instead on increasing the ego's positive standing. Indeed, this "enhancement" function is similar to Maslow's (1954) self-actualization need, which suggests that self-improvement is an ultimate human need. Thus, individuals may select volunteer activities to feel better about themselves, either because of the good work that they are doing, or because they have a need to improve themselves through volunteer work.

ASSESSING THE FUNCTIONS OF VOLUNTEERISM

The functional approach to volunteerism is predicated on the assumption that the motivations that underlie volunteer activity can be identified and measured. In the past, the lack of measuring devices has often impeded theoretical and empirical progress in the study of psychological functions (Kiesler, Collins, & Miller, 1969; Snyder & DeBono, 1987). Moreover, previous studies of volunteers' motivations have used instruments without conceptual foundation and of unknown reliability and validity (for elaboration, see Clary & Snyder, 1991; Cnaan & Goldberg-Glen, 1991). And, even though reliable and valid measures of motivations for specific kinds of volunteer service exist (e.g., the measure of motivations for AIDS volunteerism developed by Omoto & Snyder, 1995), there remains a need for an inventory that reliably and validly taps a set of motivations of generic relevance to volunteerism. Therefore, Clary et al. (1998) developed the Volunteer Function Inventory (VFI), an inventory that accomplishes this purpose.

To develop the VFI, Clary et al. (1998) generated a set of items rationally derived from the conceptualization of six psychological and social functions potentially served by involvement in volunteer work. Each function was assessed by a separate scale: Values (e.g., "I can do something for a cause that is important to me"), understanding (e.g., "volunteering lets me learn things through direct, hands-on experience"), career (e.g., "volunteering allows me to explore different career options"), social (e.g., "people I'm close to want me to volunteer"), protective (e.g., "volunteering is a good escape from my own troubles"), and enhancement (e.g., "volunteering makes me feel important"). Preliminary studies with volunteers and nonvolunteers permitted Clary et al. (1998) to identify and eliminate unreliable and ambiguous items, resulting in an instrument that consists of 30 items, with 5 items designed to assess each of the six functions.

In accord with an investigative strategy for personality and social behavior outlined by Snyder and Ickes (1985), Clary et al. (1998) sought to develop the VFI with a population for whom motivations for volunteering would be salient, accessible, and meaningful. Therefore, they administered the inventory to currently active volunteers engaged in diverse forms of volunteer service. These individuals, by virtue of having involved themselves in volunteer activity, could be presumed to possess motivations relevant to volunteerism. Participants were volunteers from five organizations that used volunteers to provide a wide range of services to children, families of cancer patients, social service and public health clients, and physically handicapped individuals, as well as blood services and disaster relief. Each participating organization's director of volunteer services administered the VFI to its volunteers. Respondents indicated "how important or accurate each of the 30 possible reasons for volunteering were for you in doing volunteer work" using a response scale anchored by 1 (*not at all important/accurate*) and 7 (*extremely important/accurate*).

To examine the structure of volunteers' motivations and to evaluate the psychometric properties of the VFI as a measure of these motivations, Clary et al. (1998) conducted a factor analysis of responses to the VFI. Beginning with an exploratory principal components analysis, they identified six components with eigenvalues greater than 1.0, suggesting six factors underlying responses to the VFI (Kim & Mueller, 1988). They then performed a principal axis factor analysis with oblique rotation to a preselected six-factor solution. The factors that emerged from this analysis clearly reflect each of the functions thought to be served by volunteering. Almost without exception, items from each scale loaded on their intended factor and did not load with items from different scales. The scales of the VFI have since been found to possess substantial internal consistency and temporal stability (see Clary et al., 1998) and to be relatively independent of social desirability responding (Clary et al., 1995). In addition, as measures of motivation for volunteerism, the scales of the VFI possess discriminant validity from the relevant motivationally oriented scales of the (Jackson, 1974) Personality Research Form (Clary et al., 1995).

Although these analyses clearly point to a six-factor solution, the question of whether there are more or fewer factors does arise. However, two additional principal axis factor analyses with oblique rotations, one to a preselected five-factor solution and one to a preselected seven-factor solution, indicated that, for the five-factor solution, the pattern of loadings for the values, career, social, and understanding items was consistent with the results of the six-factor solution, and the protective and enhancement items loaded together on one factor, whereas for the seven-factor solution, the pattern of loadings was fully identical to that for the six-factor solution, because no items loaded on Factor 5. Confirmatory factor analytic techniques, using LISREL to test each of the five-, six-, and seven-factor solutions with an oblique model in which items were constrained to load on their specified factor from the exploratory analyses, indicated that the six-factor oblique model fits the data well and is to be preferred on statistical grounds to either a five- or seven-factor solution (see Clary et al., 1998).

Thus, these findings offer support for the functional approach to volunteers' motivations and for the VFI as a measure of those motivations. Moreover, the structure of the VFI has been replicated and cross-validated on diverse samples of respondents, including a large sample of university students, many of whom were not active volunteers (Clary et al., 1998), and a group of elderly volunteers (Okun, Barr, & Herzog, 1998). In each case, the six-factor solution, measuring the values, understanding, career, social, enhancement, and protective functions of volunteering, emerged as the preferred solution. Moreover, in 1992, we were fortunate to be able to include representative items from the six VFI scales in a national survey about American adults' giving and volunteering; this survey consisted of a broad range of questions relevant to people's activities in the nonprofit sector (Clary, Snyder, & Stukas, 1996). Although not all items of the VFI were present in this national survey, we were again able to replicate the six-factor structure of the VFI in a larger sample of 2,125 adults. We again found that the six functions best represented the pattern of responses for both current volunteers and nonvolunteers (including those who had never volunteered).

THE FUNCTIONS IN ACTION

The VFI has proven its utility in a series of investigations of the hypothesized relations between the underlying functions of volunteering and the actual processes of volunteerism. Specifically, these studies have examined the usefulness of taking a functional perspective to understand the initiation of volunteer service, the selection of particular volunteer tasks, volunteers' satisfaction with their experiences, and volunteers' commitment to sustained service. These studies examine, from a variety of converging perspectives, the importance of matching the motivations of the individual and the opportunities afforded by the environment for the initiation and maintenance of voluntary prosocial action. Thus, this matching hypothesis permits an evaluation of the usefulness of attending to the psychological functions served by volunteerism, the inventory that has been developed to measure these functions, and, by extension, the functional approach to motivation itself.

Initiating Volunteer Activity

Functionalist theorizing generates the hypothesis that individuals initiate volunteer behavior to the extent that they believe it can fulfill their underlying motivations. Since the opportunities to satisfy such motivations through volunteerism may not be salient to some individuals, it follows that persuasive messages can be used to encourage people to volunteer. The functional approach offers a clear interactionist prediction: persuasive messages are effective to the extent that they speak to, or are matched with, the specific motivations important to individual recipients of the message.

To test whether individuals who were presented with persuasive messages that matched their underlying functions for volunteering would indicate greater intent to become volunteers than individuals who were presented with persuasive messages that did not match their underlying functions, Clary, Snyder, Ridge, Miene, and Haugen (1994) created a series of videotaped advertising messages, each of which depicted a female university student browsing through a library, happening upon a poster promoting volunteerism, and commenting on it. The woman read the text of the poster aloud, turned to the camera, and recounted how she had satisfied her personal goals through volunteerism; that is, she provided a firsthand account of what functions volunteerism served for her. Naturally, each of the advertising messages created for this study differed in its functional content. For example, in a message designed to highlight the values-relevant benefits of volunteerism, the spokesperson reported that volunteerism had provided her with opportunities to act on personally relevant concerns, to express a unique part of herself, and to work for a cause she cared about. In a message designed to highlight career-relevant benefits, the spokesperson focused instead on the opportunities to learn about jobs and career options, to strengthen her résumé, and to make herself more marketable to potential employers she gained through volunteering.

Based on an earlier assessment of the functions of volunteerism of greatest and least importance for each of the university students who participated in this study, Clary et al. (1994) randomly assigned each of them to either a "functionally matched" or a "functionally mismatched" experimental condition. That is, participants viewed either a videotaped message that highlighted the psychological function of volunteerism of greatest importance to them (the matched condition) or a videotaped message that highlighted the psychological function of least importance to them (the mismatched condition). Participants were asked to evaluate the persuasive appeal of the advertisement they watched and to indicate how likely they were to volunteer in the future. As functional theory would predict, participants who received a message that matched a motivation of great importance to them were more likely to feel that the ad was appealing and persuasive and more likely to intend to volunteer in the future than participants who received a mismatched message. In addition, participants' emotions appear to have been influential in their ratings: participants reported more positive feelings in the matched conditions than in the mismatched conditions.

In a related study, Clary et al. (1998) created a set of brochures to inform students about a university volunteer fair; each brochure highlighted one of the six functions of volunteerism represented by the VFI. A main goal of this investigation was to evaluate each of the six scales of the VFI separately, both to provide validation of the measure and to demonstrate that the matching of messages to motivations would work for each of the functions individually. University students, whose motivations for volunteering had been previously assessed, rated each of the six brochures in accordance with the following question: "How effective is this brochure in getting you motivated to volunteer? That is, how appealing, persuasive, and influential is this brochure in getting you motivated to volunteer?" Clary et al. (1998) predicted that each brochure's overall rating would be best predicted by participants' scores on the relevant (matched) motivation from the VFI, and, as expected, for four of the six brochures (save only the career and social brochures), these predictions were confirmed. Thus, by and large, the best predictor of each advertisement's evaluation was that advertisement's corresponding VFI scale score; that is, participants judged each advertisement to be effective and persuasive to the extent that it matched their personal motivations.

In a separate study, Ridge (in press) found that individuals, who were either high or low on the career and enhancement functions as measured by the VFI, judged print advertisements that matched their own underlying motivation to be more persuasively appealing than advertisements that did not match their own motivation. Additionally, individuals were more likely to indicate that they would contact the sponsoring organization referred to in matched ads than in mismatched ads. Finally, Day, Omoto, and Snyder (1998) found evidence of the matching of messages to motivations in evaluative reactions to print advertisements designed to recruit AIDS volunteers by appealing to diverse motivations potentially served by volunteering to help persons living with HIV.

Thus, these investigations provide added support for a principal tenet of the functional approach, namely that attempts to persuade (or to recruit volunteers) succeed to the extent that they address the specific motivational functions underlying behavior and attitudes. In addition to their theoretical relevance for the functional approach to persuasion, these findings also have clear implications for the practice of volunteerism: recruitment of volunteers should be most effective when organizations tailor their recruiting messages to appeal to the psychological motives of prospective volunteers. Although knowing the most important function or functions for a specific individual would make this strategy most effective, one might also be able to make fairly accurate guesses about which functions are most important for particular groups of people. For example, career-oriented considerations may be more salient for younger people, so a persuasive campaign targeted at this group might be advised to emphasize the ways in which career-related functional concerns can be served through volunteer work. For those who are already settled in a career, however, this message would not be particularly appealing; this group, may be receptive instead to a message that discusses opportunities afforded by volunteerism for learning new skills or exercising skills and talents that are little used in one's current job or career.

Engaging in Volunteer Activities

As an ongoing and sustained activity, volunteerism affords an opportunity to study an important implication of functional theorizing, namely that individuals whose motivational concerns are served by participation in a particular activity should derive greater satisfaction from that activity than those whose concerns are not met. For example, a person most motivated by the understanding function would be more satisfied by a task that provides opportunities to learn about new people than by a task that involves little that is new to that person.

In a field study designed to examine whether individuals who received benefits from volunteer work that matched their initial motivations would be more satisfied than those who received mismatched benefits, Clary et al. (1998) administered the VFI to elderly volunteers at a local hospital to identify the functions important to these volunteers. Several months later, these volunteers indicated the extent to which they received function-specific benefits during their service; they also indicated the degree to which they found their volunteerism personally satisfying and rewarding. Building on the logic of the functional hypothesis about the matching of benefits to motives, Clary et al. (1998) predicted that, for each of the six VFI functions, those volunteers who reported receiving relatively greater amounts of functionally relevant benefits (that is, the benefits that they received were related to functions important to them) would report relatively greater satisfaction with their volunteerism than those volunteers who received fewer functionally relevant benefits or those volunteers who received functionally irrelevant benefits (i.e., the benefits that they received were related to a functional dimension that was not important to them).

Participants' perceptions of the type and quantity of functionally relevant benefits that they received from their volunteer service were assessed with items based on each of the six VFI functions. For example, the items for the understanding function benefits were as follows: "I learned more about the cause for which I worked," "I learned how to deal with a greater variety of people," and "I was able to explore my own personal strengths." Additionally, respondents indicated their level of satisfaction and personal fulfillment gained from serving in the program on six items (e.g., "How much did you enjoy your volunteer experience?"). In accord with functionalist theorizing, volunteers for whom a particular function was important and who perceived relatively greater benefits related to that function were more satisfied with their volunteerism than those who did not receive as much in the way of relevant benefits and those for whom that functional dimension was not important. Thus, results from this field study support the hypothesis that functionally relevant benefits are directly related to the quality of the experiences of volunteers. Volunteers' satisfaction with and fulfillment from their volunteer service were more likely to be associated with receiving functionally relevant benefits than with failing to receive such benefits or with receiving functionally irrelevant benefits; furthermore, this pattern held most strongly for the motivations that were of greatest importance to these elderly volunteers.

As part of a longitudinal study of the volunteer process, Crain, Omoto, and Snyder (1998) examined the role that the matching between volunteers' motivations, expectations, and experiences plays in determining volunteers' satisfaction and burnout. In their study, AIDS volunteers completed four questionnaires in which they reported the importance of each of a set of functional motivations for their volunteering (prior to their training to serve as volunteers), the extent to which they expected that their volunteering would fulfill their motivations (following training), the extent to which their experiences met these expectations (after having volunteered for 3 months), and their feelings of satisfaction and burnout (after having volunteered for 6 months). Overall matching between motivations, expectations, and experiences was predictive of greater satisfaction and lesser burnout, which suggests that a stronger match is associated with more positive consequences of volunteerism.

Given that positive consequences of volunteerism (e.g., more satisfaction, less burnout) are affected by functional matching, it may also be that the actual quality of volunteer service is similarly influenced. That is, volunteers who are not receiving (or do not expect to receive) benefits relevant to their underlying motivations are not as invested in their tasks nor do they perform as well as those who receive (or expect to receive) relevant benefits. To examine this hypothesis, Ridge (1993) asked students (whose levels of values and career motivation had been premeasured with the VFI) to stuff envelopes for an environmental group after the study for which they were recruited was canceled. Students were randomly assigned to hear a confederate tell the experimenter the types of career benefits or values benefits she had already gotten out of such volunteerism in the past. Thus, students were placed in either a matched condition, hearing that the activity could meet their needs, or a mismatched condition, hearing that the activity could meet a different need. For both groups, however, the task remained the same—envelope stuffing.

After the study, participants in the career condition were more likely to report the possible career benefits attainable through such envelope stuffing than were participants in the values condition. This finding suggests that the explicit framing of a volunteer task as providing certain benefits can lead individuals to be more likely to actually see the possibility of such benefits. In addition, Ridge found that individuals placed in matched conditions actually did better quality work (i.e., the letters they were stuffing were folded more neatly) than did individuals placed in mismatched conditions. Therefore, the importance of selecting tasks that provide for important motivations is not solely for the sake of satisfaction but may result in better performance as well.

The facilitating effects of functional matching on satisfaction and task performance are, in addition to their relevance to functionalist theorizing, of potential practical importance, both to individuals who seek out volunteer opportunities and to organizations that rely on the services of volunteers. In either case, there may be clear benefits to matching individuals and volunteer opportunities. More satisfied and more effective volunteers should result to the extent that individuals can seek out and gravitate toward volunteer opportunities that provide experiences that match their own motivations and to the extent that volunteer service organizations can systematically counsel their volunteers into roles that provide experiences matched to their volunteers' motivations.

Sustaining Volunteer Activities

If volunteers' satisfaction with and effectiveness in their volunteer service are associated with receiving functionally relevant benefits, then perhaps their intentions to continue serving as volunteer helpers are also linked to the matching of their experiences as volunteers with their motivations for volunteering. To investigate this possibility, Clary et al. (1998) examined, from a functional perspective, the roles of individuals' motivations for volunteering and the benefits they receive for volunteering in influencing their intentions to continue their involvement in, and commitment to, volunteerism. In accord with functional theorizing, they predicted that volunteers who received functionally relevant benefits would also reveal greater intentions to continue as volunteers, both in the short-term and in the long-term future, than would volunteers who did not receive functionally relevant benefits or who received functionally irrelevant benefits.

Clary et al. (1998) examined this prediction prospectively with a sample of university students who were required to engage in community service to obtain their degrees. They measured short- and long-term intentions with two sets of items that focused on what students thought was the probability that they would be volunteers during a future time period (e.g., "I will be a volunteer 1 year from now"). Once again, in keeping with functional theory, volunteers who received benefits relevant to their primary functional motivations not only were satisfied with their service (replicating the results of the previous study of elderly volunteers) but also intended to continue to volunteer in both the short- and long-term future. Volunteers in this study provided a wide array of services under the auspices of many different organizations; however, those who found service opportunities that provided benefits matching their initial motivations more strongly believed that they would make volunteerism a continuing part of their lives than did individuals who chose opportunities that did not provide functionally relevant benefits or that provided functionally irrelevant benefits.

Does the functional matching effect extend beyond the formation of intentions and manifest itself in actual sustained patterns of continuing service as a volunteer? Relevant to this issue are longitudinal investigations that have examined actual commitment to volunteering. In one such study that focused on crisis-counseling volunteers, Clary and Miller (1986) found that volunteers with a background akin to the social function were more likely to complete their 6 months of service when they had participated in a cohesive training group that provided greater levels of social benefits (a matching of motivation and training context) than when they had participated in a less cohesive training group (a mismatching of motivation and training). In contrast, volunteers with a background suggesting the values function (which would be neither matched nor mismatched to training groups that differ in their cohesiveness and other social benefits) were equally likely to complete their service regardless of the social cohesiveness of their training group experiences.

In addition to this study of the matching effect in predicting behavior, a study of AIDS volunteers that involved successive follow-ups to determine who was still active as a volunteer and who had quit is also relevant to understanding the role of psychological functions in predicting patterns of sustained action (Omoto & Snyder, 1995). In this study, Omoto and Snyder found that volunteers' scores on measures of "self-oriented" functions for volunteering (e.g., esteem enhancement, personal development) predicted their continued activity as volunteers at 1 year and 2½ years after the original measurement of the functions served by their involvement in AIDS volunteerism.

Thus, the results of studies of intentions to continue serving as a volunteer and of studies of actual patterns of sustained involvement represent important extensions of the functional analysis of volunteerism. In each case, outcomes crucial to volunteerism can be connected to the planfulness and agenda-setting aspects of motivation. And yet again, these findings may have practical implications as well as theoretical ones, with organizations that rely on volunteers perhaps being able to foster intentions for continued service and actual continued service by creating organizational climates that help their volunteers to link up the benefits they receive from volunteerism to their own functional motivations for serving as volunteers.

LESSONS FROM THE FUNCTIONAL
APPROACH TO VOLUNTEERISM

Taken together, the investigations that we have reviewed provide empirical support for a functional approach that focuses on the psychological purposes served by sustained prosocial behavior. Functional motivations have been identified and investigated in terms of their roles in guiding people toward volunteer activities (as suggested by studies of the recruitment of volunteers with persuasive messages), influencing the unfolding dynamics at play during their tenure as volunteers (as indicated by studies of the determinants of the satisfaction and task performance of volunteers), and in sustaining involvement in volunteer activities (as suggested by studies of volunteers' intentions to commit themselves to further service and by longitudinal studies of volunteers).

Clearly, a functional perspective is of great value in understanding the dynamics and processes of volunteerism. But, we believe that studies of volunteerism can also cast their light on functionalist theorizing itself. It is to such considerations that we now turn. We discuss the importance of considering the functions served by behavior as well as the functions served by attitudes, issues associated with the diversity of motivations in functionalist theorizing, the role of a diversity of functions in the motivation of a single attitude or behavior, and a motivationally oriented conceptualization of psychological functions as agendas for action.

Functions of Attitudes and Functions of Behavior

Arguably, the most familiar examples of functionalist theorizing are the functional approaches to attitudes, as exemplified by the classic functional accounts offered by Katz (1960) and Smith et al. (1956) and by the contemporary neo-functional perspectives offered by Herek (1987) and others. These theoretical approaches answer the question, "Of what use to people are their attitudes?" with lists of functions served by attitudes. The emphasis, in other words, has been on attitudes themselves and on the functions served by attitudes. In consideration of volunteerism as a form of sustained prosocial action, however, our main concern is with behavior and the functions served by behavior.

This concern with the functions of behaviors as well as the functions of attitudes harks back to similar concerns expressed in the early discussions of the functional approach. Consider, for example, Katz's (1960) description of Himmelstrand's work:

> (His) work is concerned with all aspects of the relationship between attitude and behavior, but he deals with the action structure of the attitude itself by distinguishing between attitudes where the affect is tied to verbal expression and attitudes where the affect is tied to behavior concerned with more objective referents of the attitude. In the first case an individual derives satisfaction from talking about a problem; in the second case he derives satisfaction from taking some form of concrete action. (p. 169)

Observations such as these point to the need to understand when attitudes will lead to action and when they will not. That there may be substantial gaps between attitudes and actions (e.g., Eagly & Chaiken, 1993; Wicker, 1969) suggests, at the very least, that one ask both about the functions served by attitudes and about the functions served by behavior. But, the gaps between attitudes and actions also suggest that functional theorizing should attempt to address the matter of bridging the gaps between attitudes and behavior.

With respect to the matter of bridging the gaps between attitudes and behavior, in the specific case of volunteerism, a functional approach may help to elucidate meaningful differences in the underlying motivations that volunteerism serves for individuals who believe it is important and do act and those who believe volunteerism is important but do not act. Recall that attitudes favorable toward the idea of volunteerism are substantially more prevalent than actual involvement in volunteerism (Independent Sector, 1988). The data from another national survey of Americans' attitudes and behaviors with respect to giving and volunteering suggest that at least part of the answer to the question of when these favorable attitudes toward volunteerism are translated into action and when they are not is to be found in the importance of the psychological functions served by volunteerism for individuals (Clary et al., 1996). In this survey, volunteers reported that the functions that volunteerism can serve were of greater importance to them than did nonvolunteers; this was especially the case for the values, understanding, social, and enhancement functions. Furthermore, volunteers with more experience rated the functions as more important than did volunteers with less experience. Current volunteers held the values and social functions to be of greater importance than did past volunteers, who saw them as more important than individuals who had never volunteered.

Thus, if we generalize from the case of volunteerism, it may be that, when greater importance is attributed to a psychological function, action will be more likely to be taken to satisfy the needs or achieve the goals associated with that function. A functional approach, therefore, provides a motivational link between attitudes and behavior, which suggests that behavior is enacted when individuals feel not only that a particular activity is valuable, but also that it serves particularly important psychological and social functions for them.

The Diversity of Motivations in Functionalist Theorizing

A central feature of functionalist theorizing is that the same attitudes and the same actions may serve different functions for different people; that is, a functional approach emphasizes the diversity of motivations that underlie attitudes and actions. Consequently, knowledge of how individuals vary in their motivations can give us important information about the expression of their attitudes and actions. Inevitably, attempts to catalogue the functions that attitudes and actions may serve lead to a discussion of the optimal number of functions that may be documented and that may be relatively independent of one another. In this chapter, we have focused our attention on six functions potentially served by volunteerism as identified by Clary et al. (1998) in their theorizing and as measured by the VFI that they developed. But is six really the optimal number of functions?

We recognize that the theories of Katz (1960) and Smith et al. (1956), which have served as launching pads for many functional analyses, each employed only four functions. We are also mindful of the fact that our own preliminary considerations of the functional bases of volunteerism began with examinations of four functions (Clary & Snyder, 1991). However, our efforts to integrate the shared and distinct functions proposed in previous theorizing (including our own), and to articulate important distinctions in ego functioning, have now led us to six motivational functions served by volunteerism. And, as we have detailed here, the findings of both laboratory and field studies are highly supportive of this six motive conceptualization and its operationalization in the VFI.

Nevertheless, we emphasize that, both in our theoretical and in our empirical activity, we have sought to identify motivations of generic relevance to volunteerism. Thus, the items in the VFI never speak of particular kinds of volunteerism; moreover, research with the VFI has included both volunteers and nonvolunteers, has emphasized demographic diversity within and between samples, and has deliberately included volunteers engaged in a wide range of tasks. However, we fully expect that there are circumstances in which either fewer functions or more functions emerge as important. This may be particularly likely when distinctions relevant to specific forms of volunteerism are highly prominent; for example, in the case of AIDS volunteers, research has identified five specific motivations (which, although measured with items that sometimes make specific reference to the AIDS context, nonetheless bear a family resemblance to the motivations of the VFI; Omoto & Snyder, 1995). Thus, although it may be possible to identify a core set of functions that underlie volunteerism in general, there very well may also be meaningful variations in the extent to which these core functions can be served by specific volunteer activities.

The Diversity of Motivations in Individual Functioning

In addition to the matter of how many motivations should be incorporated in functionalist theorizing, there is the related matter of how many functions are served by the attitudes and behaviors of individuals. Specifically, it is quite possible, as functionalist theory suggests, that some attitudes and behaviors "may serve more than one purpose for the individual" (Katz, 1960, p. 170), whereas in other cases an individual's attitudes and actions may be undertaken in the service of a single function. To address the matter of the diversity of motivations involved in individuals' actions, we can turn to data collected in earlier studies. Thus, as another way of exploring the diversity of functions potentially served by volunteer activity, we sought to discover whether individual volunteers approach volunteerism as an opportunity to meet a multiplicity of their needs. By using the VFI to operationalize functions, it is now possible to ask whether individuals volunteer to serve multiple psychological and social functions.

As a simple way of investigating whether individuals seek to serve multiple functions through volunteerism, we utilized data provided by Stukas, Snyder, and Clary (1996). Specifically, let us consider the frequencies with which students, who were participating in volunteer work as part of a requirement for their undergraduate degrees in business, reported two or more important motives, as opposed to only one important motive or no important motives. Defining importance as indicated by a score in the upper one third of the distribution for a function, we found that 58% of this sample reported two or more important motives, 20% reported a single important motive, and 22% indicated that none of the six functions was important. Similarly, in a sample of more than 450 adult volunteers (Clary et al., 1998), 66% reported two or more important motivations, 18% reported a single important motivation, and 16% revealed no important motivation. Moreover, for a sample of students that included current volunteers, past volunteers, and those who had never volunteered (Clary et al., 1998), 65% reported two or more important functions, 19% had one important motive, and 16% reported no high motives. Thus, in diverse samples (with very different experiences with volunteering), nearly two thirds of participants reported two or more important motives that they could serve through volunteer activity.

These findings suggest that many people volunteer in the service of fulfilling multiple motivations; these findings also raise questions about whether those with two or more important motives differ in some fundamental way from those with a single important motive. Do volunteers with multiple motives differ from volunteers with a single motive in important outcomes of volunteering? Do those with multiple motives move through the processes of volunteerism, from initiation to task selection to eventual attrition or sustained helping, in a way different from those with a single motive? Could those with multiple motives be easier to recruit than those with a single motive? Could they be more likely to persist in a specific volunteer activity? Such questions potentially provide new directions for functionalist theorizing.

In addition to asking about the presence of multiple motivations, we may also ask about the patterns of these multiple motivations. For example, we may ask whether individuals with particular combinations of motives are likely to gravitate to particular volunteer tasks. To address this question, we turn again to data from the national survey about volunteerism (Clary et al., 1996), which included indicators of each of the six functions tapped by the VFI. Respondents to this survey who had volunteered in the previous year indicated in which of 15 areas (such as health, education, religion, human services, and the environment) they had served. For each activity area, we examined, through logistic regression, whether each of the six functions was able to predict involvement in that area (vs. involvement in all other areas). These analyses revealed that, on the whole, different combinations of motivations were associated with volunteerism in different activity areas. Given that these analyses were exploratory, we cannot precisely say which specific set of functions is most compatible with a specific activity; however, a strong possibility, and reasonable hypothesis, remains that specific combinations of functions are associated with and guide behaviors toward specific activities. The use of a perspective that suggests that meaningful variations in the expression of attitudes and behavior can be explained not only by understanding the motivational foundations of these phenomena but also by examining the particular combinations and patterns of these motivations adds a heretofore unexplored dimension to functional theorizing that could prove fruitful, not only in the domain of volunteerism but in other domains of individual and social functioning as well.

Psychological Functions and Agendas for Action

From a functionalist perspective, motivations can be conceptualized as representing the agentic pursuit of ends and goals important to the individual. Furthermore, from this perspective, it is important to recognize that what diverse functions have in common is that they guide and direct the actions of individuals, that is, they may constitute "agendas for action" (e.g., Snyder & Cantor, 1998). Indeed, few activities so overtly suggest a conceptualization of individuals as active, purposeful, and agenda-setting as does volunteerism; this is because, volunteerism is an activity that is, by its very nature, planned and voluntary. The use of a functional approach to volunteerism thus seems logical and suggests that when individuals choose to volunteer, they do so in an effort to serve important psychological and social functions. Thus, volunteers may deliberately seek out activities that they believe can best satisfy their needs, or volunteers may respond to efforts to recruit them— but only to the extent that these efforts explicitly "speak" to their functional motivations for volunteering. That is, individuals' psychological functions may be viewed as setting agendas for the kinds of events that will stir these individuals to action.

But the guiding influence of an individual's motivational functions on behavior does not end once the individual has initiated an activity. Instead, these functions may now serve as a template for determining the specific duties and responsibilities that individuals find most satisfying in their volunteer activity. As we have seen, if individuals select or are guided into an activity that provides them with functionally relevant benefits, they will be more satisfied than individuals who receive functionally irrelevant benefits. Benefits, in other words, are not all equal, and "what warms one ego, chills another" (Allport, 1945, p. 127). Similarly, individuals who find that they are receiving benefits matched to their needs are more likely to sustain (or intend to sustain) their volunteer activity than are those who receive benefits that do not match their needs.

Indeed, ongoing longitudinal studies of AIDS volunteers (e.g., Omoto & Snyder, 1995) are examining the extent to which volunteers' premeasured motivations can serve as predictors of their experiences as volunteers and of their lasting involvement in volunteer service. Longitudinal research also has the potential to reveal whether, over time, the functional motivations served by volunteerism can and do change. For example, career motivations may cease to be as salient to people once they have settled into stable and satisfying careers, and may become even less important to people who have entered their retirement years. Over the course of their lives, then, people's agendas for action, and the psychological and social functions that they find meaningful, may evolve and change in systematic ways.

These possibilities of evolution and change of motives over time and over the course of volunteer service suggest that burnout or attrition by volunteers may be productively examined as the result of a change in the underlying motivations of volunteers or of the satisfaction of their motivations to the point of satiation (as when individuals motivated by the understanding function eventually find that there are no longer new things to learn from their current volunteer activity). Such outcomes suggest that the interplay between the motives of volunteers and the benefits afforded by volunteer activities is a dynamic one, with both the needs of volunteers and the opportunities to receive benefits changing over time as motivations are fulfilled or exhausted.

Thus, at each step of the volunteer process, it appears that volunteers' own psychological functions may play a critical role in setting agendas for initiating and sustaining voluntary action. That is, they may determine what draws people into volunteering, whether their experiences as volunteers are satisfying and effective ones, and whether the benefits they accrue from volunteering are translated into intentions to continue to be active as volunteers over extended periods of time. As such, a conceptualization of the volunteer process in terms of agendas for action is congruent with approaches to motivation that emphasize the active role of individuals in the setting and pursuing of agendas that reflect important features of self and identity (e.g., Cantor, 1994; Snyder, 1993; Snyder & Cantor, 1998).

CONCLUSION

In this chapter, we have considered the motivational foundations of the sustained, ongoing helping that is characteristic of involvement in volunteerism. These considerations have been guided by a functional approach, that focuses on the psychological purposes served by participation in volunteer activities. First, the functional approach directs attention to the motivations that generate psychological phenomena, and emphasizes that attitudes and actions are purposeful and goal directed. Moreover, the functional approach underscores the importance of attending to the match between individuals' motivations and the opportunities provided by situational contexts to fulfill those motivations. As we have tried to demonstrate in this chapter, there exists a mutually beneficial arrangement between the functional approach as a general perspective on atti tudes and behavior, and the specific approach represented by the functional approach to volunteerism, with a functional perspective informing the psychology of volunteerism and the functional approach to volunteerism providing perspectives on issues of critical concern to functionalist theorizing.

Considerations of ongoing, planned helping behavior from a functional perspective clearly point to the influence of person-based processes (e.g., individuals' psychological functions) on helping; this influence has often been found lacking relative to the situational determinants typically studied in spontaneous helping situations (e.g., Clary & Snyder, 1991). Planned helpfulness represents a phenomenon in which the salient cues for action are less demanding, at least in comparison to spontaneous helping situations. Instead, planned helpfulness involves processes that encourage people to look inward to their own motivations for guidance in deciding whether to get involved in helping, in selecting a helping opportunity matched to their own motivations, and in maintaining helping over extended time periods.

However, at the same time as the study of volunteerism directs us to consider person-based processes, the functional perspective reminds us that behavior (in this case planned, sustained helpfulness) is not simply a matter of being influenced by dispositions or by situational forces, but rather is jointly determined. Moreover, functionalist theorizing provides the outlines of the manner of this joint determination. From the functionalist perspective, people come equipped with needs and motives important to them, and volunteer service tasks do or do not afford opportunities to fulfill those needs and motives. Together, these features of persons and of situations are integrated in the agendas that individuals construct and enact as they seek out, become involved in, and continue to be involved in the sustained helpfulness of volunteerism.

ACKNOWLEDGMENTS

This research was supported by grants from the Gannett Foundation and the Aspen Institute's Nonprofit Sector Research Fund to Clary and Snyder, and grants from the National Science Foundation and the National Institute of Mental Health to Snyder. This chapter was written while Snyder held the Chaire Francqui Interuniversitaire au Titre Étranger at the Université Catholique de Louvain (Louvain-la-Neuve, Belgium).

REFERENCES

Allen, N., & Rushton, J. P. (1983). Personality characteristics of community mental health volunteers. *Journal of Voluntary Action Research, 12,* 36–49.

Allport, G. W. (1945). The psychology of participation. *Psychological Review, 53,* 117–132.

Anderson, J. C., & Moore, L. (1978). The motivation to volunteer. *Journal of Voluntary Action Research, 7,* 51–60.

Bar-Tal, D. (1984). American study of helping behavior: What? Why? and Where? In E. Staub, D. Bar-Tal, J. Karylowski, & J. Reykowski (Eds.), *Development and maintenance of prosocial behavior: International perspectives on positive morality*. New York: Plenum Press.

Batson, C. D. (1991). *The altruism question: Toward a social-psychological answer*. Hillsdale, NJ: Lawrence Erlbaum Associates.

Benson, P., Dohority, J., Garman, L., Hanson, E., Hochschwender, M., Lebold, C., Rohr, R., & Sullivan, J. (1980). Intrapersonal correlates of nonspontaneous helping behavior. *Journal of Social Psychology, 110*, 87–95.

Cantor, N. (1994). Life task problem solving: Situational affordances and personal needs. *Personality and Social Psychology Bulletin, 20*, 235–243.

Carlson, M., Charlin, V., & Miller, N. (1988). Positive mood and helping behavior: A test of six hypotheses. *Journal of Personality and Social Psychology, 55*, 211–229.

Clary, E. G., & Miller, J. (1986). Socialization and situational influences on sustained altruism. *Child Development, 57*, 1358–1369.

Clary, E. G., & Orenstein, L. (1991). The amount and effectiveness of help: The relationship of motives and abilities to helping behavior. *Personality and Social Psychology Bulletin, 17*, 58–64.

Clary, E. G., & Snyder, M. (1991). A functional analysis of altruism and prosocial behavior: The case of volunteerism. In M. Clark (Ed.), *Review of Personality and Social Psychology: Vol. 12*. Newbury Park, CA: Sage.

Clary, E. G. , Snyder, M., Ridge, R. D., Copeland, J., Stukas, A. A., Haugen, J., & Miene, P. (1998). Understanding and assessing the motivations of volunteers: A functional approach. *Journal of Personality and Social Psychology, 74*, 1516–1530.

Clary, E., Snyder, M., Ridge, R., Haugen, J., & Miene, P. (1995). [Responses to the VFI and PRF as predictors of evaluations of persuasive messages]. Unpublished raw data.

Clary, E. G., Snyder, M., Ridge, R. D., Miene, P., & Haugen, J. (1994). Matching messages to motives in persuasion: A functional approach to promoting volunteerism. *Journal of Applied Social Psychology, 24*, 1129–1149.

Clary, E. G., Snyder, M., & Stukas, A. A. (1996). Volunteers' motivations: Findings from a national survey. *Nonprofit and Voluntary Sector Quarterly, 25*, 485–505.

Cnaan, R. A., & Goldberg-Glen, R. S (1991). Measuring motivation to volunteer in human services. *Journal of Applied Behavioral Science, 27*, 269–284.

Crain, A. L., Omoto, A. M., & Snyder, M. (1998, April). *What if you can't always get what you want? Testing a functional approach to volunteerism*. Paper presented at the annual meetings of the Midwestern Psychological Association, Chicago, IL.

Curtis, J. E., Grabb, E., & Baer, D. (1992). Voluntary association membership in fifteen countries: A comparative analysis. *American Sociological Review, 57*, 139–152.

Day, E. N., Omoto, A. M., & Snyder, M. (1998, April). *Targeting motivations in the recruitment of volunteers*. Paper presented at the annual meetings of the Midwestern Psychological Association, Chicago, IL.

Eagly, A. H., & Chaiken, S. (1993). *The psychology of attitudes*. Fort Worth, TX: Harcourt, Brace, Jovanovich.

Eisenberg, N. (1986). *Altruistic emotion, cognition, and behavior*. Hillsdale, NJ: Lawrence Erlbaum Associates.

Frisch, M. B., & Gerard, M. (1981). Natural helping systems: A survey of Red Cross volunteers. *American Journal of Community Psychology, 9*, 567–579.

Gidron, B. (1978). Volunteer work and its rewards. *Volunteer Administration, 11*, 18–32.

Herek, G. M. (1987). Can the functions be measured? A new perspective on the functional approach to attitudes. *Social Psychology Quarterly, 50*, 285–303.

Independent Sector. (1988). *Giving and volunteering in the United States: Findings from a national survey, 1988*. Washington, DC: Author.

Independent Sector. (1992). *Giving and volunteering in the United States: Findings from a national survey, 1992.* Washington, DC: Author.

Independent Sector. (1994). *Giving and volunteering in the United States: Findings from a national survey, 1994.* Washington, DC: Author.

Jackson, D. N. (1974). *Personality research form* (2nd ed.). Port Huron, MI: Research Psychologists Press.

Jenner, J. R. (1982). Participation, leadership, and the role of volunteerism among selected women volunteers. *Journal of Voluntary Action Research, 11,* 27–38.

Katz, D. (1960). The functional approach to the study of attitudes. *Public Opinion Quarterly, 24,* 163–204.

Kiesler, C. A., Collins, B. E., & Miller, N. (1969). *Attitude change: A critical analysis of theoretical approaches.* New York: Wiley.

Kim, J., & Mueller, C. W. (1988). *Factor analysis: Statistical methods and practical issues.* Beverly Hills, CA: Sage.

Latané, B., & Darley, J. M. (1970). *The unresponsive bystander: Why doesn't he help?* New York: Appleton–Century–Crofts.

Maslow, A. H. (1954). *Motivation and personality.* New York: Harper.

Okun, M. A., Barr, A., & Herzog, A. R. (1998). Motivation to volunteer by older adults: A test of competing measurement models. *Psychology and Aging, 13,* 608–621.

Omoto, A. M., & Snyder, M. (1995). Sustained helping without obligation: Motivation, longevity of service, and perceived attitude change among AIDS volunteers. *Journal of Personality and Social Psychology, 68,* 671–686.

Piliavin, J. A., & Charng, H. (1990). Altruism: A review of recent theory and research. *Annual Review of Sociology, 16,* 27–65.

Piliavin, J. A., Dovidio, J. F., Gaertner, S. L., & Clark, R. D. (1981). *Emergency intervention.* New York: Academic Press.

Ridge, R. D. (1993). *A motivation-based approach for investigating planned helping behavior.* Unpublished doctoral dissertation, University of Minnesota, Minneapolis.

Ridge, R. D. (in press). Targeting egoistic motivations: A functional strategy for recruiting volunteers. *Contemporary Social Psychology.*

Rosenhan, D. L. (1970). The natural socialization of altruistic autonomy. In J. Macauley & L. Berkowitz (Eds.), *Altruism and helping behavior* (pp. 251–268).

Schroeder, D. A., Penner, L. A., Dovidio, J. F., & Piliavin, J. A. (1995). *The psychology of helping and altruism: Problems and puzzles.* New York: McGraw-Hill.

Smith, M., Bruner, J., & White, R. (1956). *Opinions and personality.* New York: Wiley.

Snyder, M. (1992). Motivational foundations of behavioral confirmation. In M. P. Zanna (Ed.), *Advances in experimental social psychology* (Vol. 25). San Diego, CA: Academic Press, 67–114.

Snyder, M. (1993). Basic research and practical problems: The promise of a "functional" personality and social psychology. *Personality and Social Psychology Bulletin, 19,* 251–264.

Snyder, M., & Cantor, N. (1998). Understanding personality and social behavior: A functionalist strategy. In D. Gilbert, S. Fiske, & G. Lindzey (Eds.), *The handbook of social psychology* (4th ed., Vol. 1, pp. 635–679). Boston: McGraw-Hill.

Snyder, M., & DeBono, K. G. (1987). A functional approach to attitudes and persuasion. In M. P. Zanna, J. M. Olson, & C. P. Herman (Eds.), *Social influence: The Ontario symposium* (Vol. 5). Hillsdale, NJ Lawrence Erlbaum Associates, 107–125.

Snyder, M., & Ickes, W. (1985). Personality and social behavior. In G. Lindzey & E. Aronson (Eds.), *The handbook of social psychology* (3rd ed., Vol. 2, pp. 883–948). New York: McGraw-Hill.

Snyder, M., & Omoto, A. M. (1992). Who helps and why? The psychology of AIDS volunteerism. In S. Spacapan & S. Oskamp (Eds.), *Helping and being helped: Naturalistic studies* (pp. 213–239). Newbury Park, CA: Sage.

Staub, E. (1978). *Positive social behavior and morality: Social and personal influences* (Vol. 1). New York: Academic Press.

Stukas, A. A., Snyder, M., & Clary, E. G. (1996, July). *The effects of "mandatory volunteerism" on motivation to volunteer: A field study.* Presented at the annual meetings of the American Psychological Society, San Francisco, CA.

Watson, D., Clark, L. A., McIntyre, C. W., & Hamaker, S. (1992). Affect, personality, and social activity. *Journal of Personality and Social Psychology, 63,* 1011–1025.

Watson, D., Clark, L. A., & Tellegen, A. (1988). Development and validation of brief measures of positive and negative affect: The PANAS scales. *Journal of Personality and Social Psychology, 54,* 1063–1070.

Wicker, A. W. (1969). Attitudes vs. actions: The relationship of verbal and overt behavioral responses to attitude objects. *Journal of Social Issues, 41,* 41–78.

14

Attitude Function and the Automobile

Richard Ennis
Mark P. Zanna
University of Waterloo

> It seems peculiar that psychologists should make such obstinate attempts to evade the directional or finalistic aspect of living processes, in the name of science, when most sciences have recorded and conceptualized such tendencies. Physiologists, for example, have always been guided by the notion of function. They have always asked themselves, "What is the function of this process?"
>
> –Murray (1938, p. 67)

We all have attitudes and they are directed toward virtually everything in our environment: people, places, events, actions, issues, objects, and consumer products such as the automobile. The very prevalence and ubiquity of attitudinal evaluations suggest they must serve some psychological purpose. The scientific exploration of the motives that underlie the formation and expression of attitudes is known collectively as the functional approach. Although evident some 40 years ago (Katz, 1960; Smith, Bruner, & White, 1956), interest in attitude function disappeared from the mainstream of psychological research, which is surprising, because it seems to be an elementary and crucial domain for investigation, as noted by Murray in the opening quotation.

Fortunately, there has been a recent revival of research interest that has demonstrated the worth of the functional approach. For example, there is evidence that a knowledge of attitude function improves the prediction of behavior toward possessions (Abelson, 1986; Abelson & Prentice, 1989; Prentice, 1987; Richins, 1994; Wallendorf & Arnould, 1988); groups (Herek, 1986a, 1986b; Pryor, Reeder, Vinacco, & Kott, 1989; Shavitt, 1985, 1989, 1990); and consumer products (Belk, 1985, 1988, 1989; DeBono, 1987, 1989; DeBono & Packer, 1990; Ennis & Zanna, 1990, 1991; Johar & Sirgy, 1991; Krugman, 1965; Shavitt, 1985, 1989, 1990; Snyder & DeBono, 1989). There also appears to be a consistency in the needs served by attitudes and other belief structures such as values (Kristiansen & Zanna, 1988; Maio & Olson, 1994) and stereotypes toward out-groups (Haddock, Zanna, & Esses, 1993; Herek, 1984, 1986b; Pryor et al., 1989). The personality construct of self-monitoring (Snyder, 1974) has also been used effectively to predict different functional orientations toward consumer products (DeBono, 1987, 1989; DeBono & Packer, 1990; Shavitt, Lowrey, & Han, 1992; Snyder & DeBono, 1989).

ATTITUDE FUNCTIONS

Although functional taxonomies differ in their classifications and terminology (e.g., Herek, 1986a; Katz, 1960; Prentice, 1987; Richins, 1994; Shavitt, 1989; Smith et al., 1956), there is a unanimous distinction between instrumental and symbolic functions. The instrumental function, for example, has been termed *object appraisal* (Smith et al., 1956), *adjustive and knowledge* (Katz, 1960), *experiential* (Herek, 1986a) *instrumental* (Abelson, 1986; Prentice, 1987), and *utilitarian* (Richins, 1994; Shavitt, 1985). As these labels imply, the focus is on the features and attributes of the target object and its utility in providing better functioning in the environment. Features of the automobile such as gas mileage, reliability, and cost address instrumental needs. Utilitarian beliefs are directly related to the attitude item in the sense that they do not link the object to other mental structures such as values, norms, or other attitudes.

Symbolic beliefs, however, serve to connect the stimulus object to other psychological constructs. Given the complexity of symbolism, it is not surprising to find less taxonomic consensus about the psychological needs met by attitudes. Early theorists, for example, focused on psychodynamic motives such as externalization (Smith et al., 1956) and ego defense

(Katz, 1960). The notion of intrapsychic needs persists in modern schemes with Herek's defensive function (Herek, 1986a, 1987) and Shavitt's self-esteem maintenance function. To facilitate our research, we adopted a two-stage approach to identifying symbolic functions. Initially, we attempted to make the simple distinction between instrumental and symbolic needs. Then we explored the more subtle discrimination between social- expressive and value-expressive motives.

At the crude level, symbolic attitudes are assumed to serve all noninstrumental functions (Prentice, 1987). We, however, have limited this category to the expressive needs suggested by Herek (1986a, 1987). The attitude object serves as a means to an end, rather than as an end in itself (i.e., instrumental), by symbolically representing events, relationships, thoughts, or feelings that are important or meaningful for self-expression. Items that serve expressive needs are evaluated for more than their utilitarian attributes. Thus, the automobile becomes a vehicle for self-expression.

Herek (1986a) divided the expressive motives into those that serve either social or value needs. Social-expressive attitudes facilitate social interaction and acceptance by others. Based on Smith et al.'s (1956) social-expressive function, these attitudes represent the norms and values of important reference groups. Expression of such evaluations, therefore, foster social alignment and identification. An automobile, for example, can signify demographic information such as age, status, and lifestyle. Based on Katz (1960), value-expressive attitudes serve to give positive articulation to the important central values of the individual. Attitudinal beliefs that serve this psychological purpose feature aspects of self-concept, and expression meets needs such as self-disclosure and personal identity. Environmental and conservation values, for example, can be reflected in the purchasing decisions of car buyers.

THE AUTOMOBILE: FUNCTIONS OF THE OBJECT

As noted earlier, the automobile serves as a means to our research ends. We sought an object that allowed us to examine functional distinctions within the belief structure of attitudes and their relative contributions to overall attitudinal evaluations. Previous research (e.g., Shavitt, 1985, 1989, 1990) employed different consumer products that might address distinct psychological needs. We chose the automobile because it is a multifunctional product (Blass, Danseco, Greenberg, & Scher, 1994; Evans, 1959; Jacobson & Kossoff, 1963; Richins, 1994) that meets, to varying degrees, all the psychological needs that we have defined. Furthermore, this broad class of attitude objects contains various subcategories (i.e., car models) that should be distinct in the extent to which they engage specific functions. Although all vehicles meet certain instrumental purposes, such as transportation, specific models differ in their potential for meeting a variety of value-expressive and social-expressive needs. In other words, this consumer item offers a range of motivational profiles that may illustrate the function of the attitude process.

We selected four automobile models that we assumed would offer distinct functional profiles. Subcompact and family styles were chosen to represent vehicles that are basically unifunctional in the sense that they are predominantly utilitarian in nature. Luxury and sports models, on the other hand, are more multifunctional to the extent that they offer greater opportunity for satisfying symbolic needs. This gives us two representatives of each function for broad comparisons between the instrumental and the symbolic.

The goal of our ongoing research program is the identification of the motivational links among objects, attitudes toward those objects, and the belief structures that comprise those attitudes. The potential of a stimulus item to satisfy certain psychological needs should be an important determinant of attitude. The status conferred by owning a luxury car, for example, is valued positively by those who seek social rank and valued negatively by those who view displays of wealth as pretentious. Furthermore, this functional consistency should be evident in the system of beliefs that form the structure of the attitude (Ajzen & Fishbein, 1980; Boninger, Krosnick, & Berent, 1995; Zanna & Rempel, 1988). The related set of thoughts, feelings, and behaviors should reflect what the stimulus object does for the individual. In other words, we should be able to distinguish and classify these basic entities according to their functional nature. Multifunctional automobiles, therefore, produce more symbolic associations than do unifunctional models.

To explore these connections, however, it was necessary to establish the validity of our a priori assumptions about the motivational diversity of the chosen models. In several studies (Ennis & Zanna, 1990, 1991, 1992a, 1992b, 1993), research participants have been provided with definitions of instrumental ("how useful the vehicle will be"), social-expressive ("what the vehicle expresses to others"), and value-expressive ("what the vehicle means to the person") needs and asked to rate the relative importance of each in their evaluations of the four types of automobiles. This direct measure of object function was adapted from Shavitt's research (1985) and has consistently supported our basic distinction between unifunctional and multifunctional models. In four separate studies with a combined total of 248 participants, subcompact and family cars were rated as more instrumental than luxury and sports models, whereas the latter received higher evaluations for serving both social-expressive and value-expressive needs. In all cases, these results were statistically significant.

ATTITUDE STRUCTURE AND THE AUTOMOBILE: DOES FUNCTION INFLUENCE STRUCTURE?

Given the clear empirical evidence that automobiles are distinguished by function, at least for the basic symbolic–instrumental dichotomy, we turned our attention to how this might be reflected in attitude structure. We hoped to discover functional patterns that paralleled the direct measures of needs met by the various automobiles. This required a procedure that would allow us to identify the salient beliefs that underlie attitude. A standard thought-listing technique (Cacioppo & Petty, 1981) was used to elicit free associations for each model of car. In previous research (Ennis, 1989) we found that this procedure was biased toward the generation of utilitarian notions to the exclusion of others that might indicate expressive beliefs and feelings. Given the direct relationship between object and utility, this is not surprising. Over the course of our research, we found it necessary to provide instructions that explicitly pull for thoughts associated with social-expressive and value-expressive needs. This was accomplished by providing a detailed description of each function and requesting participants to list their thoughts and feelings that are relevant to that purpose. Table 14.1 provides the various elicitation instructions used throughout our research, including those for the expressive functions.

We developed a manual for coding the psychological motives associated with the elicited beliefs (see the Appendix). To date, more than 2,000 statements have been categorized as addressing instrumental, social-expressive, or value-expressive needs. The coding manual has proven effective, with an impressive agreement rate of 90.2% between two judges who were not aware of which car model had generated the statements.

TABLE 14.1

Belief Elicitation Instructions

Instrumental Beliefs

An automobile can be a useful tool in our everyday functioning. There are many benefits and costs associated with owning and operating a car. Using the car in the picture, list the utilitarian qualities of owning this automobile. In other words, list the features, attributes, characteristics, etc., that contribute to, or detract from, the usefulness of this automobile. What are the costs and benefits of this car?

Social-Expressive Beliefs

An automobile can tell other people something about us. We can select a car to specifically send a particular social image to other people. Using the car in the picture, list the social attributes of someone who owns this automobile. In other words, list the impressions about lifestyle, group memberships, occupation, social status, image, etc., that you might associate with this automobile. What does this car express to others?

Value-Expressive Beliefs

An automobile can be important and meaningful to us. As a valued possession, a car can be viewed as an expression of our "inner" self. Using the car in the picture, list the "inner" characteristics of someone who owns this automobile. In other words, list the attitudes, central values, personal standards, personality characteristics, etc., that you might associate with this automobile. What type of person drives this car?

Affect

An automobile has an ability to elicit emotional reactions in people. We can enjoy or suffer a range of different feelings when driving a certain kind of car. Using the car in the picture, list the feelings and emotions that you might associate with this automobile. In others words, list the sensations, moods, passions, feelings, etc., that might associate with driving or owning this car. What emotions does this car stir?

The belief-elicitation results provided some initial evidence of a functional consistency between attitude structure and stimulus object. To the extent that a product meets a specific need, this need should be reflected in the functional categorization of the beliefs associated with the product. In other words, instrumental items should produce instrumental beliefs; symbolic items should produce symbolic beliefs, and multifunctional items should produce both instrumental and symbolic beliefs. Although multifunctional, the automobile models should generate beliefs that duplicate the functional discriminations evident in the direct assessments reported earlier. Indeed, we found that participants more frequently provided self-expressive statements for symbolic (luxury and sports) models than for the functionally restricted instrumental (subcompact and family) models, $\chi^2(1) = 21.01$, p .01. For example, references to status, occupation, and materialism, were more common. There was no significant difference in the frequency of utilitarian beliefs elicited. Overall, people readily provided an array of instrumental features of any make of automobile, but symbolic associations were more readily accessible and salient when the model was capable of meeting expressive needs. This offers some indication that psychological function may influence important aspects of an attitude, such as accessibility and salience (Alwitt, 1990; Boninger, Krosnick & Berent, 1995; Fishbein & Ajzen, 1975; McGuire, 1985, 1989; Schuette & Fazio, 1995; Zanna & Rempel, 1988). The ease with which people generated their thoughts, and the success of coding them according to need served, indicates that the functionally consistent beliefs are both important and readily available.

ATTITUDE STRUCTURE AND THE AUTOMOBILE: DOES STRUCTURE INFLUENCE FUNCTION?

In a discussion of multifunctional products, such as automobiles, the psychological function of attitudinal beliefs becomes more intriguing. We have seen that the automobile elicits a network of thoughts, feelings, and ideas that are related to a range of needs including instrumental, value-expressive, and social-expressive needs. The preceding data support the notion that attitudes and associated beliefs are functionally related, but we do not have any evidence that the functional makeup of the underlying beliefs can influence the needs met by overall attitude. Indeed, it is assumed that belief structures are formed largely on the bases of experience with stimulus objects and, in particular, the ability of those objects to meet specific needs.

To test the notion that a change in the salience of individual beliefs changes the function of the attitude, we (Ennis & Zanna, 1992a) adopted a priming procedure similar to that used by Shavitt (1990) and DeBono (1987, 1989; DeBono & Packer, 1990). Our intent was to prime people with instrumental, value-expressive, or social-expressive beliefs about a novel and nondescript automobile, and then assess their perceptions about the functional capacities of the attitude object. In essence, we hoped to create product profiles that parallel our unifunctional and multifunctional models.

We introduced individuals to the fictitious "DL-22" as a prototype model and provided no further information about the vehicle. For our priming task we generated three sets of advertising slogans, each set appealing to one of the psychological needs, and randomly assigned participants to receive one set of slogans. Each promotional phrase was a brief statement that was worded identically across conditions except for a word or two that appealed to a specific function. For example, one slogan had the following three versions: "seize the wheel of the DL-22 and experience the performance" (instrumental), "seize the wheel of the DL-22 and experience the freedom" (value-expressive), and "seize the wheel of the

DL-22 and experience the glory" (social expressive). The pertinent words were chosen from the statements elicited in earlier studies.

Participants were primed by having to rate the advertisements on two irrelevant dimensions (how "appealing" and how "convincing" they were). We predicted that, in the absence of previous knowledge of the fictitious model of car, people would perceive it as meeting the needs consistent with the beliefs expressed in the specific set of slogans. Those given the instrumental version would rate the DL-22 as relatively uni-functional and similar in profile to our subcompact and family models. Given the social-expressive and value-expressive versions, however, we hypothesized that individuals would rate the DL-22 as comparable to the more multifunctional luxury and sports models.

As in other studies, these participants also provided direct assessments of the functions of the four models of cars. These data were consistent with the results reported earlier and thus provided profiles of each model that could be used to compare the functional perceptions of the fictitious DL-22. Because these measures were obtained after the priming task, these data indicate that our priming manipulation did not influence the percep-tions of familiar automobiles. The priming manipulation was, however, effective in producing different functional perceptions of the unknown and unfamiliar DL-22. As seen in Table 14.2, people rated the hypotheti-cal vehicle as serving a pattern of needs consistent with our hypothesis. A repeated measures ANOVA revealed a significant interaction between priming condition and function, $F(4,114) = 4.01, p < .01$. Generally, the symbolic primes resulted in lower instrumental and higher symbolic ratings of the DL-22 than did the instrumental prime. Conversely, given either of the symbolic primes, participants perceived the DL-22 as serving a pattern of needs similar to that of the luxury and sports models.

It is worth repeating that the priming effect was limited to the DL-22. It appears that the manipulation was subtle enough to have an impact on the functional nature of a novel, but not an existing, attitudinal belief

TABLE 14.2

Mean Function Ratings By Priming Condition For The DL-22.

	Function		
Prime	*Instrumental*	*Social-Expressive*	*Value-Expressive*
Instrumental	4.75	2.90	3.55
Social-expressive	4.40	3.10	3.80
Value-expressive	4.15	3.80	4.10

Note. Function rated on a 5-point scale with higher score indicating greater function. $N = 60$.

structure. Yet the subsequent effects on functional perceptions were noteworthy. Recall that for the vast majority of slogans only one word was unique to each version or condition. Furthermore, the exposure to the slogans was fairly innocuous and brief. Despite these minimal manipulations, people perceived the DL-22 in a manner that was functionally consistent with the motives profiled in the slogans.

These conclusions are based on the assumption that the priming slogans led participants to form new belief structures about a novel attitude object, the DL-22, which directly influenced their perceptions of the psychological needs met by that product. It is conceivable that the advertising slogans led participants to categorize the unkown DL-22 according to familiar automobile models with similar features. Existing attitudes and associated belief structures could then be substituted for the novel attitude object, resulting in the functional consistency noted in this study. Although less direct than the hypothesized process, this heuristic alternative still illustrates the potential for influencing functional perceptions by manipulating the relevant attitudinal belief structure.

In itself, it is not surprising to discover that attitude function is reflected in the thoughts and feelings that constitute the attitudinal structure. The important discovery is that the influence may also work in the other direction! By introducing new items into a belief structure or by manipulating the importance of existing items, one may be able to influence the functional capacities of the attitude toward some object. Such a finding has obvious advertising applications. We can assume that consumers purchase most products to satisfy certain needs and that buying decisions might be influenced by persuasive techniques that change the functional constitution of belief structures.

A MULTIPLE REGRESSION MODEL
OF ATTITUDE FUNCTION

Before proceeding too far with these motivational prospects, however, we continue with our attempts to come to a fuller understanding of the structural relationship between attitude function and individual beliefs. Combined with multiple regression, the theoretical work and measurement techniques articulated by Fishbein and Ajzen (1975; Ajzen & Fishbein, 1980; Fishbein, 1963) seemed particularly suited to the task. Fishbein and Ajzen have proposed an expectancy-value (ExV) model of attitude structure in which attitude toward a target item is the sum of the products of belief strength (expectancy) and belief evaluation (value).

Belief strength is the certainty or confidence that the belief is truly a feature or attribute of the stimulus object. The evaluative component is simply the judgment of the positive or negative quality of each attribute. By measuring the strength and evaluative components of beliefs, the resulting ExV index can then be used to predict attitude in a multiple regression equation. Lutz (1977) has argued that functional theory is strongly grounded in expectancy-value principles: "To the extent that an attitude is serving a particular function, then the corresponding ExV index for that function is expected to be well-formed in the individual's mind and generally consistent with overall attitude" (p. 44).

For multifunctional items, such as the automobile, a multiple regression equation permits the simultaneous examination of the diverse needs served with regression coefficients that measure the relative correlation of each function with the overall attitude (Ennis, 1989; Fishbein & Ajzen, 1975; Lutz, 1977; Pedhazur, 1982). Given our functional profiles, for example, we hypothesized that salient instrumental beliefs would be significant predictors of attitudes toward both unifunctional and multifunctional vehicles, based on the assumption that all vehicles are utilitarian products. For multifunctional cars, as the designation implies, we anticipated that the inclusion of symbolic predictors would significantly improve the multiple regression equation.

Our initial attempts to demonstrate the functional dynamics with regression models were disappointing. We began by carefully selecting a set of eight beliefs that were representative of the instrumental, value-expressive, and social-expressive statements elicited in an earlier study. In that study, which used a within-subjects design, research participants then provided belief strength and evaluation ratings of each belief across all four car models. In all cases, instrumental beliefs were statistically significant predictors of attitude. Unfortunately, the expressive predictors did not make a unique contribution to the regressions regardless of the functional dynamics of the automobile in question. Combined with similar difficulties in earlier research using different products (Ennis, 1989), these results have led us to explore various methodological improvements involving both the criterion and predictor sides of the multiple regression model.

We began by addressing some concerns that the approach of Fishbein and Ajzen may impose some severe impediments to studying attitude function (Ennis, 1989; Lutz, 1977; Slovic, 1995). Conceptually and methodologically, this traditional approach has focussed on the utilitarian needs served by attitude objects, which results in a unidimensional and unifunctional belief structure. Belief elicitation procedures, for example, explicitly call for instrumental thoughts and ideas to the exclusion of beliefs that might reflect other psychological functions. This unifunctional bias may be further compounded by the measurement of belief strength. Symbolic ideas are, by definition, not direct characteristics of the stimulus object and may be less accessible and receive lower strength rating than utilitarian features. Two procedural modifications were made to improve the quality of the predictor variables.

In our earlier work, participants provided expectancy and value ratings of attitudinal beliefs provided by other people in previous belief-elicitation research. This was in accordance with the procedures recommended by Fishbein and Ajzen (1975). It is conceivable, however, that the use of a predetermined subset of belief statements might severely limit the functional complexity of attitudes by forcing individuals to consider a restricted sample of expressive ideas. Combined with lower strength, this could reduce both the magnitude and the variance of the expectancy-value ratings and, in turn, adversely affect the regression coefficients of the symbolic predictors (Pedhazur, 1982). To counter this possibility, we now allow each participant to generate and rate their own belief statements. This is accomplished by having them record their thoughts on self-stick notes that can be moved onto boards designed to assess the strength and evaluation measures. Presumably people will recognize the strength of their own symbolic associations, which should enhance both the internal validity and the functional richness of the belief sets.

The second modification was the inclusion of another predictor in the regression model. Further review of the belief-elicitation procedures suggested another possible bias. We were impressed by the small proportion of statements that expressed any feelings or emotions about the stimulus objects despite specific instructions for individuals to list "all of your thoughts and feelings." Although some emotion was expressed, the vast majority of statements can best be characterized as cognitive rather than affective. As a result, the attitudinal belief set chosen from these procedures may inadvertently reflect a unidimensional view of attitudes. Recent theorization has criticized such a perspective and has offered conceptualizations of attitude as a multidimensional dimension concept. Zanna and Rempel (1988), for example, suggest a tripartite model in which attitudes have cognitive, affective, and behavioral components that may be quite distinct from one another. The affective component of attitude may be particularly important for our conceptualization of expressive functions and beliefs (Breckler & Wiggins, 1989). In fact, many symbolic associations may be purely affective, such as treasured mementos of a loved one (Basin, Darken, & Griffin, 1994; Lang, 1995; Prentice, 1987; Richins, 1994).

Even the direct measures of motivation, which have consistently demonstrated functional diversity among the car models, have operationalized the social-expressive function as "my social identity: what the item tells others about me," and the value-expressive need as "my values: what the item means to me." These descriptions are in contrast to the instrumental function presented as "my past experiences with the object: how useful I found the item." The affective overtones of the symbolic notions are in sharp contrast to the cognitive simplicity of the utilitarian definition. This perhaps indicates that these direct measures of function have repeatedly supported our theoretical notions, whereas the regression formulation has not.

To counter this possible bias, we used our strategy of modifying elicitation procedures to explicitly pull for the desired kind of information. In addition to instrumental and expressive thoughts, we have begun to blatantly request emotions and feelings associated with the attitude object (see Table 14.1). The subsequent ratings of these affective statements provide another predictor that we hoped would improve the relationship between attitude structure and function. This should be particularly true in the case of multifunctional automobiles, where a better prediction equation that reflects the conceptual meaningfulness of the emotional component of the expressive functions is provided.

We have also focused on the criterion variable by expanding our measurement of overall attitude. Again, we felt that the traditional evaluative scales used to rate attitude may be functionally biased toward utilitarian needs in the same manner as attitudinal beliefs. If true, this would further impair the predictive potential of symbolic beliefs. Batra and Ahtola (1991) suggested that the evaluative semantic differential scales identified by Osgood, Suci, and Tannenbaum (1957) have assumed a unidimensional, generic attitude toward consumer products. Evaluative scales anchored by adjectives such as "good–bad," "like–dislike," and "favorable–unfavorable" fall into this class. Unfortunately, these are the same scales we have used in assessing object attitudes. Batra and Ahtola provided empirical evidence that different evaluative scales can be employed to measure the utilitarian and affective (referred to as "hedonic" in their article) components of attitudes. Following their lead, we obtained overall attitudinal evaluations using three adjective pairs to represent each of generic (bad–good, like–dislike, and favorable– unfavorable), utilitarian (impractical–practical, beneficial–harmful, and inefficient–efficient), and hedonic (pleasant–unpleasant, ugly–beautiful, and interesting–boring) aspects of attitudes toward automobiles.

Although preliminary (N = 48), the findings are very intriguing. Analysis of the criterion measures themselves suggests that the hedonic and utilitarian dimensions are quite sensitive to psychological function, whereas overall summative attitudes are not. Averaged across the four types of automobiles, the utilitarian and hedonic measures of attitude (rated on a 7-point scale ranging from -3 to +3) were not correlated, r = .06, but both varied with generic attitudes, r = .43 for utilitarian and r = .74 for hedonic. These correlations support the distinction proposed by Batra and Ahtola (1991). For our research interests, hedonic ratings of attitudes toward the unifunctional cars (0.83 for subcompact and -1.92 for family) were significantly lower than those toward the multifunctional models (3.83 for luxury and 5.08 for sporty), $F(3,44)$ = 12.01, p <.001. Although not statistically significant, utilitarian attitudinal scores were higher for the unifunctional cars (4.92 for subcompact and 5.17 for family) than for the multifunctional models (2.25 for luxury and 2.25 for sporty). These findings are consistent with our notion that compact and family models are relatively unifunctional (i.e., they serve basically instrumental needs), whereas luxury and sporty models are relatively multifunctional (i.e., they serve instrumental, symbolic, and emotional needs).

Turning to the belief elicitation procedures, we again coded the 868 statements using the previously developed coding manual. Recall that instructions were tailored to explicitly elicit instrumental, social-expressive, value-expressive, and emotional statements about the target vehicle. Table 14.3 shows that this procedure was successful. The frequencies in the diagonal of the contingency table demonstrate that significantly more statements were coded as functionally consistent, rather than inconsistent, with the instructions, $\chi^2(9)$ = 1694.9, p <.0001. This pattern of results was consistent across all four models of automobile. Regardless of stimulus object, our instructions were successful in eliciting beliefs from the desired psychological function: instrumental instructions resulted in instrumental statements, social-expressive instructions resulted in social-expressive statements, and so on.

We also examined the effect of the target automobile on the frequencies of functional statements that were elicited. There were no significant differences in the number of instrumental, social-expressive, value-expressive, or emotional beliefs elicited for the four models of cars, $\chi^2(9)$ = 2.3,

TABLE 14.3

Frequency of Functional Statements By Thought-Elicitation Instructions.

Instructions	Coded Function			
	Instrumental	Soc-Express	Val-Express	Emotion
Instrumental	209	3	1	7
Social-Expessive	6	150	76	3
Value-Expressive	2	27	200	0
Emotion	10	4	8	162

Note: $\chi^2 (9) = 1694.9, p < .0001$.

p = ns. This suggests that the instructions, rather than the attitude object, guided the function of the statements provided by the participants. Unlike our previous elicitation studies, therefore, this cannot be taken as evidence of the functional profile of the attitude function. On the other hand, this suggests that each automobile generated a rich set of associations embracing the entire spectrum of instrumental and symbolic associations. This certainly improves the possibility of identifying their unique relationships with overall attitudes.

Armed with more and better predictor variables and criterion variables, we continued to explore the regression equation as a conceptual model of attitude function. We employed a hierarchical approach in which each regression begins with the instrumental index as the single predictor of attitude. This simple, unifunctional model in which utilitarian attitudes are predicted by instrumental beliefs represents the traditional perception of attitude structure dictated by Fishbein and Ajzen's (1975) procedures. Using the success of this step as a baseline, we than added the index of symbolic beliefs in the second step. An improvement in predictability at this stage would support the contention that the automobile is a multifunctional product and underscore the inadequacy of unifunctional perceptions of attitude structure. Finally, we formed the full model by adding the affect measure as the third predictor variable in the equation. This final step tested our belief that emotion may be a meaningful predictor of attitude toward multifunctional items. The hierarchal strategy was then repeated using hedonic attitude as the criterion variable. At each step, the change in the squared multiple regression coefficient (ΔR^2) allowed us to statistically evaluate the conceptual developments of our multifunctional, multidimensional model of attitude structure.

Although it is still early, we have produced some interesting and unexpected findings. We anticipated functional consistency in which, for example, utilitarian attitudes toward utilitarian automobiles are best predicted by utilitarian beliefs. However, our results suggest something quite different. Utilitarian attitudes were not significantly correlated with the instrumental index, even for subcompact and family models. In fact, the best predictive models for these instrumental cars occured when hedonic measures of attitude were used as the criterion and then, only with the inclusion of the symbolic index as a predictor. For subcompacts, the inclusion of symbolic beliefs significantly increased the predictive ability of the equation, $\Delta R^2 = .683$, $p < .05$. As hypothesized, adding the third and final predictor, the affective index, did not make a unique contribution when predicting this unifunctional automobile. Although not statistically significant, the pattern was the same for the family car model. In other words, the best multiple regression equation for each of the unifunctional automobiles was the one we thought would capture only multifunctional relationships (i.e., multiple predictors of hedonic attitude).

For the symbolic automobiles, the best predictive models occured with the functionally inconsistent criterion, utilitarian attitudes. Even the full regressions predicting hedonic attitudes did not reach statistical significance. For utilitarian measures of attitude, the regression for luxury cars reached significance only when the symbolic index was added to the instrumental predictor, $\Delta R^2 = .492$, $p < .05$. There was a further improvement with the final addition of the emotional predictor, $\Delta R^2 = .170$, $p < .05$. For sporty automobiles, the regression increased significantly with the inclusion of the affective predictor, $\Delta R^2 = .229$, $p < .05$. These results are compatible with our theoretical model of a multidimensional belief infrastructure for multifunctional products.

To further explore these findings regarding the attitudinal measures, we repeated the analyses after collapsing the data according to the functional diversity of the automobiles. In other words, compact and family cars were combined to represent unifunctional automobiles while luxury and sports models were combined to represent multifunctional automobiles. Here we obtained clearer evidence of the contrary findings. For unifunctional vehicles, the best regression was the full model regressed predicting the hedonic measure of attitude, $R^2 = .394$, $p < .05$, and for multifunctional cars, the best regression was the prediction of utilitarian attitude by instrumental and symbolic beliefs, $R^2 = .451$, $p < .01$. The inclusion of emotional beliefs failed to improve the model.

Perhaps the regression models indicate that multifunctional products, such as automobiles, are evaluated, at least in part, by their inability to satisfy certain needs. Given the bipolar nature of our evaluative scales, the negative ratings of the hedonic dimension of unifunctional cars might be reflected by negative associations such as symbolic and emotional needs that are not being satisfied. By the same token, the less positive evaluations of the utilitarian dimension for multifunctional automobiles might indicate the sacrificed capacity to meet instrumental motives. Such a process could produce the paradoxical findings in the multiple regression models. Unfortunately, supportive evidence awaits further research.

CONCLUDING COMMENTS

Although our exploration is a work in progress, we can make a number of inferences about the functional connections between objects, attitudes, and attitude structure. With the frequency data from belief-elicitation studies, we have demonstrated a motivational similarity between models of automobiles and the related attitudinal structure. Further, we have shown that manipulation of function specific beliefs can produce changes in perceptions of the capacity of a product to fulfill certain purposes—at least for novel brands.

The adoption of different evaluative scales (Basin, Dardin, & Griffin, 1994; Batra & Ahtola, 1991) has also demonstrated that overall attitude is sensitive to the functional dimensions of the target object. The final connection, between attitude and underlying structure, has been the most elusive. Still, the evolving nature of our multiple regression model is beginning to produce some promising, albeit unexpected, results. The belief elicitation procedures we have developed permit a more comprehensive mapping of the direct and symbolic associations with any object. We have found that coding these associations according to function is a straightforward task. When subsequently weighted by strength and evaluation, the belief set offers a motivational profile of the attitude item.

The functional approach, like all attitudinal theories, must eventually explore the relationship between attitude and behavior (Greenwald, 1989). A renewed focus on the motivational aspects of the process seems a logical and promising development. It seems a reasonable assumption that if knowledge of attitude function can contribute to this understanding, then the ability to measure and map the psychological purpose of attitudinal thoughts and feelings is an essential step. Our priming study, for example, has offered some tantalizing evidence of the implications for persuasive techniques. Armed with a functional profile of a product, it may be possible to target specific beliefs in persuasive appeals. Manufacturers of a unifunctional automobile, for example, may wish to reinforce the beliefs associated with the utility of their product. On the other hand, they might promote brand differentiation by introducing symbolic associations into the functional belief set for their model. Consider manufacturers that introduce a vehicle powered by an alternative power source. With higher cost and less range than the internal-combustion engine, these models might best be promoted by developing symbolic associations with environmental concerns that allow consumers to meet value-expressive needs. Less obvious, but potentially more persuasive, are image-based appeals that address social-expressive motives such as the status and prestige of ownership. These persuasive possibilities may extend to other attitude targets and other belief structures such as stereotypes and prejudice (Haddock et al., 1993; Herek, 1984, 1986b; Pryor et al., 1989; Rokeach, 1985; Rokeach & Ball-Rokeach, 1989).

The functional approach also offers a common denominator for exploration of the other principal sources of motivation: personal and situational influences. Behavioral responses to an stimulus object are determined by its capacity for meeting the psychological requirements of an individual interacting with an environment. Attitude–behavior consistency is guided by the functional resonance of person, place, and object (Jamieson & Zanna, 1989). Again, the identification and categorization of the belief structure is a promising avenue for examining this interplay. This chapter opened with Murray (1938) encouraging us to ask, "What is the function of this process?" We hope our program of research has offered insight into the answer and, more importantly, an appreciation of the question.

ACKNOWLEDGMENTS

This project was funded by research grants from the Social Sciences and Humanities Research Council of Canada awarded to Mark P. Zanna.

APPENDIX: CODING MANUAL

Function	Beliefs	Examples
Instrumental	Comfort	comfortable; lots of leg room; cramped
	Driveability	easy to park; good around town
	Description	a big boat; lots of options
	Economics	reliable; good on gas
	Applications	good for family outings; off-road ability
Social-expressive	SES	lower class preppie; upper-class owner; run-of-the-mill person
	Status/prestige	high status; someone of importance
	Occupation	white-collar job; homemaker
	Age and gender	for a young girl; old adults
	Marital status	no children; married with kids
Value-Expressive	Conservatism	traditional values; belief in free market; carefree
	Pragmatism	practical person; common sense
	Materialism	values material things; monetary values
	Environmental	cares about environment; polluter
	Personality	outgoing person; sociable; energetic; honest; ambitious

REFERENCES

Abelson, R. P. (1986). Beliefs are like possessions. *Journal for the Theory of Social Behaviour, 16,* 223–250.

Abelson, R. P., & Prentice, D. A. (1989). Beliefs as possessions: A functional perspective. In A. R. Pratkanis, S. J. Breckler, & A. G. Greenwald (Eds.), *Attitude structure and function* (pp. 361–382). Hillsdale, NJ: Lawrence Erlbaum Associates.

Ajzen, I., & Fishbein, M. (1980). *Understanding attitudes and predicting social behavior.* Englewood Cliffs, NJ: Prentice Hall.

Alwitt, L. F. (1990, August). *Attitude strength: An extra-content aspect of attitude.* Paper presented at the annual meeting of the American Psychological Association, Boston, MA.

Basin, B. J., Darken, W. R., & Griffin, M. (1994). Work and/or fun: Measuring hedonic and utilitarian shopping value. *Journal of Consumer Research, 20,* 644–656.

Batra, R., & Ahtola, O. T. (1991). Measuring the hedonic and utilitarian sources of consumer attitudes. *Marketing Letters, 2,* 159–170.

Belk, R. W. (1985). Materialism: Trait aspects of living in the material world. *Journal of Consumer Research, 12,* 265–280.

Belk, R. W. (1988). Possessions and the extended self. *Journal of Consumer Research, 15,* 139–168.

Belk, R. W. (1989). Extended self and extending paradigmatic perspective. *Journal of Consumer Research, 16,* 129–132.

Boninger, D. S., Krosnick, J. A., & Berent, M. K. (1995). Origins of attitude importance: Self-interest, social identification, and value relevance. *Journal of Personality and Social Psychology, 68*, 61–80.

Breckler, S. J., & Wiggins, E. C. (1989). The structure of individual attitudes and attitude systems. In A. R. Pratkanis, S. J. Breckler, & A. G. Greenwald (Eds.), *Attitude structure and function* (pp. 407–427). Hillsdale, NJ: Lawrence Erlbaum Associates.

Cacioppo, J. T., & Petty, R. E. (1981). Social psychological procedures for cognitive response assessment: The thought-listing technique. In T. Merluzzi, C. Glass & M. Genest (Eds.), *Cognitive assessment* (pp. 309–342). New York: Guilford Press.

DeBono, K. G. (1987). Investigating the social-expressive and value-expressive functions of attitudes: Implications for persuasion processes. *Journal of Personality and Social Psychology, 52*, 279–287.

DeBono, K. G. (1989). On the processing of functionally-relevant consumer information: Another look at source factors. *Advances in Consumer Research, 16*, 312–317.

DeBono, K. G., & Packer, M. (1990). The effects of advertising appeal on perceptions of product quality. *Personality and Social Psychology Bulletin, 17*, 194–200.

Ennis, R. (1989). *Attitude function: A procedure for its identification and measurement*. Unpublished master's thesis, University of Waterloo, Waterloo, Canada.

Ennis, R., & Zanna, M. P. (1990, August). *The measurement of attitude function at the belief level*. Paper presented at the annual meeting of the American Psychological Association, Boston, MA.

Ennis, R., & Zanna, M. P. (1991, June). *Psychological function and attitudes toward automobiles*. Paper presented at the annual meeting of the Canadian Psychological Association, Calgary, Canada.

Ennis, R., & Zanna, M. P. (1992a, June). *Automobile advertising: Changing the psychological function of attitudes*. Paper presented at the annual meeting of the Canadian Psychological Association, Quebec City, Canada.

Ennis, R., & Zanna, M. P. (1992b, October). *Attitudes, advertising, and automobiles: A functional approach*. Paper presented at the annual conference of the Association for Consumer Research, Vancouver, Canada.

Ennis, R., & Zanna, M. P. (1993). Attitudes, advertising, and automobiles: A functional approach. *Advances in Consumer Research, 20*, 662–666.

Evans, F. B. (1959). Psychological and objective factors in the prediction of brand choice: Ford versus Chevrolet. *Journal of Business, 32*, 340–369.

Fishbein, M. (1963). An investigation of the relationships between beliefs about an object and the attitude toward that object. *Human Relations, 16*, 233–240.

Fishbein, M., & Ajzen, I. (1975). *Belief, attitude, intention, and behavior*. Reading, MA: Addison-Wesley.

Greenwald, A. G. (1989). The structure of individual attitudes and attitude systems. In A. R. Pratkanis, S. J. Breckler, & A. G. Greenwald (Eds.), *Attitude structure and function* (pp. 1–10). Hillsdale, NJ: Lawrence Erlbaum Associates.

Haddock, G., Zanna, M. P., & Esses, V. M. (1993). Assessing the structure of prejudicial attitudes: The case of attitudes toward homosexuals. *Journal of Personality and Social Psychology, 65*, 1105–1118.

Herek, G. M. (1984). Beyond "homophobia": A social psychological perspective on attitudes toward lesbians and gay men. *Journal of Homosexuality, 10*, 1–21.

Herek, G. M. (1986a). The instrumentality of attitudes: Toward a neofunctional theory. *Journal of Social Issues, 42*, 99–114.

Herek, G. M. (1986b). On heterosexual masculinity: Some psychical consequences of the social construction of gender and sexuality. *American Behavioral Scientist, 29*, 563–577.

Herek, G. M. (1987). *Can functions be measured? A new perspective on the functional approach to attitudes*. Unpublished manuscript, Yale University, New Haven, CT.

Jacobson, E., & Kossoff, J. (1963). Self-percept and consumer attitudes toward small cars. *Journal of Applied Psychology, 47*, 242–245.

Jamieson, D. W., & Zanna, M. P. (1989). The structure of individual attitudes and attitude systems. In A. R. Pratkanis, S. J. Breckler, & A. G. Greenwald (Eds.), *Attitude structure and function* (pp. 383–406). Hillsdale, NJ: Lawrence Erlbaum Associates.

Katz, D. (1960). The functional approach to the study of attitudes. *Public Opinion Quarterly, 24,* 163–204.

Kristiansen, C. M., & Zanna, M. P. (1988). Justifying attitudes by appealing to values: A functional perspective. *British Journal of Social Psychology, 27,* 247–256.

Krugman, H. E. (1965). The impact of television advertising: Learning without involvement. *Public Opinion Quarterly, 29,* 349–365.

Lang, P. J. (1995). The emotion probe: Studies of motivation and attention. *American Psychologist, 50,* 372–385.

Lutz, R. J. (1977). *The functional approach to attitudes: A reconceptualization with operational implications* (Working Paper No. 53). Los Angeles: University of California, Center for Marketing Studies.

Maio, G. R., & Olson, J. M. (1994). Value–attitude–behaviour relations: The moderating role of attitude function. *British Journal of Social Psychology, 33,* 301–312.

McGuire, W. J. (1985). Attitudes and attitude change. In G. Lindzey & E. Aronson (Eds.), *Handbook of social psychology* (pp. 233–346). New York: Random House.

McGuire, W. J. (1989). The structure of individual attitudes and attitude systems. In A. R. Pratkanis, S. J. Breckler, & A. G. Greenwald (Eds.), *Attitude structure and function* (pp. 37–70). Hillsdale, NJ: Lawrence Erlbaum Associates.

Murray, H. A. (1938). *Explorations in personality.* New York: Oxford University Press.

Osgood, C. E., Suci, G. J., & Tannenbaum, P. H. (1957). *The measurement of meaning.* Urbana, IL: University of Illinois Press.

Pedhazur, E. J. (1982). *Multiple regression in behavioral research.* New York: Holt, Rinehart, Winston.

Prentice, D. A. (1987). Psychological correspondence of possessions, attitudes, and values. *Journal of Personality and Social Psychology, 53,* 993–1003.

Pryor, J. B., Reeder, G. D., Vinacco, R., & Kott, T. L. (1989). The instrumental and symbolic functions of attitudes toward persons with AIDS. *Journal of Applied Social Psychology, 19,* 377–404.

Richins, M. (1994). Valuing things: The public and private meanings of possessions. *Journal of Consumer Research, 21,* 504–521.

Rokeach, M. (1985). Inducing change and stability in belief systems and personality structures. *Journal of Social Issues, 41,* 153–171.

Rokeach, M., & Ball-Rokeach, S. J. (1989). Stability and change in American value priorities, 1968–1981. *American Psychologist, 44,* 775–784.

Schuette, R. A., & Fazio, R. H. (1995). Attitude accessibility and motivation as determinants of biased processing: A test of the MODE model. *Personality and Social Psychology Bulletin, 21,* 704–710.

Shavitt, S. (1985). *Operationalizing functional theory: Focusing on attitude functions inherent in objects.* Unpublished doctoral dissertation, Ohio State University, Columbus, OH.

Shavitt, S. (1989). Operationalizing functional theories of attitude. In A. R. Pratkanis, S. J. Breckler, & A. G. Greenwald (Eds.), *Attitude structure and function* (pp. 311–338). Hillsdale, NJ: Lawrence Erlbaum Associates.

Shavitt, S. (1990). The role of attitude objects in attitude function. *Journal of Experimental Social Psychology, 26,* 124–148.

Shavitt, S., Lowrey, T. M., & Han, S. (1992). Attitude functions in advertising: The interactive role of products and self-monitoring. *Journal of Consumer Psychology, 1,* 337–364.

Slovic, P. (1995). The construction of preference. *American Psychologist, 50,* 364–371.

Smith, M. B., Bruner, J. S., & White, R. W. (1956). *Opinions and personality.* New York: Wiley.

Snyder, M. (1974). Self-monitoring of expressive behavior. *Journal of Personality and Social Psychology, 30,* 526–537.

Snyder, M., & DeBono, K. G. (1989). Understanding the functions of attitudes: Lessons from personality and social behavior. In A. R. Pratkanis, S. J. Breckler, & A. G. Greenwald (Eds.), *Attitude structure and function* (pp. 339– 360). Hillsdale, NJ: Lawrence Erlbaum Associates.

Wallendorf, M., & Arnould, E. J. (1988). "My favorite things": A cross-cultural inquiry into object attachment, possessiveness, and social linkage. *Journal of Consumer Research, 14,* 531–547.

Zanna, M. P., & Rempel, J. K. (1988). Attitudes: A new look at an old concept. In D. Bar-Tal & A. Kruglanski (Eds.), *The social psychology of knowledge* (pp. 315–334). New York: Cambridge University Press.

15

Emergent Themes and Potential Approaches to Attitude Function: The Function-Structure Model of Attitudes

Gregory R. Maio
Cardiff University

James M. Olson
University of Western Ontario

Attitudes toward driving can be used to illustrate attitude functions, which are the psychological needs that attitudes fulfill. One can ask why people hold positive attitudes toward driving: What interests are served by these attitudes? At a deeper level, why do people bother to form positive or negative attitudes toward driving in the first place? Both of these questions inquire into the motivations that underlie such attitudes.

The answers to these questions appear to be complex. For example, it is interesting to consider why people often form positive attitudes toward driving, because there are many reasons why people should dislike driving, at least in comparison to other modes of transportation. For example, cars cost a lot of money to fuel, maintain, and insure; a lot of driving occurs in rush hour traffic; and alternative modes of transport (e.g., bus, train, cycling) are more environmentally friendly and cheaper, and offer an individual free time to pursue other activities (e.g., reading, studying). Yet, despite these disadvantages, people are frequently devoted to their cars. Consequently, it seems unlikely that positive attitudes toward driving are always the product of a simple cost–benefit analysis that is aimed at maximizing utilitarian interests; other motivations must also be relevant. For example, when people originally form attitudes toward driving, positive attitudes might develop because driving fulfills particular values, such as freedom and independence. In addition, after experiencing hardships because of their cars (e.g., costs of repairs), people might feel motivated to justify the hardships that they have endured, perhaps by increasing their affection for driving (see Aronson & Mills, 1959).

These ideas about the functions served by attitudes toward driving illustrate the point that different motivations can be expressed by attitudes (e.g., value expression, self-justification). In fact, seminal theories of attitude function (Katz, 1960; Smith, Bruner, & White, 1956) proposed several relevant motivations. Smith et al. suggested that attitudes can serve one or some combination of three functions: object appraisal, social adjustment, and externalization. Object appraisal refers to the ability of attitudes to summarize the positive and negative characteristics of objects in our environment; that is, attitudes cause people to approach things that are good for them and avoid things that are bad for them. Social adjustment is served by attitudes that help us to identify with people whom we admire and to dissociate from people whom we dislike. For example, teenagers often wear the style of clothing that is most preferred by their friends. Externalization is served by attitudes that defend the self against internal conflict. For example, a student who performs badly on tests might dislike tests because they threaten the student's self-esteem.

In a separate program of research, Katz (1960) proposed that attitudes serve four functions: ego defense, knowledge, utility, and value expression. In combination, the knowledge and utilitarian functions are similar to Smith et al.'s (1956) object appraisal function: the knowledge function represents the ability of attitudes to summarize information about objects in the environment, and the utilitarian function exists in attitudes that maximize rewards and minimize punishments obtained from the environment. In addition, the ego-defensive function is similar to the externalization function, because both functions involve protecting self-esteem. In contrast, the value-expressive function is more unique; it exists in attitudes that express the self-concept and central values, that is, abstract ideals that people consider to be important guiding principles in their lives (e.g., equality, freedom; Rokeach, 1973; Schwartz, 1992). For example, some people favor legalized abortion because they consider the individual freedom of women to be important, whereas others oppose legalized abortion because they value the sanctity of life or because they are committed to a religion that proscribes abortion.

By postulating the existence of many attitude functions, Smith et al. (1956) and Katz (1960) illustrated the complexities inherent in the study of attitude function. Unfortunately, although these original theories were provocative, early research on attitudes did not explore attitude function in great depth, partly because it appeared difficult to measure and study the functions of attitudes (see, e.g., Insko, 1967). Contemporary research however, has made progress in the measurement of attitude function. Research has measured and manipulated attitude function across attitude objects (e.g., Shavitt, 1990), individuals (e.g., Snyder & DeBono, 1985), and situations (e.g., Maio & Olson, 1995a; Murray, Haddock, & Zanna, 1996). For example, attitude function is often measured by asking people to list their thoughts about the attitude object, and these thoughts are coded according to the motivations that they express (e.g., Herek, 1987; Maio & Olson, 1994; Shavitt, 1990).

Such measures have enabled researchers to apply the construct of attitude function to many practical issues, including attitudes toward victims of AIDS (Pryor, Reeder, Vinacco, & Kott, 1989), attitudes toward the automobile (Ennis & Zanna, 1993), and advertising (Shavitt, 1990). In addition, as is evident in this volume, new techniques in operationalizing attitude function have assisted basic research. Consequently, a large amount of new empirical evidence has accumulated.

Of course, as is the case with any nascent field of study, this evidence has produced at least as many questions as answers. Fortunately, these questions (and answers) have the potential to stimulate new theory and research. Given this potential, the present chapter highlights some themes and issues that have emerged in recent research on attitude function, and we introduce a new theoretical model that attempts to integrate these themes and issues.

EMERGENT THEMES

Although attitude function has been investigated in a variety of theoretical and applied contexts, several consistent themes have emerged. We briefly describe two important themes.

Primacy of Object Appraisal

Researchers have frequently proposed that the most basic function of attitudes is to simplify interactions with the environment (Allport, 1935; Smith et al., 1956). This notion was present in Smith et al.'s seminal description of the object appraisal attitude function:

> ...attitudes aid us in classifying for action the objects of the environment, and they make appropriate response tendencies available for coping with these objects. This feature is a basis for holding attitudes in general as well as any particular array of attitudes. In it lies the function served by holding attitudes *per se* (p. 41).

This description reflects the ability of attitudes to serve as ready-made indicators of whether one should approach or avoid an attitude object. In addition, this description emphasizes the notion that all attitudes simplify interaction with the environment, regardless of whether the attitudes are positive or negative in valence. For example, people who have no attitudes toward candy should have more difficulty deciding whether to purchase candy than people who like or dislike candy. From an evolutionary perspective, the object appraisal function probably explains why humans evolved to form attitudes.

These ideas have been reflected in other theories of attitude function. For example, Katz's (1960) notion of a knowledge function suggested that all attitudes summarize the positive and negative features of objects in the environment. Similarly, Herek (1986) argued that all attitudes help to organize objects according to the extent to which the objects help or hinder one's self-interest. In general, research on attitude function has reflected an acceptance of the view that object appraisal is an important function served by attitudes (see Eagly & Chaiken, 1998; Olson & Zanna, 1993).

Research has also demonstrated empirically the importance of the object appraisal function. The empirical evidence is interesting partly because much of the evidence has arisen more than 30 years after Smith et al. (1956) postulated some important characteristics of this function:

> Insofar as attitudes are predispositions to experience certain classes of objects, to be motivated by them, and to respond to them, it is evident that their existence permits

the individual to check more quickly and efficiently the action-relevancy of the events in the environment around him. Presented with an object or event, he may categorize it in some class of objects and events for which a predisposition to action and experience exists. Once thus categorized, it becomes the focus of an already-established repertory of reactions and feelings, and the person is saved the energy-consuming and sometimes painful process of figuring out *de novo* how he shall relate himself to it (p. 41).

In summary, Smith et al. predicted that attitudes make attitude-relevant judgments faster and easier to perform.

Interestingly, research has found that the speed and ease with which people make attitude-relevant judgments are affected by prior repeated expression of their attitude. For example, people who have been asked to repeatedly indicate their attitude toward an abstract painting are subsequently faster at deciding whether they prefer the painting over another painting than are people who have not been asked to repeatedly express their attitude (Fazio, Blascovich, & Driscoll, 1992). In addition, people who have repeatedly indicated their attitude toward an abstract painting exhibit less physiological arousal during subsequent preference decisions than do people who have not repeatedly expressed their attitude (Blascovich et al., 1993).

These findings are interesting because repeated expression strengthens the association in memory between an attitude object and one's attitude (Fazio, 1990). Consequently, the attitude becomes more accessible (i.e., easy to retrieve) from memory (e.g., Powell & Fazio, 1984). Once accessed from memory, attitudes can serve as a guide to attitude-relevant judgments, making these judgments quicker and easier. Thus, the effect of repeated expression on the speed and ease of attitude-relevant judgments suggests that accessible attitudes are more likely to serve an object appraisal function than are less accessible attitudes. In fact, studies that measured attitude accessibility have yielded results that are consistent with this conclusion (see Fazio chap. 1, this volume).

Research on the effects of need for closure (see Kruglanski, 1996) is also relevant to the object appraisal function. Need for closure is a "desire for a definite answer on some topic, *any* answer as opposed to confusion and ambiguity" (Kruglanski, 1989, p. 14). This construct is relevant to the object appraisal function because attitudes are capable of providing such answers. That is, attitudes help people make decisions about attitude objects. As a result, the object appraisal motivation should be strong when need for closure is high, which should motivate people to form attitudes and protect them.

This hypothesis has been tested by using both individual difference measures of need for closure and situational manipulations of need for closure (Kruglanski, Webster, & Klem, 1993). For example, Kruglanski et al. (1993) measured individual differences in need for closure and then gave participants either sufficient information or insufficient information with which to form an opinion regarding a legal case. A confederate of the experimenter then presented participants with new information about the case, and participants' subsequent attitudes were measured. Results indicated that, if participants had previously been given insufficient information, those who scored high in need for closure were more persuaded by new information (from a confederate) than were participants who scored low in need for closure. In contrast, if participants had been given sufficient information, those who were high in need for closure were more resistant to persuasion than were participants who were low in need for closure. Thus, when given insufficient information for forming an opinion, participants who were high in need for closure were more likely to utilize new information as a basis for forming attitudes, and, after being given sufficient information to form an opinion, they were more likely to defend the attitudes that they had formed.

These results were replicated in an additional experiment that used an experimental manipulation of need for closure (Kruglanski et al., 1993). High need for closure was induced by placing participants in a noisy environment, whereas low need for closure was induced by placing participants in a quiet environment. Presumably, the noisy environment made it difficult to engage in information processing and heightened the need for closure. Indeed, participants were more likely to form or maintain attitudes in the situation that elicited high need for closure than in the situation that induced low need for closure.

Overall, then, there is interesting evidence pertaining to the object appraisal function. It appears that accessible attitudes are particularly likely to serve an object appraisal function. In addition, high need for closure may induce an object appraisal motivation, which causes people to form and protect their attitudes.[1] These findings provide an initial

---

[1]Interestingly, it has been suggested that several motives may contribute to need for closure (Kruglanski et al., 1997). In particular, some researchers have argued that the Need for Closure Scale taps a need for structure and order as well as a need for decisiveness (Neuberg, Judice, & West, 1997; Neuberg, West, Judice, & Thompson, 1997), which can be measured using the Personal Need for Structure Scale and the Personal Fear of Invalidity Scale (Thompson, Naccarato, & Parker, 1989). In addition, the construct of uncertainty orientation is relevant (Sorrentino & Short, 1986). This construct reflects the extent to which people seek to discover and resolve uncertainty about themselves or their world, and it is assessed using a projective measure (e.g., Sorrentino, Bobocel, Gitta, Olson, & Hewitt, 1988).

sketch of the object appraisal function and potentially stimulate additional research.

Instrumental Versus Symbolic Distinction

An additional theme in recent research is the distinction between instrumental and symbolic attitudes (e.g., Herek, 1986; Prentice, 1987; Sears, 1988). Instrumental attitudes focus on classifying attitude objects according to their ability to promote self-interest. Thus, instrumental attitudes promote the object appraisal function. In contrast, symbolic attitudes are based on concerns other than self-interest, including concerns about self-image and the ability of an attitude object to promote or threaten personal values (e.g., political attitudes; Herek, 1986; Sears, 1988).

Research has frequently supported this distinction. For example, using a thought-listing measure of attitude function, Shavitt (1990) predicted and found that some attitude objects fulfill primarily a single attitude function. For example, when people listed their thoughts about air conditioners and coffee, their thoughts focused on the utility of the objects (e.g., air conditioners keep people cool, coffee increases alertness). In contrast, when people listed their thoughts about greeting cards and perfume, their thoughts tended to focus on the objects' capacity to symbolize one's identity and values. These results revealed that some objects were distinctly instrumental, whereas others were symbolic.

Shavitt (1990) also obtained evidence that this distinction has predictive validity. She presented participants with persuasive ads for (fictitious) brands of each attitude object, and these ads utilized either instrumental or symbolic arguments. Analysis of post message attitudes indicated that participants were more persuaded by the ads containing arguments that matched the functions of attitudes toward the objects than by ads containing arguments that did not match the functions of attitudes toward the objects. For example, instrumental ads for an air conditioner were more persuasive than were symbolic ads for an air conditioner. Similar results have been obtained in other persuasion research (e.g., Prentice, 1987; Snyder & DeBono, 1985) that has employed different research paradigms. Such findings indicate that the instrumental or symbolic basis of the targeted attitude should be considered when one designs a persuasive message.

This distinction has also been examined as a predictor of the manner in which people process persuasive messages. For example, recent evidence suggests that match effects occur because people scrutinize arguments that match the function of their attitude more than they scrutinize arguments that do not match the function of their attitude (Petty & Wegener, 1998; see also Petty, Wheeler, & Bizer, chap. 5, this volume). As a result, match effects occur when the persuasive arguments are strong, but not when the persuasive arguments are weak. In addition, a meta-analysis of research (Johnson & Eagly, 1989) found that people tend to process messages in an objective, unbiased manner when the messages address an issue that is relevant to personal outcomes, whereas people are more resistant to persuasive messages when the messages address an issue that is relevant to values (i.e., symbolic concerns; see also Maio & Olson, 1995a). Although the exact mechanism producing this difference is unknown (Johnson & Eagly, 1990; Petty & Cacioppo, 1990), such findings support the distinction between instrumental and symbolic attitudes.

Finally, the instrumental/symbolic distinction has been emphasized in research on political attitudes. Political attitudes tend to be symbolic, rather than instrumental (e.g., Kinder & Sears, 1985). For example, voters' attitudes toward political candidates depend more on voters' party affiliations than on the personal gains that a candidate might provide. Interestingly, however, recent research (e.g., Young, Thomsen, Borgida, Sullivan, & Aldrich, 1991) indicates that political attitudes become more self-serving when self-interest is made salient. Thus, it is possible that situational factors can influence the extent to which political attitudes are symbolic.

GENERAL ISSUES

Despite the advances in research on attitude function, there are numerous issues that remain unresolved and many questions that have been raised. In this section, we summarize some important issues that future research should address.

Comprehensiveness and Distinctiveness of Motivations

One important issue that research has not determined unequivocally is the precise number of relevant motivations. It is unlikely that the ego-defensive, knowledge, social-adjustive, utilitarian, and value-expressive functions represent all possible motivational bases of attitudes. Similarly, it is uncertain whether the instrumental/symbolic distinction encompasses all or even most of the functions fulfilled by attitudes. Additional attitude functions could be derived from the attitudes literature. For example, research on cognitive dissonance theory (Festinger, 1957) has found that people attempt to form attitudes that are consistent with their attitude-relevant beliefs and behaviors, because inconsistencies elicit an aversive arousal (dissonance; see Elliot & Devine, 1994). Perhaps, then, the maximization of consistency is a basic function of attitudes. In fact, there is evidence that individual differences in a preference for consistency may moderate many important social psychological processes (Cialdini, Trost, & Newsom, 1995). Consequently, need for consistency could be postulated as a basic attitude function.

Many other areas in psychology have faced the challenge of enumerating relevant motivations. For example, some personality researchers have attempted to identify the basic dimensions of human personality by using a motivational perspective. Murray's (1938, 1951) motivational theory of personality is particularly well known. He postulated the existence of many basic human motivations, some of which are similar to proposed attitude functions. For example, he suggested that there is a motivation to attain social recognition, which is similar to the social-adjustive function. Other proposed motivations were less similar to proposed attitude functions. For example, he postulated a motivation to dominate others, which is not immediately apparent in theories of attitude function.

Murray's (1938) theory is particularly interesting because the hypothesized motivations map on to five factors that have been found in other personality research: neuroticism, extraversion, openness to experience, agreeableness, and conscientiousness (Paunonen, 1993; Piedmont, McCrae, & Costa, 1992). This finding is important because it has been argued that these five factors are basic dimensions of personality (see McCrae & John, 1992). The primary support for this argument comes from research that has used a technique called the lexical approach (see Goldberg, 1990), which involves constructing a list of personality traits that are representative of the trait words contained in the English language and then asking people to rate themselves or others on these traits. Factor analyses of these self- or other-ratings have frequently revealed five similar factors. Because the factors represent all traits, it has been suggested that these factors provide a comprehensive list of the basic dimensions of personality (see Goldberg).

Given the relations between Murray's (1938) motivations and the five factors, one could argue that these motivations should be used to derive a list of all possible, distinct attitude functions. An ensuing dilemma is that of whether motivations should be classified at a higher order level (e.g., as one of five factors) or at a lower order level (e.g., as one of some set of more specific motivations). It could be argued that relevant motivations can include a very large set of more specific, concrete goals (e.g., to eat, to sleep). Thus, research on attitude functions should explore the possibility that the motivations served by attitudes are varied and can be conceptualized at different levels, ranging from a few basic motivations to numerous concrete goals.

Evidence of Motivation

It can be argued that distinctions between some attitude functions are unnecessary or redundant because similar distinctions can be made simply through an examination of the beliefs that underlie attitudes (see Eagly & Chaiken, 1998). For example, if attitudes toward an air conditioner fulfill an instrumental function because they serve a need to stay cool at low cost, then these attitudes should be based on beliefs about the extent to which an air conditioner can keep one cool at low cost. Similarly, if attitudes toward a brand of perfume fulfill a psychological need to enhance social relations, then these attitudes should be based on beliefs about the extent to which the brand of perfume will facilitate social relations. Thus, it could be argued that attitudes that serve different functions differ in the content of the beliefs that support them. These differences in the beliefs that underlie attitudes could be given primary conceptual or theoretical significance, rather than there being allocated special significance to motivations per se.

In practice, it may be difficult to distinguish the functions that underlie attitudes from the beliefs that underlie attitudes, because function and beliefs are closely related. If a particular motivation (e.g., social adjustment) is relevant to an attitude object (e.g., perfume), people should possess beliefs about the attitude object's ability to fulfill the motivation. Therefore, the motivations that underlie attitudes and the content of attitude-relevant beliefs should be similar.

Most research has not tried to distinguish the effects of attitude function from the effects of attitude-relevant beliefs (e.g., Maio & Olson, 1995b; Shavitt, 1990). Of course, such research does not suggest that it is impossible to disentangle the effects of function and structure. One can arouse different motivations before presenting people with identical information about the object. For example, one could make salient either the motivation to live long or the motivation to seek pleasure prior to presenting information about a new health food. Presumably, the health food would be perceived by everyone as being healthy. Nonetheless, individuals for whom the motivation to live long is made salient might consider this attribute to be more important than individuals for whom the motivation to seek pleasure is made salient. With this technique, any observed effects could be more clearly attributed to attitude function. In fact, some recent experiments have successfully used similar techniques (e.g., Maio & Olson, chap. 9, this volume; Marsh & Julka, chap. 10, this volume; Murray et al., 1996), which suggests that effects of attitude function can be disentangled from effects of attitude structure. Thus, such techniques provide a useful option for future research.

Development of Motives Across Situations

It is also important to investigate whether and how situations might bring about changes in attitude function. In other words, is it possible that a single attitude can fulfill different functions in different situations? If so, what factors influence this transformation?

There are several interesting perspectives on this question. For instance, research by Seligman and Katz (1996) indicates that ratings of the importance of values (e.g., equality, freedom) depend on the situations that people consider when they rate the values. For example, people rate the value of freedom differently when they rate its importance as a guiding principle in their life than when they rate its importance as a guiding principle in the issue of legalized abortion. In general, the importance of any particular value may depend on context. Because values represent important motivational goals, such findings suggest that the perceived importance of motivations can vary across contexts (Schwartz, 1992).

Put simply, even if a motivation is important, there is no guarantee that the motive will always influence attitudes. For example, most people probably experience some motivation to be healthy, but people do not necessarily experience this motivation when they enter an all-you-can-eat buffet. Instead, the abundance of food on such occasions might cause people to experience the utilitarian goal of pleasure and therefore to eat more food than is healthy. Such instances illustrate the importance of discovering the situational factors that govern the activation and application of relevant motivations.

Research on the nonconscious activation of motivations from memory is particularly interesting and relevant to this issue. Specifically, Bargh and his colleagues (e.g., Bargh, 1990; Bargh & Chartrand, 1996) have suggested that situational cues can automatically activate motivations from memory. Once activated, the motives can affect cognitive processes (e.g., memory) and behavior, and these influences can sometimes occur outside of conscious awareness. Early evidence is supportive of this prediction (e.g., Bargh & Chartrand, 1996), and additional research is needed to reveal exactly which motives are activated by which situational cues.

Development of Motives Over Time

Research on attitude function has generally taken a static approach to the study of attitude function. That is, research has focused on identifying the effects of particular attitude functions at a set point in time, rather than examining how attitude functions might evolve and change over time. It is important to examine how attitude functions change over time, partly because practitioners of attitude change rely heavily on the tendency for attitude functions to change. For example, the "low-ball" attitude change technique involves giving people a strong incentive (i.e., motivation) to form a particular attitude and then removing this motivation (see Cialdini, 1993). Remarkably, the newly formed attitude tends to persist even after the original motivation is removed, which suggests that the attitude is supported by new motivations.

In an interesting study of this technique (Pallak, Cook, & Sullivan, 1980), an interviewer approached homeowners at the beginning of winter and asked them to try to reduce their fuel consumption for home heating. All participants were given information about how to reduce fuel consumption. Some participants, however, were given an added incentive to reduce their bills: they were told that their names would be favorably cited in upcoming newspaper articles. From a functional point of view, these participants were given a social-adjustive reason to save fuel (i.e., social recognition). Not surprisingly, these participants saved more energy over the first month than did control participants. After one month, however, the participants who expected publicity were informed that it would not be possible to publish their names. Despite the removal of the social-adjustive motivation for reducing fuel consumption, participants saved even more fuel over the remaining months, which suggests that participants had found a new reason to save fuel. In particular, participants might have become motivated by their values (e.g., a world of beauty) or by utilitarian needs (lower fuel bills).

Such changes in the motivations that underlie attitudes might occur frequently in everyday life. It would be interesting to discover whether some functions change more easily than others. For example, people might be reluctant to admit that their attitudes fulfill social-adjustive goals, because such an admittance might make the attitudes seem superficial and insincere. Consequently, people might form new reasons for their attitudes—reasons that reflect different motivations. Future research could test whether there are such systematic changes in attitude function.

Attitude Structure

It is also important to consider the relations between attitude function and attitude structure, that is, the informational bases of attitudes. It has been suggested that people infer their attitudes from their beliefs, feelings, and past behavior (Zanna & Rempel, 1988) and that the amount of support that is provided by each of these three components varies across attitude objects and individuals (e.g., Esses, Haddock, & Zanna, 1993; Haddock, Zanna, & Esses, 1993). In addition, the consistency between the components varies across attitude objects and individuals (Pomerantz, Chaiken, & Tordesillas, 1995). These three components might all reflect similar (e.g., positive) reactions to an attitude object or dissimilar (e.g., positive and negative) reactions to an attitude object.

It is likely that attitude function influences attitude structure and vice versa. For example, symbolic attitudes may be more strongly based on affect than instrumental attitudes (see also Ennis & Zanna, chap. 14, this volume; Kinder & Sears, 1985; Reeder & Pryor, chap. 11, this volume).[2] In addition, attitude function might affect the conflict within the components of attitudes. In other words, attitude function might affect the extent to which both positive and negative reactions to the attitude object are subsumed in a specific component. Bidimensional perspectives on attitudes suggest that people's positive and negative responses toward an attitude object can be independent (see Cacioppo, Gardner, & Berntson, 1997). That is, people do not necessarily feel only positively or only

---

[2]This point is consistent with the notion that symbolic attitudes are based on values, because values arouse strong affect and motivations (Maio & Olson, 1995a; Schwartz, 1992).

negatively toward an attitude object; people sometimes feel positively and negatively toward the object. In such instances, people are said to have ambivalent (or conflicted) attitudes (Kaplan, 1972).

The functions fulfilled by ambivalent attitudes are particularly interesting because ambivalence should be aversive to individuals (Maio, Bell, & Esses, 1996). Perhaps such attitudes fulfill additional functions, such as a motivation to be open minded (see Thompson & Zanna, 1995). Alternatively, it is possible that the positive and negative dimensions of ambivalent attitudes fulfill distinct functions. This hypothesis is consistent with evidence that positive and negative affective responses to attitude objects are related to distinct approach and avoidance motivations and are located in different regions of the brain (Cacioppo et al., 1997; see also Sutton & Davidson, 1997).[3] A challenge for future research is to further explore the functions fulfilled by ambivalent attitudes.

Attitude Strength

Another important issue is that of whether attitude functions change as attitudes become stronger. For example, there might be a general shift in motivations after attitudes have formed and become accessible from memory. In particular, as indicated earlier, strong and accessible attitudes appear to fulfill an object appraisal function more clearly than do weaker and less accessible attitudes.

This observation raises an additional possibility: Does the emergence of the object appraisal function overwhelm other attitude functions, causing them to play a smaller role in supporting strong, accessible attitudes? This is an interesting issue because, on the one hand, we suggested in a preceding section that attitude functions can change over time; consequently, people might "forget" the original motivations underlying their attitudes, and the object appraisal function might then provide the principal motivation supporting strong attitudes. On the other hand, the original motivations might be reactivated when strong attitudes are attacked, and the motivations might assist in defending the attitudes. For example, people often form strong value-based attitudes toward legalized abortion. Attacks against such value-relevant attitudes

---

[3]This distinction between approach and avoidance is also important in other areas, including the study of achievement motivation (see Elliot & Church, 1997) and the neuropsychological base of emotions (e.g., Davidson, 1998, Lang, 1995). Thus, the distinction extends beyond basic attitudes research.

tend to evoke defensive reactions (see Johnson & Eagly, 1989; cf. Maio & Olson, 1995a, 1998), which might reflect the arousal of a motivation to protect values. In fact, attitudes are rated as more important when they are highly relevant to values, utilitarian concerns, and social goals than when these concerns are less relevant (e.g., Boninger, Krosnick, & Berent, 1995; Thomsen, Borgida, & Lavine, 1995). Thus, rather than serving only the object appraisal function, strong attitudes might fulfill value-expressive, utilitarian, and social-adjustive functions more powerfully than weak attitudes.

THE FUNCTION–STRUCTURE MODEL OF ATTITUDES

Notwithstanding the recent progress in research on attitude function, we believe that the functional perspective should be integrated with a broader conceptual model of attitudes in order to provide a clearer picture of the motivational bases of attitudes. In the following we introduce a model of attitudes and attitude function that attempts such an integration.

Effects of Motivations

A central assumption of our model is that motivations affect attitudes to the extent that the motivations are salient. There are several circumstances in which motives might be salient. First, particular motives might be chronically accessible for some individuals. For example, people who are classified as high self-monitors attempt to adapt their behavior to the social environment (Snyder & Campbell, 1982), and, therefore, this social-adjustive goal should influence their attitudes toward many attitude objects (Snyder & DeBono, 1985). Second, motives can be made temporarily accessible. Motives might be made temporarily accessible by features of the situation that are associated in memory with a particular motive (e.g., Young et al., 1991). For example, the presence of money might activate utilitarian motivations to pursue wealth. Third, a motive might become accessible if it is associated in memory with the attitude object. Such an association would enable the motivation to be activated when the attitude object is encountered.

These three routes to the activation of a motive facilitate predictions about the persistence of attitude functions across situations and time. For example, a motive that was influential during attitude formation can also be influential after the attitude becomes strong and completely formed, provided that the original motivation is accessible at both stages. The original motivation is likely to be accessible at both stages if it is chronically accessible to the individual, primed by the situation at both time periods, or associated in memory with the attitude.

Functions of Attitudes

Given our hypotheses about the activation of attitude functions, we next describe possible attitude functions, distinguishing between the functions fulfilled by the formation of attitudes per se and the functions fulfilled by holding particular attitude positions. This distinction is important because many attitude functions do not explain why people form attitudes; instead, they explain why people adopt particular attitude positions (Fazio, chap. 1, this volume; Herek, 1986; Smith et al., 1956). For example, the social-adjustive function might explain why someone likes clothes that are trendy, but it does not explain why that person found it necessary to form attitudes toward clothing in the first place.

Attitude Formation. We propose that the formation of attitudes serves two basic functions. First, as noted at the beginning of this chapter, there is consensus among theorists that all attitudes serve to simplify our interactions with objects in the environment by providing us with summaries of the positive and negative characteristics of the objects. Put simply, the formation of attitudes fulfills an object appraisal function.

We believe, however, that the object appraisal function does not provide a complete account of the functions fulfilled by attitude formation. This function reveals the manner in which attitudes simplify the cognitive processing of attitude objects, but does not completely explain the intensity of people's affective reactions to attitude objects. Theoretically, the entire attitude–behavior process could be cold and devoid of feeling. For example, when contemplating their attitudes toward an ethnic group, people could simply recall an abstract, emotionless evaluation indicating varying degrees of favorability or unfavorability. Such recalled favorability or unfavorability could direct responses to the group without the elicitation of strong negative or positive feelings per se. Affective reactions are elicited, however (e.g., Cacioppo & Petty, 1979; Dijker, Kok, & Koomen, 1996; Fazio, Jackson, Dunton, & Williams,

1995, Reeder & Pryor, this volume), and the psychological function of these reactions should be addressed.

Perhaps these reactions can be explained using Zajonc's (1980) proposal that the experience of affect is basic and that affective reactions give meaning to the world around us. Affect keeps us aroused and it provides motivational impetus to our attitudes and behavior. Consequently, people may have a built-in need to experience emotions, and the experience of emotions may be intrinsically satisfying (see Maio & Esses, 1999).

Therefore, we propose that the formation of attitudes fulfills a need for cognitive simplicity and a need for affect. In addition, people might vary in the extent to which they experience these needs. For example, individual differences such as need for closure, personal need for structure, fear of invalidity, and uncertainty orientation may reflect individual differences in a need for cognitive simplicity (see footnote 1). Similarly, there may be individual differences in need for affect (see Maio & Esses, 1999). That is, people may vary in the extent to which they approach and enjoy objects and situations that arouse positive or negative emotions. Theoretically, people who are high in these needs should be more likely to spontaneously form attitudes than people who are low in these needs.[4]

Attitude Valence. Explanation of the functions fulfilled by particular attitude positions requires the consideration of attitude structure. Attitude structure is relevant because attitude positions should be influenced by the information that people possess about an attitude object. Specifically, according to the three-component model of attitudes (see Zanna & Rempel, 1988), attitude valence should depend on affective, cognitive, and behavioral information about the attitude object. These three sources of information are integrated to form an overall attitude.

As previously indicated, however, the relative weighting of these sources of information can vary across individuals and attitude objects (e.g., Eagly, Mladinic, & Otto, 1994; Esses et al., 1993; Haddock et al., 1993), and it is possible that psychological motivations influence the weighting of these components. For example, Haddock et al. found that value-relevant beliefs and past experiences were more important predictors of high right-wing authoritarians' attitudes toward homosexuals than

---

[4]Jarvis and Petty (1996) suggested that people vary in their need to evaluate, that is, their need to form attitudes. In our model, the need to evaluate could be influenced either by a need for cognitive simplicity or by a need for affect (or both).

of low right-wing authoritarians' attitudes toward homosexuals. This result may have occurred because high right-wing authoritarians' experiences and beliefs about homosexuals reflect a perception that homosexuals threaten conventional values and because high right-wing authoritarians are highly motivated to adhere to these values (Altemeyer, 1988). In other words, high right-wing authoritarians' values might have motivated them to strongly weight their value-relevant beliefs and experiences in the computation of their attitudes.

In Fig. 15.1, we depict a general model of how motivations and attitude structure might interact. According to this model, attitudes are based on experiences with the attitude object, beliefs about the positive and negative features of the attitude object, and affective reactions to the attitude object. The experience component contains the episodic memories of positive and negative experiences with the attitude object; the belief component represents perceptions of the positive and negative features of the attitude object, and the affective component contains the feelings that are elicited by the attitude object.

Importantly, the experience, belief, and affect components can contain information that is relevant to attitude function. For example, when contemplating their attitude toward public speaking, people might recall that past speeches had negative social consequences (e.g., embarrassment), might believe that future speeches will have positive utilitarian conse-

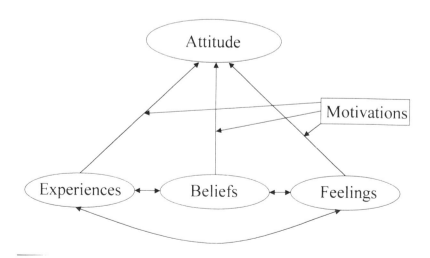

FIG. 15.1. The function–structure model of attitudes: Motivations moderate the effects of beliefs, feelings, and experiences on attitudes.

quences (e.g., promotion by an employer), and might feel anxious about the prospect of speaking. The relative weighting of these experiences, beliefs, and feelings should depend on accessible motivations. If an individual is experiencing a strong motivation to get along with others, the recollections of negative social consequences might have a strong effect on the person's attitude, causing unfavorability toward public speaking. In contrast, if a person is experiencing a strong motivation to maximize personal interests (e.g., acquire wealth), the anticipated positive consequences should be weighted more strongly, causing favorability toward public speaking. If a person is motivated to minimize negative affect, the anxiety experienced at the prospect of speaking should be weighted heavily, causing unfavorable attitudes. In summary, motivations should affect the weights assigned to various past experiences, beliefs, and feelings, and these components should, in turn, affect the overall attitude to the object.

Importantly, this model not only builds on the three-component model, but also extends the well-known expectancy-value model of attitudes (e.g., Fishbein & Ajzen, 1975). The expectancy-value model proposes that attitudes are based on beliefs about the characteristics of an attitude object and evaluations of these characteristics. For example, as previously described, people might believe that public speaking facilitates a promotion, which would be evaluated positively. Our model suggests that, in addition to these beliefs and their associated evaluations, the subjective importance of the beliefs (which is determined by salient motivations) should be considered. In the current example, the relative importance of the promotion might vary, dependent on the extent to which a utilitarian motivation is salient and strong. Thus, it is the addition of an importance weighting that provides this model with a means for integrating attitude function with attitude structure.[5]

Further, the importance weightings provide a flexible means for integrating attitude function with attitude structure, because the motivations that might affect these weightings can be diverse and wide ranging. Thus, rather than offer a limited taxonomy of motivations, we highlight some psychological constructs that could be used as a guide to relevant motivations. For example, relevant motivations might be revealed through

---

[5]Our model is also relevant to a perspective on attitudes that is based on information integration theory (see Anderson, 1991). According to this theory, an attitude is based on evaluations of the features of an attitude object, and these evaluations are differentially weighted in judgments of the attitude object. According to our model, attitude function is one factor that affects the weighting of feature evaluations.

values because values are abstract concepts (e.g., freedom, equality) that people consider to be important guiding principles in their lives (Feather, 1995; Rokeach, 1973; Schwartz, 1992). It has been suggested that values reflect 10 different motivations: achievement, benevolence, conformity, hedonism, power, security, self-direction, stimulation, tradition, and universalism (Schwartz, 1992, 1996). These motivations resemble some of the motivations that were described in classic theories of attitude function (Katz, 1960; Smith et al., 1956). For example, achievement and hedonism are integral to utilitarian concerns. In addition, conformity, security, and tradition are relevant to social-adjustive concerns. Also, benevolence and universalism (concern for all, not just the individual) are relevant to Katz's original conceptualization of the value-expressive attitude function, which emphasized the role of abstract concerns that are irrelevant to personal and social interests.

Nevertheless, the 10 motivations revealed by values may have distinct effects that are not encompassed by basic categorizations of attitude function. Such distinct effects were revealed in an experiment where we asked students to contemplate two utilitarian values: the value of achievement or the value of enjoying life (Maio & Olson, chap. 9, this volume). After completing this manipulation, students were given a persuasive message advocating a tuition increase. One of the messages indicated that a portion of the fee increase would be used to help students enjoy their time at university, by providing a fund that would reduce the price of student vacations abroad. The other message indicated that part of the fee increase would be used to create workshops on study skills, which would enable students to achieve better grades. Results indicated that the effect of the persuasive message depended on which value had been primed. For example, students who were asked to contemplate the value of achievement were more persuaded by the fee proposal that enhanced their achievement than were students who had contemplated the value of enjoying life. Thus, the utilitarian motivations of achievement and enjoying life had distinct effects on participants' attitudes: The achievement motivation caused participants to weight the effect of the increased fees on achievement more strongly than did the motivation to enjoy life, which indicates that these two utilitarian values had distinct effects that could not be subsumed by a single, "utilitarian" motivation.

Although our experiment used values to elicit attitude functions, other psychological constructs might also tap motivations that can be expressed by attitudes. In particular, as previously indicated, personality traits might reveal motivations that attitudes can fulfill. For example, people who are motivated to maintain consistency or predictability in their world view (e.g., people high in need for structure; Thompson, Naccarato, & Parker, 1989) may be more likely to base their attitudes on their past experiences. Future research could explore such possibilities.

Attitude Strength

Not only should attitude function and structure interact to determine attitude valence, but they should also influence attitude strength. Specifically, strong attitudes should maintain consistency between the elements of attitude structure. In other words, employing a term from Gestalt psychology, strong attitudes exist within *balanced* networks of experiences, beliefs, or feelings.

Indeed, there is evidence that attitudes are more resistant to persuasion and predictive of behavior when they are consistent with attitude-relevant beliefs (Pomerantz et al., 1995). In addition, attitudes are more resistant to persuasion and predictive of behavioral intentions when there is little conflict within the beliefs and/or feelings that underlie the attitudes (Jonas, Diehl, & Bromer, 1997; Maio et al., 1996). Thus, balance within attitude structure does appear to contribute to attitude strength.

Importantly, however, our model predicts that this balance should be a function of the weights connecting the experiences, beliefs, and feelings to one another and to overall attitudes, because the weights that are assigned to different elements can magnify or attenuate preexisting inconsistencies. If little weight is assigned to inconsistent experiences, beliefs, or feelings, the resulting balanced structure should provide better support for attitudes than if great weight is placed on the inconsistent components. Future research could test this prediction.[6]

CONCLUSION

This chapter has highlighted several themes and issues in research on attitude function. To address some of these themes and issues, we pro-

---

[6]This idea that strong attitudes exist within balanced attitude structures is consistent with the connectionist perspective on the formation and maintenance of attitudes (Read, Vanman, & Miller, 1997). With neural networks as a model for cognitive processing, this perspective suggests that attitudes are patterns of activation of knowledge in memory and that attitudes represent the most balanced (or organized) pattern of activation that is possible. Presumably, attitudes are stronger to the extent that this balance exists.

posed the function–structure model. This model can be used to generate hypotheses regarding several important issues, including the stability of attitude function across situations and time, as well as the relation of attitude function to attitude structure. Our hope is that this framework will stimulate further progress in research on attitude function, so that this interesting and vital topic can continue to develop. An understanding of why people possess their attitudes is one of the central questions that still faces attitude researchers.

REFERENCES

Allport, G. W. (1935). Attitudes. In C. Murchison (Ed.) *Handbook of social psychology* (pp. 798–844). Worcester, MA: Clark University Press.

Altemeyer, B. (1988). *Enemies of freedom: Understanding right-wing authoritarianism.* San Francisco: Jossey-Bass.

Anderson, N. H. (Ed.). (1991). *Contributions to information integration theory* (Vols. 1, 2, & 3). Hillsdale, NJ: Lawrence Erlbaum Associates.

Aronson, E., & Mills, J. (1959). The effect of severity of initiation on liking for a group. *Journal of Abnormal and Social Psychology, 59,* 177–181.

Bargh, J. A. (1990). Auto-motives: Preconscious determinants of social interaction. In E. T. Higgins & R. M. Sorrentino (Eds.), *Handbook of motivation and cognition: Foundations of social behavior* (Vol. 2, pp. 93–130). New York: Guilford Press.

Bargh, J. A., & Chartrand, T. L. (1996). Automatic activation of impression formation and motivation goals: Nonconscious goal priming reproduces effects of explicit task instructions. *Journal of Personality and Social Psychology, 71,* 464–478.

Blascovich, J., Ernst, J. M., Tomaka, J., Kelsey, R. M., Salomon, K. L., & Fazio, R. H. (1993). Attitude accessibility as a moderator of autonomic reactivity during decision making. *Journal of Personality and Social Psychology, 64,* 165–176.

Boninger, D. S., Krosnick, J. A., & Berent, M. K. (1995). Origins of attitude importance: Self-interest, social identification, and value relevance. *Journal of Personality and Social Psychology, 68,* 61–80.

Cacioppo, J. T., Gardner, W. L., & Berntson, G. G. (1997). Beyond bipolar conceptualizations and measures: The case of attitudes and evaluative space. *Personality and Social Psychology Review, 1,* 3–25.

Cacioppo, J. T., & Petty, R. E. (1979). Attitudes and cognitive response: An electrophysiological approach. *Journal of Personality and Social Psychology, 37,* 2181–2199.

Cialdini, R. B. (1993). *Influence: Science and practice.* New York: HarperCollins College.

Cialdini, R. B., Trost, M. R., & Newsom, J. T. (1995). Preference for consistency: The development of a valid measure and the discovery of surprising behavioral implications. *Journal of Personality and Social Psychology, 69,* 318–328.

Davidson, R. J. (1998). Affective style and affective disorders: Perspective from affective neuroscience. *Cognition and Emotion, 12,* 307–330.

Dijker, A. J., Kok, G., & Koomen, W. (1996). Emotional-reactions to people with aids. *Journal of Applied Social Psychology, 26,* 731–748

Eagly, A., Chaiken, S. (1998). Attitude structure and function. In D. T. Gilbert, S. T. Fiske, & G. Lindzey (Eds.), *The handbook of social psychology* (4th ed.) (Vol, 1). Boston, MA: McGraw-Hill.

Eagly, A., Mladinic, A., & Otto, S. (1994). Cognitive and affective bases of attitudes toward social groups and social policies. *Journal of Experimental Social Psychology, 30,* 113–137.

Elliot, A. J., & Church, M. A. (1997). A hierarchical model of approach and avoidance achievement motivation. *Journal of Personality and Social Psychology, 72*, 218–232.

Elliot, A. J., & Devine, P. G. (1994). On the motivational nature of cognitive dissonance: Dissonance as psychological discomfort. *Journal of Personality and Social Psychology, 67*, 382–394.

Ennis, R., & Zanna, M. P. (1993). Attitudes, advertising, and automobiles—A functional approach. *Advances in Consumer Research, 20*, 662–666.

Esses, V. M., Haddock, G., & Zanna, M. P. (1993). Values, stereotypes, and emotions as determinants of intergroup attitudes. In D. M. Mackie & D. L. Hamilton (Eds.), *Affect, cognition, and stereotyping: Interactive processes in group perception* (pp. 137–166). New York: Academic Press.

Fazio, R. H. (1990). Multiple processes by which attitudes guide behavior. In L. Berkowitz (Ed.), *Advances in Experimental Social Psychology* (Vol. 23, pp. 75–109). New York: Academic Press.

Fazio, R. H. (1995). Attitudes as object-evaluation associations: Determinants, consequences, and correlates of attitude accessibility. In R. E. Petty & J. A. Krosnick (Eds.), *Attitude strength: Antecedents and consequences* (pp. 247–252). Mahwah, NJ: Lawrence Erlbaum Associates.

Fazio, R. H., Blascovich, J., & Driscoll, D. (1992). On the functional value of attitudes: The influence of accessible attitudes upon the ease and quality of decision making. *Personality and Social Psychology Bulletin, 18*, 388–401.

Fazio, R. H., Jackson, J. R., Dunton, B. C., & Williams, C. J. (1995). Variability in automatic activation as an unobtrusive measure of racial attitudes: A bona fide pipeline? *Journal of Personality and Social Psychology, 69*, 1013–1027.

Feather, N. T. (1995). Values, valences, and choice: The influence of values on the perceived attractiveness and choice of alternatives. *Journal of Personality and Social Psychology, 68*, 1135–1151.

Festinger, L. (1957). *A theory of cognitive dissonance.* Evanston, IL: Row, Peterson.

Fishbein, M., & Ajzen, I. (1975). *Belief, attitude, intention, and behavior: An introduction to theory and research.* Reading, MA: Addison-Wesley.

Goldberg, L. R. (1990). An alternative "description of personality": The big-five factor structure. *Journal of Personality and Social Psychology, 59*, 1216–1229.

Haddock, G., Zanna, M. P., & Esses, V. M. (1993). Assessing the structure of prejudicial attitudes: The case of attitudes toward homosexuals. *Journal of Personality and Social Psychology, 65*, 1105–1118.

Herek, G. M. (1986). The instrumentality of attitudes: Toward a neofunctional theory. *Journal of Social Issues, 42*(2), 99–114.

Herek, G. M. (1987). Can functions be measured? A new perspective on the functional approach to attitudes. *Social Psychology Quarterly, 50*, 285–303.

Insko, C. (1967). *Theories of attitude change.* New York: Appleton–Century–Crofts.

Jarvis, W. B. G., & Petty, R. E. (1996). The need to evaluate. *Journal of Personality and Social Psychology, 70*, 172–194.

Johnson, B. T., & Eagly, A. H. (1989). Effects of involvement on persuasion: A meta-analysis. *Psychological Bulletin, 106*, 290–314.

Johnson, B. T., & Eagly, A. H. (1990). Involvement and persuasion: Types, traditions, and the evidence. *Psychological Bulletin, 107*, 375–384.

Jonas, K., Diehl, M., & Bromer, P. (1997). Effects of attitudinal ambivalence on information processing and attitude-intention consistency. *Journal of Experimental Social Psychology, 33*, 190–210.

Kaplan, K. L. (1972). On the ambivalence–indifference problem in attitude theory and measurement: A suggested modification of the semantic differential technique. *Psychological Bulletin, 77*(5), 361–372.

Katz, D. (1960). The functional approach to the study of attitudes. *Public Opinion Quarterly, 24*, 163–204.

Kinder, D. R., & Sears, D. O. (1985). Public opinion and political action. In G. Lindzey & E. Aronson (Eds.), *Handbook of social psychology* (Vol. 2, pp. 659–742). New York: Random House.

Kruglanski, A. W. (1989). *Lay epistemics and human knowledge: Cognitive and motivational bases.* New York: Plenum Press.

Kruglanski, A. W. (1996). A motivated gatekeeper of our minds: Need for closure effects on interpersonal and group processes. In R. M. Sorrentino & E. T. Higgins (Eds.), *Handbook of motivation and cognition: Foundations of social behaviour* (Vol. 3, pp. 465–496). New York: Guilford Press.

Kruglanski, A. W., Atash, M. N., DeGrada, E., Mannetti, L., Pierro, A., & Webster, D. M. (1997). Psychological theory versus psychometric nay-saying: Comment on Neuberg et al.'s (1997) critique of the need for closure scale. *Journal of Personality and Social Psychology, 73,* 1005–1016.

Kruglanski, A. W., Webster, D. M., & Klem, A. (1993). Motivated resistance and openness to persuasion in the presence or absence of prior information. *Journal of Personality and Social Psychology, 65,* 861–876.

Lang, P. J. (1995). The motion probe: Studies of emotion and attention. *American Psychologist, 50,* 372–385.

Maio, G. R., Bell, D. W., & Esses, V. M. (1996). Ambivalence and persuasion: The processing of messages about immigrant groups. *Journal of Experimental Social Psychology, 32,* 513–536.

Maio, G. R., & Esses, V. M. (1999). *The need for affect: Individual differences in the motivation to approach or avoid emotion-inducing situations.* Manuscript submitted for publication.

Maio, G. R., & Olson, J. M. (1994). Value-attitude–behaviour relations: The moderating role of attitude functions. *British Journal of Social Psychology, 33,* 301–312.

Maio, G. R., & Olson, J. M. (1995a). Involvement and persuasion: Evidence for different types of involvement. *Canadian Journal of Behavioural Science, 27,* 64–78.

Maio, G. R., & Olson, J. M. (1995b). Relations between values, attitudes, and behavioral intentions: The moderating role of attitude function. *Journal of Experimental Social Psychology, 31,* 266–285.

Maio, G. R., & Olson, J. M. (1998). Values as truisms: Evidence and implications. *Journal of Personality and Social Psychology, 74*(2), 294–311.

McCrae, R. R., & John, O. P. (1992). An introduction to the five-factor model and its applications. *Journal of Personality, 60,* 175–215.

Murray, H. (1938). *Explorations in personality.* New York: Oxford University Press.

Murray, H. (1951). Toward a classification of interaction. In T. Parsons & E. A. Shils (Eds.), *Toward a general theory of action* (pp. 434–464). Cambridge, MA: Harvard University Press.

Murray, S. H., Haddock, G., & Zanna, M. P. (1996). On creating value-expressive attitudes: An experimental approach. In C. Seligman, J. M. Olson, & M. P. Zanna (Eds.), *The psychology of values: The Ontario symposium* (Vol. 8, pp. 107–133). Mahwah, NJ: Lawrence Erlbaum Associates.

Neuberg, S. L., Judice, T. N., & West, S. G. (1997). What the need for closure scale measures and what it does not: Toward differentiating among related epistemic motives. *Journal of Personality and Social Psychology, 72,* 1396–1412.

Neuberg, S. L., West, S. G., Judice, T. N., & Thompson, M. M. (1997). On dimensionality, discriminant validity, and the role of psychometric analyses in personality theory and measurement: Reply to Kruglanski et al.'s (1997) defense of the Need for Closure Scale. *Journal of Personality and Social Psychology, 73,* 1017–1029.

Olson, J. M., & Zanna, M. P. (1993). Attitudes and attitude change. *Annual Review of Psychology, 44,* 117–154.

Pallak, M. S., Cook, D. A., & Sullivan, J. J. (1980). Commitment and energy conservation. *Applied Social Psychology Annual, 1,* 235–253.

Paunonen, S. V. (1993). *Sense, nonsense, and the Big Five factors of personality.* Paper presented at the annual meeting of the American Psychological Association, Toronto, Canada.

Petty, R. E., & Cacioppo, J. T. (1990). Involvement and persuasion: Tradition versus integration. *Psychological Bulletin, 107*, 367–374.

Petty, R. E., & Wegener, D. T. (1998). Matching versus mismatching attitude functions: Implications for scrutiny of persuasive messages. *Personality and Social Psychology Bulletin, 24*, 227–240.

Piedmont, R. L., McCrae, R. R., & Costa, P. T. Jr. (1992). An assessment of the Edwards Preference Schedule from the perspective of the five-factor model. *Journal of Personality Assessment, 58*, 67–78.

Pomerantz, E. M., Chaiken, S., & Tordesillas, R. S. (1995). Attitude strength and resistance processes. *Journal of Personality and Social Psychology, 69*, 408–419.

Powell, M. C., & Fazio, R. H. (1984). Attitude accessibility as a function of repeated attitude expression. *Personality and Social Psychology Bulletin, 10*, 139–148.

Prentice, D. A. (1987). Psychological correspondence of possessions, attitudes, and values. *Journal of Personality and Social Psychology, 53*, 993–1003.

Pryor, J. B., Reeder, G. D., Vinacco, J. R., & Kott, T. L. (1989). The instrumental and symbolic functions of attitudes toward persons with AIDS. *Journal of Applied Social Psychology, 19*, 377–404.

Read, S. J., Vanman, E. J., Miller, L. C. (1997). Connectionism, parallel constraint satisfaction processes, and gestalt principles: (Re)introducing cognitive dynamics to social psychology. *Personality and Social Psychology Review, 1*, 26–53.

Rokeach, M. (1973). *The nature of human values.* New York: Free Press.

Schwartz, S. H. (1992). Universals in the content and structure of values: Theoretical advances and empirical tests in 20 countries. In M. P. Zanna (Ed.), *Advances in experimental social psychology* (Vol. 25, 1–65). San Diego, CA: Academic Press.

Schwartz, S. H. (1996). Value priorities and behavior: Applying a theory of integrated value systems. In C. Seligman, J. Olson, & M. P. Zanna (Eds.), *The psychology of values: The Ontario symposium* (Vol. 8, pp. 1–24). Mahwah, NJ: Lawrence Erlbaum Associates.

Sears, D. O. (1988). Symbolic racism. In P. A. Katz & D. A. Taylor (Eds.), *Eliminating racism: Profiles in controversy* (pp. 53–84). New York: Plenum Press.

Seligman, C., & Katz, A. N. (1996). The dynamics of value systems. In C. Seligman, J. M. Olson, & M. P. Zanna (Eds.), *The psychology of values: The Ontario symposium* (Vol. 8, pp. 53–75). Mahwah, NJ: Lawrence Erlbaum Associates.

Shavitt, S. (1990). The role of attitude objects in attitude functions. *Journal of Experimental Social Psychology, 26*, 124–148.

Smith, M. B., Bruner, J. S., & White, R. W. (1956). *Opinions and personality.* New York: Wiley.

Snyder, M., & Campbell, B. H. (1982). Self-monitoring: The self in action. In J. Suls (Ed.), *Psychological perspectives on the self* (Vol. 1, pp. 185–207). Mahwah, NJ: Lawrence Erlbaum Associates.

Snyder, M., & DeBono, K. G. (1985). Appeals to image and claims about quality: Understanding the psychology of advertising. *Journal of Personality and Social Psychology, 49*, 586–597.

Sorrentino, R. M., Bobocel, D. R., Gitta, M. Z., Olson, J. M., & Hewitt, E. C. (1988). Uncertainty orientation and persuasion: Individual differences in the effects of personal relevance on social judgments. *Journal of Personality and Social Psychology, 55*, 357–371.

Sorrentino, R. M., & Short, J. C. (1986). Uncertainty orientation, motivation, and cognition. In R. M. Sorrentino & E. T. Higgins (Eds.), *The handbook of motivation and cognition: Foundations of social behavior* (Vol. 1, pp. 379–403). New York: Guilford Press.

Sutton, S. K., & Davidson, R. J. (1997). Prefrontal brain asymmetry: A biological substrate of the behavioral approach and inhibition systems. *Psychological Science, 8*, 204–210.

Thompson, M. M., Naccarato, M. E., & Parker, K. E. (1989, June). *Assessing cognitive need: The development of the personal need for structure and personal fear of invalidity scales.* Paper presented at the annual meeting of the Canadian Psychology Association, Halifax, Canada.

Thompson, M. M., & Zanna, M. P. (1995). The conflicted individual: Personality-based and domain-specific antecedents of ambivalent social attitudes. *Journal of Personality, 63*, 260–288.

Thomsen, C. J., Borgida, E., & Lavine, H. (1995). The causes and consequences of personal involvement. In R. E. Petty & J. A. Krosnick, *Attitude strength: Antecedents and consequences.* Mahwah, NJ: Lawrence Erlbaum Associates.

Young, J., Thomsen, C. J., Borgida, E., Sullivan, J., & Aldrich, J. H. (1991). When self-interest makes a difference: The role of construct accessibility in political reasoning. *Journal of Experimental Social Psychology, 27,* 271–296.

Zajonc, R. B. (1980). Feeling and thinking: Preferences need no inferences. *American Psychologist, 35,* 151–175.

Zanna, M. P., & Rempel, J. K. (1988). Attitudes: a new look at an old concept. In D. Bar-Tal & A. W. Kruglanski (Eds.), *The Social Psychology of Knowledge,* (pp. 315–334). Cambridge, England: Cambridge University Press.

Author Index

Subject Index

A